Afghanistan

DATE DUE

DEMCO 38-296

Afghanistan

The Soviet Invasion and the
Afghan Response, 1979–1982

M. Hassan Kakar

UNIVERSITY OF CALIFORNIA PRESS
Berkeley · Los Angeles · London

© 1995 by the Regents of the University of California

First Paperback Printing 1997

Library of Congress Cataloging-in-Publication Data

Kakar, M. Hassan.
    Afghanistan : the Soviet invasion and the Afghan response, 1979–1982 / M. Hassan Kakar.
        p.   cm.   Includes bibliographical references (p.) and index.
    ISBN 0–520–20893–5 (alk. paper)
    1. Afghanistan—History—Soviet occupation, 1979–1989.   I. Title.
BP163.A95   1995
958.104′5—dc20   93–36111
                                                         CIP

Printed in the United States of America
9 8 7 6 5 4 3 2 1

The paper used in this publication meets the minimum requirements of American National Standard for Information Sciences—Permanence of Paper for Printed Library Materials, ANSI Z39.48-1984. ∞

To Sayd Bahauddin Majruh, Ghulam Ghaus Shujaee, Abdur Rahim Chinzay, Naheed Azadah, Aziz ur Rahman Ulfat, Ghulam Shah Sarshar Shamali, Sa'adat Shigaywal, Mohammad Wali Karokhel, and other Afghans who died for us in defending freedom and independence.

Contents

Preface

In 1989, after I had fled from Kabul in late 1987, the American Center in Peshawar, Pakistan, provided me with a Fulbright grant to write my prison memoirs at the East-West Center in Honolulu, Hawaii. Before doing so, I went through the journal that I kept from 1979 until the Kabul regime arrested me in 1982. By reviving the events of the period in my mind, the journal proved so impressive that I decided to write instead a political history of the period. The result is this work, the first draft of which I composed during the six months of my fellowship with the center.

I acknowledge my special indebtedness to Kent Obee, director of the United States Information Service in the American embassy in Islamabad; Richard Hoagland, head of the American Center in Peshawar; and John Dixon, director of Afghan Section at the U.S. Information Agency in Washington, D.C. These three men made the Fulbright grant possible. During my stay in Honolulu, Mr. Dixon also provided me with press clippings on Afghanistan, for which I am also grateful. In the East-West Center, Mr. Robert Hewett (director of the center), Meg White, Mrs. Joy Teraoka, and Joyce Gruhn were very helpful, and I am grateful. I also wish to thank Professor Alden Mosshammer, chair of the History Department of the University of California, San Diego, for giving me access to the main library of the university, which enabled me to broaden my vision of the subject. I also want to thank David Christine, a computer specialist neighbor from New Zealand who helped me learn the computer technique while editing the work. His ready help eased my work very much for which I am grateful. I also want to express my thanks and appreciation to Stanley Barton for going through the manuscript and making useful suggestions regarding its style and editing. First as my student in a course on contemporary Afghan history that I taught at UCSD, and subsequently as my friend, Mr. Barton has been very helpful indeed, for which I am thankful. My gratitude also goes to Dan Gunter for his thorough editing of my work and to the University of California Press for making my work accessible to the readers. Last but not least, I am grateful to Mr. Zamin Mohmand for sending me press clippings on Afghanistan and the region.

Afghanistan

International boundary
Province boundary
★ National capital
⊙ Province capital
Railroad
Road

| 0 | 100 | 200 Kilometers |
| 0 | 100 | 200 Miles |

SOVIET UNION

Andizhan
Osh
Fergana
Leninabad

Kashi

CHINA

Navoi

Bukhara

Samarkand

Chardzhou

Karshi

Dushanbe

Taxkorgan

Mary

Kurgan-
Tyube
Kulyab

Khorog

Pamir

Mashhad

Termez
Keleft
Jeyretān
Nizhniy
Pyandzh
Feyzābād
Khorog

Lasht

Ayvadzh
KONDŪZ
Tāloqān

Kondūz

Eshkāshem

BADAKHSHĀN

Sheberghān
Mazār-e
Sharif
Samangān

TAKHĀR

IRAN

FĀRYĀB
JOWZJĀN
BALKH

SAMANGĀN

Baghlān

BAGHLĀN

Meymaneh

Chitrāl

Indus

Towraghondi

BĀDGHĪS

KAPISĀ
Mahmūd-
Rāqī
LAGHMĀN
KONARHĀ

Ceasefire Line

Tayyebāt

Qal'eh-ye Now

Chārīkār
PARVĀN
Asadābād

Herāt

Harīrūd

Chaghcharān

Bāmīān
BĀMĪĀN
Kowt-e
Ashrow
VARDAK
KĀBOL
Mehtarlām

Mazār-e

Srinagar

HERĀT

GHOWR

Farāh Rūd

Kabul

NANGARHĀR
Khyber Pass
Jalālābād
Landi Kotal

Islāmābād

Khān Rūd

Baraki
LOWGAR

Gardeyz

Peshāwar

INDIA

FARĀH

ORŪZGĀN

Ghazni

Pārachinār

Islāmābād

Rāwalpindi

Farāh

Tarīn
Kowt

GHAZNĪ

Zareh
Sharan

PAKTĪĀ

Kohāt

Jammu

Daryā-ye
Arghandāb

PAKTĪKĀ

Thal

Bannu

Jhelum

Chenab

Zaranj

Lashkar
Gāh

Qalāt
ZĀBOL

Qandahār

Tānk

Sargodha

Zābol

NĪMRŪZ

HELMAND
QANDAHĀR

Fort
Sandeman

Indus

Chaman

PAKISTAN

Daryā-ye Helmand

Quetta
Khost

Zāhedān

Gowd-e Zereh
(intermittent lake)

Nok
Kundi
Dālbandīn

IRAN

Sukkur

Boundary representation is
not necessarily authoritative.

Kābul

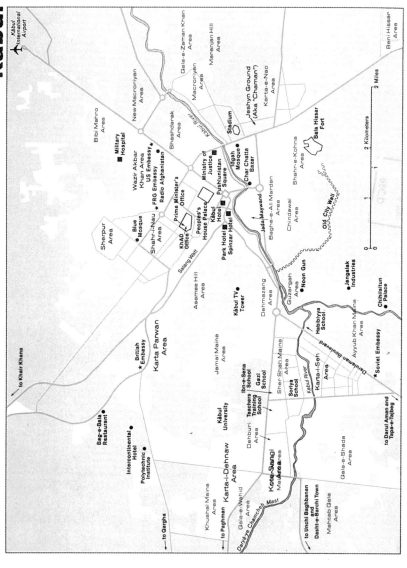

Introduction

Landlocked Afghanistan links Central Asia with South Asia and, to some extent, with West Asia or the Middle East. The latter is also connected through Afghanistan to China. In this important crossroads have lived from ancient times many ethnic groups, known in recent times as Afghans. They speak about thirty languages and dialects belonging to four main linguistic groups: Indo-Aryan, Turkic-Mongolian, Semitic, and Dravidian. The Indo-Aryan languages Pashto and Dari (Afghan Persian) serve as lingua francas, hence the significance of their speakers, that is, Pashtuns and Tajiks. These two groups constitute the overwhelming majority of Afghanistan's inhabitants, who numbered 15.5 million in 1979. Among these groups, in particular the Pashtuns, bilingualism is high. The Pashtuns outnumber all the other groups combined.

For centuries the Pashtuns have played the dominant role in politics. Their main division, the Durrani, provided Afghanistan with the ruling dynasties of Sadozay in the eighteenth century and Mohammadzay from then until recently. The main Turkic group is the Uzbeks, who speak the Uzbeki language. Just more numerous than the Uzbeks are the Turko-Mongol Hazaras, who speak Dari and adhere to the Shi'ite faith of Islam. Ethnic identity among the illiterate Afghans who constitute the majority is strong. Pashtuns, Tajiks, Uzbeks, and Turkomen have kin in the neighboring lands of Pakistan, Iran, Turkmenistan, Uzbekistan, and Tajikistan. They also share with them the religion of Islam. Except for the small group of Afghan Hindus and Sikhs, about 90 percent of Afghans are Sunnis and 10 percent Shi'as.

The ratio of ethnic groups is unknown because of the inroads of the main languages in each other's domains, particularly in the mixed areas where Pashtuns and Tajiks have lived for thousands of years and where intermarriage is common, as it is among the educated Afghans. This and the universalist religion of Islam, the assimilation of ethnic minorities within the dominant linguistic and ethnic communities, and the economic interconnectedness of regions, which is the result mainly of the introduction of a modern transportation network, have softened the notion of ethnicity and contributed to the solidarity of Afghans as a nation. The centuries-old dynastic rule and the enforcement throughout the land of a unified set of laws by a central government through a bureaucracy backed by a national standing army have also worked in the same direction.

An ancient land, Afghanistan has a long and eventful history. Its neighbors have influenced its history as it has theirs. Afghanistan has, mainly in its outlying regions, people of common descent with those of its neighboring countries. They were officially separated from each other when Afghanistan's boundaries were delimited in the second part of the nineteenth century. The boundaries, particularly that with Pakistan, are precarious. The latter was marked by the so-called Durand Line, which separated Afghanistan from its own Pashtuns, that is, the ethnic majority that had played a leading role in creating Afghanistan in the eighteenth century. The boundaries were then (and still are) so artificial that when people on either side of the line were hard-pressed for any reason, they crossed the line and settled across the border among their ethnic and coreligionist brothers. Besides, about two million Pashtun nomads crossed the Durand Line twice a year as a matter of course. The line was officially observed, although the Afghans did not truly accept it, and their successive governments, particularly after the British left India in 1947, helped their Pashtun brothers on the other side of it to constitute an independent land of their own, Pashtunistan. This meant that the frontier problems, particularly the Pashtunistan issue, deeply affected the political as well as diplomatic history of Afghanistan. The frontier problem is thus an important element of Afghan history.

Also important for Afghan history was the fact that two major European colonial powers, Russia (later the Soviet Union), and Britain, controlled her neighboring lands in the north and southeast. In the nineteenth century both powers grabbed vast territories from Afghanistan, reducing it to its present size; they then looked on it as a buffer state. Britain was the more aggressive, warring with Afghanistan three times (in 1838, 1878, and 1918), conducting foreign relations for it (1880–1918), and imposing the aforementioned Durand Line (1893). Seeing their country reduced in size and sandwiched between two "infidel" giants, the Afghans became xenophobic, inward-looking, and jealous of the independence of their country.

The delimitation of the boundaries of Afghanistan coincided with the efforts of Amir Abdur Rahman Khan (1880–1901) to lay the foundation of a strong central government, which marked the emergence of a nation-state. A movement started by which the central government concentrated power at the expense of a centuries-old traditional system that assigned power and concessions to secular rural magnates and religious groups. The consolidation of the nation-state, as well as of his dynastic rule, made it necessary for Amir Abdur Rahman Khan to build up a strong standing army aided by an expanded bureaucracy and an extensive intelligence service, a stupendous task considering the meager state income based mainly on an agricultural economy. In this initial phase the state became absolute, monopolistic, protectionist, and indifferent to modernization schemes in fields other than the military. Suspicious of the outside world in the age of European imperialism, Afghanistan remained distant from it. Although it always had a sophisticated literary and political elite and a rich literature in both national languages, Pashto and Dari, modern science and education did not touch Afghanistan. Instead, it receded into the world of conservative medievalism.[1]

The dawn of the new century coincided with the opening of Afghanistan to the outside world, the introduction of modern education, and the emergence of a small but assertive educated and bureaucratic middle class that was nationalist and constitutionalist in outlook. In the age of revolutions elsewhere, the prolific anti-imperialist journalist Mahmud Tarzi led the way in the domain of thought and propaganda. But after Afghanistan's successful war of independence, when the new reformist King Amanullah (1919–29) began to implement the first radical comprehensive schemes of modernization, they proved to be unrealistic and unpopular. They made him so unpopular that finally in 1929 a social bandit, Habibullah, commonly known as Bacha-e-Saqqao, overthrew him. With his downfall ended Afghanistan's first constitution, which Amanullah had promulgated in 1923, as well as the dynastic rule established by his grandfather Amir Abdur Rahman in 1880. As the new ethnic Tajik amir, Habibullah ruled for only nine turbulent months. Mohammad Nadir, a former military general of another Mohammadzay section of the Pashtun Durrani tribe, toppled the new amir in October 1929 and established his own dynasty of the Musahiban or Yahyakhel section.

The failure of the reforms and the rule of a Tajik amir for the first time in modern Afghanistan had serious repercussions that became manifest during the reign of King Nadir (1929–33). The Pashtun-Tajik relationship became strained for a while, and the conservative elements, represented by spiritual leaders and tribal elders, were granted scores of concessions and high positions in the government. Scholars and writers were organized in a new literary association, and religious scholars in a new association of the 'ulama. Modern education was reintroduced, though on a smaller scale, and the foundation for the future Kabul University laid down, but female education was neglected. Government-controlled dailies and weeklies were established in Kabul as well as provincial capitals. Some of the many supporters of the reformist king and the smaller group of constitutionalists were suppressed; others were imprisoned, and a few were even executed. Although he established a family rule by granting high posts to his four brothers and other relatives, King Nadir structured the government on the basis of a new constitution. Instituted in 1931, it provided for an elected National Consultative Assembly and an appointed House of Elders. The monarchy was called constitutional. But the new nation-building movement came to an abrupt halt in November 1933, when a student shot the king dead.

The sudden death of the top person of the new dynasty did not create chaos, although a number of pro-Amanullah, constitutionalist, and anti-British radical Afghans known as the "Young Afghans" had carried out terroristic attacks against its members for some time (one had killed the eldest brother of the late king). They accused the new rulers of being under British influence. The situation was brought under control when Shah Mahmud, the minister of defense and a brother of the late king, arrested the assassin and declared the nineteen-year-old Mohammad Zahir, the only son of the late king, the new ruler. The notables followed him in paying homage to the new king. No other change took place, and the late king's three brothers and nephews, led by Mohammad Hashim Khan as prime minister, ruled the country uninterruptedly for thirteen years until 1946.

Prime Minister Mohammad Hashim Khan worked tirelessly in maintaining law and order. He did not tolerate opposition, although he allowed provincial assemblies and the national parliament to function as provided by the constitution. Their members, however, were hand-picked. He permitted King Mohammad Zahir, his nephew, to enjoy life, but not to rule; by contrast, he trained his full nephews, Mohammad Daoud and Mohammad Na'eem, in the art of government by giving them responsible positions. The assassin and his nearest relations were executed and scores of others imprisoned. With the help of the intelligence service (*zabt-e-ahwalat*) backed by a strong army, the government arrested many constitutionalists and other persons, often for no apparent reason; they were detained in filthy prison cells for years without trial. After the late king was assassinated, the ruling circle had decided not to execute its opponents for fear of revenge.

Modern education was developed, but only gradually. After the fall of Amanullah people made no demand for it. The authorities were also not enthusiastic about education, fearing that it might produce radicals. Besides, the government had to restart education from scratch, since the 322 primary and vocational schools, which had a total of 54,000 students in 1927, had been closed after the fall of Amanullah.[2] In 1945, after a quarter of a century of the new dynasty, only 98,000 students studied in 346 primary and secondary schools, and Kabul University had only four colleges. Besides, schools were controlled lest they become the source of too liberal thought. Meanwhile, the government opened courses for officials to learn Pashto, the language of the majority; the policy was to make it, along with Persian, an official language, thus speeding the process of nation-building and consolidating ties with the transfrontier Pashtuns.[3]

Notable progress was made in the national economy, which had been destroyed during the rebellion. Masterminded by the businessman Abdul Majid Zabuli, a banking system was introduced, and joint stock companies for export and import were set up. By 1946 more than fifty such companies operated.[4] The resulting accumulation of capital made it possible for the National Bank and private companies to set up a number of factories for textile, woolen, sugar, and fruit processing. Cotton and sugar beets were grown in vast areas brought under cultivation in Qunduz in the northern part of the country. This region was connected to the southern part of the land for the first time by a vehicle-passable road crossing the Hindu Kush, an accomplishment that helped make these developments possible. Zabuli's success was partly due to his policy of making members of the dynasty, in particular the prime minister, partners in business.

Unwilling to grant concessions to its immediate neighbors, the government failed to obtain from distant governments and private companies major credits or capital for investment, in spite of the fact that it offered favorable concessions to the American Inland Exploration Company for the exploration and exploitation of oil and mineral deposits.[5] Deterrents were Afghanistan's distant, landlocked position, its difficult regions, its primitive transportation system, and, above all, its closeness to the Soviet Union. Only Nazi Germany, from 1937 onward, undertook to survey mineral deposits and extend a large amount of credit for Afghanistan to purchase German machinery. Germany sent a large number of specialists to Afghanistan, but they, along with others from Japan and Italy working on smaller projects, were expelled under pressure from the Allies during World War II.[6] Advised by a *loya jirga* (grand assembly), Prime Minister Mohammad Hashim followed a policy of "correct neutrality" during the war. After the war, when conditions both at home and abroad had changed, the king asked him to step down; thus ended Prime Minister Mohammad Hashim's long, suppressive rule. A brief democratic interlude followed.

The new prime minister, Shah Mahmud, another uncle of the king, was a mild person suitable to rule at a time when Afghanistan was applying for membership to the United Nations. His first act was to release the many political prisoners who had long languished in prisons. Significant also was the passage in 1947 of a law allowing the election of mayors by secret ballot. More significant, in 1949 the government refrained almost completely from interfering in parliamentary elections. The result was a national assembly dominated by liberal democrats who stood for constitutional monarchy. Progovernment conservatives and others reacted against the democrats, and stormy sessions marked the first freely elected assembly based on the constitution of 1931. The political atmosphere became euphoric when, following the enactment of a free press law, a number of nongovernmental weeklies—*Angar, Ulus, Watan,* and *Niday-e-Khalq*—caught the imagination of the emerging and receptive intelligentsia; among them were students of Kabul University, who formed an active organization of their own. The weeklies were significant more as a mouthpiece for the new political parties—the Awakened Youth, the Fatherland, the People, and the National Club— than for being a vehicle of propaganda among a largely illiterate people. By means of the press, reformist members of the assembly became so outspoken that the government felt it could no longer govern democratically. On the eve of the next general election, when former members of the assembly had no parliamentary immunity, they and scores of other dissidents were arrested. The rising group from the second generation of the dynasty had concluded that a strong government was needed to deal with the new situation. Led by the king and his two first cousins and brothers-in-law, Mohammad Daoud and Mohammad Na'eem, this group decided to rule with Mohammad Daoud as the new prime minister. Events in the newly created Pakistan also influenced this decision.[7]

The creation of Pakistan following the British withdrawal from the subcontinent of India in 1947 prompted Afghanistan to raise the question of the principle of self-determination in regard to Pashtunistan, now claimed by Pakistan. Afghanistan disputed Pakistan's claim over the territory, but the latter was unwilling to consider the complaint, despite the fact that it demanded itself the application of the same principle with regard to Kashmir, a territory disputed between Pakistan and India. Against the unwavering stand of Afghanistan over the issue, Pakistan retaliated by creating problems for the former's commercial goods in transit through her territory, the main route to Afghanistan. Pakistan also bombarded an Afghan village in 1949, an incident that injured Afghan pride beyond imagination. The radio war between the two countries intensified, much to the disadvantage of Pakistan. Afghan propagandists were on the offensive. Mediation efforts by friendly countries came to nothing. To decrease its dependence on Pakistan, the Afghan government concluded a number of commercial agreements with the willing Soviet Union, a new beginning in the atmosphere of cold war with a neighboring superpower with far-reaching consequences. As an ardent nationalist, the new prime minister was expected to resolve the Pashtunistan problem with Pakistan.[8]

Mohammad Daoud (1910–78) served as prime minister for ten years, 1953–63. During this decade Afghanistan experienced fundamental changes that were initiated more under his direction than under either his brother or the king. From the age of eighteen Daoud held more military positions than civilian. Like Amanullah, Daoud was a reformist, but he also stood for law and order. He introduced changes through the state, not individual or corporate channels. However, the state he relied on was not totalitarian but authoritarian. He disliked the notion of a democratic state based on individual freedom.

With the rise to power of Mohammad Daoud, the nongovernmental press ceased publication, and political parties became inactive. Elections for the national assembly were held, but they were manipulated. Once again the intelligence service (*masuniyat-e-milli*) was expanded as it had been under Prime Minister Mohammad Hashim. In 1957, when first a cabinet minister along with his colleagues and later a number of dissidents were arrested on flimsy charges, the sense of security that had prevailed with the beginning of the democratic interlude evaporated.

But progress in the economic field was visible. It started with the launching of the first Five-Year Economic Development Plan in 1957, financed partly by a Soviet loan of $100 million; a second plan was launched in 1962. Under the plans the main roads throughout the country were paved, some hydroelectric dams built, irrigation projects launched, education and health services improved or expanded, and some industries developed. Agricultural and commercial development banks were also set up. The expanding bureaucracy absorbed the increasing number of educated elements, as the state traditionally had undertaken to employ such people. But the overall development fell short of the targets originally set under the system of a "guided, mixed economy" because of the lack of statistical data, insufficient capital, and a shortage of qualified personnel. In fact, the economic development schemes were the almost total concern of the state, not of private development banks or companies, whether foreign or indigenous.[9] The foundation of the planned development was laid down, and the state became more comprehensive than ever before. Also, since the plans were financed mainly by foreign credit, the country was opened to foreign influence. No longer was Afghanistan the isolated land it had been traditionally.

In 1959 women were allowed to unveil. The unveiling proceeded smoothly in Kabul because of the increase in the number of educated women, who worked mainly as nurses, midwives, and teachers. The desire to unveil had become a marked tendency, particularly among the intelligentsia. Also, the government did not make a provocative fanfare on the occasion as did Amanullah in the 1920s, nor was the unveiling compulsory. When women members of the dynasty and spouses of senior government officials appeared unveiled in public functions, others followed suit. Only in the city of Kandahar did people rise up, but the rebellion there was due to the stupidity of the governor, whose tactless attitude regarding the unveiling provoked strong reaction. The revolt, suppressed at a cost of about sixty lives, remained local. The government was capable of dealing with such emergencies, since it had already equipped the army with modern weapons obtained from the Soviet Union.

On the Pashtunistan issue, by contrast, the government failed. Premier Daoud had set as one of his principal tasks the settlement of the Pashtunistan issue. In the beginning Pakistan's leaders showed interest in reaching a modus vivendi with Afghanistan over Pashtunistan, since they had a similar problem with India over Kashmir. However, because of unstable internal conditions Pakistan's leaders limited the traditional autonomy of its provinces, including the hitherto autonomous region of Pashtunistan, and joined the two regional military alliances, SEATO (Southeast Asia Treaty Organization) and CENTO (Central Treaty Organization), which the United States supported as an extension of the military arrangement to contain the Soviet Union. The Pakistani authorities not only discarded the Afghan claim over Pashtunistan (called the Northwest Frontier Province in Pakistan) but also curtailed its traditional autonomy. Diplomatic efforts of the two governments and mediation by friendly governments could not move either side from its position. In 1958 the Pakistani president Mohammad Ayyub, also a Pashtun, even threatened Afghanistan when, "instead of listening to the Afghan views," he "lectured Na'eem [the Afghan foreign minister] about Pakistan's military might and its ability to take Kabul within a few hours." [10] In 1954 U.S. Secretary of State John Foster Dulles, seeing Afghanistan as a country of no "security interest" to America, not only did not allow Afghanistan to purchase military hardware from the United States but even advised the Afghan foreign minister to settle the dispute with Pakistan, stating, "After careful consideration, extending military aid to Afghanistan would create problems not offset by the strength it would generate." [11]

Premier Daoud was left no choice but to approach the Soviet Union for economic as well as military aid. For its part the Soviet Union, under the leadership of Nikita Khrushchev, was willing to extend aid, hoping to keep Afghanistan outside the American-dominated military blocs. Khrushchev also supported Afghanistan's stand on Pashtunistan. Afghanistan intensified its propaganda war against Pakistan, and in 1961 it incited a major clash in Bajaur across the Durand Line. In the battle between adherents of both countries, pro-Afghan tribesmen were beaten and heavy casualties inflicted on them. Subsequently, Pakistan asked the Afghan government to close its consulates in that country, as it had closed its own consulates in Afghanistan. The Afghan government retaliated by severing diplomatic ties with Pakistan. For two years Afghanistan did not receive commercial goods either from Pakistan or through it from Western countries, some of whom had undertaken projects in Afghanistan. This isolation hit the Afghans severely, in particular the business community and the development programs. It increased Afghanistan's dependence on the Soviet Union, an ominous situation that the king and others could not tolerate. Pressured by the monarch, Premier Daoud resigned in 1963. But by then Afghanistan had become so much entangled with the Soviet Union in economic, military, and educational fields that it could not free itself unless there were an alternative and a strong will to change the course the Soviet Union had exploited to its advantage, although the government of Daoud had stood firm in its course of "positive nonalignment."

In the constitutional decade, 1963–73, the king was the central figure, although this statement may appear contradictory. King Mohammad Zahir decided that the time was ripe for Afghanistan to be ruled democratically. He supported a constitutional monarchy based on a constitution that provided for the autonomy of the three branches of the state and that guaranteed the freedom of the individual. Also, he arranged that members of the royal house (including the king's male first cousins) were to be barred from taking part in politics. The election for the national assembly was to be free, direct, general, and secret, while the senate was to be composed of members chosen partly through direct election, partly through indirect election, and partly through appointment. These were the central points of the new constitution composed by a committee of experts, passed by a loya jirga, and signed in 1964 by the king.[12]

Except for a few cases, the government did not interfere in the elections, and the two elections that were held in 1965 and 1969 produced representative national assemblies. The majority of their members were from the rural secular and religious elite, mainly interested in pressuring the executive to further their own interests and those of their own constituencies. Most had won their seats by spending money. Members of the educated middle class had little chance of success in the elections. Among the national and liberal democrats, who were elected mainly from the urban constituencies, a few were leftists, and four of the urban members were women. Thus, contrary to the spirit of a liberal constitution, the assembly was dominated by nonliberals and nondemocrats who did not know the workings of the constitution. They often failed to form a quorum and frequently fought the government, a situation that contributed to instability.

In contrast with the past, in the constitutional decade the governments—or, more precisely, the executive branches—had short lives: an average of two years for each of the five governments. They were also weaker, with no basis of power of their own; they had only the king to rely on. But the king, though supported by his younger son-in-law and cousin, Abdul Wali, and others, now had opponents in the persons of his other first cousins and brothers-in-law, Daoud and Na'eem, who had turned against the new arrangement because it excluded them from politics. Daoud skillfully joined hands with a faction of the pro-Moscow communists in opposition to the government. The king failed either to win him over to his side or to neutralize him. In addition, the government had to meet challenges from the national assemblies and unruly students incited by political parties. Although the political parties were not legal, they were active nonetheless. The government was also exposed to a free and critical press that mushroomed overnight.

The king chose premiers from among those whose loyalty to him was beyond question; however, they were not delegated the authority to choose their cabinet colleagues. Also, they did not have control over the army, nor could they stop members of the royal house from interfering in government affairs. One such interference led to the downfall in October 1965 of the first government, headed by Premier Mohammad Yusuf, an ominous beginning. Not all the premiers were qualified. Prime Minister Abdul Zahir resigned because his government was unable to deal with the emergency caused by a drought in 1972; Premier Nur Ahmad E'temadi was given the post because through him the king intended to mollify Mohammad Daoud. E'temadi was pro-Daoud and also partly anticonstitution. He permitted a faction of the pro-Moscow communists to proceed with their activities whereas he oppressed others, particularly the religious groups. This situation discouraged others from acting against a small but determined number of pro-Moscow leftists who, with others, tried to undermine the democratic arrangement.

The king's failure to sign the Political Parties Bill, the Municipalities Bill, and the Provincial Councils Bill, all passed by the parliament, prevented national, provincial, and municipal governments from taking root. The premiers relied on his goodwill. The king had no privy council and consulted certain dignitaries individually. Anarchy resulted from his failure to grant authority to the government and the latter's failure to establish a working relationship with the national assembly as well as to deal with the uncontrollable students and the problems that followed a drought in 1972. (Students who were under the spell of mainly subversive leftist parties spent more time in demonstrating than studying.) Only then did the king empower Musa Shafiq, who took bold steps in establishing the authority of the government. The new prime minister accomplished in seven months what others had failed to do in years. He was on the way to resolving the essential problems against which the previous governments had struggled, but before he was able to do so Mohammad Daoud, with the cooperation of pro-Moscow leftist military officers, overthrew the constitutional monarchy and declared Afghanistan a republic in July 1973.

The accomplishments of the constitutional decade were many. The most important accomplishment was security from government interference and the freedom to live within the bounds of law. This made it possible for a number of political parties to emerge: the People's Democratic Party of Afghanistan (PDPA), the Islamic Association (IA), the People's New Democratic Party, the Voice of the People, the Social Democratic Party, the National Unity, the Progressive Democratic Party, and the National Oppression Party. From the turmoil of these parties, which tended to split into factions, the radical pro-Moscow leftists (the PDPA), and the radical Islamic fundamentalists (the IA) came to the forefront. The IA and PDPA were supported more by their foreign patrons than by their own Afghan constituencies. Parties with no outside patrons and moderate programs did not play a major role: hence the radicalization of Afghan politics and the intolerance and violence in the decades ahead. Also, these events led to the influence of foreign powers in Afghan politics, beginning with the communist coup in 1978. I describe these and other parties in chapters 3, 4, and 5.

Also during the constitutional period, for the first time in Afghan history the government ceased to be authoritarian and its agents ceased to boss individuals. Prisoners of the previous regime were released, and no one could be imprisoned before being tried as law required. The government no longer spied on Afghans, who now enjoyed freedom as never before. Afghanistan became a haven for the unrestricted movement not only of Afghans but also of tourists, particularly the hippies of the decade. The tourist industry developed overnight, a result of the economic policy of the government, which encouraged the private sector. In the industrial and agricultural fields Afghan entrepreneurs showed dynamism. This became possible when, at the beginning of the decade, the government restored diplomatic ties with Pakistan and improved relations with Iran. The policy was to support Pashtunistan on the basis of the principle of self-determination, but without endangering Afghanistan's interests. Premier Shafiq took this point seriously and tried to develop Afghanistan's ties with Iran and Pakistan.[13]

Mohammad Daoud ruled Afghanistan as president under conditions different from those that prevailed when he served as prime minister. He now had to share power with members of the pro-Moscow communist Parcham faction of the PDPA, whose military wing helped him to usurp power. The suspension of the constitution and the coup created a power vacuum that had to be filled if stability was to become real. In the beginning the vacuum did not create problems, since the king, who was vacationing at the time of the coup in Italy, abdicated in Daoud's favor. But the coup and his reliance on the communists deprived Daoud of the service of the members of his former ruling dynasty; it also estranged him from the liberals and democrats and the fundamentalists of the Islamic Association. The free press and the security of the constitutional decade vanished. A former premier and leader of the Progressive Democratic Party was arrested, as were his colleagues and some leading members of the Islamic Association; some were executed. Hoping to make Afghanistan more dependent on the Soviet Union, the communists pressured President Daoud to adopt a policy of brinksmanship with Pakistan over the problem of Pashtunistan.

The first reaction was shown by the Islamic fundamentalists, who arose in 1975. Though suppressed, the uprising disillusioned Daoud about his comradeship with the communists and his policies in general. He then began to change his internal and external policies. Having consolidated his position, he expelled communists from the ministerial posts. To make his regime legitimate, he summoned a loya jirga of notables in 1977 and asked it to approve a constitution and elect a president for the republic. The jirga passed the constitution and elected him president for seven years, but the intrigues that were played even by Daoud damaged his credibility. Besides, a one-party system was introduced that was to be led by the official National Revolutionary Party, a bunch of bureaucrats. This system made the democratic rights granted by the constitution meaningless. Also, the president gave key posts in the new cabinet to minions of doubtful loyalty. Later a criminal code was enacted that banned political activities and empowered security officials. Although not acted on at the time, the code created fear, particularly among the communists for whose suppression it had been enacted.

Fundamental changes were introduced in foreign relations. President Daoud visited Arab countries and obtained loan commitments for his seven-year development plan from Iran, Saudi Arabia, Yemen, and Libya. More important, the confrontational attitude with Pakistan was abandoned, and after the exchange of visits to Islamabad and Kabul by leaders of both countries, the ground was prepared for the settlement of outstanding issues, including Pashtunistan. In the words of an Afghan diplomat who had attended the meetings, "In three to four years the Afghan-Pakistani dispute would have ceased to exist."[14]

The change in relations with the Soviet Union meant distancing Afghanistan from it when "the Russians had become increasingly disturbed by the emergence of new and expanded ties between Afghanistan and its Islamic neighbors." Until then Soviet-Afghan relations had improved because of the grant by the Soviet Union of new economic credit and the increase in trade between the two countries. But President Daoud was now "increasingly annoyed" at the Soviet "clandestine activities" and their efforts to unite the two factions—the Khalq and the Parcham—of the pro-Moscow PDPA. He intended to ask the Soviet leader Leonid Brezhnev "whether Soviet subversive actions in Afghanistan had received his sanction or were carried out without his knowledge." But before Daoud was able to do so, Brezhnev, in their last official meeting in the Kremlin in April 1977, lectured him, asking why Afghanistan had allowed experts from the United Nations, NATO countries, and other multilateral aid projects into northern Afghanistan adjacent to the Soviet Union. Further, he "wanted the Afghan government to get rid of those experts, who were nothing more than spies bent on promoting the cause of imperialism." Daoud was surprised. After a pause he lectured Brezhnev in return in these words; "We will never allow you to dictate to us how to run our country and whom to employ in Afghanistan. How and where we employ foreign experts will remain the exclusive prerogative of the Afghan state. Afghanistan shall remain poor, if necessary, but free in its acts and decisions."[15]

In 1977 a series of terroristic attacks by Islamic fundamentalists and leftists disturbed the peace in Kabul. On 17 April 1978 Mier Akbar Khybar, a prominent member of the PDPA, fell victim to such an attack. The PDPA's leaders held a funeral procession in which some spoke against the government. Since the procession was a demonstration of strength and in violation of the criminal code, the government took action. On 25 April 1978 the police detained seven members of the PDPA's politburo as ordinary prisoners in the mud-walled prison cells in the center of the city. The police delayed arresting Hafizullah Amin, a military liaison officer of the Khalq faction of PDPA, until the next day, when they searched his house. This gave Amin time to draw up a plan of operation for overthrowing the government, an order that was carried out on 27 and 28 April, while he was still in prison, by military officers who were almost all Khalqis. Unwilling to submit, President Daoud was killed, as were eighteen members of his family and a number of his ministers.

Thus ended the dominance of the Durranis, who had ruled Afghanistan since 1747. The persons now destined to govern had different ethnolinguistic backgrounds. They were a cross-section of society, but as part of the educated middle class, particularly as communists, they had alienated themselves from their origins. None had lofty social standing. Except for Nur Mohammad Taraki, general secretary of the PDPA, they were more or less of the same age and thus unwilling to submit to any of themselves as a ruler. The communist ideology had tied them to the party, the medium of power, but this solidarity reflected more their desire to acquire power than their desire to unite in a common cause— hence their potential for divisiveness. The potential exploded into hostile forces after they became a political ruling class. Besides, most had no administrative experience, but each was convinced that the PDPA blueprint was the guideline for reorganizing both society and state. Thus, they relied on Soviet, not Afghan, experience, and thus, too, they broke with the Afghan past. This may explain why, after they rose to power, they became ever more alienated from their own people and ever more disunited among themselves. As of 1994, the political vacuum they created remained unfilled.

Following the coup, the PDPA ruled Afghanistan with Nur Mohammad Taraki as president of the Revolutionary Council, prime minister, and general secretary of the PDPA. Intolerant of opposition, the government began to implement socialistic programs by issuing a series of eight decrees, including the land reform decree, in an authoritarian manner without regard for consensus and social conventions. The government relied on the army, the police, the party, and, of course, the support of the Soviet Union. The government's socialistic programs, its single-party dictatorship, and the excesses its officials and party personnel committed resulted not in winning over the populace, as it had hoped, but in popular uprisings, all of which the government suppressed, just as it suppressed rival political parties of the right and left. Even within the PDPA, the ruling Khalqi faction suppressed the Parcham faction and sent its leaders abroad as ambassadors, later dismissing them. Within the Khalq faction, too, rifts occurred, and the strong Hafizullah Amin replaced Taraki as head of government and the party. All this weakened the government and made it still more dependent on the Soviet Union.

After Amin tried to rule Afghanistan the way Marshall Tito had ruled Yugoslavia, the Soviet Union intervened.

What follows in this book is based mainly on a journal of events, written in Pashto and exceeding a thousand pages, that I kept from mid–1979 to my imprisonment in 1982. My prison life (1982–87) gave me an unparalleled opportunity to interview many well-informed inmates, including some Khalqi senior officials. Because I was known to be a historian, many inmates trusted me with information, as did other well-informed Afghans after my release from the prison. I have lived through the period about which, as a student of Afghan history, I was curious to know.

This work covers the period from 1979 until 1982. A chapter on the events before the invasion has been added to describe the circumstances under which the Soviet Union decided to invade. Although the period is arbitrary, the richness of events, the abundance of data, and my personal experience of it make it important enough to warrant a separate study. The richness of the period is due to the determination of the occupation forces to suppress the resistance quickly before the occupation could become an issue and the outside world could justify its assistance to it.

Despite the sheer quantity of interesting events, no historian in any language has so far studied the period as a unit in detail. Impressed by the Soviet determination to subdue the Afghans, the English-speaking world paid only marginal attention to the resistance forces of a geographically remote neighbor of the Soviet Union. The Western world was under the impression that since the Soviets had dominated their neighbor countries in Eastern Europe, they would also dominate their neighbor country of Afghanistan. Afghan resistance was held to be unviable. With that impression in mind, the Soviet Union and the regime it installed tried to isolate the hitherto nonaligned, independent, and Muslim Afghanistan from the outside world. Under these circumstances there unfolded a story of conflict between the fighting men of a Third World country, determined to preserve their national and Islamic identity, and the fighting men of a superpower that wished to bring them into the orbit of a communist state. This work deals with this confrontation. It is a political history that revolves around men, policies, and events. I describe only those aspects of the government and society that the Kabul regime tried to change. The work is, in short, an epitome of a political and military dynamism—or a dynamic vandalism—in which people are the central theme.

The account is divided into four parts. Part 1 deals with why and how the Soviets invaded Afghanistan. The intervention unleashed powerful forces of resistance to the invaders and the client government; this resistance and the reaction of the Kabul regime are the subject of parts 2 and 3. Part 4 concerns a more intensified degree of this confrontation, an account of genocide that the occupation forces committed in an attempt to uproot the resistance.

PART ONE

A Client Government in Afghanistan

CHAPTER ONE

The Soviet Invasion of Afghanistan

At half past six on the evening of Thursday, 27 December 1979, an explosion occurred in the central part of the general communications system in the city of Kabul. Three days before, the minister of communications of the Soviet Union had been a guest of honor of the Democratic Republic of Afghanistan. He had been given the chance to see the hub of the communications system for a reason. The purpose of the host government was to obtain technical assistance from the Soviet Union. But the purpose of the minister was to pinpoint the center of the system in order to paralyze the whole communications network later, when the Soviet invasion began.

After darkness set in, about five thousand Soviet soldiers, who had been landing during the past three days at the International Airport of Kabul,[1] headed toward Tapa-e-Tajbeg palace, where Hafizullah Amin, president of the Revolutionary Council, prime minister of the Democratic Republic of Afghanistan, and general secretary of the People's Democratic Party of Afghanistan, had transferred his seat from the city palace on 19 December 1979. The new palace had originally been the seat of the reformist King Amanullah (1919–29). Before Amin became the head of state, the Khalqi government had spent more than one billion afghanis (approximately $20 million) to repair the palace and make it a suitable seat for his predecessor, Nur Mohammad Taraki. President Amin moved into it at the urging of his Soviet advisers. He also wanted to be away from the old palace, which reminded him of the many bloody events that had taken place there. But Tapa-e-Tajbeg, situated on a mound two miles south of the city, could easily be attacked should the Soviet Union decide to do so. That evening, the Soviet military units in Kabul carried out such an order.

STORMING OF THE PRESIDENTIAL PALACE

At twenty minutes past seven, Tapa-e-Tajbeg was shelled by rockets from the west side. That evening under a clear sky the fertile Chardi Basin, where Tajbeg is located, became a scene of carnage. The sounds of rockets prompted many people in the city, myself among them, to climb onto the flat rooftops of their houses to see what was happening. Because of the tyranny of the government, the people had turned against it and hoped to see it toppled. They were, however, disappointed. Instead of Afghans, the Alpha antiterrorist squad of the KGB, dressed in Afghan uniforms and commanded by Colonel Boyarinov, had gone into operation.[2] Leaders of both the party and the government were also caught unaware. They had a blind faith in the Kremlin rulers and did not expect that their supporters would overthrow them by force. An exception may have been President Amin, but on this point his views had not become known.

The rocket attack was the external sign of the operations. The scene of the major operations was on the ground. The armored units had already started moving from Kabul International Airport, located on the opposite side of the city. They needed time to reach Tajbeg and other strategic places. The operation began on one of the longest nights of the year. From Kabul International Airport the units headed to the various places in the outskirts of the city where Afghan army divisions had been stationed. The movements of these units made the earth shake as if Kabul had been hit by one of its periodic tremors.

The sounds of these movements were heard as far as Khushal Maina, in the western outskirts of the city, from where I was watching the scene. The Russian military units headed toward the various military and strategic centers, such as tank units number four and fifteen in the Pul-e-Charkhi area, the Qargha Division, the Rishkhor Division, the police force of the Ministry of Interior, the television and radio station, and, of course, the presidential palace. These were all the organized military and strategic centers in and around the capital city from which immediate opposition could be offered; occupying them would ensure immediate success.

The Soviets intended to occupy the nerve centers of the city unaware. "Russian advisers already attached to Afghan army units repeated tricks used during the 1968 invasion of Czechoslovakia. Turn in all live ammunition and substitute blank rounds for a 'training exercise,' the Afghan soldiers had been told. Batteries were removed from vehicles for winterization. . . . Due to an alleged shortage, the diesel fuel in the older tanks had to be siphoned off for the replacement armor."[3] Also, Soviet advisers had persuaded some of the personnel of the Kabul air base to go on vacation and then had given their duties to the newly arrived Soviet experts. Although Soviet advisers did not directly control the units, as they had before Amin came to power, they succeeded in persuading the Afghan personnel to do their bidding.

Some former leading members of the faction of the party to which President Amin belonged accompanied the invading units. Being influential with the army, they had turned against Amin when, in September of the same year, a split in the leadership occurred that led to their expulsion. They then took refuge in the Soviet embassy. When the invading military units attacked Tajbeg, two of them, Sayyed Mohammad Gulabzoy and Asadullah Sarwari, guided the invaders. But the presidential guards stationed near the palace held them back with counterattacks.

A POISONED LUNCHEON IN THE PRESIDENTIAL PALACE

All this time President Amin was lying half-conscious in the palace, incapacitated by KGB agents. Around one o'clock that day, Amin, with a number of his leading party and government officials, had been poisoned when consuming a special luncheon that the palace had arranged in honor of Ghulam Dastagir Panjsheri, a member of the central committee of the party. Panjsheri had returned from a long trip to the Soviet Union. Although not on good terms with Amin, Panjsheri had told him that he had brought good tidings and wished to discuss them with him and other comrades. Since Panjsheri was the only one who did not consume the poisoned food, he was suspected. Some kind of light poison had been mixed with the soup and *ashak* (a special Afghan dish) served by two Russian girls who were working as waitresses in the palace. Also, "a number of Afghan leaders were arrested at a Soviet-hosted reception staged at the Intercontinental Hotel. . . . Similarly, Afghan army liaison officers were isolated at a reception party."[4]

The chief cook of the palace was Michail Talebov, a native of Soviet Azerbaijan, who, as a lieutenant colonel, was in the pay of the KGB.[5]

He had been employed at the urging of Soviet advisers. Amin was unwilling to have either the waitresses or the cook, but his Soviet comrades had told him that because his personal safety was a matter of utmost significance, these persons were necessary to perform such sensitive jobs. Amin was still reluctant to accept the advice. At last he acquiesced, but he made it known that they were welcome only until he found some trustworthy Afghan employees.

At the time of the attack Amin was conscious but groggy. After the effects of the poisoning had been felt, a team of physicians, including an old Russian physician from the Four-Hundred-Bed Hospital, began treating Amin. The hospital, which had been built with Russian funds, was the most modern hospital in Afghanistan. The physicians and nurses were still in the palace when it came under fire. Because the communication lines had been cut, Amin did not know what was happening.

PRESIDENT AMIN'S FAITH IN HIS SOVIET COMRADES

At this time Jahandad, commander of the eighteen hundred presidential guards, presented himself to Amin and asked for instructions. Amin wanted to know who the attackers were. When told that they were the comrades from the north, Amin was stunned. He did not believe his communist comrades would overthrow his government by force, even though he had earlier confided to one of his senior surviving officials that the Soviets might do away with him personally. As will be described in the next chapter, early in 1979 Soviet Premier Alexi Kosygin had made clear to Kabul that the Soviet government did not wish to send its troops to Afghanistan. That was why, even in the gravest minutes of his life, Amin did not believe Jahandad, to whom he had entrusted his own life and the lives of his dearest ones. He even admonished Jahandad for his report.

There are two versions of what Amin told his protecting commander. One version is that Amin said the attackers might be the Ikhwanis, that is, the Muslim fundamentalists who are the irreconcilable enemies of the communists. This version cannot be taken seriously, because the Ikhwanis in the army were not strong enough to make a coup. During the twenty-month rule of the Khalqis, the army had been purged of Ikhwanis.

More likely is the second version, according to which Amin told Jahandad, "It is the work of Paktiawal"—that is, people from the province of Paktia. In the present context "Paktiawal" referred to Sayyed

Mohammad Gulabzoy, Asadullah Sarwari, and Aslam Watanjar. Except for Sarwari, who was from the province of Ghazni bordering the province of Paktia, the others were from Paktia. All three were military officers who had played prominent roles in the communist coup as well as the coup that overthrew the constitutional monarchy. They had influence with the army, which was officered by a considerable number of persons from Paktia. Until their break with Amin, Sarwari was head of the Intelligence Department (AGSA), while the others were cabinet ministers. At first close friends of Amin, they later turned against him, siding with President Nur Mohammad Taraki in opposition to Amin. When Amin overcame them, they took refuge in the Soviet embassy.

On this point, as well as a number of others that will be described in the next chapter, Amin's relations with the Soviets became strained. The Soviets, however, showed no signs of displeasure. Although the initial warmth of the relationships that existed between them had evaporated, the Soviets showed interest in supporting Amin's government. In particular, during the last weeks of Amin's rule the Soviet Union sent a number of missions to Kabul to help the government organize its five-year development plan, which it intended to launch at the beginning of the new Afghan year (21 March 1980), and also to assess the amount of credit that it wished to extend. The three opponents of Amin now assisted the invading forces. Amin was thus partly correct in saying that the attack was the work of Paktiawal.

It is unknown what specific instructions, if any, Amin gave to Jahandad. What is known is that Jahandad, who was of the Sabari tribe from the district of Khost of Paktia Province, had decided that the time had come to prove his loyalty to the land of his birth and defy the invaders, even though they were the Soviets. On returning to his brigade, Jahandad ordered his men, who were a select corps of the loyal party members and close relatives of Amin, to fight the aggressors. They counterattacked and halted the initial advance of the invaders. The confrontation was intense and prolonged. Both sides sustained losses until the Afghans were finally overcome by some kind of nerve gas. The Afghans were in a commanding position in the nine-kilometer-long perimeter of the palace. The palace is, as already noted, situated on a mound. Also, the Soviet soldiers did not overwhelm the Afghan soldiers in numbers, although they were, of course, better armed. The invaders feared that if the Afghans were not soon overcome, forces from the nearby military divisions of Rishkhor and Qargha might join them.

According to eyewitnesses, "The Soviet soldiers then launched, from a sort of large gun, a grey gas in the direction of the Afghan soldiers, causing dizziness, nausea and paralysis of the limbs."[6] According to Ghulam M. Zurmulwal, the Afghan troops were overcome by the use of "napalm bombs and incendiary bombs."[7] This still did not bring an end to the fighting. Troops from the nearby Rishkhor Division arrived and started firing toward the enemies. But by that time the invaders had entered the palace and were themselves in a commanding position. Firing in the surrounding area of the palace was heard throughout the night and even into the next morning. Of the eighteen hundred soldiers of the presidential guards, none survived. "Boyarinov ordered that no witnesses in the palace were to survive to tell the tale."[8] Those who were still alive but unconscious were killed by the invaders after they entered the palace. They carried their bodies to the foot of nearby hills, where they buried them; the burial sites were forbidden areas throughout the occupation. To distort the truth, the new regime spread rumors that the presidential guards dispersed after they were defeated. In fact, those who dispersed were soldiers from the Rishkhor Division. Only Jahandad was taken alive; he was then imprisoned in the Pul-e-Charkhi prison with other members of the government and later executed.

THE ELIMINATION OF PRESIDENT AMIN

The actual target of the attack was President Amin. After the return of Jahandad, nothing was heard of Amin. After overcoming the presidential guards, the invaders, accompanied by Gulabzoy and Sarwari, entered the palace. The medical team—including the old Russian physician and the head of the team, physician Wilayat Khan—was still attending to Amin. When the invaders entered the palace, they shot at random, but not as thoroughly as elsewhere. The Soviet physician was killed in the frenzy. So was the wife of Foreign Minister Shah Wali, who, along with her husband, was among the guests. The physician Wilayat Khan, speaking in the Ukrainian language, pleaded with the attackers from behind the Soviet nurses and was spared. Shah Wali was lucky to escape death; he, along with a number of others, had already been taken to the Four-Hundred-Bed-Hospital for treatment.

What happened to Amin is not known for sure. Sarwari and Gulabzoy have been quoted as saying that before they entered the palace Amin was already dead, killed either by soldiers under their command or by his own hand.[9] This is not true. As guides accompanying the invading units, Sarwari and Gulabzoy had no soldiers under their command. That

Amin did not kill himself is clear from a statement by Nikolai Berlev, a member of the attacking Alpha group. According to Berlev, "Dressed in an Adidas T-shirt and blue boxing shorts, Amin rushed out of the room with a gun in his hand, and was instantly shot dead." Besides, according to Berlev, "Sarwari was frightened and completely broken, [but] when he was led upstairs and shown Amin's dead body, he felt as if someone had attached wings to his back. He cheered up almost at once."[10] Yet Berlev's account is also unreliable: Afghans do not wear T-shirts and boxing shorts in the winter. Besides, such outfits are not fashionable among Afghans, particularly among their rulers, who want to look dignified; Amin himself wore the loose national costume at home. Still more important, Amin and others, as already described, had been poisoned, and thus he was unable to "rush out of the room with a gun in his hand." I am certain that the luncheon in the palace on that day had been poisoned. Of my many informants, one had consumed the luncheon and had been treated in the hospital. All this does not make clear how Amin was killed. According to one source, the invaders took Amin and a few others into the grounds, where they shot them dead. According to a number of other sources, Amin was seized alive and taken to the Soviet embassy in a black limousine guarded by two tanks. Whatever the truth, "When it was all over, Amin's bullet-riddled body was displayed to the half-jubilant, half-petrified leaders of the new Soviet client state."[11]

While President Daoud lost eighteen members of his family in the coup, Amin lost only a few: himself and two of his eldest sons. He was survived by his wife, Patmanay, his youngest son, two daughters, and a grandson. His wife, perhaps by chance, had not eaten the poisoned food. On the eve of the communist coup, she helped Amin by safeguarding incriminating documents while their house was being searched by the police; in the present coup she managed to call for a medical team. She also opposed the transfer of the sick Amin to a Soviet medical center, as the Soviets, presumably through the old physician, had urged. "It appears the Soviets originally intended to incapacitate and kidnap Amin."[12]

OCCUPATION OF OTHER MILITARY CENTERS

Meanwhile, the invading units carried on operations in other parts of the city. Below the palace was the headquarters of the Ministry of Defense. Since Amin served also as the minister of defense, the next important person was Mohammad Ya'qub, the chief of staff. Since he was

sent food from the presidential palace, he too had been poisoned, but
he was still in his office when the building came under fire. Here the
invading units showed no concern for human life. On entering the building, soldiers threw hand grenades and fired wildly. An unknown number
of people were killed. Only a small number survived, having been left
for dead. The police officers and men of the Ministry of Interior also
perished in a matter of hours. A Soviet adviser of the police department
asked its director, Sayyed Ali Shah Paiman, to be his guest that evening
without giving him a hint of the impending catastrophe. Sensing something unpleasant in the air, Paiman declined the invitation so that he
could remain in his office.

At the Kabul radio and television building, the guards, who had been
stationed in two tanks, offered resistance until they were overcome. The
heroism shown by a Kandahari guard stationed in an inaccessible point
somewhere near the entrance is worth mentioning. He refused to let
anybody in without instructions from his superiors. Unwilling to damage the building, the aggressors halted. The guard felt he had accomplished his duty. However, a station adviser known as Paichalov, whom
the guard knew and trusted, approached him and stabbed him to death.

Asadullah Sarwari was later commissioned to bring about the submission of the Intelligence Department. Since he was its first president,
and since the incumbent, Asadullah Amin, nephew and son-in-law of
President Amin, was in Moscow at the time, Sarwari fulfilled his mission. According to Khalqi sources, Soviet advisers had persuaded Asadullah Amin to go to Moscow for treatment after he had consumed a
poisoned apple; this was the work of KGB agents. Other sources have
said that he had been injured in a shootout in mid-December in the
presidential palace. In any case, his absence impaired the job of intelligence collection during the days preceding the invasion. Aslam Watanjar
had accompanied the Soviet military force to the Afghan armored units
near the Pul-e-Charkhi prison, where he persuaded the garrisons not to
resist Soviet troops because Amin's removal was, in his words, "for the
good of the country."[13] Watanjar had initiated the first communist coup
from there when he was commander of one of its units.

The invading units must have been concerned with the possible reaction by Division Eight of Qargha and Division Seven of Rishkhor. Neither showed any determined opposition. As already noted, General
Aziem Ahmadzay, chief of staff of the Rishkhor Division, sent some
troops to reinforce the besieged palace guards, but they could not accomplish anything decisive. Abdul Sattar, commander of the Qargha

Division, at first was unwilling to submit. His units even attacked the invaders, damaging two Soviet tanks. Unwilling to retaliate, they sent Aslam Watanjar to Abdul Sattar. Whatever was exchanged between them, Sattar accepted the coup as a fait accompli.

THE DEFIANT ATTITUDE OF THE GHAZNI MILITARY DIVISION

The defiant military division of the province of Ghazni, numbering thirteen thousand soldiers, soon became a source of concern for the new rulers. Its commandant, Ja'far Sartairay (Zadran), argued that the division was loyal to Amin and did not believe the accusations that the new rulers had brought against him. The authorities summoned the commandant to Kabul, but he refused to go, reasoning that in his absence the division might rebel. On the fourth day of the invasion, Marshal Sergei Sokolov, the Soviet supreme commander in Kabul, set out for Ghazni at the head of a joint Russo-Afghan mission. There Sokolov told a gathering of military officers that Amin had established connections with the CIA and the Ikhwanis and that he wanted to turn Afghanistan into another Chile. Sokolov also said that Amin intended to do away with progressive officers and establish a fascist regime. To convince the skeptical officers, he told them that the Soviet government had in its possession evidence to prove the accusations, which it would disclose at an appropriate time. The new regime and the Soviet Union would repeat these accusations against Amin in the years ahead. In private, however, Sokolov warned the commandant that if the division opposed the government, it would be wiped out, and he would be held responsible for it. The commandant then acquiesced. He remained in his position for the next four months, after which he was transferred to Kabul to serve as a teacher. In 1990 he was killed in one of the coup attempts.

MILITARY OFFICERS AND THE INVASION: AN EVALUATION

In the next chapter I discuss Amin's relations with the Soviets and to describe why they invaded Afghanistan. Here I want to evaluate the attitude of the military officers toward the invasion. To understand this matter, the following points about the army must be borne in mind. When the Khalqis came to power, they tried to make the army a "Khalqi army," that is, the army of the people. They purged the army of the non-Khalqi officers and promoted their own officers. This was the biggest source of tension, which, along with other problems, led to major abortive uprisings, all of which weakened the army.

Added to this was the alienation of many officers, particularly in Division Seven of Rishkhor, who were loyal to President Taraki, replaced by Amin after their differences had led to a confrontation that will be detailed in the next chapter. The pro-Taraki officers rebelled after Taraki was suffocated on 9 October 1979. Although pro-Amin officers were more numerous than any other committed group of officers, and although they were more determined than either the pro-Taraki or Parchami officers, they declined to oppose the invaders, despite the fact that of all communist officers the pro-Amin officers were the most patriotic and the least communist. The presence in the invading army of Sarwari, Watanjar, and Gulabzoy might have influenced the officers not to respond actively. More important was the faith these officers had in communism and the Soviet Union. Even officers loyal to Amin did not know of his disillusionment with the Soviets. Also, the effects of the indoctrination courses on communism and friendship with the Soviet Union carried out in the army cells cannot be discounted. On the point of winning Soviet friendship, the two main factions of the party, Khalqi and Parchami, competed with each other so much that people sarcastically remarked that in order to win the Soviet favor, they behaved as if they were cowives.

All this led to a naive belief among the communist officers that the Soviet Union was the true friend of the Afghans and that whatever its rulers did was for their good. Whether these officers were communists is open to question, but their faith in the Soviet Union was total. Their sudden rise to power had intoxicated them. After the invasion some officers argued that because Amin had betrayed communism, the Soviet Union was forced to do what it did. Also, the commanding officers were confounded by events because they did not have instructions from Amin on what to do if the Soviet Union invaded their country. Besides, unlike most Afghans, they were aware of the Soviet military might, and they had been influenced by propaganda about the dangers posed to the "glorious April Revolution" by "reactionary forces" and "imperialists" led by "the world-consuming imperialist," that is, the United States of America. This meant that their country, their compatriots, and their dignity, which required them to stand against invaders as their predecessors had stood, were sacrificed for an ideology that served the national interest of Russia.

Never before have the Afghan defenders of national dignity failed in their duty as these communist officers failed. Never before have uniformed Afghan military officers been insulted so much as these officers were by individual men and women, particularly the latter, in public places in the city of Kabul for months after the invasion. To escape the sarcastic remarks of women, these officers avoided going by public buses in the city in uniform, as is the custom in Afghanistan. Indeed, the expression *Mairmun Mansabdar* (Mrs. Officer) became a common insult in the months after the invasion.

CHAPTER TWO

Why Did the Soviet Union Invade?

In the events that led to the Soviet invasion, Hafizullah Amin played a major role, particularly after he replaced Taraki as president of the Revolutionary Council and general secretary of the party. Amin (1929–79) was a Kharotay Ghilzay Pashtun from the Qazi Khel village of the Paghman district to the west of Kabul. His father had served as a police officer in the constitutional period. Amin had graduated from the College of Sciences of Kabul University and had twice been on American educational grants to the United States for higher studies. He had obtained a master's degree at Columbia University and been elected president of the Afghan Students Association; in 1965, just as he was about to start work on his doctoral dissertation, he was called home. Before leaving for the United States he had been a teacher at two government-run high schools, Ibn-e-Sena and Teacher's Training; afterward he continued teaching there and served as principal of Ibn-e-Sena. Both schools had students mainly from the countryside, which gave Amin a chance to influence the future teachers and military officers.

Amin returned to Afghanistan in late 1965 a bitter man but determined to stand up against the political establishment, which he thought to have deprived him of his right to higher education. He joined the PDPA, and thereafter the bitter man turned into a dynamic political man—particularly after the 1969 general election, when he won a seat in parliament from his Paghman constituency. But within the PDPA he had opponents who accused him of being a CIA agent. They had turned against him because Amin pursued a policy of creating a power base for himself, particularly among the Pashtun recruits. His opponents feared the prospect of Amin coming to power. On the eve of the coup when the Parcham and Khalq factions united, they asked Taraki to relieve Amin of the post of liaison officer with the military, but before the latter could do so Amin made the coup and stood head and shoulders high among his rival peers.

Amin was anxious to be on good terms with the Soviets. This he had ensured even before the coup had been made. The villa of the Soviet TASS correspondent in Kabul was the meeting place between Karmal and Taraki and the KGB men. When Amin became important as a military liaison officer, Taraki introduced him to the KGB man in Kabul. "The KGB began . . . to see Amin regularly at the TASS villa. During those secret meetings, Amin told the KGB about Khalq members in the army, and brought all in all about 300 names of servicemen."[1] After the coup Amin was a deputy premier and minister of foreign affairs, and, thanks to his influence with the army, he was able to extend control over the Ministry of Defense and Ministry of Interior and bypass their Parchami ministers in reshuffling their personnel.[2] He also "skillfully influenced the opinions of the Soviet ambassador [Alexander Puzanov] and numerous Soviet advisers who were sent to Afghanistan on his and Taraki's requests. . . . Amin isolated the advisers from . . . Karmal, and quickly indoctrinated [Nikolai] Simonenko, turning him into a supporter of the Khalq faction."[3] Simonenko was chief of the Soviet advisers in Kabul. Amin felt confident that "the Soviets would not interfere with his plans," particularly after Puzanov declined to meet with Karmal, who—along with his brother, Mahmud Baryalay, and Anahita Ratibzad—had spent a night at the villa of the correspondent to meet with the ambassador, secretly going there after Amin had decided to send them abroad as ambassadors.[4] However, Amin's amicable relations with the Soviets did not last long. His differences with the Kremlin masters became apparent on two fronts: ideological and political.

Amin held that in developing countries such as Afghanistan the military, not workers or peasants, could bring about revolution. In such societies, Amin believed, the workers were few, and the peasants, though numerous, were scattered, unorganized, and politically unaware. It would take too long to wait for them to become aware and organized so that they could play a role in overthrowing the established order. In such a situation, the ideologically advanced communists should concentrate on the military officers, whose profession tends to make them modernists and secularists. Using Marxist theory and Leninist organization to transform society from feudalism to socialism, these vanguards of the working-class movement should organize the military. In a speech at the Institute of Polytechnic after the coup in 1978, Amin propounded his views along these lines, indicating that his comrades in the socialist camp might not accept his theory but that he was willing to discuss his beliefs with them.

For Amin, this theory had practical implications. As a military liaison member he had recruited, trained, and mobilized military officers with whose help he had toppled the government of Mohammad Daoud. The military support also enabled Amin to send abroad his Parcham opponents, including Karmal. It was on this point that the rift began between Amin and Karmal, first appearing in a politburo meeting after the coup. As an orthodox internationalist Marxist with no substantial support among the military, Karmal argued that the military officers were unable to absorb Marxist theory. Karmal's purpose was to weaken Amin's position. Although Soviet theoreticians had expounded a similar thesis in connection with Africa, Amin's notion of making Afghanistan a Third World model for passage to socialism without the direct support of the Soviet Union was bound to be considered heresy.[5] Still, had other differences not arisen, "the Soviet Union would scarcely have launched its invasion, with all its enormous political, economic, and psychological costs, for the sake of semantics."[6]

RIFT IN THE KHALQ LEADERSHIP

Amin's relations with Taraki and the Soviet Union became strained simultaneously; it is thus necessary to trace them a little more closely. The strain in relations appeared during the Herat uprising in March 1979, in which about twenty-five thousand people were killed.[7] The uprising was so serious that "the Soviets stepped in to support their puppet Kabul regime. Squadrons of ground-attack bombers, . . . based at Doshanbe in Russian Tajikistan, . . . drop[ped] their payloads on Herat."[8] But Taraki wanted full Soviet involvement. To suppress the uprising and "save the revolution," Taraki told the Soviet premier Alexi Kosygin, "We need practical and technical help in both men and weapons." To get that aid, Taraki importuned "like a merchant in the Kabul market, using flattery and cajolery." During a secret trip, he assured his host, "We will never be as close to anyone else as we are to you. We are the pupils of Lenin." But Premier Kosygin could not be moved, arguing,

"If our troops were sent in, the situation in your country would not improve. On the contrary, it would get worse." Kosygin, however, promised him additional military experts as well as grain and credit.[9] The recently disclosed Soviet archives on Afghanistan have no reference to Amin on this point. Perhaps he did not know of Taraki's request, but one reported incident suggests that he was against it.

After the Herat uprising, the difference between Amin and Taraki became evident; nevertheless, because of his role in suppressing it, Amin was promoted to the position of first minister (Lomray Wazir), not prime minister, as is generally understood. Also, from then on Soviet advisers who favored Taraki worked to enlarge the differences. They preferred Taraki because he wanted a closer relationship with the Soviet Union, particularly in foreign affairs. "Whereas Amin did not favor the idea of Afghanistan being pushed into the Soviet bloc, Taraki did. Similarly, with regard to the pursuit of the policy of non-alignment, Taraki preferred that Afghanistan should be non-aligned on the model of Cuba with the active support of the Soviet bloc, whereas Amin intended to keep away from the Soviet bloc, and forge friendly relations with all countries."[10]

Amin's domestic policy also created friction. After he got the new post as well as the post of minister of defense, Amin tried to monopolize power, thereby alienating not only Taraki but also his close friends, Asadullah Sarwari, Aslam Watanjar, Sayyed Mohammad Gulabzoy, and Sher Jan Mizdooryar, known as the "Gang of Four." Mizdooryar, although a member of the Gang of Four, was insignificant. Each of the first three, however, having played a role in the communist coup and being more or less of the same age as Amin, felt a sense of rivalry with him. They rallied behind Taraki, who, as a cofounder of the party and as an elder, was like a father to them.

In this context the role played by the Soviet advisers proved crucial. Raja Anwar states that "Sarwari's defection from the Khalq chessboard was not the handiwork of Soviet advisers."[11] This is not true. First, Sarwari had not defected from "the Khalq chessboard." Sarwari defected from Amin's side to Taraki's, but he remained within the same chessboard. Second, AGSA's chief adviser, Colonel Bogdanov, who was at the same time the KGB chief in Kabul, influenced Sarwari to the extent that the latter would use abusive language against Amin. With Taraki's support and the encouragement by his own advisers, Sarwari worked as if he were the head of an autonomous body. The Soviet advisers in AGSA worked on instructions only from Taraki. The great amount of human blood that AGSA shed was the work more of Sarwari than of anyone else. Of all the Khalqi leaders, Sarwari was the most radical and the most adventurous. His superior, Amin, could not restrain him; indeed, he and his associates feared AGSA.

Despite these developments, Amin still needed Taraki. Amin was anxious to keep him pleased, but at the same time he tried to strip him of power. In public, however, he praised the old man, who had developed a cult of personality. To alienate Taraki from the triumvirate, Amin concentrated on building up Taraki's public image by calling him the "genius of the East," "the powerful master," and "the body and soul of the party," while referring to himself as "his loyal disciple" (*shagird-e-wafadar*). Amin raised Taraki to the status of Romania's Ceausescu, whose admirers praised him as the "Genius of the Carpathians" and the "Danube of Thought." It was depressing to see the grinning image of yesterday's Afghan plebeian projected from the huge framed photos fixed on the front of numerous public buildings in the city of Kabul. Even in the early stage of their rule, I noted the name of Taraki with lofty titles thirty times in three pages of the government-controlled newspaper, *Anis*.

Taraki, however, could not be pleased, especially when Amin engaged in nepotism. Taraki was unwilling to serve as a figurehead under "his loyal disciple," whom he had, before their rise to power, saved from his opponents. The climax came in July 1979: in a politburo meeting, Amin pronounced Taraki responsible for the government's failures. In August, Taraki accused Amin of nepotism.[12] It seemed impossible for them to iron out their differences along the democratic principles on which their Marxist-Leninist party was based, even though recently they had reaffirmed their faith in the principle of "collective leadership and collective decision." So far, however, their struggle was confined within their own circle.

SOVIET SCHEME FOR A NEW AFGHAN GOVERNMENT

The Soviet leaders, through their agents in AGSA, must have known of the rift. The ambassador Alexander Puzanov worked to promote the Soviet scheme. That scheme was to unite the two factions of the party by sending Amin abroad as an ambassador and preparing the ground for the formation of a new government to be composed of the Taraki and Karmal factions. The scheme made it necessary for Taraki and Karmal to meet. The task of arranging a meeting between the two was made easier when Taraki stopped in Moscow on 10 September 1979 on his way home from Havana, where he had attended a meeting of the heads of the nonaligned countries. Karmal had been summoned from his hide-out somewhere in Czechoslovakia, where he was spending his life of exile after the same Taraki had deprived him of Afghan citizenship a year earlier.

Anwar states that at the Moscow airport a meeting chaired by Gro-myko was arranged between the hitherto antagonistic leaders.[13] This is not true. Taraki stayed in Moscow for two days (10 and 11 September) and met twice with Brezhnev, Gromyko, and Brezhnev's foreign affairs adviser, Andrey Alexander, in the Kremlin. The first meeting was also attended by Afghan Foreign Minister Shah Wali and Sayyed Moham-mad Daoud Tarun, President Taraki's aide de camp. This meant that it was an ordinary meeting. But the second meeting went awry. When the Afghans, as before, took seats, they were told that all should leave ex-cept for President Taraki. Shah Wali and Tarun still remained, thinking that as senior officials they would also be taking part as before. But the security guards roughly pushed them out.[14] The meeting must have been exceptional. The exclusion of Shah Wali probably meant the inclusion of Karmal. The joint communiqué issued following the meetings made no reference to the formation of a government representing a "national democratic front." Afghan sources stated that Taraki and Brezhnev had agreed to change the Afghan government. Probably, as Anwar states, Soviet leaders had advised Taraki to send Amin and his supporters into diplomatic exile and appoint Karmal prime minister and deputy general secretary of the party, while he was to remain as head of the party and the state. What is now certain is that "Moscow urged Taraki to put Amin in his place, with help from ambassador Puzanov, . . . General Iva-nov, and General Pavlovsky." At the time, the latter two were on mis-sions in Kabul as representatives of the KGB and the Soviet Ministry of Defense respectively.[15] The phrase "to put Amin in his place" could mean anything. It was hoped that these changes would result in a gov-ernment representing a "national democratic front."[16] Taraki had to put the scheme into operation.

On the day when Taraki's plane was about to land at Kabul airport, Sarwari had arranged that a death squad would gun down Amin when he was on his way to receive Taraki. But in this game Amin proved supe-rior to his rivals. Since the official next to Sarwari in AGSA worked secretly for him, Amin knew of Sarwari's moves against him. Also, through the efforts of Sayyed Daoud Tarun, Amin was informed of Taraki's moves. Amin had received an encoded telegram from Tarun in Moscow, stating that the Moscow meeting had decided on his elimination. Although barred from the meeting, Tarun knew of its content through a minute intelligence device that he had planted in his master's (Taraki's) pocket. Tarun served more as an attendant of Taraki than as a member of the delegation. Not long afterwards, what had allegedly gone on in Moscow was known in Kabul, and the news of the meeting between Taraki and Karmal spread like wildfire. On the day of Taraki's arrival in Kabul, Amin had taken control of the airport, replacing its personnel with persons loyal to him. He himself wore an armored shield under his clothes. On that occasion no incident occurred.

THE PALACE PLOT

Between 11 and 14 September the rival groups plotted against each other. While Amin worked to weaken Taraki by removing Sarwari, Watanjar, and Gulabzoy from their posts, the latter tried to do away with him. Taraki told his associates that Amin intended to remove him by a coup. When Amin's supporters tried to bring AGSA under their thumb, Taraki's supporters gunned them down. Amin's associates, Nawab Helmandi, Sur Gul Khateez, and Khair Mohammad were the victims. Amin asked Taraki to dismiss Sarwari and others from their posts; Taraki proposed a compromise, but by then a compromise had become unworkable. Amin insisted on his demand. As the first minister and the strong man in the party and the government, Amin could dismiss his enemies, but he preferred that Taraki do it, not only to wean him from his partisans but also to help unify the party. Taraki was, after all, general secretary of the party, president of the Revolutionary Council, chief commander of the armed forces, and president of the Defense Committee of Afghanistan. He had let himself become entangled with men who had become Amin's uncompromising enemies. Finally Taraki decided, with Sarwari and others, that Amin was to be invited to the palace to resolve the differences in line with the principle of inner democracy and collective leadership. He was to be given guarantees for his safety, but when he arrived he would be done away with. To persuade Amin to come, Alexander Puzanov was to be invited and asked to mediate.

Anwar was the first to describe the incident in the palace. In his book, which is an apologia for the Soviet policies on Afghanistan, he implies that what happened on 14 September occurred without the presence of the Soviet ambassador.[17] The reports leaked out of the palace, the two-sheet publication issued for the benefit of party members, and the events themselves speak otherwise. The publication states that Amin, having received "assurances" from Puzanov and his own "comrades," accepted the invitation, much against the advice of Sayyed Daoud Tarun. Amin arrived at half-past five in the afternoon at the palace entrance. When he entered the corridor of the second floor, the presidential guards fired at him, but shot Tarun instead, killing him. Amin escaped. Puzanov and the two generals were present with Taraki. Amin rushed to the head-quarters of the Ministry of Defense and took control of the situation, ordering a siege of the presidential palace, where Taraki was. In the confusion the ambassador and the two generals left. By Amin's order Taraki was detained and, on 9 October, suffocated. The hastily convened meeting of the politburo replaced Taraki with Amin as head of party and the state. Amin formed a new government of persons loyal to him.

Amin implicated Puzanov in the plot. It seems inconceivable that Amin would have made such a charge had it not been true. It was a matter of common sense for Amin to be wary of the consequences of accusing the representative of the Soviet Union. It is a fact that not only Puzanov but also Generals Ivanov and Pavlovsky were present at the time of the incident. The KGB official Alexander Morozov writes, "The generals and Ambassador Puzanov took off for yet another meeting at the House of the Nation. Taraki asked Amin to attend it as well. However, the latter refused point blank, citing the possibility of an attempt on his life as an excuse. But yielding to Taraki's insistence he agreed and demanded guarantees of his safety from Puzanov. The latter gave him the guarantee, speaking to Amin over the phone."[18]

The triumphant Amin started to rule with the view that the Soviet Union would back him. Once again he was mistaken. The Soviet leader, Leonid Brezhnev, looked on the killing of Taraki as a personal insult.[19] Afterward the Soviet leaders changed their policy on Afghanistan.

The whereabouts of Sarwari and his associates—with the exception of Mizdooryar, who had been arrested—was a source of concern for Amin. The conspirators first stayed at the villa of the TASS correspondent, and later Puzanov managed to smuggle them to the Soviet Union in nailed wooden boxes. Amin asked Puzanov to hand them over, but the latter was unwilling. In this connection a story was told that is apparently unbelievable. According to the story, Amin one day summoned Puzanov to his presence and accused him not only of having hidden his opponents in the embassy but also of having plotted against him. When Puzanov denied the accusations and, further, argued that as a diplomat he could not be treated as an accused person under investigation, Amin slapped him in the face and poured forth insulting words in Pashto on Marx, Lenin, and Brezhnev.[20] This impulsive outburst should have made Amin more cautious in his dealing with the Soviets. In any case, Amin's relations with Moscow became strained.

Amin must have concluded that with Puzanov in Kabul, his relations with Moscow were not likely to improve. But after the failed palace coup Puzanov became supportive of Amin, concluding, "We are facing a fait accompli: Amin has come to power. Taraki failed to withstand Amin's push for power. Frankly, Taraki was a weakling and a dawdler. He never was as good as his word. On the contrary Amin is strong, and we must do business with him and support him."[21] Amin's displeasure with Puzanov surfaced on 6 October, when Foreign Minister Shah Wali, while addressing ambassadors of the communist countries with the exception of China, "accused Puzanov of complicity in the abortive attempt to remove Amin, saying Puzanov was in Taraki's office when he assured him on the phone that it was safe to go to the palace."[22] Puzanov was represented at the meeting by Vasily Safronchuck, another embassy diplomat. "As a result of the distrust of Puzanov, and as a warning to the Kremlin about meddling in Afghan affairs, Wali as foreign minister officially asked the Soviet Union to replace its ambassador."[23] Shah Wali also said that Moscow had invited Amin to Moscow to discuss the Afghan domestic issue, but he had refused to go. It was another event that the Kremlin leaders could not digest. Other events also adversely affected Amin's relations with Moscow.

RIFT WITH THE SOVIET UNION

During the 104 days of Amin's rule, Kabul was apparently enthusiastic about the Soviet Union, commemorating with fervor the public events related to it and repeating in its mass media its newly adopted slogan that friendship with the Soviet Union was an integral part of "Afghan patriotism." Hoping to obtain economic assistance as well as military aid, the government appeared anxious to have a close relationship with Moscow. The Soviet leaders likewise appeared anxious to cooperate, despite the impersonal tone of their congratulatory messages to President Amin. But the latter showed that he wanted to govern as an independent ruler.

Amin's assertiveness appeared in more than one form. By the time he took over the reins of government, Soviet advisers had obtained for themselves such a commanding position that

> no significant decision was made, no important order issued in either the civilian ministries in Kabul or the Afghan armed forces without the clearance of Soviet advisers. The advisers had obtained the authority to hold up orders until they countersigned them. What had started in 1978 as the Soviets' helping out by replacing purged officers and officials had developed into a general dependence upon them that must having been as galling for Amin as it was needed by him.[24]

Amin had tried to downgrade the Soviet experts, to make them function as advisers as their titles suggested. However, there was no question of either replacing them or decreasing their numbers, which continued to increase. Before the April coup they numbered 2,100, but on the eve of the invasion their numbers had risen to more than 5,500. Their presence was a source of concern not only for the Afghan people but also for the government. Amin had instructed his officers that they should only listen to the advisers, not act on their advice. It is not known whether or not his instruction was general and whether or not it was carried out by all civilian and military officials; however, by the time of the invasion the advisers attached to the military section of the Intelligence Department were indeed working as advisers only.

Another problem that Amin had with the Soviet Union was the price of Afghan natural gas, which the Soviet Union had imported since 1968 below the international rate. Despite Afghan protests, the gas has been metered for accounting and crediting purposes on the Soviet side of the border and under the supervision of Soviet personnel. Afghan officials were forced to accept Moscow's price schedule and its word on the amount being transported into the Soviet Union and the credit due Afghanistan.[25] Afghanistan lost a large portion of its income on this product, which was its biggest source of revenue. Three ministers, including Abdul Karim Meesaq, minister of finance, sent a polite letter to the Soviet government to this effect. While expressing the hope that the friendship between the two countries would last forever, they asked the Soviets to revise the gas price.[26] The Soviet response is not known. What is known is that a day before his fall, Amin confided in one of his senior officials that the Soviet Union had asked his government to pay three times the price of gasoline that it used to pay. Amin had told them that because of their weak finances the Afghans were unable to pay such a

high price; if the Soviets insisted, the Afghans would have to use bi-
cycles.[27]

Being a communist, and seeing that Afghanistan had been made dependent on the Soviet Union, Amin hoped that the Soviet Union would
assist Afghanistan in its development schemes. He had submitted a list
of projects to the Soviets, including plans to extract oil and to set up
new factories. He also asked that these projects be completed by certain
dates.[28] At the same time Amin began to remove pro-Soviet officials
from sensitive positions and recruited Western-educated Afghans to
higher positions.

THE DILEMMA OF AFGHAN REFORMIST RULERS

President Amin showed concern about the independence of the country.
While addressing a group of university professors whom he had invited
to dine with him, he assured them, "You professors may or may not be
with us, but as long as I am alive I will never allow any foreign power
to dominate our fatherland."[29] To his trusted military officers he was
even more open, saying that he did not understand why the Soviets were
working against his government. Even in the early days of the coup
Amin had reprimanded Puzanov. One day Amin asked him, "What kind
of communist are you that you make such demands of me? The people
of Afghanistan," he argued, "will never accept your demands, and if
pressed, will make trouble for our governments."[30] Puzanov's response
and the nature of the "demand" are unknown. On another occasion
Amin was more emphatic. In October 1979 he told the American chargé
d'affaires, "If Brezhnev himself should ask him [Amin] to take any action against Afghan independence, . . . he would not hesitate 'to sacrifice his life' in opposition to such a request."[31] This was in fact what
he did.

It was, however, Amin's naivete, lack of experience, and belief in communist comradeship that prevented him from questioning how independence would be maintained once the Soviet Union had been allowed to
penetrate the state. He failed to understand that the Soviet leaders preferred compliant rulers in countries such as Afghanistan. Their attitude
toward rulers of the East European countries should have been a lesson
for him. He and others also erred by depriving themselves of the advice
of Afghans experienced in diplomacy and the art of government. Although a tyro in diplomacy, Amin felt confident in it. An observer has
said of Amin, "His confident attitude, reflected in numerous off-the-

record comments, was that he knew how to handle the Russians, who needed him as much or more than he needed them."[32]

Amin faced the same fundamental problem that his reformist predecessors had faced before him: how to preserve the country's independence and at the same time develop it with the credit and technical assistance of the Soviet Union, when other governments did not want to assist it substantially.[33] This dilemma has baffled all reformist Afghan rulers. Although concerned about independence, Amin wanted to develop Afghanistan with Soviet help, stating, "We are convinced that if there were no vast economic and military aid from the Soviet Union, we could not resist the aggression and conspiracies of imperialism, its leftist-looking allies [China and others] and international reaction, and could not move our country toward the construction of a socialist society."[34]

By "military aid" Amin meant military weapons. From the April coup onward, Amin often stated that the Khalqis had made "the April Revolution" and that they were able to defend it. This claim was addressed both to the Khalqis' home critics, who worried that the government had made the country so dependent on the Soviet Union that its leaders might one day make it part of their empire, and also to the Soviet leaders, in effect telling them that Afghanistan did not need their military help in defending the revolution. After Amin came to power, he made his view clear on this, saying, "We will ourselves defend our country . . . [and will] never give this trouble to our international brothers to fight for us."[35]

Although the government was under pressure and the party divided, Amin had the wisdom and the courage to seek solutions through negotiation with adversaries, an approach that the Soviet Union opposed at the time but supported after ten years of war. Amin "was following in the footsteps of Moosa Shafiq's government and Daoud, turning to a non-Communist neighbor in an effort to balance and reduce Soviet influence."[36] This "non-Communist" country was Pakistan, which held a key position in balancing the already unbalanced situation in the region.

Amin knew that the Durand Line could be used by either Pakistan or Afghanistan against the other, depending on circumstances. When Amin usurped power, it was Pakistan's turn. By that time nearly 400,000 Afghans had fled to Pakistan, and it was from among them that the Afghan Islamic organizations recruited men to fight the government. To make Afghanistan stable, Amin needed an understanding with Pakistan. In early December, Amin sought a meeting with General Zia al-Haq of Pakistan. On 19 December he announced that Pakistan's foreign minister, Agha Shahi, was due to make an official visit on 22 December. Apparently because of snow in Kabul, Agha Shahi did not arrive on that day. Foreign Minister Shah Wali appeared desperate, anxious to see Agha Shahi in Kabul soon. A new date, 31 December, was set for his arrival at Kabul, but by that time the Russians had moved in.[37]

Amin also moved to negotiate with Afghan opponents. Reportedly through the mediation of a former member of parliament, Mohammad A'zam Shinwaray, representatives of the Islamic Party (led by Gulbuddin Hekmatyar) and the government met somewhere in the frontier province of Kunar. An agreement for the formation of a coalition government was said to have been reached between them.[38] Amin's moves were, however, noticed by the watchful eyes of the Soviet Union. On 31 October 1979 the Soviet politburo noted: "Disturbing signals are coming about Amin's efforts to make contracts [contacts] with representatives of conservative Muslim opposition and leaders of tribes hostile to the government, in the course of which he shows readiness to come to an agreement on compromise conditions that are to the detriment of the country's progressive development." It also stated that Amin intended "to pursue a more balanced policy in relations with the Western powers"; indeed, "U.S.A. representatives after their contacts with the Afghans have come to the conclusion that it is possible to change Afghanistan's political line in the direction which is favorable to Washington." Calling Amin "insincere and two-faced," the politburo held that he "not only does not stop anti-Soviet moods but in fact encourages them." This comment referred to Amin's disclosure that the Soviet ambassador had taken part against him in the abortive palace coup. Calling this disclosure of a fact to be "slanderous inventions," the politburo concluded that "in Amin we have come across an ambitious, cruel, treacherous person who may change the political orientation of the regime."[39]

Despite these misgivings, the Soviet Union instructed its officials to do business as usual with Amin until the Kremlin rulers were certain about his true intentions. For them it was not hard to become certain about those intentions: Taraki had assured his Kremlin comrades that "we will never be as close to anyone else as we are to you";[40] by contrast, Amin proceeded to follow, in the words of the Kremlin masters, "a more balanced policy." This was the broad line of policy that Afghan rulers had pursued in the past; but the Kremlin rulers held this policy to be "detrimental" to Afghanistan, as if they were also Afghan rulers. It was a plain fact that they were not the rulers of Afghanistan, yet they persisted in thinking that they were and, more ominously, in acting on that mistaken belief. Thus, on 12 December 1979 they decided that Amin must go and that they would rule Afghanistan through Karmal and his Parchami group.

In early December rumors circulated in Kabul that the Soviets intended to seek an alternative to the government of Amin. The situation at home and in the region seemed ripe for such a move.

Having suppressed many uprisings, the government had alienated the public. It had also eliminated public figures in the name of "socialism," "revolution," "progress," and "toiling men and women," and it had proclaimed the creation of a society "free of exploitation of man by man." By labeling their opponents "counterrevolutionaries," "reactionaries," "narrow-minded nationalists," "courtiers," "feudals," and so on, the new rulers provided themselves grounds to liquidate them. Actually, the Soviet advisers had initiated the program, but when the dogmatic, rough-edged rural plebeians directed the police state, they took the rhetoric more seriously than the Soviet advisers had probably imagined. The official party, because it had been split into factions, was in disarray. There was, in short, a power vacuum, and since there was no known figure around whom the opponents could rally, the Soviet leaders apparently assumed that with Amin removed, the compliant Karmal, backed by the Soviet might, would fill the vacuum.

The turmoil in the region also seemed conducive to such a move. The military regime in Pakistan, led by General Zia al-Haq, who came to power in 1977, and the religious regime in Iran, led by the Ayatullah Khomeini, who came to power in 1979, were grappling with serious problems. No outside power, especially the United States of America, was present in the region to counter the Soviet Union, as the British in India had countered Russia in the past. The United States, which had contained the Soviet Union in the 1950s by sponsoring the military pacts of SEATO and CENTO and had kept a presence in Iran since the end of World War II, had already backed away. Besides, in November 1979 the United States found itself confronted with the Khomeini regime over the problem of diplomats taken hostage by Iran. More important, the U.S. administrations had always considered Afghanistan to be within the Soviet influence. Still, the Soviet Union preferred to see its troops invited before moving militarily. The question thus arises, were the Soviet troops invited, or did the Soviet Union invade Afghanistan without an invitation?

INVASION WITHOUT INVITATION

Since the Soviet Union invaded Afghanistan when Amin was in power, the invitation for its troops should have come from him. As prime minister and minister of defense, president of the Revolutionary Council, and general secretary of the party, Amin was the central figure. Having probed this question, which encompasses the whole aspect of Afghan national life and, to some extent, international relations as well, I have concluded that neither Amin nor the Revolutionary Council had either orally or in writing asked the Soviet Union to send its troops into Afghanistan, although Soviet officials had made extensive efforts to frighten them about an imaginary danger directed at Afghanistan. But the Soviet government as well as the Karmal regime have fabricated stories contrary to this conclusion.

In December 1979 Soviet officials told Amin that the "revolution" was in danger from the United States, which was about to launch a massive assault from the Persian Gulf. To meet the assault, Afghanistan should be prepared militarily. Amin then requested Soviet *military weapons* on a large scale, a request that was granted. But the Soviet officials made it known that the effective use of a variety of advanced weapons required the presence of Soviet military experts and instructors to train the Afghans, a proposal that had already been accepted and was once again confirmed.[41] Already on 7 July 1979, a Soviet battalion disguised as aircraft technicians had landed at the Bagram air base north of Kabul "to protect and defend the airfield where our [the Soviet] aircraft were landing bringing aid cargo to Afghanistan. . . . The place was a sort of bridgehead where Soviet specialists and advisers with their families could assemble if the situation got worse."[42] By 6 December the number had increased to 2,500.[43] Amin demanded an explanation from the new Soviet ambassador, Fikrat A. Tabeyev, who explained that the buildup was in response to increased activity by the imperialists along the frontiers. Tabeyev also said that the Soviet experts were at the base to train the Afghans in the use of weapons. Amin seemed concerned but made no comment. On 18 December, A. H. Hakeemi, commander of the Bagram airbase, informed Amin that the Soviets seemed to be up to something sinister, similar to what they had done in Czechoslovakia in 1968. Amin assured him that things would be all right shortly. Amin was probably hopeful about the outcome of his scheduled meeting with the foreign minister of Pakistan, Agha Shahi. The meeting did not take place. Amin planned to summon political officials in the military together with commanding officers of the Kabul area to the headquarters of the Ministry of National Defense. He intended to tell them that of late the Soviet attitude toward Afghanistan had changed and that on all important matters they were to act only on his orders. But hours before the scheduled meeting, the Soviet cook and waitresses poisoned Amin, and the occupation began.[44]

The Soviet government and the regime of Karmal have claimed that the troops sent into Afghanistan were in line with article four of the Treaty of Friendship, Good Neighborliness, and Cooperation, which Taraki and Brezhnev had concluded in Moscow on 5 December 1978. Leaving aside whether or not the treaty was legally valid, we may note that the article stipulates that in the case of military cooperation, appropriate agreements should be concluded in advance. The treaty reads in part, "In the interests of strengthening the defense capacity of the high contracting parties, they shall continue to develop cooperation in the military field on the basis of appropriate agreements concluded between them." First, "cooperation in the military field" is a vague phrase that may or may not be taken to mean the dispatch of troops by one contracting party to the assistance of another. Second, even if this phrase does mean the dispatch of troops, the treaty nevertheless stipulates that "appropriate agreements" be concluded between the parties. Such agreements had not been concluded, nor had the Kabul government indicated a willingness for them. Contrary to the general view, during Amin's rule the government was not so weak that its opponents could overthrow it. Except for a disturbance in the Rishkhor military division by pro-Taraki officers, a disturbance that was quickly suppressed, no major uprising took place while Amin was in power. "Until the invasion the [Islamic opposition] parties were more or less dormant, because they received virtually no assistance from outside."[45] The security situation in Afghanistan was far from being so desperate as to need Soviet troops. The Soviet Union, before the invasion, had not officially raised the issue with the government of Amin. Had Amin requested military aid, as distinct from weapons, the Soviet Union would have obtained a document about it, a point so significant that it was bound to affect, as it did, its relations with Afghanistan and to some extent also with the region and the world. The Soviet Union never produced such a document. After the invasion the Soviet Union fabricated stories justifying its actions, one of which said that members of the Revolutionary Council had asked the Soviets to send troops to Afghanistan.

Since Amin was the central figure both in the party hierarchy and the state, and since he had driven away his rivals, and since he had assigned his own men to key positions in the party as well as the government, it is inconceivable that someone else would have dared to invite Soviet troops. The subsequent claims by Karmal and the Soviet Union are groundless. Henry Bradsher has described and analyzed these claims in detail.[46] Here I only evaluate the claims. According to an official Soviet declaration, the military assistance was in the form of "a limited contingent" that "[would] be used exclusively in rebuffing the armed interference from the outside." It was also declared that the "limited contingent [would] be completely pulled out of Afghanistan when the reason that necessitated such an action exists no longer."[47] In subsequent declarations, the word *contingent* was changed to *contingents*. By making this statement, the Soviet leaders put themselves into such a position that to justify their actions they had to tell lies about this as well as related issues. When the Soviet Union withdrew its forces in 1989, after ten years of war, it declared that the "limited military contingent" in Afghanistan numbered 105,000 men. If this number can be described, as the Soviet Union so described it, as a "limited contingent," then ordinary language is obviously inadequate.

Also, in ordinary language the phrase "armed interference from the outside" means interference by one country in the internal affairs of another—in the present case, in the internal affairs of Afghanistan. The Soviet Union never substantiated its claim, because the armed forces of no other country had intervened. By "armed interference from the outside" the Soviet Union in fact meant the Afghan mujahideen who struggled against the government, which had usurped power. As many uprisings had shown, most Afghans (with the exception of a small number of pro-Moscow communists) considered the communist government illegitimate, a usurper. While a civil war was going on among the contending Afghan groups, the Soviet Union intervened in favor of its surrogates. Its intervention was therefore nothing but an unprovoked, armed aggression. Besides, the Soviet government committed the aggression at a time when a government friendly to it was in power. In the course of the ten years that the Soviet troops were in Afghanistan, they fought against Afghans, not against the army of another country.

If the Soviet Union sent troops to Afghanistan to be used "exclusively for assistance in rebuffing the armed interference from the outside," why did they kill President Amin and topple his government, which they claimed to have invited them? On this point the Soviet argument was that Amin had been overthrown not by its forces but by the true Afghan revolutionaries. However, the Soviet Union itself repudiated this fabrication. On 23 December 1989 the Soviet Supreme Council declared the dispatch of troops to Afghanistan unconstitutional. While castigating Leonid Brezhnev and others for sending the troops into Afghanistan, it declared that the decision to invade Afghanistan "was made by a small circle of people in violation of the Soviet constitution, according to which such matters belong to the jurisdiction of higher state bodies."[48]

Another "reason" was given more prominence in the Soviet official declarations. According to this claim, the southern flanks of the Soviet Union had become "insecure" and "the Pentagon and the U.S. Central Intelligence Agency were counting on stealthily approaching our territory more closely through Afghanistan"; thus, the Soviets "had no choice but to send troops."[49] First, this claim is not in line with the allegation that the troops were sent to repel foreign aggression. Second, the Soviet Union provided no evidence to substantiate the claim. How could Afghanistan pose a threat to the Soviet Union when a government led by their own comrades was in power there when the Soviets intervened? Moreover, when a government feels its boundaries have become insecure, does it then have the right to invade other countries? If this were to be accepted as a norm of behavior, what would happen to international relations? In such a case any stronger country could justify invading its weaker neighbors. The law of the jungle would prevail.

More specifically, across the wide Soviet empire no other country except Turkey had as geographically distinct boundaries as Afghanistan had with it. Afghanistan was separated from the Soviet empire for 2,300 kilometers, for the greater part by the River Oxus and then by an uninhabitable desert. It is strange to think that the Soviet state would have been unable to safeguard its boundaries against a smaller country, even if a hostile government were in power. After all, the Soviet Union had adjusted boundaries with its much bigger neighbors, notably China, and coexisted with them. Throughout history, conquests and massive migrations occurred as nomadic hordes descended from the north on the settled populations in the south—not the other way around. The concern that the Soviet leaders showed about the "insecurity" of their southern borders was a mere rationalization for their drive for expansion, a drive reminiscent of nineteenth-century colonialism. It was also a reflection of the problems that they had with the Muslim nations of the Central Asian Republics, such as the Tajiks, Uzbeks, Turkmen, and other groups whose kinsmen live across the border in Afghanistan.

The claims were a cover-up for an agenda the Kremlin decision makers had for Afghanistan. The agenda was to rule it through an outcast group of communists, much as the Soviets had dominated Bukhara in the early 1920s. Since the independent-minded Amin and his government stood in the way, they had to be removed. On 12 December 1979 the Soviet politburo, chaired by Leonid Brezhnev, endorsed the KGB view and decided to invade. In the KGB's view, "The situation [in Afghanistan] [could] be saved only by the removal of Amin from power and the restoration of unity" in the ruling party. The Kremlin ruling group adopted this view because it considered Amin to be "insincere" toward the Soviet Union; he was pursuing "a more balanced foreign policy" and was bent on purging the party and state of potential opponents. "The Soviets had never trusted Amin, regarding him as a power-hungry politician of dubious ideological convictions."[50] In waging an undeclared war on the Afghans in what historian Barbara Tuchman has called "The March of Folly," a few superannuated Soviet leaders ignored the sound advice that their own premier Kosygin had given to Taraki earlier in the year: "If our troops were sent in, the situation in your country would not improve. On the contrary, it would get worse. Our troops would have to struggle not only with an external aggressor, but with a significant part of your own people. And the people would never forgive such things."[51]

In the present interdependent world, a secret decision made by a few irresponsible men in the Soviet empire to wage an unprovoked war on Afghanistan was bound to be opposed by millions of men and women; it also led to the intensification of the cold war. Luckily, this was the last decision of its kind the Soviet leaders would make.

In installing Karmal, the Kremlin decision makers acted on the view that what counted was success, and that before the god of success the scruples of human behavior did not count. The Soviets had built their empire with this precept in mind. But could they succeed in Afghanistan with the outcast Karmal and his faction of Parcham?

CHAPTER THREE

Under the Soviet Shadow

When the Soviet forces started operations in Kabul, Babrak Karmal, the outcast leader of the Parcham faction of the PDPA, was in Doshanbay, the capital city of the Soviet republic of Tajikistan bordering Afghanistan. Afterward Karmal broadcast over radio a statement on a frequency close to that of Radio Afghanistan in which he said, "Today the torture machine of Amin has been broken." In the name of the Revolutionary Council of the Democratic Republic of Afghanistan, he asked Afghans, especially the security and army officers, to remain vigilant and maintain security and order.

At three o'clock in the morning the news of the formation of a new government was broadcast over the radio. A statement to this effect was made in the name of Karmal, but at the time he was not in Kabul. Instead, a tape recording of his voice was used. Karmal was later brought "in a tank or armored personnel carrier from Bagram to Kabul by the airborne troops."[1] He took residence in the old palace in the city. Between eight and nine o'clock on 28 December 1979, a helicopter landed in the Soviet embassy compound and after a pause of fifteen minutes or so flew back. It is believed that the helicopter brought Marshal Sergei Sokolov, who had organized the operation from Termez (the border town of Soviet Uzbekistan) and who was now the supreme commander of Soviet forces in Afghanistan. The marshal took up his residence in the Chilsitun Palace to the southeast of the city; a reception was held there, attended by Karmal and other leading members of the PDPA and the new government. The warm messages of the Soviet government and party leaders addressed to Karmal, now called president of the Revolutionary Council of Afghanistan, president of the Council of Ministers of the Democratic Republic of Afghanistan, and general secretary of the People's Democratic Party of Afghanistan, were read by General Abdul Qadir, who had just been released from a term of life imprisonment along with other members of the Parcham faction. Sokolov stayed in Chilsitun until early 1982, when he was forced to abandon it for a residence in Wazir Akbar Khan Maina, near the old palace, because the mujahideen's rocket attacks had made it unsafe for him.

The morning announcement of the formation of the new government was brief. It included, besides Karmal, the names of Asadullah Sarwari, as vice president and deputy premier, and of Sultan Ali Kishtmand as deputy prime minister. The appointments were strange: Sarwari, when chief of AGSA, had tortured Kishtmand in the prison so much that he had to be sent to Moscow for medical treatment.

The second official announcement was also brief but stunning. It read in part, "The Democratic Republic of Afghanistan earnestly demands that the USSR render urgent political, moral, and economic assistance, including military aid, to Afghanistan. The government of the USSR has accepted the proposal of the Afghan side." The reason for the request was described thus: "Because of the continuation and expansion of aggression, intervention, and provocations by foreign enemies of Afghanistan."[2]

At this time the new government existed only on paper. Its head, Karmal, was still in the Soviet Union, not in Afghanistan. The year before, the Khalqi government, which the Soviet Union had recognized, had deprived him of Afghan citizenship. Now that the Soviet forces had overthrown the Khalqi government, only they were in power in Kabul. The statement admitted this also when it said the Soviet Union had "accepted the proposal." More important, the Soviet Union had already given the "military aid" now requested in the name of the nonexistent government. Indeed, this "military aid" had made the declaration possible in the first place.

On 10 January 1980 the names of ministers of the new government were announced. The new government was composed of Parchamis, Khalqis, and a few pro-Parcham individuals. Amin's senior ministers, with the exception of two, were imprisoned. The Taraki faction, now led by Sarwari and Gulabzoy, called itself "the principled Khalqis." Before the major policies of the new government are described, it is necessary to discuss the Peoples Democratic Party of Afghanistan (PDPA) and dwell on the relationship between its Parcham faction and Moscow.

RULE BY SURROGATES

Rule by surrogates has become more common in modern times than at any time before. So long as the Soviet Union had not found surrogates in Afghanistan, it showed due respect to that country's independence, territorial integrity, and nonaligned foreign policy. Before the invasion the Soviets declared time and again that they wished to grant disinterested assistance to Afghanistan, but they wanted nothing to do with its politics. They cited Afghanistan as a model of cooperation between two countries with different social and political systems. Some Soviet leaders went even further. During an official tour of Afghanistan in December 1955, while visiting cadets in Kabul, Soviet Premier Nikita Khrushchev advised Afghan Premier Mohammad Daoud to eliminate any cadet found to be a communist.[3] Such assurances were credible to the Afghans, perhaps because they lacked experience in dealing with the outside world, owing to their short period of diplomatic history, and perhaps also because of their national and Islamic values, which require them to accept the words of others, and especially high dignitaries.

The Afghans had yet to learn the saying about the Russians: they think one thing, say something else, and do yet another. After Khrushchev's visit, the Soviet Union encouraged receptive educated Afghans to organize a party of their own. In particular, it encouraged a group of Afghan leftists for such a purpose after 1960, when Karmal performed a service to the Soviet Union as well as to Premier Mohammad Daoud. In that year Karmal informed Premier Daoud that Sibgatullah Mojaddidi had plotted to blow up the bridge of Pul-e-Artan in Kabul when the motorcade of a Soviet delegation was to cross it. Rahmatullah Mojaddidi, a leftist brother of Sibgatullah Mojaddidi, had passed on the information to Karmal through some Parchami leaders, Sulaiman Laweq and Mier Akbar Khybar. While the incident resulted in the imprisonment of Sibgatullah Mojaddidi, it made Karmal and his circle of leftists a serviceable group to Premier Daoud and the Soviet Union.[4] In general, the leftists became active after the Soviets extended economic assistance to Afghanistan in 1956, and the government, though harsh toward others, tolerated them. In the constitutional period they as well as others emerged in the open.

On 1 January 1965 twenty-eight educated Afghans assembled secretly in the residence of Nur Mohammad Taraki in Karta-e-Char in the city of Kabul, and there they founded the PDPA along the lines of the pro-Moscow communist parties. In this first party congress they named Nur Mohammad Taraki as general secretary and Babrak Karmal as secretary of the PDPA. The charter reads, "The PDPA, whose ideology is the practical experience of Marxism-Leninism, is founded on the voluntary union of the progressive and informed people of Afghanistan: the workers, peasants, artisans, and intellectuals." In real life, unable to win the tradition-bound Muslim peasants and workers to its cause, the PDPA tried to win over the Afghan elite and to "maintain control [influence] over the state apparatus and to eliminate any Western presence."[5] It followed the Soviet's policy toward the Afghan governments. After 1956, when the Soviet Union extended financial assistance to Afghanistan, Soviet policy called for closer cooperation with the Afghan governments. Party activists worked within the existing framework of government rather than outside it, agitating only against those governments that tried to distance Afghanistan from the Soviet Union and to bring it closer to the Western and Arab worlds. The PDPA showed respect to the monarchy. Taraki, for instance, kissed the hands of the Afghan king, and Karmal, in a parliamentary session, called the king the most progressive monarch in Asia.[6] In his compliments, Karmal used words that Lenin had first employed toward the "revolutionary" King Amanullah.

The PDPA was, however, unable to make progress in society. Its original name was the Association of National Democrats,[7] and its leaders associated themselves with national issues such as Pashtunistan. Karmal had been first a member of the Union for the Independence of Pashtunistan; Taraki had been a founding member of the Awakened Youth (Weekh Zalmyan), a group of national democrats. After adopting its present name with its leftist connotation, the PDPA was subjected to pressure from within and without. The pressure from society on it was strong. In the constitutional period, when the free press mushroomed, the PDPA began to disseminate its views in its periodical *Khalq,* first published in April 1966. The public reacted against it. The House of Elders of parliament considered the periodical against the public interest and asked the government to ban it. The government did so in May 1966, after six issues had come out.[8] In November of the same year Karmal expressed pro-Soviet sentiments in the House of Representatives; some of its members beat him. In 1970 a member of the PDPA praised Lenin in the commemoration of his centenary in words that custom had preserved for the Prophet Mohammad; in response, the *'ulama* (religious scholars) from all over the country held protest rallies lasting over a month in Kabul against the communists.

To pressure the communists, the government of Premier Nur Ahmad E'temadi initially encouraged these rallies. But the rallies turned into a two-edged sword, denouncing both the PDPA and the government. In a twenty-two-clause proposal, the 'ulama asked the government not only to suppress the communists but also to forego social reforms, including coeducation and the unveiling of women. The proposal also demanded that women not be permitted to hold public office. When the government rejected the proposal, the 'ulama—led by such persons as Mawlana Fayzani—denounced the government as well and dropped the name of the king from Friday sermons, a sign of rebellion. The government repressed the rallies, and the communists were thus spared.[9] Had the premier (probably at the advice of the former premier, Mohammad Daoud) not suppressed the rallies, the PDPA would probably have been dissolved.[10]

Pressures from within the PDPA were disruptive. The leftist implications of the new name alerted the public to the danger of communism. The national elements of the party broke off with it. Among them was the historian Mier Ghulam Mohammad Ghobar. As a founding member of the Fatherland Party, Ghobar had played a leading role in parliament and national politics in the 1950s; now he too turned against the PDPA. More disruptive was its split in 1967 into four groups: the Khalq faction, led by Taraki; the Parcham faction, led by Karmal; the Sitam-e-Milli faction, led by Tahir Badakhshi; and the Goroh-e-Kar faction, led by Dastagir Panjsheri. Dastagir later joined the Khalq faction, but then the Khalq faction lost two of its leading members, who formed factions of their own: Jawanan-e-Zahmatkash (Industrious Youth), led by Zahir Ofuq, and another, which had no specific name but was more radical, led by Abdul Karim Zarghun.[11]

THE SITAM-E-MILLI

The PDPA groups were Marxist-Leninist proponents of the Moscow line. The Sitam-e-Milli, however, placed more emphasis on the problem of ethnicity than class struggle. Its leader, Tahir Badakhshi, held that the emancipation of the "oppressed nationalities" from Pashtun "domination" was the main problem and thus needed to be addressed first. Toward this end, he worked for Uzbek-Tajik unity, identifying himself with the Tajik although he was the son of an Uzbek father. A founder of the PDPA, Badakhshi broke off with it to promote his own view. The educated sectarian elements of some ethnic groups rallied behind him, but Sitam-e-Milli remained insignificant, although in the beginning it had attracted some followers in Badakhshan.

Like most opposition groups, the Sitam-e-Milli failed to remain solid for long, soon splitting into two subgroups. Its radical wing, led by Ab-haruddin Baw'ess, followed a revolutionary line, while Badakhshi stood for moderation. A talented and dynamic man, Baw'ess trained his followers in a militant spirit; with their help, for a short time he occupied the frontier district of Darwaz in the abortive uprisings in 1975. A Tajik from the same locality, Baw'ess afterward lived in hiding until the Khalqis did away with him when he escaped from the Ali Abad hospital, where he had been transferred from prison for medical treatment, and was arrested again.

On 14 February 1979 four followers of Baw'ess kidnapped U.S. Ambassador Adolph Dubs and took him hostage in a hotel to pressure the government to release their leader. Directed by Soviet advisers, the Khalqi police stormed the hotel, where all perished. The incident brought the Sitam-e-Milli to the front line of national and international attention for the first time; it also worsened relations between Afghanistan and the United States. The Carter administration first announced the withdrawal of most of its diplomats from Kabul; later President Carter signed a law that prohibited any further aid to Afghanistan until the government apologized and assumed responsibility for Dubs's death.[12] This action drew the Khalqi government closer to the Soviet Union. Sitam-e-Milli also declined in strength, which may account for the change of its name to the Organization of the Toilers of Afghanistan, or SAZA (Sazman-e-Zahmatkashan-e-Afghanistan), for the followers of Badakhshi, and the Commando Organization of the Liberation of Afghanistan, or SARFA (Sazman-e-Rehaeebakhsh-e-Fedayee-e-Afghanistan), for the followers of Baw'ess. Encouraged by a few Tajikized Russian interpreters and the Parchami Premier Kisht-mand, they subsequently entered the Parchami government and formed some militia units.[13]

Internal pressure on the Sitam-e-Milli proved crucial. In the Khalqi period the government imprisoned or executed many officers in the army uprisings on suspicion of being Sitamis. During the resistance period after the invasion, the Islamic organizations hunted the Sitamis down for their leftist views, although the Islamic Association sympathized with their notion of "national oppression."

The suppression of Sitamis did not create a stir. Common Afghans did not sympathize with them. One reason for this lack of sympathy was the linguistic and social integration that the society had undergone with improvements in the system of transportation, particularly after the opening of the Salang tunnel in 1965, when the northern and southern regions were brought closer. Until then the northeastern region, the most distant from Kabul, had been isolated by the deterioration of relations with Pakistan over the problem of Pashtunistan, cutting it off from Chitral, with which it had trade and other ties. Before that the Bolshevik revolution had done much the same to its ties with the regions beyond the Oxus, where people of the same stock lived. This isolation, and the fact that in this poor region no major development project had been undertaken, accounted for the discontent among its educated elements.

Serious also was the exploitation of the locals by government officials. But they were not the only people who had been exploited, nor was theirs the only region that had remained undeveloped. Besides, the exploiters were not only Pashtun officials but all officials, since the bureaucracy—particularly after the spread of modern free education—was open to all ethnic groups. Also, since Afghan Dari (Persian) was the medium of bureaucracy, Persian-speaking Afghans dominated it. With the extension of the government's direct control over the country since the days of Amir Abdur Rahman, Afghan Persian has made steady progress. This fact is significant because the Pashtun Mohammadzay ruling dynasty had become linguistically Persianized and thus more at home with the Persian-speaking Afghans than the Pashto-speaking Afghans, that is, Pashtuns. This linguistic preference, coupled with the fact that the ruling dynasty preferred that clients run the government, may account for the fact that it gave a disproportionately high number of cabinet posts to Persian-speaking Afghans. This was the case since the days of Ahmad Shah Durrani, who founded modern Afghanistan in the middle of the eighteenth century. Persian-speaking Afghans have at times served as alter egos to kings, as Mohammad Wali did in the reign of King Amanullah and Ali Mohammad in the reign of King Mohammad Zahir. Both were Tajiks from Badakhshan. The "sitam-e-milli" or "national oppression" becomes relevant when it is understood as a reflection of the tyranny of the illiberal state. To view it as an oppression of the ethnic Pashtuns is to misread it. This was one of the reasons why, like the Maoist groups, the Sitam-e-Milli, after its initial upsurge, declined even in Badakhshan, and its leaders had to rely for survival on the Soviets.

In conclusion, the Sitamis aroused an awareness to a problem that needed to be tackled constitutionally, but they also sensationalized divisiveness and hatred.

THE KHALQ AND PARCHAM FACTIONS

The main factions of the PDPA were the Khalq and the Parcham, each of which claimed to represent the "true" PDPA.[14] Their composition, too, was influenced by ethnic, regional, and social considerations. The Parcham faction was distinct from the Khalq faction in its composition, the social background of its members, and their views on national policies and matters of morality and general behavior.

The Parchamis were mainly from cities, with some from the countryside. The Khalqis were almost all from rural areas, with a significant number from ethnic and client minorities integrated among the Pashtuns. Most Khalqis belonged to poor rural groups, and most Parchamis to well-off groups. A number of the latter arose from the landowning, bureaucratic, and wealthy families. Also, some Parchamis were from urban ethnic minorities. Unlike the Khalqis, most Parchamis were non-Pashtuns (the Pashtuns being the main ethnic group, as already noted). Thus, the Parchamis were—again unlike the Khalqis—less rooted in society, more internationalist and less nationalist in outlook. They also had many women in their ranks. In the upper echelons they were indifferent to the moral dictates of society, where such norms had been the code of conduct for thousands of years. Believing in a good relationship with the establishment, the Parchamis preferred to work within it rather than to oppose it from the outside, whereas the Khalqis opposed it. Both Khalqis and Parchamis were educated, and through education the Marxist ideology bound them loosely, but they had acquired their dogmatic Marxism from the literature of the Communist Party of the Soviet Union and the Tudeh Party of Iran, mainly in Russian, Pashto, and Persian. Daoud Malikyar has described the Parchamis as "characters"— that is, as marionettes who have no independence of their own but are directed by others behind the scene. The characterization is a reference to the uprooted and opportunistic urban Parchamis, who adopted the Leninist tactics of achieving the end by any possible means.

As a socially baseless political group, the Parchamis could not be expected to be influential in society, but they did influence the state frame-work in the city of Kabul. There, too, they could exercise influence only in times of stability; in times of disturbance they could not play a deci-sive role. The significance of this statement can be appreciated when it is borne in mind that so far in Afghan history the rural Afghans have been, in times of disturbance, more decisive than the urban Afghans in shaping events. In such times the urban Afghans have been at the mercy of the rural people, except when foreign powers protected the urban centers. The urban-rural dynamic has always been a distinctive feature of Afghan society.

Relations between the Khalqi and Parcham factions were inharmoni-ous and ill disposed. In their short history they were more disunited than united, and even when they were united, they were distinct from each other. They never integrated. The Parcham faction was smaller, particu-larly in the army, than the Khalqi faction.

In 1967, eighteen months after its founding, the PDPA split into the Khalq (people) and Parcham (banner) factions. The split continued until 1977, when the Kremlin masters pressured them to reunite. But the de-cade-long split hardened the attitude of their members toward each other, since during its course they were more acrimonious and less than comradely. In documents that leaders of both factions addressed to their Kremlin comrades, they accused each other on points of theory. The Parchamis charged the Khalqis with adhering to the cult of individual-ism; with promoting the notion of alliance of the revolutionaries with only two classes of workers and peasants; and with calling for the dicta-torship of the proletariat. The Parchamis described themselves as revolu-tionaries opposed to the cult of individualism and in favor of alliance not only with workers and peasants but also with national patriotic forces. During the initial stage of the revolution they claimed they stood for democratic change, not the dictatorship of the proletariat. The Khalqis, by contrast, denounced the Parchamis as collaborators and conciliators with the wealthy, the upper crust of the ruling regimes, and described themselves as opposed to the "suppressing regimes of Zahir Shah and Daoud." Referring to themselves as communists imbued with the spirit of class struggle and close to the poor people, the Khalqis elsewhere called the Parchamis "royalist pseudocommunists." In the same document addressed to the Soviets, the Khalqis also announced themselves "devoted to everything associated with the Soviet Union" and doubted the sincerity of the Parchami leaders toward the Soviet leaders.[15]

After the split, both the Khalqis and the Parchamis found themselves
unable to make headway in society. Thus, Parchami leaders tried to
court a closer relationship with the former premier Mohammad Daoud
and, during the constitutional decade, with Premier Nur Ahmad E'temadi, who, of the five prime ministers of the decade, served longest (1967–
71). In this period the Parcham made noteworthy progress, particularly
through its periodical, *Parcham* (1968–70), whereas the Khalq faction
was barred from publishing another periodical.[16] The purpose of this
political marriage was to disrupt the nascent democratic system that
helped Mohammad Daoud to overthrow the monarchy.

The Parcham faction became a partner in the new republic. Half of
the cabinet ministers were Parchamis, and hundreds more entered the
government as junior officials and rural district officers. In this euphoria
Karmal went so far as to dissolve his faction, hoping that by forging an
alliance with the aged President Daoud (1910–78) he would succeed in
raising his faction to power.[17] In the names of the republic and the president, the Parchami officials, through the police forces that they controlled, instituted a reign of terror, imprisoning and torturing hundreds
of their Islamist and other opponents. President Daoud was either unwilling or unable to curb his Parchami partners. This failure led him to
be associated with the Parchami communists. However, once Daoud felt
secure in his position, he removed the Parchamis one by one from their
cabinet posts and declared that he was opposed to any party that served
the interest of "foreigners." But by then the Parchamis had succeeded in
alienating President Daoud from the Islamic movement. They had also
endeared themselves to the Soviets by passing on official secrets. Colonel
Alexander Morozov, a KGB officer in Kabul at the time, writes, "Almost
all Parchamis mentioned in Amin's document as members of Daoud's
Central Committee shared information with Soviet secret agencies."
And he adds that their "participation in the Daoud's administration . . .
had been sanctioned by Soviet intelligence."[18]

Because of their pro-Soviet activities, and their institution of the reign
of terror, the Parchamis made themselves unpopular. Their junior officials in the rural areas became corrupt. In losing the patronage of Mohammad Daoud, the Parchamis lost one of their two sources of support,
the other being the Soviet Union. While the Khalqi leaders supported
the republic and while their military officers took part in instituting it,
they themselves did not join it. By allying himself with the Parchamis,
President Daoud alienated the Khalqis. In addition to underestimating
the Khalqis, President Daoud, like Karmal, suspected Taraki of being "a

spy of the United States of America."[19] Having gotten rid of the Parchamis, President Daoud thought he would also suppress the Khalqis. But having concentrated on the army, the Khalqis instead toppled him. When the Khalqis usurped power, the discredited Parchamis were no match for them.

THE PARCHAMIS DURING THE KHALQ RULE

Twice during their rule the Khalqis suppressed the Parchamis. Why the Khalqis suppressed the Parchamis the first time, after a short-lived honeymoon between them following the coup, is unknown. The outer signs of the rift were obvious. For a few weeks following the coup, the Parchamis served in the government, apparently on an equal basis with the Khalqis but actually as their junior partners. Then Amin and Watanjar, in a meeting at the Institute of Polytechnic, gave out that the revolution was the work of Khalqis and that the Parchamis had no part in it. In an official pamphlet detailing this statement, it was further alleged that on the day of the coup Karmal, not knowing what was happening, did not want to be released from prison. He had asked whether or not it was safe to be out.

The Parchamis, in particular Karmal, were active on another level, establishing a special relationship with the Soviet ambassador, Alexander Puzanov. Puzanov was so fond of Karmal that he believed the revolution was due to his statesmanship. In June 1978 Amin told the Soviet leaders that the Khalqis, not the Parchamis, had made the revolution. At the time Amin had stopped in Moscow on the way home from a trip to Havana. It was said that Soviet Foreign Minister Gromyko, deeply impressed by Amin, told him that if he wished he might remove Puzanov from Kabul. But Amin replied that he could get along with him.[20]

The issue that revealed the difference between Amin and Karmal was that of military officers, as noted before. After the coup Amin introduced some military officers to the membership of the central committee. Sensing danger to his faction, Karmal opposed this movement on the ground that the army officers were unable to absorb Marxism-Leninism. This opposition was unacceptable to Amin, since the officers were his bastion of support.

At some point Amin decided to send the Parchami leaders abroad as ambassadors. In one of the politburo meetings he put forward this suggestion. Karmal at first said that he wished to give up politics. Already he had complained in vain to Taraki that "since no one seemed to accept his authority as the nation's second in command" he wished to resign and "devote himself to development of modifications of the PDPA's strategy and tactics to suit the present condition."[21] Amin's response was prompt. Addressing Karmal, he said, "Dear Babrak, you have got a number of followers. When you stay at home they might make some trouble, and the trouble might be traced to your door in which case you will find it difficult to exonerate yourself." Karmal accepted the proposal, which was passed by a majority of the votes cast. Indeed, Karmal had no choice. As already noted, he had spent a night at the villa of the TASS correspondent to meet with the Soviet ambassador, but the latter had declined. On this point Amin had even ignored the advice of the International Affairs Department of the Soviet Central Committee, which had counseled that "Lenin emphasized that a revolution could be worth anything [only] if it knew how to protect itself." According to the advice, "This great mission can be fulfilled only if the PDPA acts as a united and closely-knit political organization held together by one will and a common goal."[22] In the aforementioned document, entitled "Preliminary Proposals Concerning Changes in the Organizational Structure of the PDPA," Amin told his Soviet comrades that the Parchamis had made themselves "notorious for their participation in the work of the Daoud administration."[23] But Amin did not know that the Parchamis had done so on instruction from the Soviets. In any case, six Parchami leaders, including Karmal, soon left for their ambassadorial posts. This marked the beginning of the second split of the PDPA into Parcham and Khalq factions. The scene was now set for events with serious consequences.

In early September the government announced that it had foiled a Parchami plot to overthrow it. The government either arrested or dismissed the remaining Parchami ministers in the cabinet, accusing them of holding rallies to promote a coup. The rallies were alleged to have been scheduled in collaboration with the Sitam-e-Milli, who were to disturb Badakhshan. According to the plan, when the government dispatched forces to that remote province, Kabul's defenses would have been weakened and the way paved for the success of the plotters. Handwritten "confessions" made by Sultan Ali Kishtmand, minister of planning, and Mohammad Rafi, minister of public works, appeared in the press along with their photos; although the confessions confirmed these allegations, they were useless, having been obtained under torture.

The Parchami ambassadors were dismissed from their posts and deprived of Afghan citizenship. Except for Mahmud Baryalay, the rest, including Karmal, took with them the cash assets of the embassies.[24] At home the crackdown on the Parchamis began. Since Amin had earlier obtained a list of Parchami military officers through Sayyed Daoud Tarun, the suppression of the Parchami officers might have been complete. Their known officers were imprisoned, and overzealous Khalqi interrogators in the provinces eliminated a considerable number of them. In Kabul only a few were eliminated, among them the junior university professors Khanabad, Amier Mohammad, and Abdur Razaq. Soviet advisers were against their elimination. None of the leading Parchamis was executed. Of the "conspirators," only the military chief of staff, Shahpur Ahmadzay, and the physician Mier Akbar were executed. The former was executed on the advice of Soviet advisers not because he had plotted but because he was an influential person in his locality. The remaining Parchamis "began to form underground organizations to resist the regime."[25]

The authorities meanwhile started an anti-Parchami campaign in the mass media. For the anti-Parchami Afghans, it was a golden chance. Even unsuspected Parchamis and their sympathizers, out of fear of losing jobs, took part in the crusade. Opportunistic Parchamis and those who had been associated with them also joined the chorus. They made Karmal the special target of attack. In a televised meeting of party and government officials, an eloquent member of the politburo denounced Karmal as a traitor who had abandoned his fatherland in return for life under the "dark umbrella of imperialism." For an impartial spectator, all this was amusing and distressing. It was amusing because skill in oratory, writing, drama, and art was demonstrated. It was depressing because the whole episode was a reflection of opportunism and lack of integrity. Anyone for whom politics was a profession of decent people was a misfit.

A second wave of arrests engulfed the Parchamis following the Karmal-Taraki meeting in Moscow, as already noted. The Parchamis had been suppressed but not eliminated. As a faction they were still organized. Since Kabul was their stronghold, it was impossible for the rural Khalqis to trace them, despite their wide networks of intelligence. From October onward the Parchamis became active once again, but their distribution of propaganda leaflets helped the government to trace and arrest them. Around six hundred Parchamis were arrested. By the time of the invasion the Parchamis had been impoverished as never before. I myself saw clear evidence of their impoverishment. On the second day of the invasion, I toured Kabul in the company of my university colleagues Sayd Bahauddin Majruh, Rasul Amin, and Hakeem Taniwal and a friend, Farouq Safay. As revolutionary guards the Parchamis were patrolling the streets as lean figures in shabby garb with rifles behind their backs. Karmal was now destined to rule the country with their help.

BABRAK KARMAL

Babrak Karmal was popular with his followers, particularly the urbanized Parchamis, some of whom were emotionally attached to him. To them he was the symbol of defiance to social injustice and absolutism as well as a comrade of the downtrodden and the impoverished. His followers looked on him as the leader of the new-style pioneers who felt they had liberated themselves from the shackles of religion, tribe, region, and social customs, which restricted individuals in every corner of life. Karmal's career of political struggle, his years of imprisonment, his perseverance in the hard profession of politics, his polished manners and convincing reasoning—all these endeared him still further to his followers. It was the force of their attachment that twice won for him seats in parliament in the constitutional decade. But all this is an incomplete picture of his personality and his social standing.

Karmal's loyalty to the Soviet Union was well known. He would say even in the presence of non-Parchamis that he wished to make Afghanistan the sixteenth republic of the Soviet Union.[26] He was in the pay of the Soviet Union. He had been accused of this by Soraya Baha, a Parchami woman activist who had become disillusioned and who was therefore under investigation by some members of the central committee, including Karmal. She told him to his face that he was paid 35,000 rubles a month in the name of the party.[27]

Karmal was widely believed to be a man without scruples. Following the death of his mother, he left home and lived with his widowed maternal aunt. He was said to be living in disregard of the society's moral values. Karmal's father, a general in the Afghan army, had disowned him, apparently for his leftist views.[28] In his mature life, too, there was talk about Karmal's debauchery. To his critics Karmal would say, "Among us these issues have been resolved." Karmal resembled Mulla Zakki, whose licentious views permeated the court of Shah Mahmud Sadozay in the early years of the nineteenth century. Zakki's actions led to a commotion that resulted in the overthrow of the monarch. Afghan society was no longer as rigid as it had been during the previous century, but it was not so liberal as to accept as its ruler a commoner with such a record.

Karmal's behavior created a problem for his faction, despite the fact that some urban Parchamis were "loose." Karmal's behavior intensified a rift between himself and Mier Akbar Khybar, the number two man in the faction. Khybar once slapped Karmal in his face because Karmal had tried to seduce the unwilling wife of their host comrade. Khybar said to him, "You aspire for Afghan rulership, but do such base things."[29] The incident had wider—and, for Khybar, fatal—implications. All this lowered the status of the Parchamis in the public eye.

The incident had wider consequences for Karmal as well. All peoples want to know the identity of their rulers, and that desire is particularly strong among the genealogy-conscious Afghans. When Karmal was raised to power, his background became a subject of inquiry. Karmal was born in 1929 in the village of Kamari to the east of the city of Kabul. He had graduated from the College of Law and Political Sciences of Kabul University. Karmal's family was believed to be Tajik, the second main ethnic group after the Pashtuns, because linguistically and culturally the family was Tajik and was integrated into the urban community of Kabul. But Karmal's father did not say so and "would skillfully conceal his Tajik identity."[30] In 1986 Karmal announced that he and his full brother, Mahmud Baryalay, were Pashtuns. He said so because they were the sons of a linguistically Persianized Pashtun mother of the Mullakhel section of the Ghilzays. But in the patriarchal society of Afghanistan, descent is traced only through the patriarchal line. Karmal should have stated that he was a Tajik if he was a Tajik. Karmal's announcement was political in that he wanted to attach himself to the Pashtuns, but it confounded the issue of his identity. Karmal's forefathers had immigrated from Kashmir to Kabul, as many Kashmiris had settled there over a long period of time. Kashmir was a part of the Afghan Durrani empire until its dissolution in 1818. This descent is reinforced by the fact that Karmal and his brother's original names resemble the names of Indian Muslims. Karmal's first full name was Sultan Hussayn, and his brother's name was Sultan Mahmud; their father was named Mohammad Hussayn. The brothers changed their names to sound more like Afghan names.

The fact that Karmal's ancestors had immigrated to Kabul, Karmal's statement that he was a Pashtun, the fact that his father was not a Pashtun, and his father's reluctance to admit that he was a Tajik—all these make it doubtful that the family was Tajik originally, although they were integrated into that group. It is a custom in Afghanistan for a person of no ethnic significance to relate himself to the ethnic group into which he has been integrated. Not all Pashto-speaking Afghans are Pashtuns, and not all Persian-speaking Afghans are Tajiks. Karmal went against the custom. This means that, ethnically speaking, the family was insignificant. Among the educated Afghans this was not so damaging to the social standing of Karmal and Baryalay. More damaging was the view that they were the descendants of Hindu ancestors.

Some claimed that Karmal was descended from Hindu ancestors, but no evidence has substantiated the claim. However, it was said that Karmal and his two younger brothers looked like Hindus. Another supportive point can be traced in Karmal's relationship with the government of India. Before the coup the Indian embassy in Kabul used to invite Karmal to its receptions, whereas it did not invite Taraki, although he, unlike Karmal, had spent some time in India. When Karmal was raised to power, India was, of all the nonaligned countries, the only one to establish full diplomatic relations with the Kabul regime. This is not to suggest that India did so for personal reasons. In maintaining a relationship with Kabul, India intended to promote its own regional interests. But in these relationships Karmal's personal role was striking.

For the first time in Kabul, the small Hindu and Sikh communities were officially encouraged to hold religious ceremonies openly. Senior officials participated in televised ceremonies. It might have been in line with their communist creed to encourage religious minorities. The Soviet advisers might also have instructed them to please India, their ally in the region. But the fanfare that they made on these occasions irritated the Afghans. In addition to being known as a self-indulgent communist, Karmal was said to be a promoter of Hinduism. Even if nothing else counted against Karmal, these labels were enough for the Afghans to distrust him.

KARMAL AS A RULER

Karmal's immediate problems were within the party. He was the chosen man of the Kremlin, and no one within the party could openly oppose him. However, scheming men devise ways to oppose even under the strictest of circumstances. Within the closed frame of government, the opposition, in order to seize power, may resort to whatever means available to it. After the fall of Amin and the suppression of his faction, Karmal had new rivals in the persons of Sarwari and Gulabzoy, the heads

of the Taraki faction that called itself the "principled Khalqis." Sarwari
and Gulabzoy had endeared themselves to the Soviets by helping them
in the invasion. They had done so not for the sake of Karmal but for
their own agenda, which was to get rid of Karmal and his faction.[31]

The scheme was to dispose of the Parchami leaders in their offices by
a synchronized action. Since the Parchamis were few in number, since
they were not as bold as the Khalqis were, and since the Khalqis had
battered them twice before, they did not think much of them. This was
what Sarwari thought. He was, however, so naive as to disregard the
Soviet factor. In June 1980, before Sarwari was able to put his scheme
into operation, he was sent as ambassador to Mongolia. This still did
not mean that Karmal became the general secretary of a unified party,
as he claimed.

The Soviet Union, by overthrowing the Khalq government and raising
the Parcham faction to its place, had split the PDPA into irreconcilable
factions. The KGB's view that the removal of Amin would ensure unity
in the PDPA remained dominant in Moscow. But as minister of interior
and a leader of the Taraki faction, Gulabzoy acted as if he were the head
of a state within a state. He acted on the view that both he and Karmal
had gotten their posts from Moscow, thus claiming himself Karmal's
equal.

Because of all these problems, Karmal was raised to the position of
head of state without ceremony to legitimize his rule. But in Afghanistan
the head of state must gain legitimacy either directly from the constituencies or through their representatives, in accord with social conventions. This approach becomes a necessity when a dynasty is replaced. In
the case of Karmal, though, such legitimation was impossible. No attempt was made to convene an assembly of the notables to bestow on
him the position of the head of state. Instead, the government in its mass
media reported that people from various walks of life had expressed
their allegiance to their leader, Karmal. Except for some messages from
party cadres and some government employees, these messages were fab-
rications. No attempt was made to televise the process by which, even
within the official party and the Revolutionary Council, Karmal was
elected head of the party and of the state. Only official communiqués
were issued to the effect that the central committee of the party and the
Revolutionary Council "almost unanimously" agreed to elect Karmal
as head of the party and the state.[32]

After the Afghans demonstrated in opposition to Karmal, and when
other governments, except for those of the Soviet bloc countries, de-

clined to recognize the regime, Karmal invented stories that he hoped
would legitimize his rule. According to one of these stories, he entered
Afghanistan "through revolutionary pathways" and along with the true
members of the party organized opposition with whose help he overthrew the government of Amin. By the phrase "through revolutionary
pathways," Karmal meant his two secret flights aboard Soviet military
aircraft to the Bagram military airport. The Soviets first flew him in on
13 December 1979, when they expected opponents would topple Amin
by a coup. "But when the operation to kill Amin failed, Babrak [Karmal]
was hurriedly brought back . . . to the Soviet Union."[33] The Soviets again
flew him in after the invasion. So to Karmal the Soviet interference in
Afghan affairs, its invasion of Afghanistan, and his becoming a tool of
its policy were a "revolution"—but this view could not help him legitimize his rule.

Karmal's poor performance in interviews with foreign journalists also
failed to help his public image. In the first and last televised interview
of his life, held before a large number of foreign and Afghan journalists
after he was raised to power, Karmal divided the journalists on the basis
of the cold war line distinguishing between "the imperialist bloc of the
West" and the "socialist bloc countries." In this interview his answer to
a question put by a BBC correspondent showed that he lived in the past.
Instead of answering the question he was asked, he adopted a confrontational attitude, lecturing the BBC reporter, "We know each other in history because our forefathers had defeated your forefathers in numerous
battlefields in Afghanistan." People expected that since Karmal had
served twice in parliament and since he had been abroad for over a year,
he would now act as a statesman. Instead, he proved himself to be an
exhibitionist. It was one thing for him to recite composed statements as
an actor; it was quite another for him to answer questions that touched
the lives of millions of men and women. He almost never spoke extem-
poraneously. After this interview the impression became widespread
that Karmal, in addition to being a stooge, had no qualities of a
statesman.

From the moment Karmal was raised to power, he faced tremendous
problems. Whatever weight he had he lost after the invasion. An Afghan
author has summed up Afghan feelings about Karmal by stating, "His
presence alongside the Red Army is so small that it attracts no attention.
People don't think of him, but evaluate the long-range consequences of
this political move [the invasion]."[34] Karmal's Soviet supporters reduced
him as a person and a ruler. Thus, "by the close of 1979 the PDPA no

longer ruled Afghanistan; the CPSU [the Communist Party of the Soviet Union] did."[35]

From the moment Karmal was flown in to Kabul, he was no longer his own master, still less the Afghan ruler. His Soviet cooks, waiters, and waitresses, the Soviet driver of his black limousine, and his Soviet advisers took care of him around the clock. Behind the curtain in his office were a Soviet adviser and an interpreter; his conversations were taped.[36] Contingents of Soviet guards patrolled the palace in the city where Karmal lived. Afghan guards surrounded him, but their weapons were without ammunition. The Karmal of the old days, when he roamed freely, suddenly became a pearl. The Soviets were so kind to him that he had no need to meet with members of his family, or at least to meet them without their presence. Karmal's wife, Mahbuba—a courteous woman who was once one of my students—spent most of her time in the Soviet Union. Karmal no longer needed his mistress, Anahita Ratebzad, since young Russian women gave him, as well as a select number of the politburo members, intimate company. Everything that the Soviets could provide for Karmal's personal comfort was made available to him. Under Soviet supervision Karmal found himself in surroundings he had never been in before. But then he had to live the life of an unfree ruler, and this is clear from his own words to a friend and the words of one of his friends about him. To an old leftist friend, Asif Ahang, who met him under strictly supervised conditions, the embarrassed Karmal said, "The Soviet comrades love me boundlessly, and for the sake of my personal safety, they don't obey even my own orders."[37] Another friend, Zia Majid, said of Karmal after meeting with him, "The hands, feet and tongue of the poor Sultan had been tied, and he had no right to speak [without permission] with his personal friends."[38]

THE INVISIBLE RULING CIRCLE

Like Karmal, others in the politburo, the central committee, and the Revolutionary Council did not have to trouble to formulate policies or make decisions. These matters were handled for them. Whatever the guidelines of the Kremlin rulers, they were handed over to the regime's appropriate agencies. This was done through an invisible body or council, composed of the Soviet ambassador, the local head of the KGB, and the commander of the Soviet army, and headed by the Soviet supreme commander, Marshall Sergei Sokolov. The council met regularly. As the actual ruler behind the scene, Sokolov issued directives to agents of the party and the government. He received Karmal in his presence in his own headquarters. Through his own agents Sokolov likewise supervised how the directives were implemented. In particular, policies on security matters emanated from this body, and they were handed over through its advisers to the regime's intelligence department (KhAD) for implementation.

The number of Soviet advisers was on the increase. In the first month after the invasion their numbers more than doubled, surpassing total PDPA members at the time.[39] By early 1984 they were believed to total over ten thousand.[40] They worked not only as advisers but also as executives in all the military and civilian departments to which they were assigned. Bureaucrats of the regime found that even routine orders had to be approved and countersigned by the Soviets. In fact, "no minister [could] make a single decision, even a minor one, without consulting his omnipresent shadow."[41] As noted, even Karmal was not permitted to make decisions. "Slowly his power was confined to approving dismissals or appointments which, under instructions from Soviet advisers, the Intelligence Department or his comrades in the politburo would propose. He would neither postpone nor reject such proposals."[42] But as a Persian saying has it, "Alive, the hero is happy." To comrades who complained of the domineering attitude of Soviet advisers, Karmal said, "The Soviets have enough experience in implementing socialism and social justice in Asia, Africa, Latin America, and Europe. They will never make mistakes in their accomplishments. Be patient. They have come here to develop our country as a model in the region."[43] During his stay in Czechoslovakia, Karmal's belief in the Soviet Union had become total. The Czechoslovak leaders had impressed on him that the world's progress was due to the invincible Red Army. That was why "he did not think he had made a mistake to have come [to Afghanistan] along with the Soviet army."[44]

Promotions became a source of profit for corrupt advisers. An adviser in Herat, in return for a golden necklace for his wife, released a member of the Afghan Millat Party who had been sentenced to death. A few Parchami officers were said to have obtained promotion by offering women to their Soviet comrades. Similarly, a Soviet adviser who wished to remain longer in his post sent his own wife to the arms of a senior Afghan official to obtain his recommendation. Not all advisers were qualified. When a non-PDPA official informed Karmal that the advisers attached to his ministry were unqualified, Karmal ignored him and, holding to the party line, told him that "the Soviet advisers were most qualified in their fields, and . . . Afghanistan should take advantage of their expertise."[45]

Soviet advisers composed statements in the Russian and Tajiki languages for party members and government officials to read on official occasions. Party and government experts paraphrased the Tajiki texts into Afghan Persian (Dari). Under Soviet supervision government officials also composed statements. Soviet advisers did not allow government and party officials—even Karmal or his brother Baryalay—to make statements of their own, particularly on issues relating to foreign affairs. Karmal and Baryalay were admonished after making unauthorized statements. However, within the framework of the guidelines, party members and government officials had a wide range in which to demonstrate their talents and to win over the public.

EMPTY PROMISES

In his first radio broadcasts Karmal gave hopeful promises. He said that henceforth there would be no executions and that a new constitution would be drawn up providing for the democratic election of national and local assemblies. He also promised that political parties would function freely and that both personal property and individual freedom would be safeguarded. In particular, he stressed that soon a government representing a united national front would be set up and that it would not pursue socialism. He also promised a general amnesty for prisoners. In normal circumstances these promises would have aroused expectations, but now they sounded dreadful. As noted before, Karmal announced at the same time that his government had asked the Soviet Union to give economic, political, and military assistance, a request that, he said, had been accepted and rendered. Since he had become an agent for inflicting the calamity of Soviet troops on the Afghans, Karmal had no choice but to give the promises of a democratic government. But in this he went so far as to give promises that he could not fulfill even if he wished to.

These promises were nothing but the Leninist tactical move of two steps backward and one step forward. For a Brezhnevian protégé such as Karmal, it was impossible to go ahead with a platform that his masters saw as bourgeois. Also, the Afghans had seen that the same Karmal following the communist coup had, with others, promised that private as well as personal property would remain safe, a promise that they violated. The fact was that he could not become a ruler without the

military might of the Soviet Union. Karmal, with a view to taking revenge on Amin and making himself the ruler of Afghanistan, had let
himself become an instrument in the hands of foreign masters with no
regard for the rights of his compatriots to sovereignty, their dignity as
free men and, above all, their lives. To reach his goal, this most slavish
of puppet rulers let himself be entangled in a dilemma that was beyond
his powers to solve and that brought untold suffering to millions of men,
women, and children.

Among the measures promised by Karmal, the most important were
the release of prisoners; the promulgation of the Fundamental Principles
of the Democratic Republic of Afghanistan; the change of the red,
Soviet-style banner of the Khalq period to the more orthodox one of
black, red, and green; the granting of concessions to religious leaders;
and the conditional restoration of confiscated property. Some concessions were also granted to landowners whose lands had been confiscated
in the land reform program implemented by Karmal's predecessors. Except for the release of prisoners, all these measures were taken gradually.
What lessened the bitterness of the people was the release of prisoners
on 6 January 1980. The Parchami prisoners, numbering about 600, had
been released in the early hours of the invasion; the bulk of the prisoners, released on 6 January, numbered 2,000; and about 100 prisoners
were not released. Thus, the total number of prisoners before the invasion was around 2,700. Much fanfare was made of the occasion of the
release of prisoners. People from the outside were brought in to mingle
with the prisoners to make their number appear higher. But the day
turned into a day of wailing for thousands of families who were now
convinced that they would never again see their imprisoned relatives.
After Amin came to power, he had made public a list of those already
executed; according to this list, 12,000 prisoners had been executed, but
people still hoped that since the actual number of prisoners was higher,
their imprisoned relatives might be alive. They were disappointed.
(Amin had released 850 prisoners after he became the ruler and intended to release the rest by 1 January to coincide with the sixteenth
anniversary of the party.)

After the Khalqis came to power, they ran the country by issuing a
series of eight edicts. They suspended all laws except those on civil matters. Another exception was the criminal law of the Daoud period,
which the Parchamis, like the Khalqis, retained as a repressive instrument.

In April 1980 the Karmal regime adopted a temporary constitution, the Fundamental Principles of the Democratic Republic of Afghanistan, which had been drafted while Amin was in power. The new constitution guaranteed certain democratic rights of individuals, including the right to "security and life," the right of "free expression," and the right "to form peaceful associations and demonstrations." It also declared that "no one would be accused of crime but in accord with the provisions of law," that the "accused is innocent unless the court declares him guilty," and that "crime was a personal affair, and no one else would be punished for it." It likewise declared that "torture, persecution, and punishment, contrary to human dignity, are not permissible."

Envisaged for the country was "a new-style state of the Democratic Republic of Afghanistan," guided by the PDPA. It was the only legal party, and the Revolutionary Council, as the supreme state power, was to convene twice a year to approve measures already taken by the Presidium, which was composed mostly of the politburo members of the PDPA. The state was to safeguard three forms of property: state property, cooperative property, and private property. The constitution declared that the state had the right to exploit all underground property and other resources considered state property. The constitution also declared that the state had the power to develop the economy toward the creation of a society free of the exploitation of man by man. The state was likewise empowered to take families, both parents and children, under its supervision.[46]

The constitution was inherently contradictory. On paper it was a perfectly democratic constitution, at least as far as the rights of the individuals were concerned; in reality it was a document granting a monopoly of power, since the state that it envisaged was to be steered only by the official party. More important, the way it was implemented was arbitrary. It relied on clauses in favor of the state while ignoring those in favor of individuals. The guaranteed rights of individuals were meaningless words. It was, in brief, a legal instrument of suppression in the hands of the regime. But its impact was limited. By the time it was promulgated, the mujahideen had confined the regime to cities.

Among the palliative measures that Karmal was to take, the most important was the one intended to have an immediate effect on the current situation. This was the question of forming a government representing a united national front, which Karmal had promised. By definition, such a government would be composed of those groups or individuals having the power to influence national politics. Karmal had neither the desire nor the power to form such a government. The government he did form was composed of the Parchamis, Khalqis (Taraki group), and three persons of no national significance. A number of well-known non-communist Afghans were also appointed to various ministries.[47] But these collaborators, who set the precedent of cooperation with the regime, found that they had been given posts without authority. Besides, by then it had become a fact of Afghan politics that any one who collaborated with the regime was no longer socially significant.

The next step toward the formation of the government of national front was the appointment of a large number of junior bureaucrats in various ministries. The regime made a big fanfare of this, but these officials were ordinary civil employees, not politicians. This was what Karmal and his Soviet advisers meant when they spoke of a government representing a united national front. As has been pointed out, "no totalitarian regime can afford to share real power with any group outside its own immediate control."[48] Karmal had failed to unite the party, although calling it a unified democratic party. He had also failed to form a truly national government. Yet he and his associates called their regime "a new evolutionary phase of the glorious April Revolution."

All this time armed opposition was mounting. Within weeks of the invasion the mujahideen had wrested the rural areas from the control of the regime. The regime ruled the city of Kabul, the provincial capitals, and those strategic areas where the Soviets and the regime had stationed military contingents and militia units. Even cities were unsafe for PDPA members. Worse still, the mujahideen killed Soviet soldiers in large numbers. All this was a spectacular feat for the mujahideen. (The situation remained the same until the Soviets withdrew their army in 1989.) Opponents of the regime spread rumors to the effect that the Kremlin rulers had decided to replace Karmal. But luckily for him, no one else within the party had even his meager standing.

Years later, when Karmal's inability to consolidate his government had become obvious, Mikhail Gorbachev, then general secretary of the Soviet Communist Party, said, "The main reason that there has been no national consolidation so far is that Comrade Karmal is hoping to continue sitting in Kabul with our help."[49] Colonel Nikolai Ivanov, a Soviet military writer, even wrote that "he [Karmal] was a nobody."[50] Both statements reflect the failure of Soviet foreign policy. It was because of this policy that Karmal was unable to achieve "national consolidation," that he had become "a nobody." Prior to the Soviet invasion of Afghanistan, Karmal not only was not "a nobody" but was an important somebody. Twice the people had elected him to parliament. When his Kremlin comrades used Karmal as a tool of their policy, they turned him into a nobody. Then this "nobody" was unable to achieve "national consolidation." He even had to plead with his Soviet comrades: "You brought me here [to Afghanistan], you protect me."[51] The Soviet invasion had generated forces of resistance beyond the control of even the strongest ruler with the best mind—let alone a puppet such as Karmal. In addition, Karmal was inexperienced in running the country, a particularly severe weakness at a time when the nation had turned against him. The truth of this statement Gorbachev accepted when in a politburo meeting he told his peers, "If we don't change approaches [to evacuate Afghanistan], we will be fighting there for another 20 or 30 years."[52] To make Karmal a scapegoat for the Soviet failure is wrong, but doing so was standard practice for the Soviet leaders. At any rate, the Soviet leaders stuck with him for six years. Hoping to prop him up, they received him and his delegation with pomp in October 1980 in the Kremlin, where they lectured him on how to run the country.[53] What was needed was a lecture to the Kremlin leaders themselves on why they had blundered in invading Afghanistan and raising to power a person whom their own historian called "a nobody."

PART TWO

The Afghans Against the Invaders and the Client Government

CHAPTER FOUR

Islamic Resistance Organizations

The resistance to the Soviet invasion was nationwide. But in contrast with past resistance movements, which were headed by traditional leaders, in the present resistance leaders emerged from among the modern, educated members of Afghan society. They had been organized in political parties set up in the 1960s, a by-product of the transition from a traditional to a modern society. The process of modernization on a major scale started in 1956, when Premier Daoud launched the first five-year economic development plan. Thereafter, a state-controlled mixed economy based on five-year plans became the model for development. Among other things, modernization policy led to the expansion of education and an increase in the number of students. Their total number rose from 667,500 in 1970 to 888,800 in 1976. Among them were students of both sexes in institutions of higher education; these students numbered 7,400 in 1970 and 15,000 in 1976. In 1970 there were 910 teachers of higher education and 18,138 teachers in primary and high schools.[1] There were similar numbers of military students and students enrolled abroad. By 1975 there were 115,125 Afghans with at least twelve years of formal education.[2]

In the constitutional decade, when secularization was a main current, the morphology of Afghan politics began to change. A feature of this change was the emergence of educated Afghans in the forefront of politics. No longer were traditional leaders the only actors on the political stage. Political parties composed of the intelligentsia were set up. Since the parties were not legal, their leaders employed the free press as a vehicle for their views and chose students to be their activists. The 1960s was a decade of student unrest throughout the free world. In Kabul, too, higher educational institutes—particularly Kabul University—became politicized. In the 1960s it was closed for weeks, even months, because of such activities. Following the overthrow of the monarchy and during the Khalqi rule, the parties inside the country were suppressed. Some carried on activities from Pakistan. The Soviet invasion prompted the parties to become active once again. New resistance groups also mushroomed. Following the exodus in 1980 of Afghans to Pakistan, eighty-four small and large resistance groups were set up in Peshawar. Inside Afghanistan about twenty groups and regional unions were active by July 1981.[3] They fell within a spectrum including Islamic, nationalist, and leftist tendencies. Some groups were regional. Only the groups that opposed the invasion and had platforms for ruling the country are described here.

ISLAMIC RADICALISM

The Islamic groups constituted the backbone of the resistance movement. Among them, some were traditional and others novel in composition, ideology, or platform. The novel groups were fundamentalist and revolutionary. They aimed not only to oppose the invasion but also to reorganize the state and society. They intended to do so on the basis of Islamic ideology, which they had acquired from the radical thinkers of the modern Islamic world. That was why their story did not end with the repulsion of the invasion.

In Afghanistan as elsewhere in the Islamic world, Islamic fundamentalism (or Islamism or Islamic radicalism)[4] is the story of response to a society in transition from the traditional to the modern that sets the state on the road to secularization. The overriding concern of the Afghan Islamists was to defend Islam from the encroachment of atheism, which permeated the educated population after the country became dependent on the Soviet Union for schemes of modernization in the late 1950s. As a by-product of this dependence, there emerged a group of leftists influenced by the literature of the Tudeh Party of Iran, the Communist Party of the Soviet Union, and the Communist Party of China. Supporting the Soviet-assisted schemes of modernization, the pro-Moscow leftists did not oppose the government as strongly as leftists usually do.

They chose feudalism, capitalism, imperialism, and to some extent Islam as their targets to prepare the atmosphere for intellectual change.

To undermine Islam, the leftists questioned the existence of God. Because of these efforts to spread atheism, some Afghans saw official atheism as the leftists' goal. Leftist students at the Kabul educational centers became active in this endeavor, which also touched provincial high schools. Gulbuddin Hekmatyar notes that, while a student in his hometown in the province of Qunduz, he felt the need to set up an Islamic organization to combat the atheists.[5] Students and professors of Kabul University started the Islamic movement in the 1960s and disseminated the views of Islamist thinkers through translations of their works. Since the Islamic groups were at the bottom of the resistance movement, and since the movement has deeply affected Afghan politics, it is necessary to describe first the views of the modern Islamic thinkers and then, in this and the following chapter, the Afghan resistance groups in general and their programs of resisting the invasion.

FEATURES OF ISLAMIC RADICALISM

The Islamic movement is composed of the views of three thinkers of Muslim India, Indo-Pakistan, and Egypt. They are Abul Hassan 'Ali Nadawi, Abul A'la Mawdudi (1903–79), and Sayyed Qutb (c. 1906–66), who wrote their main works in the mid–twentieth century. Based on the Quran, their views encompass aspects of society and the state. They have made the seizure of state power the main goal. The movement is political, and the Islamists are, like other revolutionaries, concerned with power. In their view, God is the source of sovereignty, and his commands are the laws of Islam. Secular concepts such as nationalism, liberalism, democracy, capitalism, socialism, communism, and the like are rejected. As Sayyed Qutb holds, Islam "has chosen its own unique and distinctive way and presented to humanity a complete cure for all its ills." Their prescriptions for the ills of humanity are to be administered by professional revolutionaries without recourse to the masses of the people and with no room for accommodation with adversaries.[6]

The Islamists stress the need to introduce reform along Islamic fundamentalist lines. This is because, according to the thinkers, religious ignorance (*jahiliyya*) has prevailed in the world, as it had before the rise of Islam.[7] Like revolutionaries, the Islamists consider the state to be an instrument of reform. The state, Mawdudi has propounded, is universal to the extent that its "sphere of activity is coextensive with the whole of human life." Also, the state is ideological: that is, its aim is to establish the ideology based on the fundamentals of Islam, which are the Quran and the Sunna (sayings of the Prophet Mohammad). In Mawdudi's writings, this is called the Islamic state, whereas in Sayyed Qutb's writings it is termed "an Islamic order." Both are coextensive with the activities of humanity. In Sayyed Qutb's view, "Religion in the Islamic understanding is synonymous with the term nizam [order] as found in modern usage, with the complete meaning of a creed in the heart, ethics in behavior, and law in society." [8]

In Mawdudi's view, the state "should be run only by those who believe in the ideology [of Islam] on which it is based and in the Divine Law which it is assigned to administer." Mere belief in the ideology of Islam is not enough for a Muslim to run the state. "The administrators of the Islamic State," Mawdudi avers, "must be those whose whole life is devoted to the observance and enforcement of this law, who not only agree with its reformatory program and fully believe in it but thoroughly comprehend its spirit and are acquainted with its details." He further states that "whoever accepts this program, no matter to what race, nation or country he may belong, can join the community that runs the Islamic State. But those who do not accept it are not entitled to have any hand in shaping the fundamental policy of the State." [9] The non-Muslim subjects of an Islamic state are thus excluded from running the Islamic state but are entitled to all the rights and benefits of second-class citizens.

The Islamic state is yet more exclusive, for women, too, would be prohibited from administering it. In Mawdudi's view, nature has made women unfit to play an active role in society, outside the home where they belong. [10] He holds this view although Muslim women, like Muslim men, are counted as first-class citizens on whose will alone the Islamic state is to be based. Among men, too, by definition only a small group of pious professionals thoroughly versed in Islamic law and the fundamentals of Islam are entitled to run the state. Thus, the Islamic state, which is to be universal in function, becomes exclusive in composition. Mawdudi calls this state a theo-democracy. He calls it so not because it offers political pluralism and equality of all citizens before the law, irrespective of religious or political beliefs; indeed, he holds these principles to be contrary to the essence of Islam. He calls the Islamic state theo-democratic because, in his view, "the entire Muslim population runs the state in accordance with the Book of God and the practice of

His Prophet." In his view a theo-democracy is "a divine democratic government, because under it the Muslims have been given a limited popular sovereignty under the suzerainty of God." [11]

This limited sovereignty entitles the Muslims to constitute the government and also to depose it when it is found to be working contrary to
Shari'a (Islamic law). In Mawdudi's view, "Every Muslim who is capable
and qualified to give a sound opinion on matters of law is entitled to
interpret the law of God when such interpretation becomes necessary."
This sovereignty is further reinforced by the principle that "all questions
about which no explicit injunction is to be found in the Shari'a are settled by the principle of consensus among the Muslims." [12] But in practical life only professionals are able to express sound judgment on matters
of law. Since the majority cannot become professionals, the field becomes restricted to a small portion of society. Also, when it comes to
the question of the head of the state, the limited sovereignty is limited
still further, since only a male Muslim is considered qualified for the
post of amir, who is to be assisted by a consultative council. Although
Mawdudi allows women the right to vote, he demarcates a permanent
division of labor in accord with the Islamic law, in which women are
assigned indoor duties. [13] On this point Sayyed Qutb is more explicit,
stating that a woman fulfills her function by being a wife and mother,
while the function of a man is to be the authority, the breadwinner, and
the active member in public life. [14] Thus, the Islamic state becomes a
prerogative of professional Muslim men only.

On the question of state power, the Islamists are more serious than
the traditional reformist religious thinkers were. This is one of the points
of their departure from the reformist thinkers of the past. Since the state
has now become more important, its seizure has been made a goal. Toward this end jehad, which traditionally is religious in the sense that it
is extreme exertion of self and property in the cause of God, is looked
on as a "continuation of God's politics by other means" not only against
infidels but also against tyrannical rulers when the tenets and rules of
Islam are neglected or violated. In this sense, jehad is a form of permanent political struggle designed, as Qutb argues, to disarm the enemy so
that Islam is allowed to apply its Shari'a unhindered by the oppressive
power of idolatrous tyrannies. [15]

Both Mawdudi and Qutb place jehad at the forefront of religious
obligations, arguing that it is a duty incumbent on all Muslim men, particularly when their religion is under attack by the spread of jahiliyya.
Mawdudi rejects the view that jehad is either a "holy war" waged by

religious zealots in order to convert infidels by force of arms or an instrument of self-defense. There is a connection between the use of force and the nature of Islam as a dynamic movement, or "a revolutionary ideology" as Mawdudi calls it. The missionary side of Islam is relegated to this ideology. Because it is "a revolutionary ideology," Islam has adherents who are an "international revolutionary party" that has as its main aim a worldwide revolution that transcends boundaries and national territories. The seizure of political power is thus the consummation of jehad and its raison d'être.[16]

The process by which political power is acquired is central to the Islamists, as it is to all revolutionaries. Since to the Islamists Islam is a "revolutionary ideology" and its adherents "revolutionaries," it is logical to assume that their immediate goal is to seize the state. They have discarded gradualist and reformist approaches, including the holding of elections and the rest of the democratic procedures for attaining state power. They have done so not only because these approaches are the contribution of the Western world, for which Islam has no need, but also because in Sayyed Qutb's view the common people are unreliable, easily swayed by demagogues, particularly in the age of mass media. In his view the seizure of power is the work of the "chosen elite," the vanguard of professional revolutionaries who dedicate their life to one purpose. Well-disciplined, highly organized, and imbued with the spirit of a new era in the long march of Islam, they cannot fail to win.[17]

To ensure victory for the vanguards, Sayyed Qutb has left them some guidelines in their "long march" toward an Islamic state. In their daily confrontations with the state, they must dissociate themselves from it. Except for a studied and purposeful interaction, neither penetration of the existing political establishment nor cooperation and accommodation with the state are to be allowed. In his own words, "the summoners to God must be distinct and a community unto themselves." As Youssef M. Choueiri points out, this attitude results in a society of the believers, represented by God's select group, that is in a perpetual conflict with the unbelievers, whose earthly concern spans both society and the state.[18] The more important point of Sayyed Qutb's views on the subject of direct struggle of the vanguards with the state has been summed up as follows: "First a small group of people accept the creed until it is firmly rooted in the hearts of its members; then this group begins to organize its life on the basis of this creed and encounters persecution from the surrounding jahili [ignorant] society, then it splits off from the surrounding jahili society and confronts it in an open struggle. Then it succeeds completely, or partially, or is defeated, as God wills."[19] As a devout Muslim, Sayyed Qutb, with the cooperation of a network of militant underground cells, intended to offer a model to his followers by trying to overthrow the socialistic government of President Jamal Abdul Nasser by a swift armed action. But before he was able to do so, he was seized and condemned to death in August 1966. His teachings and methods, however, soon invigorated Islamists throughout the Muslim world, encouraging them to set up political organizations for the same purpose.

THE ISLAMIC MOVEMENT IN AFGHANISTAN

The story of the emergence of the Islamic movement in Afghanistan, as elsewhere in the Muslim world, is a story of reaction to modernization schemes that led to an increase in state activities from a minimum, as in traditional society, to a maximum in the period of transition to a modern society. As such, the movement is recent, a by-product of the modernization schemes that began in the late 1950s. It is also more dynamic since it was at the same time a response to the rise of communism associated with the modernization schemes financed mainly by the Soviet Union. In the process of modernization, people were drawn into greater participation in the modern sector through schools, courts, economic activity, communications, the army, and urban immigration. As Professor M. E. Yapp explains in the context of the Muslim societies in general, in Afghanistan this process also led to the politicization of religion when the state took over the functions formerly the domain of the religious classes and other institutions.[20]

In the process of modernization, the Afghan middle class, composed of the educated elements, increased in numbers from a few hundred to nearly a hundred thousand.[21] These educated persons were mainly from rural areas. The state-run free educational system had made it possible for industrious students of the rural areas to have access to institutions of higher education in Kabul, where they had been concentrated. The founding members of the Islamic movement were from rural areas associated with modern educational institutes, not traditional madrases. They were neither part of the political ruling circles nor dependent on the state, a point that may account for their militancy.

Professor Ghulam Mohammad Niazi and others were the founders of the Islamic movement in Afghanistan.[22] Hekmatyar, though, states that the founders were twelve university students, including himself.[23]

He also states that the founding students invited the professors to join the movement, but most declined the invitation. He speaks specifically of the invitation to Professor Niazi, but he adds that all along, even from his prison cell, Niazi replied that while he supported the movement, he did not wish to take part in it as an official member.[24] Hekmatyar concludes that "as state employees they [the professors] did not wish to become members of a movement which opposed it."[25]

The movement began in 1957, when Ghulam Mohammad Niazi established a small cell at the Abu Haneefa seminary in Paghman. He had just returned from Egypt, where, at University of al-Azhar, he had obtained a master's degree in Islamic studies. On arriving in Paghman, he initiated a group of devout teachers to the cell and its numbers increased, especially after the fall of Premier Mohammad Daoud in 1963, when they regularly held clandestine meetings in Kabul.[26] By 1969 the Islamists had set up a political action group with Professor Niazi as its nominal leader (amir).[27] Hekmatyar's comments above probably concern the students' branch of this movement, which was founded in 1969 under the name of the Muslim Youth (jawanan-e-Musulman). He writes, "When Daoud staged a coup [in 1973] our party was very young. Only four years had passed of its founding."[28] Others called them the Islamic Brethren (ikhwan al-Muslimin). Hekmatyar probably did not know of the secret association of the professors, described by Barnet Rubin:

> At the beginning of 1973, the movement, which also included a more secret association of professors, began to register its members and formed a leadership shura (council). Burhanuddin Rabbani, a lecturer at the shar'ia faculty of Kabul University, was chosen as chairman of the council. Ghulam Mohammad Niazi, the dean of the faculty, was recognized as the ultimate leader, but, because of the sensitivity of his position, he did not formally join or attend the meetings. The council later selected the name Jam'iyyat-e-Islami [Islamic Association] . . . for the movement.[29]

In a pamphlet published by the Jam'iyyat, *Who Are We and What Do We Want?* it was stated that the movement was nothing but an attempt to liberate the people of Afghanistan from the clutches of tyranny and to bring about a renaissance in religion. In elaboration, Hekmatyar stated that the aim of the movement was "the overthrow of the ruling order, its replacement by the Islamic order *[nizam]*, and the application of Islam in political, economic, and social spheres."[30] Similarly, Rabbani states, "For us Islam is a driving force, which concerns every aspect of our life."[31] In the view of an Islamist author, Gulzarak Zadran, the Islamic order is "the implementation by the Muslims of the laws of God on the creatures [human beings]."[32] While castigating liberal democracy and socialist democracy in line with the views of Sayyed Qutb, Zadran adds, "Every other kind of law, custom, tradition, procedure, and concept has no place in Islam, because Islam is a complete religion, and the introduction in the Islamic society of the above-mentioned democracies and other similar concepts is against the Islamic injunctions and fundamentals, and a contrariety and a rebellion."[33] Reflecting Sayyed Qutb's views in an even more negative form, Mohammad Yunus Khalis rejects not only "a republican form of government" but even "general elections." In his view, the Council for Resolution and Settlement (*shura-e-ahl-e-hal wa 'aqd*), composed of pious and just Muslims, is to elect a Muslim as the leader of the community on the basis of competence and Islamic learning.[34] The Islamists had as their aim to set up the Islamic order, or "Islamic revolution," not only in each separate country but also "in the Muslim world."[35]

The views of Sayyed Qutb and other revolutionary thinkers of the Muslim world, especially leaders of the Muslim Brethren, influenced students of the colleges of law and theology of Kabul University as well as of the Madrasa of Abu Haneefa through foreign professors employed there. Also, the Afghan professors of the College of Theology who had studied at the University of al-Azhar in Cairo had disseminated these views through local journals, especially the weekly paper *Gaheez*, founded in 1968. Its editor, Minhajuddin Gaheez, had made it an anticommunist paper, but he was assassinated by a radical leftist in 1972. The Islamists also translated some works of Sayyed Qutb in vernacular languages. While most colleges of the university were affiliated with Western universities, the College of Theology was affiliated with the University of al-Azhar in Cairo.[36]

Outside the Islamist circles some traditional 'ulama and religious leaders had already founded associations such as Khuddam al-Furqan (Servants of the Quran), Jam'iyyat-e-'Ulama-e-Mohammadi (the Association of Mohammad's 'Ulama), and Qiyam-e-Islami (the Islamic Uprising) to combat atheism, wage *Jehad-e-Akbar* (great jehad), and oppose the pro-Soviet stand of the government. Among their founders were Sibgatullah Mojaddidi, the *pir* (religious leader) of Tagao; the pir of Qala-e-Biland, Hafizji Sahib of Kapisa; and Mawlawi Fayzani.[37] On the strength of the support of such dignitaries, the 'ulama held demonstrations for over a month in Kabul until the government dispersed them, as already noted. When Daoud ruled as prime minister from 1953 to

1963, he did not tolerate opposition. Nevertheless, these associations did not achieve much.

The Islamists became active after they spread a clandestine leaflet, *Tract of the Jehad,* challenged the communists to debates, and held rallies on the campus. But their rallies were smaller than any of the rallies held by their opponents. This was evident to this author, who attended the rallies and was once beaten by the police when they attacked the university. Some Islamists called for "armed jehad," but this call produced no response. Being latecomers in politics, the Islamists did not have many members until the end of the decade. Hekmatyar even states that until the Daoud coup in 1973 the Muslim Youth were engaged in cultural activities and that they became active as an organized group only afterward.[38]

The progress that leaders of the movement had made was unknown to Hekmatyar. The progress consisted of recruitments on a big scale and the preaching of the cause in the countryside as well as the city of Kabul. Premier Moosa Shafiq encouraged the Islamists to be more active.[39] During his short rule, Premier Shafiq also released Hekmatyar, who had been imprisoned for his alleged killing of a Maoist, Saidal Sukhandan. On the campus, too, the position of the Muslim Youth had improved. Hekmatyar states that "in the last years of the reign of Mohammad Zahir Shah we gained a majority of two-thirds of the seats of the Student Union."[40] By then the balance in the forces of university students had changed in favor of the Muslim Youth. "At the beginning of the 1970s the Islamic movement was stronger than the Maoists among the students, but its penetration of the army remained weak."[41] Because of the headway the Islamists had made, the leftist groups had gone on the defensive. The decline of the leftists was also evident in the results of the 1969 parliamentary election, in which only two of them were elected. The Islamic movement appeared to be on the way to becoming a party of the masses. Among other things, this threat prompted the communists to help Daoud to topple the monarchy in 1973.

UNSUCCESSFUL UPRISING AND SPLIT

The Parchamis, as already noted, dominated the security forces of the new republic. When the constitution was suspended and President Daoud was dependent on the Parchamis, they began a reign of terror with a view to eliminating their opponents. They fabricated reports accusing their opponents of destroying the republic. Since President

Daoud had usurped power in a coup and since his government was far from established, he accepted such reports. Suspicion led to official actions in this period. The first victims were former Prime Minister Mohammad Hashem Maiwandwal and about forty senior colleagues of his Progressive Democratic Party who served in the military and civilian departments of government. The Islamists were the next on the agenda. After President Daoud declined to accept Niazi and Rabbani's offer of cooperation in return for his break with the communists, the suppression of the Islamists began.[42] Some were killed; others, including Niazi, were arrested. The rest, including Rabbani and Hekmatyar, fled to Pakistan, the traditional land of refuge for Afghan dissidents.

Afghan Islamists in Peshawar lived in hardship, financed by the Jama'at-e-Islami of Pakistan under the leadership of Mawlana Abul A'la Mawdudi. But after Afghanistan's relations with Pakistan deteriorated over the issue of Pashtunistan, both countries financed and incited each other's dissidents. While Afghanistan harbored the Pashtun and Baluch dissidents of Pakistan, the latter incited Afghan Islamists. Olivier Roy states that Afghan Islamists decided to wage an armed struggle against the government of Daoud, but on this they were divided, and while the younger members stood for it with the support of Pakistan, Rabbani was against it. Roy further states that "the radicals, led by Hekmatyar, carried the day."[43] He cites no source for his statement, which is contradicted by Rabbani's account. According to Rabbani, "Among ourselves we decided that Daoud personally was not a communist, but a Muslim, surrounded by communists, who should be eliminated. For that purpose we prepared a list of eighty military and civilian communists and instructed our companions to carry it out. . . . Surprisingly news of the failure of the uprising in Laghman and other regions reached us in Peshawar." Rabbani is further quoted as having said that "leaders of the operation groups, in response to our investigation, told us that they did so on a second instruction, which they received from Hekmatyar. But the latter denied having issued such an instruction."[44] By waging the uprising, Afghan Islamists were now entangled in international politics, which affected their movement. Also, they had neither infiltrated the army nor enjoyed public support, and Pakistan had not given them a large quantity of weapons; instead, Prime Minister Bhutto of Pakistan intended simply to frighten President Daoud to change his policy toward Pakistan.

On 22 July 1975 armed Islamists attacked government headquarters in Badakhshan, Laghman, Logar, and Panjsher. Only in the districts of

Panjsher were they able to occupy government headquarters for a short while. Elsewhere they were either defeated or arrested on arrival. Nowhere did the locals or the army support them. The failure became a disaster for the Islamists. Conversely, it provided an opportunity for the Parchamis in the security forces to arrest anyone who was suspected of being an Islamist. An unknown number of Islamists were arrested. Of the ninety-three brought to trial, three were executed and sixteen acquitted. The rest received sentences ranging from life imprisonment to a year in jail.[45] Serious also was the dissension that appeared among the Islamists who escaped to Pakistan. Recrimination became common and splits unavoidable. The establishment of relationships with "some authorities" of the government of Pakistan, the acquisition of financial assistance and other concessions, personal ambitions, and scores of other points all played a role in this split.[46] Among these other points was a split along sectarian lines between the Sunni and Shi'ite activists, "who suspected one another of the subversions that led to the uncovering of their various plots."[47] Until then the two sects had been united.

Serious also was the division among the Sunni leaders. The Jam'iyyat split. Hekmatyar and Qazi Mohammad Amin Wiqad formed a new party, the Islamic Party (Hizb-e-Islami), but Rabbani stuck to the old name. In 1978 they reunited under a new name, the Movement of Islamic Revolution, with Qazi Wiqad as its leader, but it did not last. The failed attempt made leaders of both parties wary. While it influenced Rabbani to move toward moderation, it induced Hekmatyar to adopt a long-term strategy, organizing his party on rigid lines. The *Aims* of the Hizb states, "The reformation of government is the pre-requisite to the reformation of society as well as that of the individual." The *Aims* also states that the Hizb "stands for the Islamic reorganization of the state [through] its program."[48] Of all the parties, the Hizb is the most radical and Islamist. Some argue that from the onset Hekmatyar's goal was to acquire power rather than to liberate Afghanistan. Over this issue Mohammad Yunus Khalis parted company with him and formed a party of his own under the same name, because in his view the liberation of Afghanistan was more important than the conquest of power.[49] Khalis considers lack of trust among leaders a factor for the multiplicity of resistance organizations.[50]

The split also revealed ethnic and regional tendencies. At the leadership level Pashtuns dominated the Hizb and Tajiks the Jam'iyyat, although both groups could be called mixed. In the latter group regional tendencies such as Panjsheri, Badakhshi, and Herati crystallized. The passage of time made the tendencies sharper. Regionalism and ethnicity thus made inroads at the expense of Islamic ideology, which disregards such parochial proclivities.

Another weakening factor was the Islamists' loss of credit in the eyes of their patrons whose goodwill was essential for them, since they had to act from abroad inside Afghanistan. This point became serious when, following his victory over the Islamists, President Daoud took measures to distance Afghanistan from the Soviet bloc countries and to bring it closer to the Islamic world, in particular Pakistan and Iran.[51] The policy was detrimental to the Islamists, so much so that by the end of President Daoud's reign they had "run out of money, because Saudi Arabia and Iran, who were pursuing a policy of support for Daoud, did not help them, and Pakistan did not wish for an open confrontation with Kabul."[52] Until the invasion the Islamic parties were "more or less dormant." Against the Khalqis, too, they did not receive any substantial support from outside. Only the Soviet invasion enabled them to come to the forefront of politics.

Part of the Islamic movement consisted of certain groups that took into account the actual situation of society. Loosely structured, they can hardly be called political parties in the modern sense, since they generally lacked sociopolitical platforms. Based on common traditional religious and secular notions, the organizations were open to persons with different shades of opinion. The 'ulama, community elders, the intelligentsia, army officers, and former government employees joined them in the spirit of jehad to expel the invaders. Their leaders were either members of religious families or religious scholars. A degree of tolerance, compromise, and democracy was also a feature of these organizations. Islamic, national, and to a certain extent democratic, they came to be known as traditionalist or moderate as distinct from Islamist. The emergence of the traditionalists weakened the hold of the Islamists over the Afghan refugees since the fold of the former was open to those whom the Islamists suspected.

The Islamic moderate organizations were set up in various times in 1979. They included the Front for National Liberation (Jabha-e-Nejat-e-Milli), the Revolutionary Islamic Movement (Harakat-e-Inqilab-e-Islami), and the National Islamic Front (Mahaz-e-Milli-e-Islami), led respectively by Sibgatullah Mojaddidi, Mawlawi Mohammad Nabi Mohammadi, and Pir Sayyed Ahmad Gailani. Mojaddidi and Gailani are heads of religious families as well as leaders of the Islamic mystic orders of Naqshbandiyya and Qadiriyya, respectively. They have many followers, particularly among Pashtuns. Whereas the Mojaddidi family in the past played a role in politics, it is the first time for the Gailani family to emerge in the forefront. Both families have a modern outlook on life. While the Mojaddidis are, as a mark of respect, known as Hazrats, the Gailanis are known as *pirha* or *pirān* (spiritual leaders; singular, *pir*). The Khalqis executed many Mojaddidis, some of whom were more influential than the present Mojaddidi. The religious scholar Mawlawi Mohammadi served as a member of parliament in the constitutional decade. For this as well as for his assault on Babrak Karmal in the House of Representatives in 1966, he became popular, particularly among the mullas in his own province, Logar.

ATTEMPTS AT UNITY

To make the jehad a success, a coalition of the resistance forces was necessary. This was what the public demanded, as the urban uprisings showed. The demand was raised by Afghan refugees who held meetings in Peshawar in 1980, at which they demanded a united front to coordinate military activities. (These meetings will be detailed in the next chapter.) The pressure these meetings produced persuaded leaders of the Islamic groups to form a coalition.[53] A coalition of the three Islamist and three moderate organizations, the Islamic Union for the Liberation of Afghanistan, was formed. Abd al-Rasool Sayyaf, a founder of the Islamic movement who had arrived in Peshawar after he had been released from prison in Kabul, was chosen to lead the coalition. But it was not destined to last. First Hekmatyar and later the three moderate groups seceded from it. These three set up the Union of the Three. In 1981 the Islamist groups formed a broader alliance, the Union of the Seven, made up of the three Islamist groups, the newly formed organization led by Sayyaf, and three splinter groups. In 1985, under pressure from the king of Saudi Arabia, a broad coalition, the Islamic Unity of Afghan Mujahideen, was set up, comprising the four main Islamist and three moderate groups.[54] This group was in existence until 1989, when, under the patronage of Pakistan and Saudi Arabia, the Afghan Interim Government (Dawlat-e-Islami-e-Afghanistan) was set up in Rawalpindi to coincide with the withdrawal of Soviet troops from Afghanistan.

Not all resistance groups were included in the coalitions. The Tehran-based Shi'ite groups, nationalists, tribal unions, and the anti-Soviet leftists (including the pro-Chinese leftists) were excluded. The coalition was composed only of the Sunni Muslim groups approved by Pakistan. Pakistan's support was crucial since, through its military Inter-Service Intelligence and Afghan Commissionerate, it distributed weapons, cash, and materiel received from donor countries. Pakistan supported the Afghan jehad, but it manipulated it to serve its own interests. An ardent supporter of the jehad, President General Zia al-Haq of Pakistan overruled the view of the majority of his inner council to come to a modus vivendi with the Soviet presence in Afghanistan.[55] But he manipulated the jehad with a view to raising a client government to power in Afghanistan after the Soviets withdrew. For this purpose Pakistan opposed the emergence of a strong united leadership. "On the political level, the Pakistanis were obsessed with the fear that the resistance might develop in the same way as the Palestinians had done, enjoying the support of millions of refugees. It seemed to them that the best protection against this risk was a divided resistance. The Pakistanis granted the same facilities to each of the six groups and closed their eyes to the activities of minor groups, which they did not recognize. It was thus the Pakistanis who ensured the continuance of the major split in the movement, at least until 1984."[56]

The patronized coalition did not prove effective in coordinating military activities. There were no coordinated military activities, nor did they make use of the expertise of the military officers of the Kabul regime who defected. Community and tribal elders and members of the intelligentsia were hindered from working for the jehad. The Islamist groups did this in the hope of monopolizing power and Islamizing the society. The host government left them free to deal with Afghan refugees even on its own soil. Having tighter organization and discipline, the Islamist parties treated the refugees as if they were their rulers. Some groups even had courts and prisons and opposed national identity, stating that "if in both countries [Pakistan and Afghanistan] there prevailed an Islamic order we prefer that the common boundaries between us be discarded and both countries united."[57] Others wished to substitute the name Islamistan (land of Islam) for Afghanistan. In past resistance movements, the combination of such groups constituted a national force that met the emergency although they were not as widespread as they were in the present movement. Had the resistance not been strong at the grass-roots level, one wonders whether it would have made any headway. A specialist on guerrilla warfare wrote, "A visit with the rebels in Afghanistan suggests two broad conclusions about the resistance there. The first is that it is an extremely popular movement that has arisen spontaneously among many different kinds of people with varying motives. The second is that in its leadership, organization, coordination, and strategy, the Afghan movement is one of the weakest liberation struggles in the world today." [58]

SHI'ITE RESISTANCE GROUPS

The Afghan Shi'ite minority of Hazaras and Qizilbashes were for the first time as active as the Sunnis against an invasion. Among their educated, however, a considerable number sided with the Kabul regime. The Shi'ite leaders were more divided than the Sunnis. As Shi'as, their loyalty to Iran was a major reason for disunity. Some followed the Ayatullah Khomeini of Iran as a political as well as a religious leader, while others followed him only as a religious leader. With the rise of Khomeini the Afghan Shi'as became more militant. The Shi'ite faith obliges every Shi'a to follow a *mujtahid* (an authority in the interpretation of the faith), wherever he may be, an injunction not in line with principles on which a nation-state is based.

The Ayatullah Sayyed Ali Bihishti had in 1979 set up in Waras in Hazarajat the United Islamic Council (Shura-e-Ittifaq-e-Islami), comprising traditional, secular, and religious Hazaras. Through the efforts of its commander, Sayyed Mohammad Jagran, the council liberated Hazarajat from the regime following the invasion. The Islamic Movement (Harakat-e-Islami) led by Ayatullah Shaykh Mohammad Asif Muhsini was another significant organization set up in 1978. It centered around followers in Kandahar and Kabul. From the outset Muhsini's relations with Iran were strained. In 1980 Iran expelled Muhsini's followers because he followed Khomeini only in religious affairs. By contrast, the first pro-Iranian organization, the Organization of Islamic Victory (Sazman-e-Nasr-e-Islami), was set up in 1979 and received financial and military assistance from Iran. Nasr was the continuation of the New Mughal group, founded as early as 1966, which was subsequently renamed the Youth of the Hazaras (Shabab al-Hazara). Nasr has served as a mother organization from which smaller groups have sprung. Under the leadership of Karim Khalili, Mier Sadiqi Turkmani, and Abdul Ali Mazari, it was composed of ideologically committed fundamentalists. Khalili says of himself, "I do not know what part of Afghanistan I am from; my father and grandfather would tell us we are from Ghazni. I was born in Iran." [59]

Another organization set up in late 1979 was Strength (Nairo), with Qazi Safa Karimi as its leader. They all were "very successful," [60] but the Iranians did not think so. According to one observer,

The Iranians consider the Soviet invasion of Afghanistan the most favorable situation for the consolidation and extension of their influence in the country. In the beginning they decided to help all the Hazara groups without discrimination. When it did not work according to their wishes, they changed their policy and decided to federate the groups under their umbrella of one organization, Nasr. But last year [1982] the Iranians sent a delegation to Hazarajat to investigate the activities of Nasr and to see how their military and financial help was being used. The Iranians were deeply disappointed and convinced that it was impossible to accomplish anything with the Afghan parties. Then they decided to operate through their own Iranian party inside Afghanistan, and [in 1983] created the Sipah-e-Pasdaran [under Shaykh Akbari]; it has the same structure and the same organization as the Iranian Islamic Revolutionary Party, only the members are Afghans.[61]

Smaller and more rigid groups emerged from Nasr in Iran, among them Thunder, the New Generation of Hazaras, Organization of the Toiling People, and the Party of God (Hizb Allah), which was set up in Mashhad in 1981 under Qari Yakdist. Some of these attracted educated persons with conflicting extremist views, such as Maoism, racism, and religious fundamentalism. Another group, Mujahideen-e-Khalq, was founded under the influence of Iran's Mujahideen-e-Khalq. Afterward infighting became common, resulting in the death of about 26,000 Hazaras, a number higher than that the Hazaras lost in clashes with the Soviets. Hazarajat was not the scene of many clashes with the Soviets and the regime, which did not carry out major expeditions there. In the infighting the United Council was ousted from many areas, including its headquarters in Waras. Also, the Hazaras became disillusioned with Iran. Among the disillusioned ones, those who were forced to seek refuge chose Pakistan, not Iran.[62] Any hope of forging a united front among them became more unrealistic than among the Sunni organizations. However, in 1985, under the supervision of Iran, the Islamic Movement, the Islamic Victory Organization, the Revolutionary United Front, and Guards of the Islamic Jehad declared a cease-fire among themselves.[63]

CHAPTER FIVE

Nationalist Resistance Organizations

It is difficult to pinpoint which resistance groups were nationalist. Most might be called so, since they defended their homeland against the invasion and stood for the view that the people of Afghanistan alone had the right to set up the kind of state they wanted. Resistance to the invasion on this basis was the widest. The whole question centered on the point of sovereignty: whether it was to be actualized by the Afghans themselves or determined with the help of foreign might on the basis of universalist or internationalist notions. The point had never before been posed to the Afghans in such a stark form. Those Afghans who stood for the principle of popular sovereignty were never subjected to as much pressure as they now were. This is a distinguishing mark of the Afghan liberation movement. The weak point of the nationalists was the uncooperative attitude of Pakistan and their inability to unite in one organization.

AFGHAN JIRGA IN PESHAWAR

Following the invasion, a popular movement was set up whose purpose was to unite the Afghan nation, solidify the resistance organizations, liberate the land of foreign domination, topple the client regime, and establish a single political leadership. Contrary to the stand of the leftist internationalists and Islamic universalists, this movement's stand was based on the notion of Afghan solidarity as a nation, and its leaders followed a path like that followed by Afghan elders in the past on similar occasions. Every day about one thousand Afghans, led by community elders, mujahid commanders, and former members of parliament, gathered first in the Madani Mosque and later in the Mahabat Khan Mosque in Peshawar. In Waziristan and Thal, too, Afghan refugees held similar jirgas. The meetings held in Peshawar, which lasted in intervals for three months until 13 May 1980, assumed the features of a loya jirga, a traditional way of resolving a crisis on the basis of consensus. This made it necessary for tribal and community elders to unite with leaders of the Islamic organizations. The jirga focused its efforts on this essential but difficult point.

Under the leadership of Qazi Mohammad Omar Babrakzay, the jirga made two decisions: to create conditions for the convening of a *mumassila loya jirga* (a jirga akin to the loya jirga) and to invite leaders of the Islamic organizations. In a proposal to the Revolutionary Islamic Council of the Islamic organizations it stated, "Since among you important talks are being held on the fate of Afghanistan, and since these talks are about our fatherland, religion, honor [*namoas*], and independence, we propose that on the question of determination of our fate all authoritative tribal elders should take part in decisions through such a loya jirga. Any decision made in our absence would have no validity with the Afghan nation."[1] At first leaders of the Islamic organizations took the invitation lightly. However, when more than 150 tribal and community elders separated from them in protest and joined the jirga, the Islamist leaders agreed to take part.[2] At this time the Islamic organizations were not strong enough to ignore such a call. They had neither sufficient logistics nor weapons at their disposal. Also, the refugees, whose number was increasing, were more enthusiastic about the jirga than about the Islamic organizations. The clashes that the mujahid commanders—particularly the Hizb and Jam'iyyat commanders—had permitted to happen among them had disillusioned the Afghans. They wanted jehad, not internecine battles. Also, the Peshawar-based organizations had frustrated many of their mujahideen by their inability to provide arms.[3] The Islamic organizations then took part in the jirga, and their representatives supported its goals. Mohammad Hashim Mojaddidi, representative of the National Salvation Front, proposed that a united revolutionary council be set up. Its leader, Sibgatullah Mojaddidi, who alone of the leaders of the organizations participated, warned the jirga against sabotage by hypocrites and people in pursuit of self-interest.[4]

The jirga bore fruit on 21 February, when it passed a resolution of thirty-four clauses. The resolution consisted of guidelines covering all aspects of the jehad, the first of its kind to be laid down. One clause proposed setting up a revolutionary council, a government in exile. In another clause the Afghans in Kabul were asked to boycott the client regime. Well-to-do Afghans were called on to assist the mujahideen financially. In another clause the Afghans were asked, in accord with Islamic and Afghan codes, to desist from taking revenge until the jehad ended. Since the jirga was administered according to traditional codes, violators were considered subject to execution. Afghan tribes were, in line with the disciplinary codes of the jirga (*nirkh*), asked not to give asylum to perpetrators of personal revenge.[5]

Since the implementation of the resolution required the cooperation of the Islamic organizations, the jirga asked their leaders to forge unity among themselves and to allow representatives of tribes to take part in the Revolutionary Council of the Islamic Union for the Liberation of Afghanistan. It also called on the Afghan nation to solidify its ranks. Sayyed Ahmad Gailani and Sibgatullah Mojaddidi declared their support for the resolution.[6] But some from within and without opposed the jirga. A number of its founding members seceded from it to set up a rival jirga, the Loya Jirga of the Tribes of Afghanistan. This threat was soon averted, however, and the seceders rejoined. The threat from the fundamentalists was more serious. Hekmatyar opposed membership of tribal elders in the Revolutionary Council of the Islamic Unity, arguing that they wanted to snatch its leadership. He also accused certain elders of trying to destroy the Islamic Unity.[7] The Kabul regime was also quick in undermining its successes. Shaken by the February Uprising (described in the next chapter), it promulgated a new constitution and distributed conciliatory leaflets in the border regions whence many elders came. From time to time it also convened jirgas of its own.

The jirga's last round of sessions lasted from 11 May to 13 May 1980, with 916 members from the administrative units of the country, including some from nomadic groups. In a new resolution it repeated its stated goals, proposing at the same time that an Islamic National Revolutionary Council (Islami Milli Inqilabi Jirga) be set up. The Council was to have an executive committee and a series of subcommittees, which would carry on practical affairs.[8] Leaders of the Islamic organizations could become its members provided that they supported the resolution.[9] In effect, the jirga outlined a government in exile. Headed by Mohammad Omar Babrakzay as the acting president of the jirga and Asadullah Safay, a former member of parliament, as chief of the Revolutionary

Council, the structure was to remain in force until an elected government was instituted.[10] Believing in the principle of election as the foundation of state structure, the jirga declared, "It [the jirga] considers legitimate and legal only the state that is instituted in line with the national and Islamic spirit following [the restoration of] full independence, through free and impartial elections." Affirming the principle of separation of the three branches of the state, it stood for the freedom of expression within the bounds of laws and declared its opposition to an absolute order.[11]

There were now two revolutionary councils: the Revolutionary Council of the Islamic Union for the Liberation of Afghanistan, composed of the six Islamic organizations, and the National and Islamic Revolutionary Council, composed of tribal and community elders. Both were for an "Islamic republic." But the nature and composition of the two "Islamic republics" differed. While the former stood for an ideological Islamic republic, the latter stood for a national, Islamic, and democratic republic. This difference made cooperation between their supporters impossible. The Islamic Union branded the jirga "another enemy of the sacred Islamic revolution of Afghanistan."[12] In response, the National Islamic Council stated that while representatives and leaders of the Islamic organizations supported the jirga, there were a few in the unity who, because of ignorance, denounced it. It also stated that the "real Islamic groups would never do something for which they would make themselves liable to the Muslim nation of Afghanistan."[13] The jirga used such language against the Islamic Union because of its popularity with the refugees, who numbered more than 700,000 at the time. The Islamic Union withdrew its statement.[14]

Forging unity and procuring financial assistance were the two important issues to which the National Islamic Council addressed itself. But these issues sealed its doom. The council set up a commission to ensure membership of the Islamic organizations and procure financial assistance from friendly countries. Already Saudi Arabia and a few others had expressed their willingness to grant financial assistance. But they had made this assistance conditional on the creation of a unified center. The Islamic Union held that it had created such a center already, while the National Islamic Council intended to forge a larger unity. "At this juncture certain [Islamic] organizations, in order to procure [financial] assistance, tried to extend control over the National Islamic Revolutionary Council."[15] Also, some leaders of the Islamic Union feared that, because of the success of the jirga, power was slipping from them. Although in principle in favor of the jirga, Gailani and Mojaddidi competed with each other in influencing it while the Islamists tried to undermine it.[16] The attitude shown toward the jirga by the authorities of the host country proved crucial. A number of times Pakistani police warned its participants to disperse for security reasons. Once they took away many of them in two trucks after a group from a fundamentalist organization had beaten them.[17] Pakistan did not want the Afghans to set up new organizations on its soil; this point had been decreed by the Consultative Board, a high-level commission concerned with Afghan affairs and headed by President Zia al-Haq.[18] The board persuaded Afghan refugees to join the Islamic party of Hekmatyar.[19] But the jirga's coup de grâce came from within. Supported by his followers, a member of the Gailani family chaired the jirga in violation of its procedures, as a result of which the majority boycotted it.[20] Subsequent efforts aimed at creating regional unions for the same purpose also came to nothing. Thus failed the first attempt by Afghans to set up a political structure along traditional lines at a time of national crisis.

AFGHAN JIRGA IN PISHIN

This was, however, not the end of the movement, nor could it be unless there was an alternative to it. In September 1981 elders from western Afghanistan, led by the former senator Abdul Quddos and the former deputy president of parliament Abdul Ahad Karzay, attempted to convene a loya jirga. They invited the 'ulama, tribal elders, elder statesmen, and military officers to set up a political leadership. Pointing at the inability of leaders of the Islamic organizations to unite the Afghans, the initiators of the proposal stated that it was now incumbent on them to set up a council (*shura*) through which the representatives of the Muslims of Afghanistan could lay a foundation for the future. Specifically, they also stated that since party politics had disunited Afghans, they should abandon it in favor of the institution of the jirga, by which their forefathers had resolved national problems in critical times. They stated that under the leadership of an elected acting president and secretaries, the proposed jirga would adopt guidelines on the basis of which a shura and a political leadership would be set up and a government in exile formed.[21]

The response was overwhelming, despite warnings from fundamentalists to those who wished to attend the jirga. In their view the jirga was a suicidal attempt by "the enemies of Islam and leftist parties."[22]

More than three thousand influential persons from all over the country arrived at Quetta, but local authorities requested that they move to the smaller town of Pishin for security reasons. There, too, the meetings were postponed for a few days because of the arrival in the region of President Zia al-Haq. Against the opposition of the police, who argued that the jirga should not be held, the Afghans insisted that since it was an Afghan affair, others had nothing to do with it.[23] This time the moderate Islamic organizations boycotted the jirga, alleging that the Parchamis had infiltrated it. The jirga elders said that since the jirga did not intend to be an instrument in the hands of any organization, opposition to it was understandable.[24] But unlike Peshawar, where the Islamists could disrupt such meetings, Pishin was safe from such interferences. The meetings were held as scheduled in September 1981.

The question of the selection of a national leader (*mille qa'id*) dominated the meetings of the jirga. Ningrahar elders proposed the former king for the position; this motion was accepted after a debate in which the Kandahari proponents of the king argued against the advisability of the proposal at this juncture. A commission composed of five representatives from each province and major district, as well as from the nomads and Hazaras, was assigned the task of setting up local councils, provincial councils, and a central council, called the National Islamic Council.[25] But the former king was living in Rome: he could not come to landlocked Afghanistan, nor could he direct his followers there in the face of opposition from Pakistan as well as the Afghan Islamists. It is an irony of history that in 1929, under similar circumstances, the non-Muslim British government of India allowed Mohammad Nadir Khan to pass on to Afghanistan, where he founded his dynasty, while the Muslim rulers of Pakistan refused to allow his son (Mohammad Zahir) to do the same. Mohammad Zahir had neither organized support among his followers nor sympathetic listeners to his cause in the neighboring countries.

Likewise, the elders—who were the embodiment of social wisdom and experience but who, unlike their opponents, were neither organized nor supported by a foreign power—were alienated from the Islamic groups in general and the fundamentalist groups in particular. Because of that alienation, the liberation movement worked against itself, creating a situation that made it dependent on foreign powers and distanced it from its grass roots, thus leading to its weakness. At a time of struggle against foreign domination, when the neighboring supportive powers also intended to influence Afghan politics through their surrogates, those who acted on the principle of self-determination had little chance of success. But the Pishin jirga, by pinpointing the former king as an embodiment of Afghan nationalism, brought him to the focus of attention.

MOHAMMAD ZAHIR

The former king responded to the Pishin jirga in words that reflected Afghan nationalism. In a communiqué issued on the occasion, he stated that traditional jirgas were the last resort for free debates and the adoption of resolutions in a democratic fashion about national problems in times of emergencies such as the present one. In the former king's view, the resolutions of such jirgas must take into account the viewpoints and tendencies of all national groups who are engaged in the struggle for the realization of common goals—in this case, "independence, territorial integrity, restoration of the status of traditional nonalignment, the national and Islamic identity of our homeland, and the maintenance of the right to self-determination for the institution of the future government through free elections."[26]

By the "state of emergency" the former king meant the lack of a legitimate government in the country and its occupation by the Soviet Union. The king responded to the situation by convening a loya jirga and pursuing a policy of waging armed jehad and holding political negotiations, depending on the circumstances. From the elaboration of these points, the features of Afghan nationalism as envisaged by the former king become clear.

In the king's view, the jirga is a traditional institution in which all tribes and sectors of society (through their elders) take part on an equal basis to settle national problems. The jirga is convened in times of national emergency, especially when Afghanistan feels pressured by outside powers. King Amanullah even required participants of a jirga to "settle by consensus of votes all the vital problems and schemes for the uplift and progress of Afghanistan."[27] The agenda fixed for the jirga covered the entire range of foreign and domestic affairs. In general, an elderly statesman presides over the jirga until someone else is appointed for the whole session. Whatever the issue, the participants resolve it by consensus after they discuss it in a democratic way. This is a description of a national jirga (loya jirga) attended by influential people from throughout the country and by selected government officials. The national jirga is then open to influence by governments, which have frequently held them in modern times and particularly in the twentieth century. But in a particular locality everyone concerned with the issue attends the jirga, along with elders and other persons (*jirgamawr, marakchiyan*) who have special knowledge of its rules and procedures. The mullas are invited to attend the jirga not to administer it but to provide advice, if needed. The jirga is solemnly convened after the usual Muslim prayer is offered, and a Pashto verse is recited: "Events are with God, but deliberation is allowed to man." The more democratic the tribe, the larger the jirga. Part of *Pashtunwali* (the social and legal codes of the Pashtuns), the jirga is a Pashtun institution by which the Pashtuns resolve not only ordinary disputes but also issues, particularly criminal issues, that defy solutions through the Shari'a or civil courts. The decisions are enforced and, among some tribes, the violators punished by a special militia (the *arobaki*).

As noted, Mohammad Zahir held that such an assembly was to deliberate over ways and means to restore Afghan sovereignty and lay down the basis for a future government. But since the prospect for holding jirgas were dim, the former king also viewed armed jehad as a means of realizing the national goal. In his view, "Presently the people of Afghanistan are engaged in an armed jehad for the restoration of their rights and national honor. Other than that no way has been left open to them, and if this goal can be attained by a peaceful means they would consider it." For the success of jehad, in December 1981 he proposed the formation of a "united front." He appealed to his compatriots to set aside— in accord with the injunctions of Islam and the approved national traditions—whatever personal and tribal differences they might have and choose their representatives "so that if God wills through the institution of a great national assembly with the participation of the representatives of all tribes, existing unions, organizations, and associations the foundation for such a united front may be laid down which can represent all the people of Afghanistan for the purpose of waging the armed struggle, and legally representing the people in international councils and states."[28] Realizing the difficulty of convening a loya jirga under the conditions of war, the former king proposed setting up a constituent assembly to pave the way for it. For this purpose a commission was set up.

Even opponents of "a united front" could not reject overnight the proposal for its formation. Afghans were disturbed by the disunity among the jehad organizations. That was why, according to the king, by October 1984 a number of "fronts and other groups from inside and outside Afghanistan as well as a large number of Afghan refugees in

Pakistan and the majority of Afghan associations in various parts of the world" supported the proposal. The three moderate groups, the Triple Alliance, also endorsed it, suggesting at the same time that the Muslim and other interested organizations and governments should be consulted about it.[29]

Nevertheless, the proposal remained in abeyance. In particular, Pakistan was against it. As already described, although Pakistan supported the jehad, it preferred a divided leadership even among the Islamic organizations. It was even more in favor of division in the case of a national front, especially the one propounded by the former king, who was considered a symbol of Afghan nationalism. Also, the rift between the two countries on the issue of Pashtunistan might have influenced Pakistan to oppose a movement that would have helped Afghan nationalists rise to leadership. The king had favored improved relations with Pakistan, offering "his pledge to Pakistan during her wars with India that Afghanistan would not move her troops nor create any disturbance on the Pak-Afghan border";[30] even so, Pakistan did not trust him. For forty years he had been the sovereign of an independent land, and now, too, he stated, "I do not think I can become an instrument in the hands of anyone."[31]

This may have been why Pakistan discouraged those groups and persons who supported the former king as well as the cause of the Afghan nation. Among the known nationalist Afghans was Abdur Rahman Pazhwak, a diplomat and former president of the General Assembly of the United Nations. The Social Democratic Party (Afghan Millat) is a case in point of a nationalist party that—although it had opposed the Khalqi government, and although the Parcham regime had imprisoned many of its leaders—was not allowed to work independently but only under the umbrella of the National Islamic Front. Azizulla Wasifi, an influential Alkozay elder from Kandahar and a former cabinet minister and president of the last loya jirga of the precommunist period, was the only one who was able to carry on his resistance activities in the spirit of nationalism. He could do so because as an elder of the Durrani tribal confederation he enjoyed the support of his refugee tribesmen in Quetta, where in 1980 he set up the Islamic National United Front (Islami Muttahida Mille Jabha).[32] Apparently, this scheme also called for the elimination by terrorists of leaders of emerging self-reliant Afghan groups and for the discouragement of others—community elders in particular—who might otherwise undertake resistance activities beyond the aegis of the Islamic groups. Many such persons took refuge in the West.

Pakistan refused politely or deferred to an indefinite date the requests that the former king had made to visit it.[33] The Islamist organizations opposed both him and his proposals to set up a national front.

Under these circumstances it was not feasible for a united front to be formed through a jirga. It was so not because the jirga had become anachronistic, to be looked on as "a final attempt by an aristocracy in decline to oppose the rise of Islamists,"[34] but because the neighboring governments opposed the emergence of a national leadership since each followed an agenda of its own to dominate Afghanistan. For this purpose they supported the Islamist groups in their bid to restrict to themselves the right not only to wage jehad but also to be part of the future political leadership. But in the sociopolitical structure of Afghan society at the time, there was no alternative to the jirga of influential groups and magnates to set up a political leadership in accord with the social norms and conventions—unless, of course, one believed in the use of violence and the setting up of an undemocratic or client leadership.

The opposition deterred the former king from moving from Rome, where he met with foreign emissaries. Since he had neither an organization nor a dynasty nor independent financial or military means, he had no other choice. Contrary to the rumors his opponents had spread, the former king, while a ruler, was among the poorest monarchs in the world. In Rome he lived in a villa with financial assistance from the king of Saudi Arabia. A realist and unambitious, he said he would not try to restore the monarchy.[35] Like other Afghans, he was convinced that the Mohammadzay rule has become a part of history. But he was popular. In an opinion survey among the Afghan refugees in Peshawar in 1987, more than 72 percent favored him as their leader. He is, however, not the sort of person to accept risks as his father did in 1929. In his defense, he has been quoted as saying that if he became active, his followers might suffer at the hands of the opponents and he would not be able to help them.[36]

Such a statement is believable from a person who, during forty years of rule, did not sign a writ for the execution of any person for political reasons. He also used his royal influence to commute capital punishment for persons convicted in criminal cases. This is unusual for a king of the Afghans, who have in their history appreciated a strong ruler. Mohammad Zahir Shah was instead a mild ruler. A decade of his reign constituted the constitutional democracy, which had no precedent in Afghan history. He has also played an important role in demonstrating a spirit of nonpartisanship, stating that "during my reign I did not relate myself to a particular tribe or clan, but looked on the entire people of Afghanistan from the same angle."[37] His unifying efforts in these turbulent times, when other contenders of power showed themselves willing to resort to any means available, reflect that view. In the period of divisiveness, violence, and anarchy the former king was steadfast in his stand for unity, accommodation, construction, and cooperation. Now, half a decade after the withdrawal of the Soviet Union, it is unclear whether he will be able to play a role. He can do so only when the Islamic fundamentalists and the governments of Iran and Pakistan leave the Afghans to themselves to set up a political leadership in accord with their social conventions.

LEFTIST RESISTANCE GROUPS

The leftists opposed to the invasion and the Kabul regime were the Marxist or Maoist group known as the Shu'lais. Radical revolutionaries, they were also called Left of the Left (Chap-e-Chap). The original name of their organization, which was set up in 1964, was the People's New Democratic (Democratic-e-Naween-e-Khalq). Its prominent founding figures were Rahim Mahmudi, Hadi Mahmudi, and Mohammad Osman, known as Osman Landay.[38] The Mahmudis enjoyed prestige for being the brother and nephew, respectively, of Abdur Rahman Mahmudi, a revolutionary figure of the 1950s, and Landay, a teacher, was popular among students. No other teacher in Afghanistan has served the cause of modern education as much as Osman Landay. Teaching mathematics and physics in his private courses, he has trained thousands of students.

The People's New Democratic served as a mother organization of the leftist movement. It aimed at socialism through revolutionary and violent means, rejecting parliamentary ways and conversely supporting armed struggle. It also supported the ideological and political line of the Communist Party of China on national and international issues. Nevertheless, "the organization could never rise to the level of a party and offer a policy program. Lacking this, the organization could not effectively combine legal and illegal methods of struggle and ended up engaging in nothing more than political adventurism."[39] Still, it more than the PDPA concentrated its activities among peasants.

In the constitutional period the organization published a periodical, *Shu'la-e-Jawid* (The Eternal Flame), after which it came to be known. The periodical was closed shortly afterwards. In this decade of strained relations between Moscow and Beijing, both chose to spread ideological literature in Kabul. In the fervor of the Cultural Revolution, Beijing eagerly distributed Mao's works in Pashto and Persian. When Prime Minister E'timadi observed the rapid growth of the pro-Moscow leftists, he left undisturbed the free distribution of Chinese literature, hoping to encourage the Shu'lais to counterpoise the pro-Moscow communists. But this myopic policy brought about the opposite result. In the 1960s, when the university campus was in turmoil and student processions common, the Shu'lais seemed more numerous and more dynamic than the PDPA. The Shu'lais, more than other leftists, became responsible for undermining the democratic system.

The Shu'lais became active in the rural areas, particularly in Herat and closer to Kabul in Kohistan and Parwan, where Chinese experts were also working with the government on a canal project for irrigation purposes. This may explain why the Shu'lais had infiltrated the peasants of the latter areas more than other parties had. But they, too, were not immune to the law of Afghan politics, and by the time of the invasion they had split into many subgroups over theoretical as well as tactical and practical issues. The new groups, in order of significance, were Surkha (later Rihayee), SAMA, Akhgar, Paikar, SAWO, and Khurasan.[40]

Among the pro-Chinese leftist groups SAMA, the most practical, was known to the public, while the rest were known primarily to their members. Majid Kalakani founded SAMA in late 1978. In 1979, in concert with other "nationalist groups," SAMA forged a front, the National United Front of Afghanistan, or NUFA (Jabha-e-Mutahid-e-Milli-e-Afghanistan). Dominated by SAMA, NUFA was an urban guerrilla alliance. According to Khalid Duran,

> [NUFA] outlined a clear program for the war of liberation as well as subsequent political and socioeconomic reconstruction. While NUFA declared itself free of any ideology, it defined itself as "national democratic." The adherence to democracy was substantiated by a clear affirmation of universal suffrage and human rights, with full equality for women and minorities as well as freedom of worship, all within a federal state with far reaching autonomy for the various nationalities and language groups.[41]

Despite this proclamation, the public still heard the acronym SAMA, not NUFA.

SAMA's significance was largely due to the adventurousness of its leader, Majid Kalakani, who was more of a social bandit than a leader of leftists. He was a teacher, and while a student he was alleged to have killed the principal of his school, for which he spent two years in prison.

Known to his followers as Majid Agha and in the Western press as "the Afghan Robin Hood," he had become active in his region as early as the first years of the 1970s. He came from the village of Kalakan, from where in the late 1920s the social bandit Habibullah captured the throne and became the ruler of the country for nine months. Majid Kalakani stood for armed as well as cultural and political struggle. He also valued constructive traditions, in particular the custom of opposing social injustice and observing the code of social morality by accepting risk with boldness and chivalry (*'ayyari*). This attitude, which distanced him from the dogmatic revolutionaries, brought him closer to the common people. An admirer of Kalakani writes, "Unlike the intellectual revolutionaries who look at the people from above, Majid Agha lived among them. The people felt him to be with them. He was knowable to the people. His language was the language of the people and his ideal the ideal of the people."[42]

All the pro-Chinese leftist groups opposed the invading army and its client regime, and they were behind many uprisings. They also carried out terroristic attacks in daylight in Kabul, some of which were daring indeed. But their organized strength became ineffective in a short time. In cities the KGB, through the KhAD, hunted the pro-Chinese Afghan leftists more vigorously than they did the Islamic elements. Evidently it was the policy of the KGB to clear the country, particularly the city of Kabul, of pro-Chinese elements. It was a clear case of witch-hunting: a suspicion was enough for KhAD to push an educated Afghan into prison, where it would accuse him of being a pro-Chinese communist. Even I was accused of being a leading member of Rihayee, and on such an allegation the KhAD executed a well-known nuclear physicist, Professor Yunus Akbari.

In the rural areas the pro-Chinese communists were no more secure. Their partisan peasants disowned them when they found out that they were communists. Both the government forces and the Islamic opposition pursued them. When the Islamists pursued them, they surrendered to the government. Others joined the government in opposition to the Islamic resistance, while most, particularly their leaders, found their places in the Pul-e-Charkhi concentration camp, where I met many of them. Some disguised themselves and joined the moderate Islamic groups. Their fate became worse than the fate of the populists of Russia in the last part of the nineteenth century when the peasants whom they wanted to serve in their regions handed them over to the authorities. China, the distant patron of these Afghan leftists, was unable or unwilling to help them. The first group of prisoners whom the regime executed were leaders of SAWO. In June 1980 the regime also executed Majid Kalakani, who had been arrested in February of the same year. His brother, Qayyum Rahbar (b. 1942), replaced him as leader of NUFA. A graduate of the University of al-Azhar, Rahbar had specialized in Afghan constitutional development. Well-versed in five languages, including Arabic and German, he taught at the University of Kiel in Germany. A man of the pen rather than the gun, Rahbar led NUFA for ten years until he was gunned down in daylight in Peshawar in 1990.

The suppression of the pro-Chinese elements shows the fate of revolutionary leftists in Afghanistan when unsupported by the might of a foreign power.

CHAPTER SIX

Urban Uprisings and Their Suppression

The Afghans are a dynamic and excitable people. When left to their ways, they go quietly about their own pursuits. When outraged, they may go to any extreme—and, like most people, they are outraged when their values are encroached on. Since the Afghans have a long history, and since in the course of it great religions such as Zoroastrianism, Buddhism, and Islam have spread in their land, their traditional and religious values are rooted in time. During the course of history Afghans have been molded by these religions as a set of commands and prohibitions and by their own traditions. They look on these social and religious codes as sacrosanct. Because of their experiences, they lead lives centered on religious values; on a code of honor that emphasizes family, ethnicity, and country; and on a code of conduct that governs relations between individuals and groups. Most important, they prefer to live within a framework that imposes the fewest restrictions on them.

Both religious and social conventions require Afghans to have a political structure. This is particularly true of tribal Afghans. The Pashtunwali of Pashtuns, governing their individual and social life, is a code of behavior for all, including their elders. In the past, even in times of war when the central political structure had disintegrated, the Afghans have lived within their social codes. Yet, contradictory as it may seem, the Afghans are not resistant to innovation and modernization. "Afghan cultural traits enable survival because the social structure, while strongly traditional, is, at the same time, surprisingly resilient, not rigid and intractable."[1] A pragmatic people, the Afghans have shown appreciation for change when, in this period of rapid transformation elsewhere, they have become aware of their backwardness. They have, however, wanted change to happen within the framework of their value system. The Afghans can be coaxed to hell, but not forced to heaven. The truth of this saying was made clear in the constitutional decade, when governments ruled on consensus. In this period even rural Afghans demanded schemes of modernization, calling for them either directly or through their representatives. For this purpose they volunteered their services and offered contributions in cash and plots of land. Such was particularly the case with regard to schools for both boys and girls. The rapid increase in the number of schools in the 1950s and 1960s, when Ali Ahmad Popal and Abdul Kayeum were the cabinet ministers of education, was the result of such cooperation. But those who embarked on schemes of modernization after the constitutional period did not show this wisdom.

Twice in the 1970s the Afghans were outraged: in 1978 by the communist coup, and in 1979 by the Russian invasion. The Afghans regarded both as violations of their mores. Besides, the invasion occurred when a civil war was going on. The invasion turned the civil war into a war of liberation. It gave that war a new meaning, summed up in the word *jehad*, an expression particularly moving to Muslim Afghans in such times. There have been many periods of jehad before in Afghan life, such as those against the Sikhs and the British in the last century, but this was the most forceful of all. The Russians were godless communists, and their ruthless suppression of the Muslims of Central Asia had been related to the Afghans by the thousands of the Muslims of Bukhara who had taken refuge in Afghanistan.

The Afghans worried that if the Russians dominated their country, not only would they lose their independence, but their land might become a Soviet republic, as the Muslim Bukhara had become. This explains why, with the exception of pro-Moscow communists (and not all of those) and the small group of the Sitam-e-Milli, the bulk of Afghans opposed the invasion. The opposition was shown throughout the country in a form and to a degree that has not been shown before. Except for pockets of the regime's supporters here and there, every group— religious, ethnic, and social—rose in protest. Even the religious minorities of Sikhs and Hindus covertly assisted the mujahideen.

PRELUDE TO URBAN UPRISINGS

The national opposition was marked by two stages: spontaneous, disorganized urban opposition, and rural guerrilla opposition. It soon became clear that the Soviet army could suppress the former but not the latter. The mobile mujahideen could fight almost indefinitely.

Following the invasion, the Soviet army contingent increased in number. Within a week it swelled to about 85,000 and subsequently to 120,000. Its materiel included varieties of modern weapons, both chemical and strategic, which were deployed temporarily against possible attack from the outside. In addition, Soviet warplanes from bases across the Oxus also took part in operations inside Afghanistan.

Army contingents were stationed in and around cities as well as along some main roads. Some were dispatched to frontier areas such as Kunar and Gardez. The bulk of them were stationed along the main roads leading to the Soviet border. A protective line was drawn around the city of Kabul, but the army did not immediately take part in operations. Until the uprising in Kabul in February 1980, the invading army acted in self-defense. The Soviets acted on the view that since resistance to their invincible army was futile, it would be a matter only of weeks or perhaps months before the country settled. They also held that since the invading army had rid the Afghans of the tyrant Khalqis, they would accept its presence. The promises of the new regime were likewise calculated to soothe the Afghans.

With that in mind, the authorities instructed provincial governors to establish a dialogue with those who had taken up arms. They were to persuade the militants to lay down their arms and enjoy the benefits of a peaceful life. This approach, on the contrary, emboldened the mujahideen, who soon appeared close to provincial capitals and roamed about in groups in villages surrounding the cities. There they either killed Communist Party members or drove them to cities. By 24 January the province of Laghman, for example, had been cleared of party members and their collaborators, while by mid-February the whole countryside had been wrested from government control. The mujahideen even controlled some main roads in the sense that they searched transport vehicles for party members and government officers. The Karmal government became confined to cities, and even there unparalleled opposition was shown to the invading power and its client government.

HERAT AND KANDAHAR IN TURMOIL

Individual acts of opposition were first shown by urban Afghans follow-ing the invasion when Russian soldiers walked here and there in the city of Kabul, acting as though Kabul were Moscow. Ordinary Afghans ab-horred the very sight of the soldiers. In separate attacks, a butcher and a shopkeeper killed roaming soldiers in broad daylight on 3 January. The attackers also lost their lives. During the first week of January individual attacks became common in Kabul, particularly in quarters such as Khair Khana, Dasht-e-Barchi, Qala-e-Shada, and Pul-e-Sokhta. A particularly dramatic attack was made by a young villager of Qala-e-Abdullah in Kohistan in May 1980. Approaching as a peddler, he stabbed to death a patrolling Russian soldier when the latter became interested in his fan-ciful commodities. Dressed in the soldier's uniform and armed with his weapons, the "peddler" shot dead seven Russian soldiers who were swimming in the nearby river.

Such attacks were an indication of the storm that was soon to come. The movement of contingents of the invading army into cities, in addi-tion, made it clear to the ordinary Afghans that atheists had occupied their homeland. Their response to the invaders now came quicker than the response of their forefathers to the invading British army a hundred years earlier. Popular opposition in the city of Kandahar was even more dramatic. Five days after the invasion the people of the city of Kandahar, who numbered over 130,000 in 1970, rose against the Russian army. After they killed a few men, the invading army withdrew to the canton-ment. The uprising was followed by closure of the shops as a form of protest. By the first week of February the demonstrations became gen-eral. Shopkeepers closed their shops while men and women called *azan*s (calls for prayers) on their flat rooftops and recited passages from the Quran. Denouncing the Russians and their puppet regime, they headed toward public cemeteries in protest.

The inhabitants of the city of Herat, who numbered 73,700 in 1970, made an even stronger commotion. During the first week of January 1980, the men of the city, at the first sight of the Russian soldiers, left their homes for mosques and other open spaces and called for prayers. All shops, except those selling essential commodities, were closed. The city of Herat was the innovator of anticommunist commotions. Its in-habitants had been the first to arise en masse a year earlier against the Khalqi regime, as already noted. The cities of Mazar and Balkh were also disturbed, but not to the extent that Herat and Kandahar were. In

Kandahar and Herat the commotion was continual. On 22 February 1980 the population of Kabul, which numbered 513,000 in 1970, also participated in the greatest uprising in its history.

THE GREAT UPRISING OF KABUL

The commotion in Kabul was a reflection of the will of the people because it was the capital city of the country. Party activists tried to dissuade shopkeepers from closing their shops and stores, but to no effect. A day before the uprising security officials arrested about two hundred persons, including a number of Khalqis, for inciting the people. The closure of the shops had been preceded by the distribution of clandestine antigovernment leaflets (*shabnamaha*). To incite the people still further, a group of two or three young men would appear in front of each shopkeeper and warn him to close the shop. He was also told to repeat with them that "Karmal was a traitor, and the Russians should leave our fatherland." It was also said that "under-ground groups had smuggled rifles into the city beforehand."[2]

The next sign of the storm was shown in the moonlit evening, when the cry "Allah o Akbar!" (God is great) echoed and reechoed over the breadth and length of the city, something unheard before. This was said to have been ordered, but who had ordered it is not known.[3] The chanting was an extension of the practice in Herat and Kandahar, where two evenings earlier such azans had become intense. In Kabul only men, including myself and young children, called the azans. The azans sounded the whole night. Nearby villagers also took part in making them. Soon the sound and color of rockets fired into the sky accompanied the azans. The invaders from the military cantonments in the city fired the rockets to frighten the people. In response, the Afghans raised the volume of their calls. It was as if a competition was under way, and indeed it was. This protest coincided with a reception in the Soviet embassy commemorating the sixty-second anniversary of the foundation of the Soviet army. The reception was announced in the name of the military attaché of the embassy, yet Babrak Karmal had also attended as head of state. This further angered the Afghans, who saw it below the dignity of the office of the head of state, even though they now opposed that office.

Early the next morning (22 February 1980, or 3 Hoot 1358) thousands of Afghans consummated the uprising, beginning in the old part of the city. Almost simultaneously, groups of people by the thousands appeared in different quarters of the city: Dasht-e-Barchi, Pul-e-Khishti,

Mohammad Jan Khan Watt, Salang Watt, Jamal Maina, Beni Hissar, and Qala-e-Fathullah.[4] Along the way thousands of others joined the march, which made it difficult even to estimate their total number. Except for the pro-Moscow communists, the people of the city either took part in the uprising or supported it, and Kabul was the first to oppose the invaders and the regime. The marchers were determined and undaunted. Those in the front ranks carried the green flag of Islam and chanted the slogan "Allah o Akbar!" Others incited them with fiery and evocative words. In the Haji Yaqub Square a group of women also chanted anti-Soviet slogans until they were dispersed.[5]

Soon armed units that had already taken positions in streets met the column marching along the Salang Watt in the central part of the city. Some Khalqis had declined to take action against the demonstrators. The demonstrators were unarmed, marching peacefully. Security forces, speaking through loudspeakers, asked them to disperse. They declined. After firing into the air, the security forces then fired at them at random. The marchers in the front lines fell to the ground. For a while, the flags were not allowed to remain on the ground with the fallen martyrs. They were picked up by men from the rear lines, who continued the march in the face of now sporadic firing.

The demonstrators could not continue their march in the face of the cutting force. After some time they ran for safety in the adjacent narrow lanes, only to join the main body later. It was then that they looted some shops and set some transport vehicles on fire. Their targets were state property, although private property was also looted. Finally they ran to the mosque of Pul-e-Khishti to take sanctuary, as is the custom of the land. But there, too, in some places they were fired on. After the dispersal of this uprising, security forces again began firing into the air, giving the impression that they had been doing so all along.

In the Dehburi Square in the Mier Wais Maidan, many groups of demonstrators converged, forming the biggest protest rally in the western part of the city. Those who started their protest from the town of Dasht-e-Barchi were the largest of all the groups. In their long march to the area, thousands of others joined them. When they reached Pul-e-Sokhta, the security men fired at them. Some protesters were lost, but the rest continued their march. The police of the Mier Wais Maidan headquarters also fired on them. This time they lost a larger number and dispersed. At about this time another column of protesters arrived from Qala-e-Shada and headed toward the government bakery through Dehburi, where the dispersed protesters of the Dasht-e-Barchi column joined them. The combined group occupied the headquarters of the police of the Khushal Maina. Here the police not only did not oppose them but even let them have weapons. The house of the fallen Amin was looted. An armored Russian contingent then appeared in the area, and helicopters flew low over the protesters, apparently passing on information about their movements to the armored units.

Toward midday the sounds of heavy bombs exploding elsewhere shook Khushal Maina. High in the sky warplanes roared. Rockets were fired from the low-flying helicopters. Armored units on the ground also began firing. Thus, both from the sky and the ground the Russians used their weapons for the first time against common Afghans in their own city. But these protesters, protected by modern buildings, did not lose as many as the protesters in the Salang Watt. The invaders apparently intended more to frighten than to kill. At this time I fled the area for safety, feeling a sense of appreciation for those journalists who cover the forefronts of battlefields. The sound of firing in Khushal Maina was heard until six o'clock in the evening.

Another column of protesters emerged in Chindawal near the center of the old city. After taking weapons from the area police headquarters, the protesters marched toward the main road of Jada-e-Maiwand in the middle of the crowded part of the city. This section had also been the scene of clashes in the preceding summer between the locals and the Khalqi government. Both uprisings were suppressed. The column of protesters in the Bagh-e-Ali Mardan part of the old city also succeeded in acquiring weapons from the local police headquarters. A determined column of these protesters managed to reach as far as the east gate of the presidential palace (often called the People's House), but after suffering casualties they were forced to retreat and disperse. In the confrontation with the presidential guards about fifty soldiers were killed.

From the suburban interconnected villages of Deh Dana and Afshar close to Darulaman, people went out of their homes and, chanting "Allah o Akbar!" and anti-Soviet slogans, attacked a few nearby tanks. The tanks withdrew from the area, but shortly afterward a number of military jeeps containing armed men appeared at the scene. By that time the number of protesters had also increased. The men in the jeeps, speaking through loudspeakers, told the protesters that gatherings of more than four people had been declared unlawful under martial law; thus, they were required to disperse. When the people declined, they were fired on. About 120 fell dead, and the rest fled. Columns of protesters also appeared, as noted, in many other parts of the city, but information about them is not available. By nightfall calm prevailed over the city. About two thousand people were said to have been killed, but the actual number was probably about eight hundred. Four hundred bodies were seen in the morgue of the Four-Hundred-Bed Hospital.[6] Protests still continued for the next six days, but no longer in the streets. During this period shops and stores, except those for essential goods, were kept closed until the security men compelled shopkeepers to open them. Knowing in advance that the storm was coming, the authorities responded quickly. They took measures to suppress the marches, and they adopted other measures to forestall disturbances in the future. Around midday, in a special television broadcast, the government announced that martial law was in effect in the city. Declaring meetings unlawful, it forbade people to be seen in groups of more than four persons. It also declared the city to be under curfew at night and ordered people to surrender the unlicensed weapons in their possession. Further, it stated that agents of the governments of Pakistan, the United States, and China had tried to disturb security and destroy state property. "An unfortunate group of sixteen Pakistanis, with two Chinese, two Americans, and an Egyptian, were arrested in Kabul, accused of being agents to create bloody pogroms and murder."[7] The government did not mention the name of Iran, although the Afghan Shi'ite followers of the Ayatullah Khomeini were active in the uprising and had chanted his name. In the uprisings during the Khalqi period, both Iran and Pakistan had been blamed. Later in the evening the regime announced that government offices were closed until further notice; they were reopened on 25 February. "Many more Kabulis were summarily shot from among 5000 arrested after the uprising."[8] Among them were a number of pro-Amin Khalqis.

The measures opened a new stage of repression for the period when Karmal headed the regime. Common sense would have regarded the uprising as an indication of the will of the people. The policy of occupation should have been revised, as the British had done under similar circumstances about a hundred years earlier. Instead, the Soviets stressed violence in reaching the goals their rulers had set. To establish the regime, they abandoned a defensive posture in favor of offensive measures. The new posture became clear in other cities, where bands of armed agents of KhAD searched houses for suspects, while army units searched for draft evaders. During the curfew hours KhAD agents roamed the streets of Kabul. Not a night passed without shops being looted or houses searched and their inhabitants molested or insulted and their valuables taken. The Russian patrols also looted shops. In the name of security the regime created insecurity, and its measures to undo some of the repressive measures of its predecessor lost meaning. The regime became more isolated from the people and more dependent on the Soviet might.

In evaluating this uprising, we might note that no group of protesters was organized, although it has been claimed that "to oppose the Russians the whole city of Kabul had been organized to rise on 21 February."[9] Only the column of Chindawal seemed organized. No prominent figure was seen among the marchers, who were ordinary citizen. In this respect, the protesters differed from those who had risen against the British during the Second Anglo-Afghan War in the last century. At the time such men as General Mohammad Jan Khan Wardak, General Ghulam Hayder Charkhi, Mier Bacha of Kohistan, and others led the uprising. The actions of the present protesters were not coordinated.

A conspicuous feature of the opposition was the participation of the Shi'as with their Sunni brothers; together, they constituted the great majority of the city's population. The Shi'ite Qizilbashes and Hazaras dominated the columns of demonstrators emerging from the Dasht-e-Barchi, Qala-e-Shada, Deh Dana, Jamal Maina, Karta-e-Sakhi, and Chindawal. The significance of this can be understood when it is borne in mind that their role was reversed during the Second Anglo-Afghan War. A portion of the educated Qizilbashes were Parchamis, who were now called "the internal Russians." In opposing the regime and the occupation army, the Sunni followers of the Islamic Party, led by Gulbuddin Hekmatyar, and the Shi'ite followers of the Islamic Movement, led by Ayatullah Shaykh Asif Muhsini, and thousands of others joined hands. The Maoist Shu'lais likewise incited the insurgents, particularly the Qizilbashes and the Hazaras. In this they were quite successful, working as if they were competing with the Islamic movement. A number of pro-Amin Khalqis also took part in the uprising, either by inciting the insurgents or by not performing their jobs in critical hours. It was because of the unwillingness of some Khalqi officers to go against the insurgents that the Russian forces were brought in. All Parchamis and most Khalqis joined hands with the occupation forces against their own compatriots.

Although rifles were smuggled into the city, they were apparently not used. The protesters, particularly those who were from the suburban areas, carried spades, clubs, a number of antiquated rifles, and swords. A lame, middle-aged villager with an antiquated sword in his hand was seen struggling toward the city to join the multitude, denouncing the infidel Russians as he went. The voices heard among the protesters were

directed against the Soviets and infidelity (*kufr*) and showed concern for
the country. Some said, "O Muslims, infidels have come and occupied
our fatherland and endangered our religion," while others cried, "O
Russians, get out of our land!"

The number of the protesters cannot be determined. It is, however,
not difficult to say to what segment of society they belonged. The areas
from which they emerged are areas mainly of the lower professional
middle class and unskilled laborers. They are also areas of shopkeepers
and artisans of various professions. The Hazara coolies also come from
these areas. Eight of them were found dead near Dehburi with their
sacks on their backs.

This description might suggest that the protesters' grievances were
economic. Far from it. In the face of a ruthless enemy, prudence dictated
that prominent persons remain behind, while thousands of anonymous
persons—inspired by their religious values, which were now visibly
threatened by atheists, and by the values of their country, now openly
endangered by foreign occupants—confronted the occupying forces
with empty hands, even going so far as to sacrifice their lives. They did
so knowing that the army of one of the mightiest powers in the world
patrolled their city. The Afghans showed an opposition to foreign intruders that transcended religious, linguistic, and ethnic boundaries.
The ties that now bound them overshadowed their mutual differences.
That the resistance groups in the opposition camp had not yet mul-
tiplied, that the followers of the few existing ones had not aligned
against each other on party lines, and that the traditional way of waging
jehad in a collective spirit was strong may in part account for the solidarity. So against the Russian intruders the Afghans responded in unison,
despite the intimidating odds. In the entire period of national resistance,
it was the peak of Afghan solidarity.

STUDENT UPRISINGS

Educational institutions were opened after the winter holiday in March
1980 in Kabul. Kabul has a large number of high schools and professional and higher educational institutions in proportion to its population. Most are located in the western part of the city, where the student
population was conspicuous. Among these institutions is Kabul University, which before the communist coup had twelve thousand students
and eight hundred professors.[10] A month after the start of the academic
year, students demonstrated. Before that they had distributed antigov-

ernment leaflets. In one of them, *Falah* (Salvation), they demanded the
withdrawal of the invading army and proposed that until it had been
withdrawn, ideological differences should be put aside and a united
front formed. The underground periodical *Jabha-e-Danish* (The Front
of Knowledge) called on the opposition organizations even more force-
fully to set up a common front. In ordinary circumstances such activities
may pass unnoticed, but under conditions of repression it can be a sign
of an imminent storm.

One of the first waves of the storm came on 27 April 1980, when the
regime commemorated the second anniversary of the coup in a strict
ceremony attended by only a few select party members and government
officials. This restriction gave the ceremony the aura more of a funeral
than of a public festival. On the eve of the inauguration school students
had disturbed the city. During the disturbances female students had been
so agitated that they ridiculed police officers sent to silence them. Some
girls called them "Russian slaves" while others put their scarves on the
officers, telling them that now they had become "women," an insulting
word when uttered in such a manner to men in Afghanistan. Others
snatched caps from the police and accused them of having accepted slav-
ery in return for money. It was extraordinary for schoolgirls to be so
brave, but the police were sympathetic to them. The police showed reluctance to harm them, but the Parchami youths who had accompanied
them acted brutally. They had already shot dead four students at the
Omar-e-Shaheed Lycée and one at the Habibiyya High School when the
students had risen in defiance on 25 April.

On 29 April 1980 the peaceful procession that students held on the
campus of the university turned even bloodier. They shouted anti-Soviet
slogans and demanded that the Soviet army leave. When their procession, originating at the College of Engineering, reached the College of
Pharmacy, armed Parchami youths, after firing first into the air, fired at
them directly, killing three. The procession nevertheless continued until
ten students were lost to the bullets of the Parchami youths in front of
the nearby Teachers Training Institute. Among them was Miss Naheed,
a high school student, who, while holding a wounded fellow student in
her arms, was inciting others. She soon became a martyr and a symbol
of patriotism. A Parchami from a nearby building had fired at her.
Months later the assassin was also killed for the killing of Miss Naheed.
At the institute the procession dispersed without reaching the center of
the city. On that day, while the students of a number of schools had
taken to the streets, other schools had been besieged. When a procession

of the students of the Habibiyya High School reached the nearby Soviet embassy, armed Parchami youths fired at them, killing three.

Despite the repression, students were still inflamed. The majority of students continued to boycott classes. On 3 May 1980 a still greater number of university students took to the streets and headed toward the city, moving in a more organized fashion. This time they refrained from uttering provoking slogans and observed the spirit of the newly enunciated provisional constitution, the Fundamental Principles of the Democratic Republic of Afghanistan, which guaranteed the right to peaceful demonstrations. I witnessed the beginning of this march, and, although I admired the students, I felt depressed at the thought of the fate awaiting them. When the procession reached Barikot, it was encircled by a contingent of mounted army instead of by the police. After initial hesitation, the contingent dashed at the students, beating them with clubs and using tear gas. More than five hundred were arrested. On that day security forces also besieged government offices in anticipation of the rumor that government officials intended to join the procession. On 22 May 1980 the fourth and last procession by students of the College of Engineering was suppressed immediately after it started. But high schools throughout the city remained disturbed. Students went on strike, and their schools were besieged by contingents of the police. Students, particularly female students, were loud in denouncing Lenin and Brezhnev in their slogans, in spite of the fact that their parents had cautioned them not to do so.

During the second week of June 1980 a melodrama of a different kind was played out in some schools. Ever since the communist coup, many events had taken the Afghans by surprise, but the poisoning of school students was the most surprising of all. For three consecutive days a large number of students of the Soriya High School (an academy for girls) and a number of other schools were poisoned. Thirty workers at a government printing press were also poisoned. A few days later (12 June) students at ten high schools were poisoned. On that day alone more than five hundred students were taken to hospitals for treatment. No one was fatally ill. It was said that the poison was released into the air from a small "cartridge." Others said that drinking water had been poisoned. It is still unknown who did all this. The regime blamed the "agents of imperialism and reactionary forces," that is, the ikhwanis or mujahideen, while the mujahid organizations in Peshawar blamed the Soviet Union and the Kabul regime. In Kabul it was said that KhAD was responsible. According to this theory, since the month-long student agitation had discredited the regime, KhAD, in order to forestall a repetition, decided to intimidate the students and their families. It was further argued that had other people committed the act, KhAD would have caught the perpetrators and made the case public. This theory is also reinforced by the fact that a proportionally larger number of students of the Soriya High School suffered in the tragedy, for they as well as their teachers were most active in the agitation. Following the agitation and the poisoning, Kabul schools were paralyzed, and many schoolboys fled abroad.

Unlike the city uprising, the student uprising was organized. By the time the students arose, seven student unions had become active on the university campus, among them the Council of the Revolutionary Youth of the University, the Union of Liberationists, Salvation, and the General Union of Professors and Students. With about six hundred members, the Council of the Revolutionary Youth was the biggest, with branches in city high schools. The council, like the Union of Professors and Students, was composed of noncommitted students, while others were branches of political groups such as the Maoist Rihayee, the Islamic Association, and the Islamic Party. But along with two more, the council did not favor open demonstrations on the ground that by holding rallies students exposed themselves. They stood instead for strikes and boycotts. The committed unions and others carried the day by persuading others to hold rallies, but, as described, KhAD suppressed them. For this purpose KhAD, through its secret agents, had set up its own union to persuade students to hold rallies.[11] It has well been said that "pro-Khalqi students opposed Parchamis, resenting the Soviet presence, and almost equally Parchami disparagement of Amin, together with his policies. Nationalists and anti-Marxists [joined] with Muslim fundamentalist sympathizers, girls as well as boys, in riot[s] and demonstrations, which were put down only after shootings and mass arrests."[12] How many students were killed in this monthlong period of agitation is difficult to tell. Estimates have varied between seventy-two and one hundred; others put it as high as two hundred.[13] The number of those who were injured cannot be determined, because the injured students, fearful of being imprisoned, did not seek treatment in hospitals. But those arrested were said to number about two thousand. Subsequently, no more rallies were attempted, and the students concentrated on boycotts.

On 13 May the authorities released about five hundred students on certain conditions and further announced that the cases of "a few" imprisoned students were pending in the court. The "few" were many students who spent years in the Pul-e-Charkhi prison. The imprisoned students did not defend the rallies in the courts. An exception was Ashuk Kumar (a Hindu student from Kandahar), Abdul Widud, and one other. Not only did they defend the rallies, but they also opposed the Soviet invasion. Each was sentenced to eight years of imprisonment, the longest term for the imprisoned students.[14] Other measures included the dismissal and transfer of high school teachers, who were suspected of having incited their students. As for the university, no drastic measures were taken, but the regime speeded up the Sovietization program that it had already started. The program consisted of changing university curricula in line with Marxism-Leninism, of changing the administrative system to conform to that of the Soviet system and of stressing the spirit of friendship with the Soviet Union.[15] All of these changes required an increase in the number of instructors and advisers from the Soviet Union and communist bloc countries.

Although the student agitation was a minor problem, the regime feared that it might provoke the people of the city to yet another disturbance and tarnish its image in the Soviet Union. Since the students were their sons and daughters, the city's residents abhorred the use of force against them. For the same reason, the regime also tried to suppress the student processions as quickly as possible. Coming as they did in the wake of the city uprising, the agitations revealed certain matters that damaged the regime politically and morally. The Karmal faction was predominantly a city group. Until the student demonstrations, the Parchamis had claimed that the intelligentsia supported them. This claim was convincing, since the intelligentsia had twice elected Karmal to parliament in the constitutional period. The uprisings proved otherwise: now his erstwhile supporters also rejected him. By becoming the man of the Soviets, he eroded the only support he had ever had.

From yet another angle, the Parchamis were also discredited. In the 1960s they held rallies as the present protesters did, taking to the streets when they thought a government had breached a democratic right. But now they suppressed rallies permitted by their own constitution. If the regime had had any moral basis, it now disappeared. The Parchamis were, however, acting on the instructions they were receiving from the Soviets. Ominously, the Soviets could impose their client regime on the Afghans only by subduing them by force; they could secure the country only by destroying it.

CHAPTER SEVEN

Beginning of the Countrywide Armed Clashes

A true account of war is essential for understanding the policies as well as the degree of culture of the parties involved in it. To understand the war under discussion, we must examine the events on the battlefields, for it was on the battlefields that policies were exposed and tested. It was also on the battlefields that the participants revealed themselves as exemplars of their nations. Official documents on the present war are not generally available, but even when they are, one wonders whether one would be able to write the kind of work that the British historian John Kaye wrote on the First Anglo-Afghan War. That profound historian had available not only official documents but also private diaries of those who took part in the war. It seems unlikely that anyone will be able to gain access to such materials for the present war: the truth is distorted and suppressed by both the totalitarian state (or states) and the feeling of righteousness.

But the truth must be told if history is to describe the activities of men and women as they actually happened. Hoping to be exact and objective, I have described those armed confrontations of the initial stage of the war about which I have reliable information. This description, too, is unsatisfactory, since the authorities not only prevented journalists from covering the engagements but also fed the public misinformation. Also, many clashes occurred, and many of those happened virtually simultaneously in a country with an area of 250,000 square miles. Besides, while one side boasted a mobile modern army, the other consisted of a constellation of mobile human groups who were unable to confront the enemy in open battle but were well acquainted with the terrain of their land. When pressed, they would retreat to the upper parts of the long valleys, from which they could strike almost at will.

When the mujahideen were unwilling to encounter the enemy on the plains, they either hid in orchards and underground irrigation canals or spread out and mingled with the locals in villages or worked on the land as farmers. They waged a war of hit-and-run tactics until they were armed with antiaircraft weapons. Only then did they become a little more stable. An exception was in mountainous regions, where certain tribal communities known for their marksmanship, such as the Zadran, were able to repulse attacks made against them. Nevertheless, the resistance movement in the plains was as strong as that in the hilly regions. The view that the Afghans succeeded because of the mountainous nature of their land is simply not true.

A GOVERNMENT WITHOUT RURAL TERRITORIES

The Khalqi government was the government of Afghanistan in the sense that it ruled over it despite opposition. By the time of the invasion, except for the four districts of Gizao, Barak, Oaz, and one other and two subdistricts, which had been wrested from government control, all administrative units in the rural areas functioned. In certain rural areas where the opposition was strong, party members and collaborators were exposed to acts of terror. The government retaliated by sending troops there, and in the clashes that followed government forces compelled the recalcitrants to retreat to the upper parts of the valleys. They were thus safe from being crushed, but weakened. Some main roads were also unsafe, but once a week I and other university professors went to Jalalabad to teach, and we continued to do so right up to the invasion without observing any signs of insecurity. By contrast, the Parchami government was not a government even in this sense. It did not rule over the country. Within weeks of the invasion it was, as already noted, besieged in the cities. The greater part of the people lived in the countryside beyond the regime's control or fled abroad. The regime was less than a state, since *state* refers to a government ruling despotically or constitutionally over a people living within internationally accepted boundaries and recognized as such by the world community. For want of a better term, the Democratic Republic of Afghanistan, which the Parchamis stressed as the state (*dawlat*), is here referred to as the Parchami regime or the Kabul regime.

If the installment of the puppet regime was quick, so was the opposition to it. The Islamic groups were the first to descend on the plains from the upper parts of the valleys, surrounding the provincial capitals. The city of Baghlan, close to the Soviet Union, fell to them on 14 January. Soon the groups cleared the country's rural areas of party members and collaborators. In the province of Laghman the mujahideen besieged its capital city, Mihtarlam, then eliminated those party members who had remained behind and set their houses on fire. Former collaborators were also forced to leave their homes for cities. By February the city of Jalalabad, close to Pakistan, was besieged. By mid-February, when all the rural areas had been wrested away, the Kabul regime became confined to cities. The Soviets and the regime set up military posts along the main roads, but in places along those very roads resistance groups searched transport vehicles for party members and took them away when they recognized them. It was no longer safe for party members and proregime Afghans to travel between cities. To escape unharmed, they traveled in disguise. By the second week of May 1980 the Khalqis and Parchamis were no longer to be found in the rural areas. They had either been killed or fled to cities.

Most *uluswals* (heads of districts) had either been killed or fled, and those few who remained guarded themselves with armored units. *Alaqadaran* (heads of subdistricts) were no longer to be found. Some provincial governors had to spend the nights in military cantonments. By the first week of March the main roads had become unsafe for traffic in spite of the military posts stationed along them. Accompanied by contingents of the army, transport buses and other vehicles had to go in caravans.

This success of the mujahideen indicated their support by the locals, who either opposed the regime or refused to cooperate with it. Only certain small sectors supported the regime—for instance, the residents of the Nazyan Valley in Shinwar, some Uzbeks in Takhar and Dawlatabad, and some Isma'ili Tajiks of Roashan and Shighnan. The opposition to the invasion was thus national, crossing regional, ethnic, and linguistic lines. Never before in Afghan history had so many people been as united as they now were in opposition to an invader. What polarized the society was political and ideological. Those who supported the regime and the Soviets were usually educated persons drawn from various ethnic groups, particularly the urban minorities.

After the invasion, Karmal sent deputations to the frontier provinces to obtain their allegiance, but the deputations could not reach their destinations. Provincial governors were then instructed to summon local notables and explain to them that the government had plans to promote their welfare. This also failed to impress the people. On Friday, 5 April 1980, for example, the governor of Laghman addressed a meeting of about fifteen hundred worshipers in a public mosque and asked for those who supported his government to raise their hands. No one raised a hand. The notables of the city of Baghlan were more open and demanding, telling the governor that they would accept the government provided the Russians left and elections were held. They also voiced their support for an Islamic republic. In June 1980 the notables of the province of Balkh told their governor that unless the foreign troops were withdrawn, they would be unwilling to pay taxes or furnish men for military service.

MUJAHIDEEN AS LOCAL RULERS

Even in this early stage the mujahideen acted as local rulers. They replaced government officials and also local elders who acted as go-betweens for the government and the people and who settled disputes in accord with the system of jirga or consultation. The mujahideen extended control over areas with mixed population and to some extent over tribal areas. By April 1980 the province of Laghman was divided into a number of precincts (*houza*), each led by a commandant. In each precinct Shari'a became supreme, and disputes were settled on its basis. Local usage and conventions were discarded. Judgment was swift, involving heavy fines on both sides of the dispute. Theft became rare. The new rudimentary system of administration established by the Islamic party was in essence the nucleus of the Islamic republic that the Islamists intended to set up.

The success of the mujahideen meant an increase in their numbers. Since not all of them were from the area where they operated, and since jehad required large expenditures, the locals provided them with shelter, food, and clothes. But even with the best of intentions people were unable to accommodate large numbers of mujahideen. Nevertheless, since jehad required the Muslims to contribute toward it with fighting men and other necessities, the mujahideen expected them to perform their Islamic duty. Landlords paid them the Islamic tithe, while merchants paid them taxes. Another source of income for the mujahideen was a percentage from the pay of government employees, including party members who were on government payroll but who had property in the area under the control of the mujahideen.

A tragic aspect of the situation was the destruction of schools, which were destroyed with no remorse. This was because the Khalqis had turned schools into centers of communist indoctrination, espionage, and immorality, not of knowledge and education. To the Khalqis and the Parchamis, educational institutions were means for promoting ideology. Also, since the educational system was a part of the government, party members—most of whom were also party secretaries—administered educational centers. Being powerful, they played a role in eliminating government opponents. Although before the communist coup people had requested governments to open schools, as already noted, throughout the land the mujahideen now destroyed village schools, primary schools, and high schools outside provincial capitals and cities. Agents of the regime also destroyed schools with the intention of defaming the resistance groups. To infiltrate the resistance groups, some of them became overzealous in this act of vandalism. Thus, the cooperative accomplishment of governments and people over a long period of time was destroyed overnight. This was the second time in this century when modern education suffered on a major scale as a victim of politics.

PUBLIC CONCERN

The locals showed concern on a number of points that assumed many dimensions discrediting the resistance movement. The locals looked with revulsion on the summary execution by the mujahideen of party members and their associates. The same was also the case when the mujahideen burned houses, confiscated property, and compelled suspected families to leave their homes for cities. Since social bonds were strong in the rural areas, such acts adversely affected the community. Such acts became common because not all mujahideen were disinterested. Those mujahideen who bore grudges against others or who were from among the lower ranks of society let themselves be motivated by personal interest. The biggest source of disillusionment for the common Afghans was the multiplicity of the resistance organizations and their lack of unity. The clashes that occurred among some of them pained the people. This dissension was caused partly by the disunity among their leaders and partly by the jealousy of the local commanders, who wished to extend the areas they controlled with little or no regard for jehad. The flight of

local elders to cities and abroad created a vacuum which the commanders now tried to fill and over which they quarreled. The common Afghans, for whom the expulsion of the invaders was the overriding concern, did not understand why the resistance groups bickered among
themselves. It was against this background that the Soviets embarked
on military expeditions.

FEATURES OF MILITARY CONFRONTATIONS

Protected by an unmatchable air force, armored units of the invading
army were able to carry out expeditions anywhere and drive the mujahideen to the inaccessible parts of the valleys, but it was too risky for the
Soviets to remain there. Indeed, they could not stay even in the plains.
The army of the regime was also unreliable and soldiers deserted. Since
there were few Parchamis in the army and since the regime's army had
still not become reliable by recruitment, the invading army undertook
expeditions alone, hoping to break the resistance as soon as possible:
hence the intensification of confrontations, the high number of casualties, and the displacement of many Afghans. By the end of 1980, 1.4
million Afghans had fled to Pakistan alone; by the end of 1981, the number of Afghan refugees there had reached 2.3 million. Similar numbers
fled to Iran.[1]
    Since they could not differentiate the mujahideen from the locals and
since they could not engage the mujahideen in battles, the invaders tried
to detach them from their own people. Intending to destroy the rebels'
support among the civilian population, they also turned against the noncombatants, destroying their villages, their crops, and their irrigation
systems and even killing them.[2] Indiscriminate destruction of property
and human life, civilian as well as military, thus became a feature of
Soviet military expeditions. This was particularly so when the mujahideen killed Russian soldiers. In such cases the invaders massacred civilians by the droves. By the force of circumstances the invaders found
themselves in a situation in which they killed hundreds and thousands
of those for whose protection they had purportedly come. Thus, the
claim that they had come to save Afghanistan lost meaning, and Russia
found itself in a quagmire that challenged the imagination of its military
authorities more seriously than it had been challenged at any other time
during its five centuries on the Asian mainland.
    As noted earlier, until the February uprisings the invading army had
a defensive posture. There was some fighting, notably in Paktia, Badakh-

shan, Logar, and both sides of the Salang Tunnel following the invasion, but the mujahideen initiated these conflicts. After the many uprisings, particularly during the summer of 1980, units of the invading army, accompanied by air power, carried on operations in many parts of the country. The main thrust of these operations was in the regions around Kabul such as Logar, Shamali (Kohdaman, Parwan, and Kohistan), Maidan, and Ghazni and also in regions such as Ningrahar, Laghman, and Kunar, as well as the northeastern regions, south of the Soviet border.

Among the border regions with Pakistan, the province of Kunar, through which the mujahideen brought weapons, was garrisoned first. The main highways, particularly those leading from Kabul to the Soviet borders in Hairatan (Mazar) and Torghundi (Herat), became the special concern of the invading army. The road leading to Hairatan through the long Salang Tunnel in the Hindu Kush massif, constructed by Soviet engineers in the 1960s, was also considered significant, especially since a large Soviet force was now stationed in Kelagai. Connecting the northern part of the country with the southern and eastern parts, the tunnel had shortened the distance between Kabul and the Soviet border more than sixty kilometers. With Kabul now only 399 kilometers from the Soviet border, the Salang Road (or the Mazar Road) is the shortest overland route from the Soviet border to the capital of the country. In this war the regions through which the Salang Road passed became for the first time strategically as significant as the eastern regions had been during the Anglo-Afghan wars.

The invading army used air power, particularly helicopter gunships. These war machines, which also flew from bases inside the Soviet Union, fired rockets on targets inside Afghanistan, particularly in the northeastern regions. Helicopter gunships also searched for the mujahideen on the ground. During the first years of the invasion, they were a frightening menace. After the invasion, helicopter gunships by the score became a familiar sight in the air space of the city of Kabul, whence they headed to various areas at short intervals every day. Every night the deafening sounds of guns, mortars, and rifles pierced the air, mingling with the ear-splitting noise of convoys of heavy tanks moving along the roads. Thus, even Kabul itself seemed like a war zone.

ATTEMPTS AT CONTROLLING THE STRATEGIC
FRONTIER POSTS

After the February uprising the armored units of the invading army and
of the Kabul regime embarked on offensive operations in some of the
provinces. The purpose of these spring operations was to block the main
entrance routes before the snow melted along the mountain passes leading to Pakistan. It was hoped that the mujahideen then would not be
able to enter the country from Pakistan. The frontier garrison of Asmar,
situated in the upper part of the long Kunar Valley, became the center of
attention, perhaps as a demonstration of the might of the Soviet Union.

Yet Asmar, along with its surrounding districts, proved to be beyond
government control. In the previous year Abdur Rauf Safay, commander
of the garrison, had waged a successful operation from there against the
Khalqi government. The Soviets now intended to recover Asmar and at
the same time to show their strength to the people of Kunar Province,
who had risen against the Khalqi government a number of times.[3] First
helicopter gunships and warplanes rocketed and bombed the surrounding districts of the garrison. Then a large force parachuted into
the empty garrison. But when they withdrew the air force, the mujahideen of the surrounding hills poured into the garrison, wiping out all
except a small number of its new Afghan occupants, who were taken
alive. The invaders bombed and rocketed the surrounding districts of
Asmar. According to some reports, they also used napalm bombs and
chemical weapons. At the same time, they dispatched there a large force
from Asadabad, the provincial capital. The people of Asmar fled to Pakistan. The invaders occupied Asmar as well as the garrison town of Barikot, but they still could not block the entrance routes along the border.
The frontier district of Kama near the city of Jalalabad, after changing
hands a number of times, was also occupied and military posts established there. But the southern frontier belt, beginning in the Jalalabad
area, still remained open, despite the operations that the Soviet forces
carried in the Surkhrud and Khugianay regions.

Meanwhile, by blanket bombing the Soviets destroyed more than 80
percent of the villages between the district of Ghazni and Muqur along
the highway between Kabul and Kandahar. They did this to make the
road safe for traffic that passed through the populated areas between
Kabul and Kandahar. Kandahar was ultimately connected to the Soviet
border by a concrete road that the Soviet engineers had constructed in

1965. In early April the mujahideen destroyed a large number of military planes stationed on the Bagram air base near Kabul, striking at them with rockets launched from hills. They had obtained these rockets and light and heavy weapons when the garrison of Hussaynkot near Kabul deserted in mid-March. In clashes between the invading forces and the mujahideen in the northeastern provinces of Qunduz, Baghlan, and Badakhshan, hundreds were killed. The high rate of Soviet losses in Badakhshan and other areas was attributed to the inability of their soldiers to maneuver on the battleground. After they had shelled an area from the air and the ground with rockets, the Soviet soldiers would then go straight to the spot, but this tactic made them easy targets for the mujahideen, who had hidden themselves in unsuspected places. For two years the Soviet soldiers went straight ahead in battlefields. Because of this approach, they lost about 350 men in a series of clashes with the mujahideen near the Dasht-e-Saqawa in Charasia close to Kabul. The date of the battle is not known.

THE FIRST SOVIET EXPEDITION IN LAGHMAN

The Soviet military expedition in the province of Laghman, with a mixed population of 229,100 living in attached mud houses in 340 villages and a number of towns, is known in some detail. Laghman is a long, fertile river valley of 7,600 square kilometers flanked by mountains. From the middle of the main valley branch off two narrow valleys, Alingar and Alishang, reaching as far as Kawun, a branch of the Hindu Kush. Along the way glens branch off from both valleys, so that their upper parts provide safe sanctuaries. Laghman can be considered typical of the many river valleys that lie between the mountains from the Hindu Kush to the plains of Peshawar. After the invasion mujahideen spread throughout Laghman, as already noted. The exception was Mihtarlam, the provincial capital, which they kept under pressure. The purpose of the Soviet operation now was to clear the region of the mujahideen.

Units of the invading army that had been stationed in Dasht-e-Gambiri at the foot of Laghman set out on 6 April 1980 accompanied by helicopter gunships. On the way they destroyed the two collections of settlements of Qarghaee and Zeranee. The latter settlement, which is still desolate, was destroyed because some of its inhabitants acted against the invaders along the nearby main Kabul–Jalalabad road. Seeing the convoys of tanks, the mujahideen fled into the glens; those who remained behind mixed with the people. Seeing no opposition, the invaders headed toward the upper parts, spreading out in small groups when they entered villages. When they exposed themselves to attack, the mujahideen in some places fired at them. What happened to a group of six Russians in my own village of Deva (also Palwata) and a few nearby hamlets of about a hundred houses in the Alishang Valley was typical.

Having crossed the river by a swinging bridge, the Russians entered the village and appeared before a shop, asking the inhabitants, "*Dost ya dushman?*" (Friend or enemy?). They had no interpreters and knew only this phrase by which they distinguished friends from enemies of the Soviet Union and the Kabul regime. The villagers naturally replied, "Dost." At this time a mujahid stationed on a rooftop fired on the Soviets, killing one and injuring another. While retreating, the Russians reciprocated, taking their casualties with them. Meanwhile, they fired a signal shot into the air, after which the village was hit by long-range guns from the other side of the valley where a contingent of artillery had been stationed. The retreating Russians also killed two farmers working in a field.

The calamity descended the next day. Fearing reprisal, the villagers evacuated the village following the encounter, but since nothing happened after the shelling, a number of them returned later the same day. They were mistaken. The next day the village was shelled by long-range guns while a group of low-flying helicopter gunships fired rockets into its surroundings. Then a group of forty Russians in tanks besieged it. When the village was thus isolated, a group of six Russians entered the village, killing everyone in sight. Some were killed in lanes, others in mosques, and still others inside their houses. Women and children were spared.

Gul Mohammad, his newly married son, and two of his guests were killed as if in a game inside his courtyard in front of his womenfolk, apparently because the Russians had found an empty cartridge there. In the courtyard each victim was made to run to a fixed spot; when he reached it, he was shot dead. The wailing of the women of the household and their solicitation by gestures had no effect. Born into a blacksmith family, Gul Mohammad had taken to farming; he also kept a hunting hawk belonging to my father-in-law, Abdul Aziz Kakar. I had joined Gul Mohammad a number of times in hunting expeditions in the nearby hills. Always smiling and dressed in worn clothes, he was one of the finest persons I have ever known. In any case, had it not been for the sagacity of a villager, Sayyed Ahmad, who impressed the word "dost" on the assailants, the total number of those killed would have been higher than the nineteen who were slain that day. Eighteen houses were either completely or partly set on fire, and the rest were searched for weapons. Sweets, transistor radios, cash, and similar objects were looted.

The same thing happened to a few nearby villages and hamlets, which brought the total number of those killed to sixty. The nearby town of Maskura also lost twenty men on that day. As noted, what happened to the village of Deva and a few others may be taken as an example.

It is impossible to outline the events of that day in the whole valley, much less in both valleys. It is estimated that since all the villages up to the upper part of Alishang were searched in the same way as Deva, the invaders killed two thousand men. In Alingar only about sixty men lost their lives, since the mujahideen there had refrained from firing on the intruders. Three mujahideen were said to have been killed, while the loss of the Russians was said only to have been higher. The Soviet military units, after losing a few tanks at the hands of the mujahideen, evacuated Laghman and arrived in Jalalabad. The remaining mujahideen soon descended from the upper parts and spread throughout Laghman.

What can we learn from the expedition in Laghman? First, only Russians soldiers took part in the operation. The Kabul regime army was not seen with them, and the invaders did not have interpreters with them. In some places Parchamis acted as guides, but they were not with the Soviet soldiers all the time. The very appearance of the alien, armed, atheistic invaders in the midst of the rural Afghans was provocative, especially given the absence of the guides or interpreters. It was obviously unwise to send such troops among a people who had driven away government agents and were known to be fanatics. One wonders whether the purpose was to find a pretext for massacre. Still, the people remained quiet, and their militants preferred flight to encounter. Throughout the valley there was no group opposition, only occasional rifle shots. Yet many men were massacred in their own homes. This group homicide was neither made an issue nor lamented. It passed unnoticed, as did so many similar atrocities in the coming years.

The invaders perhaps thought that by eliminating the "dushman" they did their job. The Parchamis were glad that their Soviet comrades had cowed their opponents for them. Strangely, the Parchamis of the village supported the operations even though some lost relatives and one lost his father.[4] In support of the Soviets and of their party, some argued that if the mujahideen had not fired on "the forces of the comrades" (*quwwaay dost*), their term for the invading army, then the Soviets would not have fired on them. Zuhur Razimjo, a member of the central committee who was also from Laghman, said, "What we do is for the welfare of true toiling people." The grip of the Soviets over the party and of the party over its members was complete. The operation was one of many that the invading army carried out during its stay. When such were the consequences of an unprovoked expedition, the reader can imagine the consequences of the contested major operations.

The victims of the operation, as noted, were civilians. This was true of all the operations throughout the occupation: hence the killing and displacement of the highest number of Afghans in their history. Except for killing of innocent men, the present operation did nothing else. It did not lead to the pacification of Laghman. Instead, it created problems of major dimensions with dire consequences. It demonstrated the might of the Soviet Union aimed at frightening the Afghans into submission. It was an affirmation of the view that the resistance must be suppressed within weeks or, at most, months if conciliatory measures failed to persuade the people to submit. But its outcome was the opposite of what had been intended. According to Abdul Rahim, a mujahid commander from Dawlat Shah in the upper part of the valley, after this incident his small group of mujahideen, armed with primitive weapons, increased in number as many young men joined him.

THE CHANGED ROLE OF THE AFGHAN ARMY

The Afghan army did not initially oppose the invasion, but afterward it opted for a host of pro-mujahid, antigovernment, and anti-Russian activities, which upset the Soviets' calculations concerning the force needed to pacify the country. The Afghan army's changed attitude helped the resistance movement and affected the political situation despite (or because of) the presence of the invading army.

As noted earlier, the Parchamis in the army were not many. They also had no known officers in the army when the Soviets invaded Afghanistan. No Parchami officer had taken part in the invasion. This is not to suggest that they did not want to cooperate with the Russians, but because the Khalqis had suppressed them, they were unable to do so. Not all Khalqi officers supported the invasion, despite their opposition to the radical Islamists. The noncommunist elements in the army, whether officers or ordinary soldiers, were against the invasion. All this suggests that the army was not prepared to help the Parchami regime enforce its authority.

Desertions, which were frequent, took two forms: individual and group. During the invasion the whole division of Baghlan had deserted. After the invasion smaller units deserted, notably those of Nahreen and Hussaynkot. More widespread were desertions by individual soldiers. Soldiers who had almost completed their terms deserted, particularly following the Kabul uprisings. By then the view had become widespread that the regime could not last long. By mid-March 1980, of the nearly two thousand troops of the brigade stationed in Maidan Shahr only about four hundred remained. By that time the whole army, which numbered under 100,000 before the communist coup, had been reduced to about 20,000. In May the number was said to have been further reduced to about 10,000.

A number of consequences followed. The regime was completely dependent on the invading army, which found itself involved not only in military operations but also in the internal politics of the country, despite the declarations of its masters that the Soviet army was sent to repulse foreign aggression. The building of a new army by the pursuance of a policy of recruitment through conscription as well as by the employment of mercenaries and others was stressed, no matter how unpopular the policy and how serious the consequences. Along with the official party, the Parchami regime had to build a power of its own: it therefore chose to enhance KhAD (the intelligence agency).

The regime also had strained relations with the Khalqis who dominated the army. The Khalqi officers had not resisted the invasion, but the regime could not count on them to serve as pliable instruments. Besides, Khalqi officers from rural areas were sometimes more patriotic than communist. Some were Muslims, and many of these officers secretly assisted the mujahideen. The early successes of the mujahideen were partly due to the assistance rendered them by nationalist officers.

A month after the invasion the army officers of the major division of Khost in the province of Paktia made it known to the regime that if either the Russian army or Parchami officers were sent there, they would join the mujahideen. Its commander declined a summons to Kabul on the grounds that his absence would lead to disturbances in the division. Closer to Kabul, the commander of the Qargha division warned that because of the presence of the Soviet army the division was on the brink of rebellion. The regime's plan of replacing the Khalqi officers of the Kandahar division was rebuffed. Some Parchami officers who had gone there for that purpose in March were done away with. Officers of the two factions clashed, and the Parchami officers had the worst of the clashes. The situation deteriorated still further when, in June 1980, the regime executed first Amin's brother and nephew and later three of his senior ministers and a few officers.

CHAPTER EIGHT

A New Type of War Leader

The Case of Logar

The Soviet invasion disturbed Afghan society greatly. Among other things, it led to a change of political leaders at the local level. In the course of resistance, traditional leaders were being phased out, and new Islamic leaders were taking their place. Jehad and the efforts to purge the society of non-Islamic elements helped to bring about this transformation. Here this transformation is studied in the province of Logar.

INHABITANTS

A feature of the people of Logar is their solidarity. Nowhere in Afghanistan is the leveling effect of Islam as conspicuous as it is among the people of Logar, where among the well-to-do it is a custom to give to the needy the Islamic *zakat* (one-fortieth of one's property) and other donations on a regular basis. Bilingualism also influences solidarity, as does the similarity in physical appearances and clothes. Those who do not know the people may be unable to differentiate between the Dari-speaking Tajiks and the Pashto-speaking Pashtuns. The more numerous Pashtuns—Stanizays, Ahmadzays, Abdurrahimzays, Alozays, Mohmands, Gadaykhel, and Zhalozays—live in the hilly areas, and the Tajiks, Khwajas, and Sadat live in the plains together with Pashtuns, mainly in villages on both sides of the main road. In some areas of the plains the Pashtuns predominate, while in others the Tajiks predominate. Also, in Logar the Shi'ite minority and the Sunni majority are on good terms with each other. Neither the PDPA nor other leftist groups had made any significant inroads among them. The absence of disgruntled minorities has also contributed to solidarity among the people.

Before the disturbances, Logar had many *madrasas* (traditional religious seminaries) and *mawlawiyan* (religious scholars). As in the rest of the country, each of the regions's 338 villages, which together contain more than 300,000 inhabitants, had (and still has) one or more mosques where mullas lead the Muslims in prayers and teach children the essentials of Islam. Logar also had four high schools and about one hundred secondary (through ninth grade) and primary schools.[1] Like the people of other regions, the people of Logar also cooperated with the government by volunteering labor, plots of land, and money for the construction of schools for both girls and boys. On this point the people pressured the government, but the latter was unable to meet the demand for financial reasons. Also, sons and daughters of the well-to-do studied in higher civilian and military schools in Kabul.

Because of improvements in transportation, the daily contact between Kabul and Logar had begun to change the lifestyle of the people. As in other districts around the city, the daily transport of cash crops from Logar into Kabul had brought them closer together. A number of individuals from some distinguished families from Logar had served the government in various periods as senior ministers and officers, while some had become famous as generals and leaders of the resistance movements in wars against the British.[2] Before the communist coup the people of Logar were adopting modern ways of life more rapidly than the peoples of the districts around Kabul. But the coup and the invasion changed this trend. The change was apparent in the attitude of the people in the domain of politics.

Following the coup, the people of Logar were disturbed, just as were the people of other regions. They feared the ascendance of atheists in the government. Some councils of elders and mullas decided that they should be the first to wage jehad against the communists, even if they had to oppose their own relatives. The Logari officers in the army in Kabul planned to rise against the government, but before they could do so many were executed or imprisoned.[3] Thus, the first planned but unsuccessful uprising in the army was the work of officers who were all or nearly all from the province of Logar. Then, in May 1979 the people of Logar rose and overthrew the provincial government.[4]

It was, however, the Soviet invasion and the policies of the new rulers that changed the attitude of the people. Their attitude was changed not only toward the regime but also toward modern education and local leaders. As one observer writes:

> The Soviet interference and the Soviet invasion provided powerful incentives to the mullas in their opposition to modern education. The Soviets, through the Parchamis and Khalqis, deceived students in schools, and in the name of a revolutionary ideology spread atheism, a sense of obedience to foreigners [*ajnabiparasti*] and of treason to the fatherland [*watanfiroshi*]. They employed sons against fathers by sending them in tanks and warplanes to destroy their homes and villages. [Seeing this], the common people took spades and destroyed schools from the foundation. The educated persons became discredited, and the mullas became unrivaled rulers.[5]

On this point an elderly man from Zadran of the province of Paktia is more eloquent. According to him, during the reign of King Mohammad Zahir the government introduced two projects in the province of Paktia: roads and schools. At first the people of all the valleys of Zadran opposed the projects, but later they acquiesced. To continue the story in the words of the elderly man himself:

> Advised by a great mulla, the people of our valley opposed the two projects of schools and roads. Thus, neither Khalqis nor Parchamis appeared among us. But from among the schools of other valleys there emerged Khalqis and Parchamis who later, as pilots, bombarded their own people and villages, while the Russian tanks, which arrived along the roads, did much the same. But the people of our valley were immune to such destruction. May God bless the great mulla. He was so right.[6]

TRADITIONAL POLITICAL LEADERSHIP

In previous resistance movements, leaders had usually been local magnates who could muster support and who had established either a feudal relationship as khans with the central government or who had served as military officers. Spiritual persons and the 'ulama provided them with religious blessing by issuing *fatwa*s (rulings) and preaching for wars as sanctioned by Islam and tradition. The mullas incited the people. As charismatic leaders, some distinguished spiritual persons also led the faithful. But as a rule, in this combination of secular and spiritual forces the former led while the latter sanctioned, because the former had the labor and material means at its disposal, and the latter had the monopoly of spiritual power in a predominantly Sunni society, a society shaped more by traditional and conventional values than religious values. This is evident from the fact that Islamic Afghanistan had no theocracy. The anthropologist Fredrik Barth notes that "among the Afghans, Islam has never been the basis for a permanent, formal and hierarchical religious or political organization." However, as Barth also states, in the time of resistance "Islam is needed as a unifying symbol and emotive force."[7]

This situation changed, though, as the spread of communism, the Soviet invasion, the imposition of a client regime, and the Soviet massacres led to the rise of mullas and Islamists. These could not have risen to become leaders at the expense of traditional leaders had they not been part of the jehad organizations, supported by outside powers that provided weapons, logistics, and money. Traditional leaders did not have such support, nor was their bastion of power able to sustain them as it had in the past. With the disruption of the political system, they had also lost their influential position as intermediaries between the local government and the people. Having moved either to cities or Pakistan, they had been deprived of the produce of their land and of the support of local people, who had also moved out of most areas. It was beyond the means of traditional elders to obtain the weapons needed to oppose the army of a superpower. In the beginning a number of commanders rose from among the traditional leaders, but over time they either affiliated themselves with the jehad organizations or were forced out.[8]

Also important was the attitude of the Islamists, who disparaged traditional elders and tribal organizations. Another influence that worked against traditional leaders was the rise among their relatives of Khalqis and Parchamis, whom the mujahideen hunted down. In line with its dogma the regime issued propaganda attacking traditional elders as feudal, reactionary, and so on; nevertheless, it tried to win them over to its side. But ultimately the local leaders were reduced to insignificance because of the animosity showed them by the new leaders—the mullas, field commanders and Islamist organizations.

THE RISE OF MULLAS AS LEADERS

Drawn from among the poorer elements of society, the mullas were religious functionaries with little or no education. As religious functionaries, they lived in communities away from their own localities, dependent on the believers for a living. Since they had no tribal or social standing, the mullas opposed social conventions, tribal codes, and nationalism.[9] Sayd Bahauddin Majruh states that "he [the mulla] was not involved in local socio-political affairs; he did not participate in the deliberations of the council of village elders—his only function on these occasions was to perform the opening and the concluding prayers of the jirga session. While respected, he still remained the favorite target of popular jokes."[10]

The rise of the mullas to the position of political and military leaders in Logar is without parallel in modern Afghan history. Of the twenty-nine heads (*awmer*), judges, and military commanders in the Baraki Barak district (*uluswali*) of the Logar province, all were mullas. Of these, nineteen were members of the moderate Islamic Revolutionary Organization and six of the moderate National Islamic Front; the remaining four were members of the Islamic Party and Islamic Association. A number of other mullas and *akhund*s (traditional teachers, masters) also acted as "leaders of the jehad and rulers of the people."[11]

The mullas rose to power in Logar because, as noted, many mullas rallied around Mawlawi Mohammad Nabi Mohammadi, the leader of the Islamic Revolutionary Organization, who was also from Logar. However, the Islamists who surpassed them in organization, education, weapons and in making propaganda challenged them, as well as other groups. The two were radically different, as explained in chapter 5.

The resistance in Logar assumed many other dimensions as well. In the absence of government, the commanders vied not only with those outside their group but also with those within their own group. Personal rivalry and the desire to extend control played a part in this competition. The sociological composition of the Islamist and traditionalist organizations set their members at odds with each other. The mullas competed with members of the Islamic Party, who were drawn from among the Dari-speaking educated groups such as teachers, students, and government employees.[12] By comparison, the mullas were a different social group. Untouched by secular and modern ideas, concerned with their duties as religious functionaries, and looking on themselves as custodians of traditional Islamic values, the mullas were at variance with these "modernized" persons even though both groups were fighting the same enemy in the spirit of jehad. The mullas opposed modern ideas so much that they called "infidels" those who believed the earth was round.

The Islamists who were more organized and also had an ideology and a program for the transformation of society were a threat to the mullas.[13] Although the opposition among field commanders belonging to the various groups was usually personal rather than organizational or ideological,[14] the opposition between the commanders of the Islamic Revolutionary Movement and the Islamic Party was more serious. It often led to clashes even on such matters as opposing the enemy, not only in Logar but throughout the country.[15]

The mullas adopted an authoritarian style of leadership. Nominally, they settled claims and conflicts between individuals in accord with the Shari'a, while community elders, though weakened, settled cases through jirgas. In fact, however, in Logar the mulla commanders did not rule according to the Shari'a, which requires that evidence be presented and elaborate procedures be followed; rather, they ruled as they pleased. They would single out those whom they thought were collaborating with the enemy and dub such persons infidels. Once a man was so dubbed, he seldom lived long.[16] One observer writes:

> Decisions were made in the absence of the accused. In the decisions the views of the secret agents of the mullas whom they had assigned duties in villages were considered decisive. Personal considerations, distrustfulness, and animosities could influence decisions and the execution of the accused. The mujahideen who enforced the decisions wore dark glasses and covered their faces. The accused were either taken at night from their homes or seized in daylight from roads. Others were picked up from public buses running along the main road between Kabul and Gardez. To escape such an ordeal, members of the party traveled in the guise of women. Some were still recognized and executed somewhere away from the public. The executioners were not recognized, nor did any group claim responsibility.[17]

In addition to these secret executions, those who were accused of spying for the regime were publicly executed.[18]

The public was divided about the executions, particularly since the Parchamis and Khalqis had already been driven into Kabul. While some argued that those who were executed deserved the punishment, others disagreed, insisting that evidence be brought forward. The mullas combated this attitude. Their agents would spread rumors in support of the judgments, saying that the decisions had indeed been based on evidence.[19] The number of persons executed cannot be determined. In Logar alone, in the two years after the invasion it is likely that more than one hundred persons were executed. It was commonly held that revenge and personal animosity, camouflaged as jehad, were the impulse behind many executions.[20]

The executions were the result of influences connected to the jehad but rooted in society. An atmosphere of distrust and rivalry prevailed, the result of disunity among leaders of the mujahid organizations based in faraway Peshawar and among local field commanders. Through the field commanders, this ambience of distrust spread far and wide. Some leaders of the mujahid groups persuaded their commanders to clash with their rivals, and some commanders and individual mujahideen found an opportunity to settle old scores and take revenge. They disrespected the traditional leaders. Some mujahideen who had been recruited from among the uprooted groups harmed the people in pursuit of personal interest with no regard for social norms. The Islamists were more intolerant of their opponents and even of those who were not sympathetic to them, labeling them heretics. In particular, many people were denounced as Wahhabis. (The Wahhabis were followers of Mohammad bin 'Abd al-Wahhab [1703–87], whose aim was to do away with innovations later than the third century of Islam.) Former government employees were especially vulnerable to such accusations. To be safe from such accusations, they grew beards as a sign of being religious.[21] Beards thus became common throughout the country.[22]

The mujahid organizations found it difficult to get rid of the undesirable elements in the ranks of the mujahideen, particularly when they were commanders. When such mujahideen were expelled from one group, the fold of another group was open for them. Another influence that created tension was infiltration by KhAD agents and leftist elements, who worked, among other things, to prepare the groundwork for clashes. The atmosphere of distrust and disunity was also exacerbated by the inability of the organizations to set up a council composed of their representatives and of the locals to work out programs for opposing the enemy and administering the province. The tendency among the commanders to monopolize power was too strong for such a council to be set up. The mullas who had obtained power and other benefits were also unwilling to cooperate.[23] Any one group would counterbalance the activities of the others. This created a form of equilibrium,[24] a situation that checked the dominance of one organization over the rest and the region as a whole.

THE FORCE OF JEHAD

That the Afghans were in a state of jehad was obvious. Not only the Muslim Afghans but even the Hindu and Sikh minorities contributed to it. The tradition of jehad in Muslim Afghanistan has always been strong. The defense of country, of honor (*namoas*), and of cultural values— among which the demonstration of valor in a spirit of rivalry was conspicuous—turned jehad into a mighty force.[25] Added to this was the marksmanship of the Afghans, who, even in time of peace, led the world in numbers of rifles per person. When the state of jehad was believed to exist, the Muslim Afghans, in particular the patriotic believers, felt duty bound either to take part in person or to contribute otherwise. In times of jehad the number of combatant Afghans was higher than normal in proportion to the population. In such times the noncombatant Afghans, including widows, supported those fighting the invaders. The defense of the country and the faith was not the responsibility of the armed forces alone but of every adult Afghan capable of carrying weapons. Every time the country has been invaded, the regular army has disintegrated and the ranks of the irregulars strengthened in the spirit of jehad.

The jehad against the Russians was more comprehensive than any other in Afghan history. "What was at first an uncertainty about the new [Khalqi] regime became anger and frustration as unrealistic, insensitive, and oppressive policies were introduced. When the Soviets invaded, these feelings turned into widespread outrage, among traditionalists and progressives alike."[26] The combatant Afghans were determined to defend their values, while the noncombatant Afghans felt duty bound to support them. This meant that the noncombatant Afghans felt it to be their religious and patriotic duty to shelter, clothe, and feed the mujahideen, to meet their expenses for weapons, and to assist them in the problems that resulted from clashes with the enemy. The flight of the locals to Pakistan thinned this basis of support of the mujahideen.

True to their patriotic and Islamic duties, the Afghans supported the mujahideen despite the odds in fighting the army of a superpower. They paid the Islamic tithe (*'ushr*) on the produce of land and a number of other taxes to the mujahid commanders. But because of inexperience and the necessity of asserting their newly won power and of meeting the harsh requirements of jehad, the commanders often treated the locals in an authoritarian manner. Not all were harsh; some ruled in consultation with others. Nevertheless, authoritarianism generally marked their rule. There then began to develop between the commanders and the people the sour relationship that exists between the ruler and the ruled.

Like people of other areas, the Logaris were compelled to pay taxes to the financial heads not of one mujahid organization, but of all of them. Armed mujahideen would appear at the doors of the people and demand money.[27] Although the Islamic tithe was lighter than what landowners had formerly paid the government, now they paid more than before and, in addition, they paid under the threat of Kalashnikovs. Also, supported by bands of armed mujahideen, the new rulers imposed heavy fines on both sides of disputes without investigating them as required by Islamic laws.[28] Not surprisingly, the number of disputes and criminal cases dropped.[29]

SUPPRESSION OF NATIONAL CULTURE

Another set of measures adopted by the mujahideen were intended to suppress or replace customs, traditions, and social conventions with the injunctions of the Islamic Shari'a. Among other things, the new measures suppressed the tradition of singing and dancing at weddings and many other similar ceremonies; traditional games, entertainments, and racing events, including those that were militarily significant; and the custom of reciting not only lyric but also epic and mystic poetry from the classic literature in which Afghanistan is so rich, substituting for these the recitation of passages from the Quran. The measures also confined to their homes women who formerly labored in the fields, assisting their men. In addition, community elders, those who embodied traditional and social wisdom, were replaced by scholars of religion and Shari'a.[30]

These measures showed that the mujahideen's program was intended to change and Islamize those aspects of the rural society that were considered to be un-Islamic. The new local rulers set for themselves a provocative task, since the many different groups composing the Afghan society were (and are) rich in alternative mores. Indeed, the Afghans are much attached to this legacy from the civilizations of their long history. The mores constituted the main ingredients of their identity. The efforts of the new rulers were a reminder of the unsuccessful efforts of the communists, who tried to reorganize the society along Marxist-Leninist lines. Never before had the Afghan national culture been under so much pressure: on the one hand, from the internationalist culture of communism; on the other, from the universalist culture of Islam. Recent developments are probably best explained in terms of the encounter among these three types of cultures. In particular, the implementation of the two hostile sets of measures—those of the communist rulers in the urban areas and those of the religiously oriented rulers in the countryside—widened still further the existing gaps between the cities and the countryside.

THE POLITICAL SIGNIFICANCE OF WEAPONS

The new religious leaders set themselves above the locals and acted in an authoritarian manner because they had the ability to acquire weapons and thus to enforce their wills. The possession of weapons was, of course, necessary for waging jehad. The matter of weaponry was especially critical in this conflict. At no time before had the gap been so wide between the Afghans and the invaders in the quality, quantity, and range of weapons. In contrast with the past, when the Afghans provided large numbers of high-quality weapons to their combatants, they could now provide very few weapons, and those of poor quality. But to wage jehad the mujahideen must have weapons. They obtained weapons from two sources: from the army of the Kabul regime and through their own Peshawar-based organizations.

To acquire weapons, the mulla commanders of Logar, particularly of the Mohammad Agha front, would ambush enemy forces when they were in their locality. In addition, troops from the Kabul regime sometimes assisted them by defecting, bringing their advanced weapons with them. The commanders would submit such weapons to their headquarters as spoils, in contrast to the tribes of Paktia (Gurbuz, Tanay, Zadran, Mangal, and Zazay), who either quarreled over weapons or received some concessions from the regime in return for weapons.[31] The Logaris were successful in acquiring weapons from the regime forces. During the twenty months following the Soviet invasion the Kabul regime lost 25,000 Kalashnikovs to the mujahideen in Logar.[32]

The other source of weapons was beyond the border. From there weapons were sent to the mujahideen from two places: from the Darra-e-Adam Khel in the Afriday land where the Peshawar-based organizations made the purchase, and from Peshawar itself, to which the governments that supported the Afghan cause sent weapons. Jan Goodwin donned a disguised to visit this first place, a town forbidden to foreigners: "Of the 250 or so arms dealers in Darra, half that number are engaged in copying any kind of weapon from anywhere in the world you require. . . . In this dusty maze-like town, where the sound of gunfire is continuous as guns are tested and demonstrated for customers, it is possible to purchase light and heavy machine guns, mortars and rocket launchers in addition to ordinary rifles, all of which have been skillfully copied."[33]

Of the foreign sources of weapons, the United States and Egypt were the major ones during the first two years of the invasion. The United

States and some Muslim countries began to support the mujahideen, "cautiously channeling limited amounts of small arms and other military equipment to them."[34] In January 1980, after the Soviets invaded Afghanistan, the Carter administration appropriated about $30 million to supply the resistance. In December 1982 President Reagan's administration reportedly ordered the Central Intelligence Agency "to provide the Afghan insurgents for the first time with bazookas, mortars, grenade launchers, mines and recoilless rifles of Soviet origin, and possibly also shoulder-fired antiaircraft missiles."[35] But not all the aid reached the mujahideen: published estimates said between one-third and one-half of the aid was diverted by Pakistan or sold by representatives of the mujahid groups in Peshawar. Edward Girardet, who visited the mujahideen territory, wrote in September 1984 that the American military aid that was "seeping through. . . . tend[s] to be of poor quality or insufficient quantity" and that he and other visitors had not found published accounts of "a highly effective" CIA program to be true.[36] Although for many years the mujahid commanders did not receive enough weapons to fight the enemy, they still got enough to enable them to push out traditional elders from their areas and to rule over the territories under their control in an authoritarian manner. Emboldened by the moral force of the jehad that they were conducting against an atheist invader and strengthened by weapons, the new leaders acted like independent rulers, showing little or no regard for the people whom they ruled.

PUBLIC CONCERN

Logaris, like all people throughout the land, soon felt dissatisfied with the disunity of the jehad organizations, and particularly of the field commanders. This point has already been explained. People were worried about the consequences of the disunity in war against the forces of a superpower. Many people reiterated the adage that success lay in unity, but to no effect. By mid-1981 it was clear that rivalry, not cooperation, ruled the relations of the six mujahid organizations in Logar on all matters, including military operations.[37] In this atmosphere each group tried to carry on military operations separately to demonstrate its valor and acquire a heroic reputation.[38] At times the groups pursued not only separate but conflicting programs of operations, which sometimes led to clashes among them.[39] One such policy difference between the Islamic Party and the Islamic Revolutionary Movement led to the destruction of the only high school in the district of Baraki Barak.[40]

Despite complaints about the new leaders, the people of Logar cooperated with them on jehad.[41] Zahir Ghazi Alam, a native physician,
writes:

> Politically, every class and grade of the community was disgusted with the
> Kabul regime and the Russians. Among the people there was no sign of sub-
> mission either to the government or the Russians. They had acquiesced into
> submission to the commanders and heads of various organizations, showing
> patience and tolerance to the mistreatment they received from some of
> them. . . . Disunity among the organizations was daily on the increase and
> taking root. Accusations, criticisms, and provocations had become common,
> and this caused concern among the people. The people were looking forward
> to the emergence of a leader to end this anarchic state and to save the nation
> from the present dilemma. Sometimes they were looking even toward the
> former king, Mohammad Zahir. They did so because the leaders in Peshawar
> had disappointed them. The people had been frustrated by the disunity of the
> organizations and the pressure brought to bear on them by the Russians.[42]

PART THREE

The Politics of Confrontation and Suppression

CHAPTER NINE

KhAD as an Agency of Suppression

Following the Soviet invasion, the Sovietization of the state structure was expedited. The security department, known in the Khalqi period first as AGSA (Department for Safeguarding the Interests of Afghanistan) and later as KAM (Workers' Intelligence Department) was changed to KhAD (State Information Services). Dissociating themselves from AGSA and KAM, the new rulers pledged that henceforth no official organization would strangle or torture persons. They also promised that KhAD would serve to protect democratic rights and neutralize plots hatched by enemies of the state. The constitution stated that "torture, persecution, and punishment contrary to human dignity are not permissible." Babrak Karmal and his senior officials told a delegation of Amnesty International that there "would be no more torture" in Afghanistan.[1] But the promises were only words, and the Kabul regime and its Soviet patrons simply ignored them. KhAD was not set up to protect human rights; rather, it operated on principles espoused by Felix Dzerzhinsky, the founder of the Soviet Cheka (the predecessor of the KGB). In discussing how to combat counterrevolutionary activities and sabotage, Dzerzhinsky had told his fellow commisars in 1918, "Don't think that I seek forms of revolutionary justice; we are not now in need of justice. It is war now—face to face, a fight to the finish. Life or death."[2]

The name KhAD was a misnomer, just as the names of its predecessors, AGSA and KAM, had been. The scope of KhAD's activities was wider than its name suggests. Besides intelligence gathering, it took part in military operations "with its own military-style division complete with tanks, armored personnel carriers and helicopters."[3] One of its twelve main directorates, KhAD Number Five, was commissioned to encounter the "rebels." KhAD was part of the triple armed forces, the others being the regular army (with militia) and the Sarindoy (police force). It was also charged with creating instability in Pakistan and combating foreign intelligence services. But its program of intelligence gathering in an effort to eliminate active as well as potential opponents and "counterrevolutionaries" was its main area of activity.

To do its job, KhAD needed material means, persons with expertise, and power. These were provided. Providing money was easy, because Afghan bank notes were printed in the Soviet Union, which sent money directly to KhAD as well as the Sarindoy. KhAD had a budget of thirty billion afghanis, or one thousand times more than the budget of the precommunist Intelligence Department, which was thirty million afghanis.[4]

Despite KhAD's unpopularity, it readily found recruits. Material incentive, exemption from military service, and employment attracted sufficient numbers. Ideology was important only for the dedicated members of the party who served as its leading officials. Among its junior officials were uprooted educated persons who had been driven from the rural areas. Deprived of their own sources of income, they entered KhAD, because as strangers in Kabul they found it difficult to cope with life in the inflationary situation. As an extreme example, forty-two persons from my own home village of Deva in Laghman found employment with KhAD. Officials from Kabul and the province of Parwan outnumbered others in KhAD. All KhAD's officials were Parchamis.

Material incentives for KhAD's personnel were many. Professional officers, as distinct from those who did paperwork, received salaries double those that the regime paid to its other employees. As plainclothes secret police, KhAD's officials were given the status of military officers; this status entitled them to military pay, which the government had increased 100 percent in 1978. In addition, just because they were serving the KhAD, its officials were paid an extra 15 to 75 percent of their pay, depending on the nature of their jobs. The lowest rate was paid to those who worked in the offices. Other concessions included residential apartments, excellent free medical treatment, and short trips for training and other purposes to the Soviet Union.

The above were the official concessions. The illegal sources of income were many, such as searching a region following a military expedition, patrolling the city during the curfew hours, and searching the houses of those who had been, or were to be, arrested. Three examples will suffice to illustrate such activities. In 1981 a group of patrolling KhAD agents broke into the Pashtun Market in Kabul and took about eighty million afghanis (over $1 million) from the safes of businesses there. Similarly, during curfew hours Japanese articles and gadgets were looted from about forty small shops in the middle of the city; this time the looters were Soviet soldiers. In 1982, twelve bars of gold bullion were taken from the house of Haji Barat Bie in Kabul during a search.[5] KhAD's officials were required to have householders sign a form saying that nothing had been taken from their houses. But this form was meaningless, because during the search family members would be pushed inside a room, the house would be searched by armed men, and members of the family would be so terrified that they did not dare complain.

Since the Parchamis were tyros in the field, since KhAD was organized along KGB lines, and since the KGB secret police controlled this "kingdom without a crown,"[6] Soviet advisers played a dominant role in reshaping it out of KAM of the Khalq period. However, the number of Soviet advisers cannot be determined. For nine months following the invasion, Soviet advisers controlled KhAD directly, maintaining the security of prisons with their own men. KhAD's officials were unable to conduct investigations without their permission. After that period, when they handed over control of prisons to KhAD's officials, Soviet advisers kept a low profile. But since KhAD was "the key to the political and state structure of the Soviet mission in Afghanistan,"[7] Soviet advisers were behind the decisions made in it. But care had been taken to ensure that the records did not show their role.

Even Babrak Karmal could not influence the decisions of Soviet advisers in KhAD, as the following incidents show. After the arrest of a number of members of Afghan Millat in 1983, its leaders dissolved their organization and called on their followers to support the regime. Karmal issued instructions to KhAD that they be released without being tried in court; they would then cooperate with the government through the National Fatherland Front. They were, however, tried and sentenced to long terms of imprisonment.[8] Relatives of two members of the imprisoned Afghan Millat got a letter from Karmal in which he ordered that the prisoners be released, but to no effect.[9] Also, for three months Karmal insisted on the release of five detained university professors, including the author, before they were to be tried in court, but to no effect.[10] Karmal's instructions were not obeyed in a department where he had placed his trusted followers. As already noted, if any official department was loyal to him, it was KhAD. It was his stronghold of power, even more than the Parcham faction was. Lauding it with warm words, he often visited KhAD, and KhAD's officials did their best to exalt him. There was thus no question that his own cronies in KhAD would have carried out his orders. But they were under the power of the Soviet advisers, who looked on KhAD as the promoter first of the interests of the Soviet Union.

The Soviet interest was the prosecution of, in order of significance, Maoists, Islamic fundamentalists, and nationalists. Those who were accused of being agents of the CIA and other foreign intelligence services were also singled out for harsh treatment, but since they were not part of the organized resistance groups, they were not punished as severely as others. KhAD's most important program was to smash organized resistance groups with a view to drying up the breeding ground for "counterrevolutionaries." On this point no compromise was shown until the rise to power of Gorbachev in 1985. In this atmosphere every Afghan outside the regime was suspected of being a member of an organization opposed to the Soviet Union.

To stamp out resistance, KhAD was organized to assert its mastery over Afghans: hence the dominance of KhAD over other government ministries, although it was nominally a department within the prime ministry. In addition to having a broader structure, access to more money, and more numerous personnel than any other ministry, it had the power not only to look into matters of public significance but also to intrude into the private domain of persons and families and to make arrests. Except for Karmal, no Afghan under the regime was beyond its reach. It had the power and the means to torture men and women to the point of death with impunity. Although by law the execution of a prisoner after his trial in court was the prerogative of the head of state, *KhAD determined the case one way or another.* In the few cases when the head of state commuted death sentences to terms of imprisonment, he did so only with KhAD's permission. KhAD was said to be a state within a state.[11] This was true, but only partly. If the Kabul regime may be called a state, then KhAD was an agency above the state.

Under Najibullah, its president, KhAD's personnel rose from 120 during the constitutional period to 25,000, according to one source, and to 30,000, according to another.[12] With regard to KhAD's personnel, the following points should be borne in mind. The last two figures are for KhAD's staff, not for those who cooperated with it from the outside. These were regular and part-time informers whose number cannot be determined. All political and party organizations—in particular the Youth Organization, Workers' Union, and Women's Organization— were connected to it.[13] KhAD had established committees in all government departments as well as residential areas. A deputy of every ministry was a KhAD official. KhAD officials were also assigned to Afghan embassies and commercial houses.[14] Even the Khalqi-dominated Ministry of Home Affairs, after initial resistance, opened its doors to KhAD. Thus, the total number of persons serving KhAD in one capacity or another will never be known. More important, even the figures cited were disproportionately high for the number of people under the direct control of the regime, which was probably about 2.5 million. Consequently, among the people under the control of the regime, KhAD was ubiquitous. As one contemporary observation noted, "The Afghan regime and its Soviet allies maintain and enforce control in the cities through the fear of a terrorized population aware of the ever-present possibility of arbitrary arrest, torture, imprisonment and execution."[15]

The omnipresence of KhAD was an indication of the regime's need for it. "It reached the point where, without KhAD, the regime could not survive."[16] Of the regime's programs to survive, one was to neutralize its opponents by imprisoning them, but it required some reason or evidence for imprisoning anyone. During the Khalqi period the authorities viewed certain groups of people, such as feudals and the clergy, to be the irreconcilable enemies of the "revolution." So the government imprisoned many mullas and feudals simply because they were mullas and feudals. During the Parchami regime, however, some efforts were made to make arrests on the basis of "evidence," although KhAD also made arrests on the basis of mere suspicion. Those captured on the battlefield, those caught fleeing the country, and those who were members of organized antigovernment groups were considered opponents of the regime and imprisoned. Also among the imprisoned were those who did not want to cooperate with the regime, who were against the invasion and the war, or who were persons of reputation but not on the side of the regime. It was not difficult for KhAD to identify such people. The so-called Cartotic Division was made responsible for collecting the kind of information on suspected persons that would lead to their arrest. My interrogator told me that I had been under surveillance by that division for about two years before my arrest.

KhAD IN ACTION

KhAD was known to Afghans for house searches, arrests, torture, and execution. While leaving a detailed account of those activities for my prison memoirs, here I would like to describe each briefly.

To imprison a person, armed personnel from the Department of Operation would go into action. For them it was like a hunting expedition, even if the accused was to be picked up from a government office. In a serious case the locality of the accused would be cordoned off, sometimes by armored vehicles. In such a situation KhAD would detain not only the person for whose arrest a warrant had been issued but also anyone who happened to be with the accused person at the time. Also, anyone coming toward the cordoned house would be arrested. Those who were arrested without warrants were detained on the assumption that they might be members of the group to which the accused was considered to belong. Speed was of the utmost significance, and KhAD provided its personnel the means to carry out its mission as quickly as possible. The houses of the accused were searched by personnel from the Departments of Interrogation, Prosecution, and Police. These personnel were at liberty to search the house for as long as they wished, regardless of whether the accused was present.

The search of the apartment of Fahima Nassiry, a schoolteacher, was typical. "They cracked open the walls with the bayonets of their automatic rifles. They cut open all the mattresses. They broke the toilet. They poured out the cooking oil from the jars in her kitchen and tipped over bags of rice." [17] In a larger house search many more things were usually looked into. Anything that could incriminate the accused would be confiscated. Books—particularly the works of Sayyed Qutb and Mao—would be taken as proof of the accused person's "guilt." Under Khalqi and Parchami rule, private libraries were also confiscated. In most cases whole libraries were taken away; fortunately, my own library was spared. In 1973 the Parchami police had set the precedent of confiscating private libraries. At that time they confiscated the entire library of former Prime Minister Maiwandwal; among the works in the library were seven volumes in Maiwandwal's handwriting on Afghan history. [18]

In contrast with the Khalqi period, when detainees were treated violently during their interrogations, in the Parchami period torture became "part of a scientific system of intelligence rather than just a form of sadistic punishment." [19] Interrogation and torture were prolonged with the intention of forcing the detainee to implicate others. In theory, the interrogators were not to break detainees physically but to hurt them psychologically, breaking their personalities so they would admit to the crimes of which they were accused. In practice, though, interrogators did not observe these limits, sometimes going so far as to kill detainees. Among those who lost their lives under torture was the famous poet and journalist Ghulam Shah Sarshar Shamali, who, while under interrogation in Sadarat in 1982, was kicked to death.

In the city of Kabul detainees were taken to one of eight detention and torture centers, four of which were known as the KhAD-e-Sadarat (the Central Interrogation Office in the Prime Ministry), KhAD-e-Shashdarak (the KhAD Office in the Shashdarak district), KhAD-e-Panj (the KhAD Office Number Five in Darul Aman), and KhAD-e-Nezami (Military KhAD). These were the main detention centers. The remaining four were in two private houses near the Sadarat building, the Ahmad Shah Khan house, the Wazir Akbar Khan Maina, and the KhAD office in the Barikot district.[20] When a large number of people were detained, they were taken directly to the Pul-e-Charkhi concentration camp. Also, every provincial city had one or more detention and torture centers and a prison. The provincial prisons of Qunduz, Mazar, and Kandahar were the major ones. The Soviets also detained and tortured detainees in their army units before handing them over to KhAD. In Kabul the detainees were kept in the main detention centers until their interrogations were complete or almost complete.

Investigations often took weeks or months before the detainees were taken to Pul-e-Charkhi and then to the courts. Our group of professors was detained for nine months in Sadarat. This phase of detention was agonizing, since everything imaginable was likely to happen to the detainee, especially in Shashdarak. Of those detained in Shashdarak, I have neither met nor heard of anyone who was not tortured. Pul-e-Charkhi was a haven by comparison. Almost every one was taken to Shashdarak at least once for different periods of time. I was detained there for only an hour before I was transferred to Sadarat. Even during this short time I saw the Soviets in droves.

Some detainees were held in a small cell in a group of a few each, while others were herded into rooms where they could hardly move or sleep because of overcrowding and the swarms of lice. Some were held in solitary confinement, each in a cell of two and one-half meters square. Mohammad Osman Rustar, a member of our group of professors, was detained in such a cell for six weeks. He was transferred there as a punitive measure, apparently because he complained to the information officer, Rajab Ali Saighani, about the insufficiency of food. From the time prisoners detained, they were no longer their own masters. The authorities controlled everything they needed as human beings. The one exception was the air they breathed. Indeed, prisoners were deprived of fresh air, since, except when they were taken to the interrogation cells or to the washroom (three times in twenty-four hours), they were always confined. They were given rich, greasy, salty food, usually in insufficient quantities. Good medical treatment was available. The idea was to keep the inmates fit to stand up to the exacting conditions so that the interrogators could extract confessions. Detainees were cut off from contact with the outside world. Not only were they not allowed any visitors, but they were also denied access to means of communication, such as pens, books, and paper. Only when a prisoner's family sent clothes was he or she given a short pencil for a brief time to write down what had been received. When the detainees made beads from dried cooked rice or dried loaves of bread, or when they made playing cards from cigarette boxes, these items were confiscated if detected. Inmates were permitted nothing with which to pass the time. They were, however, given plenty of time to stare and brood. Guards were charged with not letting inmates laugh or talk loudly, although it was impossible for them to enforce this order completely. Powerful light bulbs were left on day and night. This almost total isolation made the detainee all of a sudden seem like a special person, regardless of his or her social status. This was because KhAD treated each detainee as if he or she were a missing link in the chain of an enemy organization.

The inmate's real ordeal started when he or she was interrogated, which commenced following arrest. First an attempt was made to make the prisoners feel overawed. In the interrogation cell the detainees were alone in the presence of one or more interrogators and a few other strong men. Soviet advisers also took part in the interrogation. According to Amnesty International, "There are consistent accounts of the complicity of Soviet personnel through their presence during interrogation under torture."[21] They did not participate in all cases. However, whether present or not, they directed the interrogation. The Afghan interrogators brought written queries with them, presumably dictated by the Soviets. Only rarely did they compose written queries in the presence of the detainee.

The queries were directed to make detainees admit not only to the crimes for which they were accused but also to specify their accomplices and the organizations to which they allegedly belonged. The detainees

were compelled to do so, as two examples show. Qari Mohammad Shar-
ief, a native of Badakhshan, who was an imam in Shakardara in Kohdaman near Kabul, listed more than two hundred persons as his associates
in the Islamic Association. Qazi Bismillah Zarif, a native of Panjsher,
listed about four hundred persons as his accomplices. The latter had
been tortured so much that he listed anyone whose name he knew. He
was said to have organized a resistance group in Panjsher. It was not in
the interest of the interrogator to establish the true state of affairs. The
establishment of the truth, which was likely to lead to the acquittal of
the detainee, would deprive the interrogator of the rewards (promotion,
cash, trips to the Soviet Union) that he was granted when he made the
detainee confess to the crime of which he or she was accused. It was in
his interest to make the detainee guilty. Since KhAD intended to suppress the opposition, the arrests were viewed necessary for the establishment of the regime. The detainees then had to be punished, and for this
they had to admit to the crimes of which they were accused. This was
why only a negligible number of those arrested were acquitted, and the
greater number were sentenced to various terms of imprisonment or
were executed.

The detainees were charged not for opposition to the invasion but for
acts that were considered crimes in the criminal code, the most repressive code there ever was in Afghanistan. This code had been promulgated in 1977 for the suppression of the communists. Now the communists who abrogated the main laws of the period not only did not annul
this code but enforced it fully. I was not charged for my attitudes and
actions: specifically, that I opposed the invasion and the violation of the
basic rights of individuals; that I and others monitored the academic
rights of professors and students; and that I maintained a critical attitude toward the regime. Of the twelve charges actually brought against
me, the main ones were that I was a founding member of the Rihayee,
a Maoist group, and of the nationalistic group Afghan Millat. Two of
the charges carried the death penalty. Although it was impossible for
my interrogator, Asad Rahmani, to substantiate any of the charges, he
persisted, hoping that he might detect some contradictions in my responses that would incriminate me. KhAD did not physically torture me
to extract a confession. Had Amnesty International not taken my case
(together with those of other professors), KhAD probably would have
accorded me more serious punishment than eight years of imprisonment. But more than 90 percent of the detainees were not as lucky as
I was.

The unlucky majority were accorded standard punishment. The accused were to confess to the charges brought against them and reveal the names of their accomplices and the organizations to which they allegedly belonged. KhAD also arrested a few foreign journalists who were covering the war, charging them with being counterrevolutionaries "in the service of imperialism . . . [who have] come to Afghanistan to gather military intelligence on behalf of the diabolical international spy organizations."[22] The accused would be told that the authorities knew all the things they had done, but that they would receive kinder treatment if they themselves confessed their crimes. When the accused, as was natural, refused to respond positively, then the interrogators would resort to torture. Psychological torture, which had begun with the detention, was common, but that was in the background and was usually insufficient to extract a confession. What was needed was effective, direct physical torture. All types of tortures previously applied in Afghanistan were used, as well as innovations on them, and new Soviet-style tortures were also introduced.

Fariduddin's description of his torture is typical, though incomplete. "They started cursing me," he says, "with foul language, then beating me with their fists and clubs. Then they kicked me. Then came the electric shocks. They [tied] wires to my feet, and they strapped my hands and legs to a chair and gave me electric shocks." Electric shocks were given even to the most sensitive parts of the body: "They also give you electric shocks in your ears, on your head, your mouth and the private parts of your body." The intensity of the torture was such that not many people could stand up to it. Again in the words of Fariduddin, "No matter how strong you are, you must confess. The only way to stop them is to say, 'Yes, yes, I am what you say I am. I did what you say I did.'" Naturally, Fariduddin's view of the interrogators is unfavorable: "No matter how much you scream and no matter how much you plead, they do not listen. They are savage human beings. They are worse than wild beasts. Even animals are not that cruel."[23] The Italian journalist Fausto Bilolavo has vividly described the condition of the victims of torture in his cell: "I was surrounded by human wreckage: people with their backs smashed to pieces, dislocated jaws, twisted nasal septa, their bodies covered with scars of every description and bearing the hallmarks of cigarettes [snuffed] out against their skins."[24]

Other tortures were applied when the lesser ones did not lead to a confession. Among the main ones were those intended to rob the accused of dignity. Men were threatened with having glass Fanta soft drink bottles forced into their rectums, while women were threatened with having hot eggs forced into their vaginas. Worse still was the situation in which accused males were threatened with having their wives or female relatives sexually assaulted in their presence. It was then that even the strongest of the accused would plead guilty to the charges brought against them. These methods were applied or threatened in more serious cases. In such cases Fariduddin is right in saying that "no matter how strong you are, you must confess."

The accused were, of course, deprived of a lawyer. If they were illiterate, the interrogator also wrote their responses to written queries. The accused were required only to place their thumbprints on the papers of inquiry. That was not all. Before the file of the accused was sent to the Special Revolutionary Tribunals, KhAD reviewed it. The tribunals were set up following the Soviet invasion. Staffed by party members trained in the Soviet Union, they were not impartial bodies but legalized instruments for suppressing the "counterrevolutionaries" in an effort to vindicate the "revolution," as Felix Dzerzhinsky had suggested.[25]

When KhAD reviewed the case of the accused for the last time, the role of the Soviet adviser was decisive. It was he who "advised" the type of punishment to be accorded to the accused. Before the actual trial, the adviser penciled in the term of the sentence in the file; another adviser in the tribunal was to see that the sentence was carried out and the penciled recommendation erased. In the Special Revolutionary Tribunal—which, except for certain cases, was held behind closed doors—the appearances of legal procedures were observed. A few days before appearing in the tribunal, defendants were handed an official statement from the state attorney, charging them with the crimes that they had allegedly committed. Again, they had access neither to a lawyer nor the law on the basis of which they had been charged. They were thus denied the basic rights of defense. Illiterate defendants were lucky if someone in their cells could write their defense for them. But condemnation in the tribunal had already been fixed, no matter how convincing the prisoner's statement of defense and no matter how convincing the defendant was in protesting the charges and the tortures he or she had gone through. The file, which was already determined, was paramount.

The rationale for ruining the life of a person and his or her family and disturbing the community of which they were an organic part could be traced to the view that the "guilty" person was a "counterrevolutionary" who had committed a crime against society and the state that the PDPA claimed to represent. Translating that view into actuality was made possible by the state structure, in which the departments of secret police, public attorney, and special tribunals, dominated apparently by the official party but in fact by the Soviet Union, worked toward the same goal: to realize the domination of the state over individuals. Persistence in such an effort was bound to intensify the existing tension to the point of rocking the society from its foundation.

PRISONERS OF PUL-E-CHARKHI

Nearly 100 inmates were left in Pul-e-Charkhi after the Parcham regime in January 1980 released 2,700 inmates of the Khalqi period. But after the February uprisings the new regime started arresting people. The number was on the increase, and the increase was an indication of opposition to the regime. At the time of my transfer in January 1983, Pul-e-Charkhi had the highest number of prisoners, about thirty thousand, held at any one time.[26] In the new Pul-e-Charkhi prison, before all the cellblocks were ready for use, about 250 inmates were accommodated in each main hall. Each hall was about 320 square meters in space. Between 180 and 200 inmates were quartered in two-level wooden beds in a hall. Probably more than ten thousand additional prisoners were held in detention centers outside Pul-e-Charkhi in Kabul and provincial capitals. The total figure—forty thousand—is terribly excessive for a regime that, as noted, had about 2.5 million people under its direct control. The upkeep of so many persons under strict conditions was bound to be troublesome.

Of the Pul-e-Charkhi inmates, the majority were from the Kabul province. Among them were also members of the official party who had committed nonpolitical crimes. Women inmates were confined in part of cellblock number three and in the detention centers in Sadarat and Shashdarak. Their total number is unknown, but they must have been a sizable number to go on a hunger strike in 1982.[27] The Pul-e-Charkhi inmates ranged in age from twelve to eighty-six years old. Some were blind. Inmates suffering from various illnesses, even tuberculosis, lived with the others. During the two years of 1980 and 1981 alone from hall number 248, in which 250 inmates had been placed, 4 died of tuberculosis.[28] An inmate with leprosy also lived with the others in cellblock number three in 1984. Some inmates were considered mad because "they were indifferent to food and water; many among them would always laugh while others sometimes would weep, and would have waste material in their trousers." In 1981, in one hall containing 250 inmates,

12 such inmates were officially listed as "mad" but were not released.[29] Pul-e-Charkhi had two clinics, but until 1983 the one in cellblock number two was in reality a resting place for imprisoned party culprits or for inmates who had paid bribes to stay there.

Inmates faced a painful situation regarding the basic necessities of life—food and toilets. While criminal inmates in cellblock number four were allowed to provide their own food, an important concession, political prisoners were dependent on the authorities. There were, however, canteens in almost every block where out-of-date cans of fish from the Soviet Union and a few other basic items of food were sold. This was because the food in the Pul-e-Charkhi was much poorer and more insufficient than the food given to the inmates in the detention centers in Kabul. This in itself would not have been a problem had the food been given purely as food. It was not. The inside of the thick bread baked in the Russian-made bakery was unbaked, but its outer skin had plenty of dust and sand. The cooked rice had plenty of sand, and the watery soup sometimes had pieces of cooked mice and always many flies. Although the food improved as a result of a hunger strike in 1982, in 1983 I saw a piece of cooked mouse in a soup pot. More agonizing was an incident before the hunger strike when some substance was mingled with the food to cause diarrhea. The inmates, who lacked antidiarrhea medication, were permitted to use the toilets—few in number anyway—outside their halls only at fixed times. The inmates thus had to use plastic bags as toilets in their living quarters. This situation—which deteriorated still further after the execution of inmates—resulted on 1 May 1982 in a prisoners' strike, the greatest in the history of Afghanistan.

The hunger strike was triggered when a teapot of hot water was given to a sick inmate by a friend who worked in the only workshop set up in cellblock number two. A guard beat both of the prisoners—standard punishment for minor infractions. Scuffles followed, but this time the enraged fellow inmates of the sick inmate drove the guard away from their hall and began a hunger strike. By evening, inmates of the whole cellblock number two had joined the strike and locked the iron gates of their halls. No amount of pleading by the authorities—something the officials had never done before—could soften the attitude of the inmates, who issued a statement demanding that their conditions be improved to meet international standards. But the authorities rejected the demands as "illegal." By then Soviet advisers were in command, and the army had encircled the cellblock. On the fourth day of the strike (24 May 1982), the inmates were overcome by commandos, who cut through the iron bars on the windows. By then, because of hunger, most inmates had grown weak. While most discontinued the strike, others persisted in it for two weeks, despite threats from the authorities. Three inmates—Mohammad Osman, Mohammad Qaseem, and Abdul Rahman—died. Various types of punishment were accorded to the striking inmates throughout the year. For instance, about 600 inmates were forced into a hall in cellblock number 3 where formerly 250 had been quartered.[30]

What most disturbed the inmates and society was the execution of prisoners. The actual number executed in the Khalqi and Parchami periods will never be known. Execution was related to the degree of opposition to the regime. In the Parchami period the inmates sentenced to death were not told of the decision of the court. Those inmates who were sentenced to death were not executed immediately but after a long time. KhAD persuaded a number of such inmates to spy for it, insinuating that their lives might thus be spared, but they were still executed. Periodically, inmates sentenced to death were taken out at night, apparently for purposes other than execution. During the years 1983 and 1984, each week between six hundred and seven hundred inmates would be taken from cellblocks number two and one. Some would be transferred to the cellblocks controlled by Sarindoy, a number would be taken back to the headquarters of KhAD, and the rest would be executed.[31] The cellblocks were soon to be filled with new inmates. The biggest execution operation was the one carried out on 23 December 1983, when from 350 to 400 inmates were picked up for execution from half past five in the evening until one o'clock the next morning, mainly from cellblock number 1, where I had been held. In a little over four years (until May 1984), between 16,500 and 17,000 inmates were taken out for execution to places in Dasht-e-Chamtala beyond Khair Khana to the north of the city.[32]

INMATES' RESPONSES

How the inmates responded to the strict prison conditions and how they behaved among themselves is a fruitful field for study. Here, though, I can examine only its barest essentials. As noted, during the first phase of detention, prisoners were kept under strictly supervised conditions with the possibility at any moment of physical injury and torture; in addition, inmates depended on the authorities for the necessities of life.

Yet among inmates the tendency to defiance was strong. Some despaired and submitted, but the majority stood up for themselves, demonstrating their honor by defying a tyrannical agency that they considered an instrument of an untenable puppet regime. Likewise, the solidarity among inmates of the opposition groups (excluding the Parchamis and Khalqis) was also remarkable despite the differences that existed among the organizations to which they belonged. What hurt the inmates most was the degree of isolation. The greater the isolation and the longer the duration, the stronger the pangs of inner pain. Here, too, inmates battled despair by clinging to hope and the feeling of righteousness in their cause. Inmates felt strong in the company of others, even if they belonged to hostile groups. Even the voices of KhAD's staff was a source of strength. Their distant voices linked the inmates with a humanity at large with whom they felt unity.

Under the changed conditions of Pul-e-Charkhi, however, the inmates behaved differently. In the overcrowded warrens of that prison, discord and divisiveness gradually took the place of the original solidarity. The inmates quarreled over space and food, since the latter was given to representatives of groups who distributed it among themselves alone. In the matter of food, the educated inmates were generally more conscious about their own health and less concerned about others, while the majority were concerned for others, sharing their meager rations in a spirit of hospitality and community. One wonders whether the opposition to the invasion would have been as strong as it was if the more educated and self-centered Afghans had predominated. A factor of considerable significance in creating the atmosphere of divisiveness was the crystallization of group behavior, particularly ideological behavior. The stricter the party, the more rigid its followers. Inmates with no attachment to a party were more open in their behavior toward others. But KhAD played a big role in creating an atmosphere of suspicion.

To forestall disturbances and to collect intelligence, KhAD directed a network of spies. For this purpose it also planted police officers in the guise of prisoners. The appointed heads (*bashis*), with their many covert and overt assistants and collaborators, worked for the same purpose. In return for concessions in food and scores of other favors, they not only collected intelligence but also played a role in defaming and intimidating others as well as distributing varieties of homemade narcotics and committing homosexual acts. Teenaged inmates were the special target of homosexual acts, perpetrated not only by them but also by others, including some educated inmates.[33] The strict conditions of prison life as well as these other factors adversely affected all groups of inmates. Not a single group of inmates remained as solid as before, but split into rival or hostile subgroups. Scuffles and quarrels among them became common. More common was the recitation of the Quran, when leaders of prayers ended with a plea to God: "So make us victorious over the infidels."

CHAPTER TEN

Military and Administrative Measures for Consolidation of the Government

Since the Soviet policy was to consolidate the regime, it tried to suppress resistance. For this purpose, among other things, the Soviets tried to build a new army. The Soviets, distrusting the Khalqi-dominated army, began to weaken the hold of the Khalqis over it, first by wresting control of weapons stores from the Khalqi officers. By late March 1980 the Soviet advisers had made the weapons, including tanks, inoperable in all the units that they controlled. Next they collected antitank weapons, antiaircraft rockets, and other heavy weapons from the army. By January 1981 the army in and around Kabul had been disarmed, and the armored units numbers four and fifteen, the pride of the Khalqis, had been removed from their headquarters near Kabul and sent to Muqur and Herat. By March 1980 about three thousand soldiers were left in the city of Kabul. The capital city was thus almost denuded of the army from which the regime felt danger. Only units of the invading army were stationed in and around the city, patrolling it at night.

The regime now set for itself the task of building a new army. But its new policy of recruitment not only failed but also created social tensions of a new kind. The regime reemployed those former officers whom the Khalqi government had dismissed. It also set up short-term courses for training new officers, enrolling its own supporters even if they lacked the proper qualifications. Known to the public as "instant officers" (*mansabdar ha-e-mashini*), they made the army inefficient. But the basic problem was the shortage of soldiers. It was difficult to recruit new soldiers to compensate for the desertions. As early as April 1980 the regime began taking the recruitment problem in earnest. Unsuccessful in its initial efforts, the regime then called to military service university graduates who had either been exempt or whose recruitment had been postponed. The call-up was accompanied by concessions and bonuses. New enticements were also devised, among them granting university entrance to high school graduates who had passed only a nominal examination; Kabul University suffered academically as a result. Also contained in the new policy of recruitment was the call-up of university professors and government employees under twenty years of age. The age of enlistment was reduced from twenty-one years to twenty, but in practice younger men were also recruited.

The method of recruitment resembled more a system of kidnapping. Since the draftees were unwilling to join, the authorities dispatched army units to search houses for them. Units of the army roamed the cities for that purpose. Conscription also became a purpose of the military expeditions in the countryside. Draft dodgers (*askar guraiz*) were on the watch, and as soon as word passed to them of an impending expedition, they would head toward the upper parts of the valleys or the nearby hills. This became a source of public concern, the more so since those draft dodgers who were caught were sent directly to the battlefields. It was said that the regime was out to kill young men. The claim was not without foundation, since the regime had authorized its military units to fire on men fleeing conscription. In the summer of 1981 a number of young men, while fleeing from the press gangs, were shot dead in front of the public in the city of Kabul. Fear spread, and senior students in high schools and in the military school in Kabul boycotted classes in August 1981 for a time until the regime assured them that students were by law exempt from military service. Nevertheless, the program of recruitment and conscription failed to work, and the regime called reservists to duties.

RECALL OF THE RESERVE ARMY

The story of the Kabul regime is a story of a regime stubbornly holding on to power in the face of popular opposition. Worse still, it is a story of subordination to the Kremlin masters. Afghan history knows of no such regime in the past. Instead of drawing lessons from the failed policy of recruitment, the rulers embarked on a more unworkable policy of recruitment because their Soviet masters had undertaken such a measure in Russia following the October Revolution.

On 8 September 1981 the regime announced that those Afghans who had completed military service between 1968 and 1978 and who were under fifty years of age should present themselves to the centers of recruitment. Chief of Staff General Baba Jan stated that since the number of "rebels" had increased, it had become necessary to take this measure to make the "revolution" a success and to ensure the security of the country. He also stated that in this way "regional reaction" and "world imperialism" led by "American imperialism" would be defeated.

If the summons had been honored, the total number of the reserve army during that ten-year period would have run well over half a million men. The regime could not have provided supplies for such a number. The Afghan regular army numbered less than 100,000. The authorities knew that because theirs was an unpopular regime, and because the reservists had to support their families in this troubled time, only a fraction of this number would be available. To get that fraction, they were willing to make their regime still more unpopular. To lessen that unpopularity, though, the regime promised the reservists not only various bonuses but also 3,000 afghanis per month, an amount of money far larger than that ever before paid to Afghan soldiers.

Reaction to the recall was swift. On the day after the announcement reservists started leaving cities, and people in Kabul denounced the measures. If they now could not oppose the regime openly, they opposed it by spreading rumors calling for a boycott of the recall. Following the announcement, students either took to the streets or held rallies inside their besieged school compounds, shouting, "You have killed our brothers, and now you want to kill our fathers." The demonstration was an act of courage because the regime had authorized security men to suppress all opposition, no matter its source.

Armed party activists entered schools, beating the striking students with rifle barrels and dragging them into waiting vans for imprisonment. About two hundred were imprisoned on that day. Students repeated their strikes the next day in the compounds of their besieged schools. Army personnel refrained from molesting the youngsters, but armed Parchamis fired at the legs of the demonstrating students. In the Jamhooriyat Hospital six students were treated for the loss of their legs. A few were killed. The city's residents were outraged, and resistance groups distributed leaflets urging them to rise against the regime. The next day shopkeepers closed their shops in protest, but later security men forced them to reopen. The regime modified the recall by exempting university and school teachers as well as students. Subsequently, other groups whose work the regime considered essential—such as drivers of state-owned trucks and government officials—were also exempted from the recall.

The regime also released most of the imprisoned students on bail. Meanwhile, it sent delegations of women to students in schools to mollify them, but without success. A student of the Jamhooriyat high school told a delegation that the present situation would continue if the Russian army did not leave. When she was told that the army had come to suppress the "rebels," her answer was brisk. She said that they were not rebels, that they were real patriots, that "we are also mujahideen, and that we are not afraid of death, and that the government is not a legal government." Among the imprisoned female students was Miss Kobra, whose courage won for her the admiration of her fellow students when she surprised everyone by answering the interrogator with courageous words. She told him that her name was "War," that her father's name was "Pul-e-Charkhi," and that her aim was "Death." The full weight of such answers can be appreciated when it is borne in mind that the interrogators could inflict terrible harm without being accountable. A student from the Zarghoona high school, Miss Kobra was fifteen years of age. Palwasha Safi, an imprisoned fellow student, said that Miss Kobra was the most undaunted girl she had ever seen. Her only fear was that of being raped.

The impact of the recall was felt among those who were ordered to present themselves to the recruitment centers. They did not. They had to be summoned, but most of them had fled. Although security forces had blocked the two main routes leading from Kabul to Logar and Ningrahar, during the three days preceding the deadline of the summons, far more than 100,000 men fled the city, either joining the mujahideen or taking refuge in Pakistan. On Friday morning, the market day on the eve of the deadline, the bazaars of Kabul filled with men hurriedly shopping; by midday the bazaars were almost empty. After the reservists fled, Kabul no longer looked like the capital city of a country. I had never seen Kabul like this before. The city had lost nearly 20 percent of its population, and it continued to lose inhabitants fleeing conscription. Meanwhile, the mujahideen increased their activities inside the city, kidnapping party members at night. In certain areas of the city the regime's men could not go out at night. But during the day the regime's military units were ubiquitous, searching houses for draft dodgers. The city looked as though it had a dual system of government, one for the day and one for the night. By recalling the reserves, the regime created serious security problems that it had to resolve if it wished to be a government. Once again it used weapons. For over a week near the end of September, government forces furiously shelled the hilly districts from which the mujahideen were penetrating the city.

Contrary to the intention of the regime, the recall of the reserves strengthened the mujahideen. Not far from the city they set up centers to receive the fleeing reserves, who were taken in buses to Pakistan. Moreover, this measure, like many previous measures, discredited the regime. Rumors soon circulated that because of the regime's unpopularity, the Soviets had decided to replace Karmal through a coup. To combat such rumors, the dispirited party activists gave out that the Soviets had decided to withdraw their forces, but before that could happen the government must have a strong army of its own. This was, however, not possible. Despite nearly desperate exertions, by mid-October the regime had recruited perhaps five thousand men. Only in Herat did many reservists present themselves to the recruitment centers. They did so to obtain weapons; when they had the weapons in hand, they defected, a practice that had become common.

MILITARY POSTS

Along with the efforts to build up the regular army, the regime tried to establish military posts and organize militias. The regime followed this policy after its efforts to build up the army failed. In this it was successful. Since the calling of tribal militias was a tradition, the governments in the past had made extensive use of it. Since the Afghans are good marksmen, the militias were equal, if not superior, to the regular army. But the success of the policy depended on the standing of the rulers. The Karmal regime could not count on the loyalty of the militia. It had to buy it for money.

The regime set up military posts first around provincial capitals and then in areas of military significance in the countryside. The military posts were manned by mercenaries whom the regime recruited from among the poor people. Each was paid 3,000 afghanis and additional bonuses. When these mercenaries searched houses, they also took away valuables. By the standard of the time and by comparison with the pay of government employees, the incomes of the mercenaries were high.

Some were even given government posts. The militiamen were equipped with sufficient weapons, including long-range guns. They fought better than did the unreliable soldiers, who sympathized with the mujahideen. The militiamen were safe in their posts, which were surrounded by barbed wire and minefields. But the posts were defensive. The increase in their number meant the mining of more areas, which, along with mines planted around military garrisons or dropped from the air, long remained a deadly legacy of the Soviet invasion.

The mujahideen were unable to overcome the military posts by frontal assault. They had to infiltrate them to effect their surrender. In this way they would dismantle the posts, but the regime would replace them with new ones. Since the militiamen in the posts were unable to move about, the regime supplied them by either helicopters or armored units. The militia posts were also unable to influence the districts where they were stationed. Their presence in the midst of the hostile rural people was merely an odious symbol of the regime. When the mujahideen attacked that symbol, the militiamen played havoc with their guns on the villages. They were so accurate in shelling that they could hit a small target miles away. I will never forget the wailing of a father, Ali Mohammad, whose only son was hit fatally when he was going shopping from the village of Deva to the town of Alishang in Laghman. Farming and other activities—weddings, funerals, and the like—became hazardous. In the villages and towns around Mihtarlam, the provincial capital of Laghman, villagers could neither put on the lights at night nor go from village to village for fear of being fired at from the nearby posts. They begged the mujahideen to leave their villages or not to fire at the posts. A rift was thus created between the villagers and the mujahideen. This was a victory for the regime. A network of military posts throughout the country would have enabled the regime to pacify the land, but the government was, of course, unable to create such a system.

RELATIONS WITH FRONTIER TRIBES

Unable to overcome by force the frontier tribes bordering on Pakistan, the regime tried to penetrate them by negotiating with them on security matters and setting up militia posts in their territories, giving them weapons and money in return. Had the policy been successful, it would have made it difficult, if not impossible, for the Peshawar-based resistance groups to use these territories as conduits for mujahideen and weapons.

In the frontier province of Paktia the regime encountered a difficulty in connection with the military posts. Before September 1980 it had set up in the frontier areas a number of military posts garrisoned by men from different tribes but officered and supervised by the Khalqis of the same area. The Parchamis could not continue this system. Being opposed to the Parchami regime, the Khalqis acted independently, although the regime gave them money and weapons. Finding this intolerable, the regime stopped paying the posts and demanded that their weapons be returned. The militiamen, as well as the Khalqis, declined, arguing that by taking up arms against their own tribes, they had made them their enemies, and now they had to have the weapons to protect themselves.

The regime commissioned Fayz Mohammad, minister of tribal affairs, to implement the new policy with the frontier tribes of the province of Paktia. Well-versed in tribal customs, he was suited for the task. A Massed Pashtun from across the border in Pakistan and educated in Kabul and the Soviet Union, Mohammad had served the interests of the Paktia tribes when he was minister of interior in the government of President Daoud. Daoud had raised Fayz Mohammad to high state positions for his leading role in helping to overthrow the monarchy. Now, having achieved some success with the tribes of Sayyed Karam and Khost, Fayz Mohammad tried to negotiate a settlement with the tribe of Zadran, which had, since spring 1979, blocked the Sitta Kandow Pass between the garrisons of Khost and Gardez. Had the regime been successful in negotiating with this tribe, it might have achieved further successes in the region, but on one of the missions a tribal police force, the *arobaki,* killed Mohammad in the Mizzi territory after he had negotiated a settlement with elders of the Zadran tribe. The regime ignored the killing of its minister. However, it scattered leaflets over Paktia calling the act a disgrace, a direct contravention of Pashtunwali, the Pashtun code of behavior. But in the tribe's view Fayz Mohammad had abandoned Pashtunwali when he sided with the invaders and distributed money. Also, Fayz Mohammad had neither been invited nor sought admittance or asylum (*ninawatay*) to the Mizzi section where he was killed. The code therefore did not apply.[1]

As among other tribes of Paktia, so among the Zadrans the arobaki, made up of young men of important families (*kahole*), is authorized to undo a settlement that it believes its elders have negotiated against the interests of the tribe. As it maintains other service groups—mullas, shepherds, and millers—the tribe maintains the arobaki to enforce the decisions of jirgas and a host of other decisions affecting the community. Supported by the community, the arobaki is a force against disorder. Among these groups, membership in the arobaki is prestigious, and its members sometimes rise to higher positions; for instance, Babrak Zadran became elder of the whole tribe and military general in the reign of King Mohammad Nadir.[2] In the present case, the "interest" of the tribe was to fight the invaders and their client regime, a decision reached by a tribal jirga after the Soviet invasion. It also had decided "to bury their differences" until the invaders had been pushed back. However, by offering money and weapons Fayz Mohammad had persuaded the heads of the tribe to maintain security in their region and to leave the Sitta Kandow Pass open. Had this agreement been implemented, the regime would probably have influenced the whole region. These terms were to be regarded as a model of negotiations with other tribes as well.

A similar deal had been made with a certain Haji Kandahari (Ahmadkhel), who had retained a large number of the militia of the Zazay tribe. Through him, the regime had distributed money among his tribe, as it had among the major Mangal tribe. By September 1981 the regime had made "peace" with the "tribes" of Paktia. It is not known which tribes these were. Presumably they were Zazays and Mangal, since they had provided the regime with a militia that had taken part in operations against the Wardak tribe. In addition, the regime was successful with these tribes in part because of their estrangement from the mawlawis of the Islamic Revolution, who had caused the execution of some of their kinsmen on the grounds that they had become renegade and had collaborated with the regime. The regime had paid them money in return for their remaining quiet, an arrangement that enabled the regime to send troops to other areas. The mujahideen and the people of Kabul grumbled about this point. But peace or no peace, as soon as military units of the Soviets or of the regime appeared in Paktia, the tribes turned against them. Haji Kandahari turned against the regime when such forces appeared in the region in November 1981. The Soviets and the regime undertook the expedition to control this area, through which passed the shortest route from the border to Kabul. This strategy clashed with the interests of the tribe—hence the estrangement of Haji Kandahari.

Toward the east of the Zazay tribal territory is the territory of the Khugianay tribe in the province of Ningrahar, divided among the three main divisions of Wazir, Kharbun, and Sherzad. The latter group (the most important division of the tribe) suffered from internal conflict between the two principal families, that of Malik Qays (who died at the age of 120 before 1978) and Mohammad Jan; this conflict had resulted in the killing of more than 150 persons from both sides. The Kabul regime tried to capitalize on this difference by resorting to the same tactics as it had with the Zadrans. It succeeded in persuading the Malik Qays faction to rule over the district as district governor (*uluswal*) in return for money and weapons, but the ploy did not work. The Malik Qays faction was interested in weapons and money with a view to opposing the regime later. Realizing this, the regime declined to meet the terms of the bargain. This move of the Malik Qays faction, led at the time by Aman Beg, was tactical: during a meeting in Peshawar, the two rival factions had already agreed to leave their enmity aside and fight the invaders. The opposition of Malik Mohammad Jan to the communists was a known fact. The Khalqi regime had imprisoned some of his sons and nephews who were serving the government as military officers and had bombed his locality; he then took refuge in the mountains and threatened retaliation unless the prisoners were released and compensation (*nagha*) paid for the damage wrought by the bombing. Unwilling to provoke the Khugianays further, Hafizullah Amin acquiesced to his demands. He also paid 50,000 afghanis as a compensation for Mohammad Jan's dog, which had been killed in the bombing—an exorbitant sum for a dog, especially since the government's hands were stained with the blood of thousands of human beings.

The relationship of the regime with the Khugianays is further explained by a story concerning Malik Khair Mohammad and others, who had conspired in the killing of seventy-two KhAD personnel from the provincial capital of Jalalabad. Apparently the KhAD personnel had been invited for the purpose of winning over the recalcitrant tribe, but when they arrived in the Khugianay territory, the Khugianays killed them. Only their chief managed to escape alive. The date is not known, but it falls within the scope of this study. In 1985 certain men posing as representatives of the Khugianay tribe attended the jirgas that the regime held in Kabul, but they carried no influence with the tribe and could not even live with their own tribesmen. They lived in the city of Jalalabad, as did many others like them. The Khugianays were also under the influence of Afghan Millat and of the Islamic Hizb, led by Mawlawi Mohammad Yunus Khalis, himself a Khugianay.

The significance of the Shinwar tribe can be understood from the fact that one of its four main divisions, Ali Sher Khan Khel, lives across the border in Pakistan. For the Shinwar tribesmen the border is not a border, because many routes pass through their territory to Pakistan. Among the Shinwars almost the whole Sangokhel (also Sunkhel) section had turned Khalqi. The man responsible for this conversion was Hafizullah Amin, who, as principal of the boarding schools of Teachers' Training and Ibn-e-Sena in Kabul, had influenced the students who had come from that valley. Throughout the district (*uluswali*) of Shinwar, Nazyan alone had a high school, which the government had opened in the 1950s to influence the major Afriday tribe beyond the border in Pakistan. The Nazyan Valley stretches over to the Afriday land in Pakistan. During the Khalqi period, the educated elements of Nazyan, whether in the military or civilian departments, were given high government positions. Any educated and skilled person from among the inhabitants of Nazyan could benefit from the regime. Most inhabitants of the infertile valley of Nazyan became well off. They pretended to be more communist than the communists themselves. This their tribesmen could not tolerate.

After the invasion the tribe held consultations. The mujahideen also participated, but they were obliged to act within the tribal code. The gathering passed a resolution condemning the Sangokhel section to death. Led by the noncommunist Sangokhel, the Shinwar tribesmen massacred the communists, looted their property, and burned their houses. Although the mob could not massacre all, no communist remained in Nazyan. A considerable number fled to Jalalabad and informed Shamladar, the Khalqi governor, of the incident. The governor— who was from Nazyan and who was at one time a teacher of the school and responsible for the spread of communism there—retaliated. For days many villages in Shinwar were bombed and many people killed. The Nazyan communists became refugees in their own land. Those among them who were fit for duty were enlisted in the militia to maintain the security of Jalalabad. Others settled in Ghani Khel or were employed in the Ningrahar Valley project. From time to time some of them acted as if they were the representatives of the tribe, giving proregime interviews, especially on television.

Among the major Mohmand tribe the institution of eldership (*khani*) has developed to a high degree, partly because of the issue of Pashtunistan, which brought the elders subsidies, and also because of the large tracts of land certain families possessed. The growing of opium poppies there had also enriched some of the tribespeople. This is not to suggest that all in the tribe were well off or that the tribe had retained its traditional significance. The bulk of the tribespeople lying on both sides of the Durand Line were poor. In the period under discussion, three groups of elders were important among the Mohmands: the khans of Ghoshta, the khans of Atamarkhel, and the descendants of the late Haji Mohammad Hassan Khan of Kama. The khans of Girdab and of Lalpura were no longer significant. To block the routes that pass through Mohmand to Peshawar, military units of the invading army as well as of the Kabul regime descended on their territory and, after some setbacks, established military posts there. The khans crossed the border and, living either with their kin in the border area or in Peshawar itself, took up the cause of resistance. Among them, particularly among the descendants of Haji Hassan Khan, many are educated, and Kama had been a town with a number of public libraries confiscated by the Khalqis. One khan, Pir Dost Atamarkhel, finding life in Peshawar difficult because of the association of his rival peers (*turboors*) with the resistance groups, went over to the side of the regime and in 1985 attended the jirgas in Kabul. But he could not organize either a militia or live with his kinsmen in Afghanistan. In the past Afghan rulers exploited the traditional rivalry (*turboori*) that existed (and still exists) among elders of the Pashtun tribes to their advantage. Even the British exploited this situation with some success after they invaded Afghanistan twice in the last century. But the Kabul regime could not make headway among the Mohmand or other tribes, although Karmal gave one of his daughters in marriage to an Afriday tribesman apparently for that purpose.

ADMINISTRATIVE MEASURES

In the Democratic Republic of Afghanistan, no clear line divided the government and the PDPA. Both had elaborate structures, and the party was supreme. Officially this was the only legal party; hence, there was no room for opposition to work for change without bloodshed. Like any other Leninist party, the PDPA was hierarchical in structure, organized on the principle of "democratic centralism," a contradictory expression for a system that was, in practice, centralist but not democratic. Local decisions were made (often the party merely implemented instructions it received from Moscow) in the party politburo, which was composed of eleven leading members and headed by the general secretary, who, in the period under discussion, was Babrak Karmal. This office, the highest in the party, in theory was elective. In fact, it was not.

As noted, Babrak Karmal was raised to this position not by members of the politburo, as he should have been, but by the Kremlin rulers. Also, the term of the office of the general secretary was not fixed or limited, depending instead on the goodwill of the Kremlin rulers. Likewise, the term of membership in the politburo and the central committee was not fixed. Members could stay on so long as they enjoyed the support of the authorities. Membership was then the result more of partisanship than of qualification. The decisions of the politburo, which acted as the governing body of the party, were discussed in the central committee, which acted as parliament of the party. A much fuller assembly of the central committee, the plenum, met from time to time to discuss issues of special significance. The decisions reached in these assemblies were channeled to the lower cells of the party. The reverse was rarely the case. The supremacy of the PDPA over the government, state, and society was laid down by the constitution, which called it "the leading and guiding force of society and the state." If these words were meant seriously, then the party was assigned an impossible task.

Until June 1981, Babrak Karmal was the general secretary of the party, president of the Revolutionary Council, president of the Council of Ministers, and commander-in-chief of the army, thus officially wielding the highest party and government positions. He appeared to be all-powerful, but in fact he was a yes man. In June 1981 the sixth plenum of the party relieved him of the post of prime minister, conferring it on Sultan Ali Kishtmand, a member of the politburo. Seen in the context of the rivalry between the two factions, Kishtmand's promotion also strengthened Karmal's position, but it created problems for the regime. Although he had a faction of his own, Kishtmand was pro-Karmal, and this was considered more important in view of the intraparty squabble, which had made it difficult for Karmal to run the administration. Before this point is discussed, it is necessary to say why Kishtmand was promoted to the post and to discuss its implications.

Kishtmand, one of Moscow's yes men, had established a special relationship with Soviet advisers. Subsequently, two of his daughters married Russians in Moscow. Kishtmand was a graduate of the Faculty of Economics of the University of Kabul and experienced in administrative and planning affairs. He was known to be a Hazara, the third largest ethnic group. As a member of a minority group, he was sympathetic to minorities as well as to Sitam-e-Milli, whose founder, Tahir Badakhshi, was his brother-in-law.

More important, Kishtmand's promotion reflected a new policy. The Soviet authorities and party leaders were worried about the success of the mujahideen and the failure of their own pacification programs. In particular, politburo members worried about their future, especially if they lost the shield of the Soviet army. They then embarked on a new policy, the essence of which was to embroil ethnic groups among themselves: the war of the people against the PDPA and the invaders would be transformed into a war of the people against the people. The shift was intended to weaken the basis of the resistance, that is, national solidarity, and prepare the ground for socialism. The Soviet ambassador Ahmad Fikrat J. Tabeyev reportedly initiated the policy. Kishtmand was to work with politburo comrades, each of whom was assigned a task in making the policy work. In *Samara-e-Dosti* (Fruit of Friendship), a booklet issued for the benefit of party comrades, Kishtmand had dwelt on the issue. He had stated how the non-Pashtun ethnic minorities could be made oversensitive to each other and how, at the same time, they could be persuaded to form an anti-Pashtun front. Politburo members and others were made responsible for the affairs of ethnic groups. Each was also to supervise contingents of militias of the ethnic group assigned to him. To implement the policy, they earmarked billions of afghanis free from state audit. In the name of "international socialism," Pashtun and non-Pashtun members of politburo alike undertook to make the policy a success. It was to be implemented through the new Ministry of Tribal Affairs and Nationalities, which replaced the former Ministry of Frontiers.[3] These persons deafened the Afghans by preaching that they toiled for the welfare of toilers, but in actuality, and on instruction from the Soviets, they devised ways and means to embroil the toilers in wars of hatred among themselves so that they themselves could stay in power. Having already sacrificed national sovereignty, they now showed that they were more loyal to socialism than to their own people or the land of their birth.

Kishtmand was known for his opposition to the Khalqis, who had tortured him while he was imprisoned in 1978. His family also shared Kishtmand's views, and one of his brothers, Asadullah Kishtmand, a newspaper editor, let a remark be published about Taraki that likened him to Dracula. The paper also called the Pashtuns "the uncultured majority" (*aksaryat-e-bayfarhang*). Although Asadullah Kishtmand was demoted because of these remarks, the Khalqis and Pashtuns were not satisfied. The remark was, of course, not valid, since every group of people has a culture, since "culture is that complex whole which includes knowledge, belief, art, morals, law, custom and any other capabilities and habits acquired by men as a member of society."[4] As the creators of Pashtunwali, their complex social code, the Pashtuns are conspicuous among their ethnic neighbors in having a distinctive culture. But as a pretext for an anti-Amin campaign, and under the shadow of Soviet might, the Kishtmands and others had started an anti-Pashtun campaign. They frequently called Amin and his cohort "fascists." The promotion of Kishtmand was also important because it would placate the Shi'ite Hazaras and improve relations with the Khomeini government of Iran. It was hoped that both would be pleased to see an Afghan Shi'a as prime minister of the country for the first time in its history. But Kishtmand had liabilities, and these outweighed his assets.

Although it was not generally known, Kishtmand was not a full-fledged Hazara, although for political reasons he had associated himself with them. He was in fact a Gadee, a mixture of the Hazaras and other low-ranking people of unknown origin; he was born in the Qala-e-Sultan village close to Unchi-e-Bagbanan in the Chardihi basin. Whether his ancestors lived in the Hazarajat proper is unknown, but the Gadees themselves, a small group, lived in the villages of Chardi. Their neighbors held the Gadees in low esteem. The Gadees were Isma'ili Shi'as, or the Seveners, as distinct from the main group of the Shi'as, or the Twelvers, who regarded the former as Ghalis or Ghalatis, that is, those who either "exaggerate" in the matter of religion or are on the "wrong" pathway. At no time had the Gadees played a role in national politics. The Isma'ilis of the northeastern part of the country in Badakhshan, as well as in Kahmard and Saighan, were also a minority living in areas surrounded by their Sunni neighbors. Under these circumstances, it was unlikely that Kishtmand could play an important role.

Kishtmand's promotion to the office of prime minister provoked the conservative, traditionalist Sunni Muslims: contrary to traditional and religious practices, an Isma'ili Gadee had become prime minister. In addition, Kishtmand and others were known to be atheists and communists, although they behaved as if they were Muslims. During the constitutional monarchy, when Kishtmand campaigned for a seat in parliament, he omitted the word "Ali" from his name in the election brochures. He did so because "Ali" represented Shi'ism, and he was concerned that, if he were so identified, the Sunnis of the Chardihi constituency would not elect him; and, indeed, he was not elected. While he was prime minister, even his own Gadees boycotted him.

Kishtmand's promotion alarmed educated Afghans for a different reason. They were alarmed because of the Soviet design on northern Afghanistan, a relatively underpopulated region but potentially rich both agriculturally and industrially. Strategically it is also significant, because it is separated from the rest of the country by the Hindu Kush and also because it is close to Central Asia. The alarm was not unfounded. In 1987 the scheme for northern and southern Afghanistan was implemented: under this plan a deputy prime minister, along with sixteen deputy ministers for the nine provinces in northern Afghanistan, began to work in Mazar, the capital city of the province of Balkh.[5] Before that, Kabul had allowed the provincial governments as well as businessmen of the area to deal with the Soviet Central Asian Republics directly, a unique concession. Among the educated minority groups of this region, the sectarian tendency was strong; for instance, the Sitamis come from this area.

The Afghans feared that an increase in the number of central Asians in Kabul, the stress of the ethnic minority issue, and the promotion of Kishtmand meant the revival of Russia's design on northern Afghanistan. They feared that through the importation of central Asians and the cooperation of Parchamis and Afghan sectarians, the Soviet Union intended to carve out a state in northern Afghanistan with a view to making it part of its empire. They also feared that with the presence of such surrogates the Soviets now intended to implement their design, as they had invaded the country when the Parcham faction provided them a pretext. Thus, the promotion of Kishtmand made the regime more unpopular, despite the view that the Soviet model of nationalities, even if applied, would not work in Afghanistan since the Afghans were socially and linguistically more integrated than were the inhabitants of the neighboring lands. Besides, the Soviet nationalities of the Central Asian Republics had been more oppressed than their brethren in Afghanistan. The émigrés from these republics had spread stories of Soviet atrocities in northern Afghanistan. This was why the central Asians who worked in Afghanistan sympathized with the mujahideen. For this reason, the Soviets recalled the approximately 32,000 troops they had sent from the Central Asian Republics into Afghanistan.[6] Still, a scheme of such magnitude was bound to have some ugly consequences.

Karmal's difficulty with the Khalqi-dominated army has already been described. His position in the civil administration was also unenviable. The source of the troubles was the party rift, which had been accentuated by the purges of the rival faction each time the other faction was dominant. Following the invasion, it was the turn of the Parchamis. The regime tried to disarm the Khalqis while it armed its own Parchamis. This made the Khalqis vulnerable to terroristic attacks by mujahideen.

Also, the Khalqis were dismissed from party and government positions or demoted. Since there is no civil service system in Afghanistan, each time a new regime comes to power new officials are employed in place of the old ones. After the communist coup, the overhaul became more general than at any time before. Party members had to have government positions even if it was at the expense of expertise. This attitude was further reinforced by the view that since the state was an instrument in the hands of the ruling class, the vanguard of the workers—that is, party members—must steer it to their own benefit: hence the justification of the view that the state should be in the hands of party members. The state was then considered sacrosanct, a monopoly of the communists. In practice this attitude meant the holding of official positions by unqualified party members.

After its rise to power, the regime tried to promote Parchamis to government positions and to remove the Khalqi officials from their posts. This proved difficult because qualified personnel were in short supply and because the regime needed unity in the party. Amin's associates were dismissed following the invasion. But the regime needed to promote its own trusted Parchamis to high positions. In September 1980 the regime ordered the removal of about eighty government officials, among them a number of departmental chiefs, judges, and the mayor of Kabul; almost all were Khalqis. But the regime could not make such changes on a large scale. The Khalqis complained to the Soviet ambassador that the move was intended to undermine the unity of the party. They carried on their duties as usual, turning away the new officials who had come to occupy their posts. On instruction from the ambassador, the regime acquiesced. However, the regime removed the Khalqi officials one by one. But the Khalqis had to have a haven in this game of survival.

Since the invasion the Ministry of Internal Affairs, headed by Sayyed Mohammad Gulabzoy, had become a haven for those Khalqi officials whom the regime had dismissed from other departments. The ministry assumed a feature distinct from all other ministries. Its top civil officials, as well as police officers and ordinary police, were almost all Khalqis, and almost all were from Paktia, the stronghold of the Khalqis. In addition, they were almost all Pashtuns and opposed to the Parchamis. The ministry functioned as a counterweight to KhAD, in which the Dari-speaking elements, mainly from the city of Kabul and Parwan, outnumbered all others. The two ministries were more rivals than cohesive organs of the regime.

In 1981 I observed that the Khalqi officials in the Ministry of Interior criticized Karmal and the Parchamis to the point of diatribe, even in the presence of strangers. Since KhAD was ruthless to the opponents of the regime, the Khalqis' attitude was amazing. But they felt safe since Gulabzoy, until then, had opposed KhAD setting up its committees in that ministry, whereas in all other government departments it had set up a network of committees. In addition, the ministry had a strong police force (Sarindoy) of its own, armed with tanks, helicopters, and other sophisticated weapons, which enabled it to take part in military operations. Finally, the ministry was financed by Moscow. All this meant that it had such an independent status that even Karmal could not influence it. It was more like a state within a state. Gulabzoy reportedly called it "the ministry of Gulabzoy." Since the Khalqis dominated the army and Sarindoy, and since the Khalqis, although divided, were more numerous than the Parchamis, Gulabzoy considered himself equal to Karmal.

A Zadran Pashtun from Paktia, Gulabzoy was by profession a tank commander. Before the communist coup he was a noncommissioned officer. His part in the communist coup was inconspicuous, since at a critical moment he had failed to perform his duty. He had been recruited to the party by Hafizullah Amin, of whom he was an associate until the latter's relation with Taraki became strained. He then turned against Amin and became one of the Gang of Four described earlier; together with Asadullah Sarwari and Aslam Watanjar, he played a part in the downfall of Amin as part of the invading forces: hence his endearment to the Soviets, and hence also his rivalry with Karmal. Confident that the latter could not harm him, Gulabzoy acted independently, building a stronghold for himself as Karmal had built a stronghold in KhAD. Being a daring person, Gulabzoy patrolled the city at night, often without bodyguards. No other leader of either the Parchami or the Khalqi factions had the courage to do so.

Gulabzoy said that since Moscow had appointed both himself and Karmal to their posts, Karmal could not remove him. Gulabzoy thus acted without reference to Karmal, especially after Sarwari had been banished to Mongolia as ambassador. Gulabzoy looked on himself as his successor, organizing the human resources at his disposal. He proved to be skillful in this job. Since the Khalqis had to struggle against so many odds, this organizational task was massive. Gulabzoy made a significant contribution to his faction since KhAD had the power and the means to suppress the Khalqis much as the Khalqis had suppressed the Parchamis in 1978. In the tradition of the Afghans, he was ambitious, hoping to fill the vacuum at the top when Karmal had failed to do so. But such an outcome was unlikely. Barely literate, Gulabzoy had no knowledge of ideology. Often drunk, like General Abdul Qadir, Gulabzoy was impolitic, more at home using muscle than brain. Also, within his own Khalqi faction the Amin group thought little of him, looking instead on Shah Wali and Abdul Karim Meesaq as its leaders.

CHAPTER ELEVEN

Victory at Any Cost

Vasily Safronchuk, the Soviet adviser at the Ministry of Foreign Affairs in Kabul, stated in 1981 that since the "Afghan revolution" was similar to the Soviet revolution, it would triumph in a matter of time. Although an adviser, Safronchuk worked as if he were the minister for foreign affairs in Kabul. His statement implied that the Soviets would support the Kabul regime until it overcame the resistance. Safronchuk echoed his government's position, which was that until armed interference in the internal affairs of Afghanistan ceased, and until the Karmal regime was recognized as the legitimate government of Afghanistan, the Soviet Union would support it. This was a reflection of Leonid Brezhnev's position that "affirmation and defence of sovereignty of states that have taken the path of socialist construction are of special significance to us communists."[1] This statement, made after the Soviet Union invaded Czechoslovakia in 1968, came to be known as the Brezhnev doctrine. It meant that the Soviet Union felt free to intervene in neighboring countries in favor of its surrogates, and once it dispatched an army to such a country, it would remain there until it accomplished its self-imposed mission.

The Soviet rulers probably believed that the resistance would be soon suppressed by the invading army's many expeditions. The Soviets as well as their clients therefore portrayed the mujahideen not as a resistance force but as a few "robbers," "bandits" gone astray. Confident of victory, the regime several times fixed dates for their disposal. When those

dates passed without victory, the regime gave up setting new deadlines
and stressed violence still more in achieving the goal. Likewise, the mujahideen were also determined to free their homeland. The scene was
thus set for violent clashes, whose consequences I described in my journal for 16 March 1982:

> Thus homicide has been adopted as a solution. This shows that an irrational
> attitude has become dominant and that beastliness is on the ascendance. On
> the one side are a small number of party members who, because of the might
> of the Soviet Union, claim that they have a mission to accomplish for the
> good of the people. They are loud in stating that "because the April revolu-
> tion is irreversible, we will not return from the road we have chosen." On
> the other side, however, are the majority of the people, represented by the
> mujahideen, who hold that the regime is a puppet of the Soviets and that the
> Soviets, in the name of bringing justice to the millions by rooting out human
> exploitation and safeguarding the country from foreign aggression, are, in
> fact, bent on dominating their homeland, their wealth, their honor, their reli-
> gion, their freedom, and all that they value.

Because the Soviets had a huge army and a vast arsenal, they felt
confident of victory. By comparison, the mujahideen were not as fortunate in terms of weaponry, but they had the will to defend their values,
and in the defense of their own country they felt invincible. One of their
many antigovernment tracts (*shabnama*), this one addressed to the
people of Kabul in February 1980, showed their spirit. The tract stated:

> Do not accept the orders of the infidels, wage jehad against them. . . . The
> Moslem people and the mujahideen of Afghanistan, with the sublime cry of
> Allah o Akbar, will bring down their iron fist on the brainless head of the
> infidel and Communist government. Mujahideen Moslems, remember that
> our weapons are the weapons of faith. These are the strongest and most effec-
> tive weapons in the world. Even the most modern weapons will be unable to
> resist ours. That is why, if we resist Soviet imperialism's infidel government
> we will be victorious, and it will suffer a crushing defeat. . . . The only path
> to happiness is faith in the jehad and martyrdom.[2]

SECURITY MEASURES FOR THE CITY OF KABUL

The regime soon found that it had to exert extraordinary efforts to protect its members from being killed. KhAD extended its network of supervision over Kabul city, increasing the number of its spies many times.
At the same time, members of the youth and women's organizations and
also party members began reporting on the people. Every police precinct
was matched by a KhAD precinct. Also, city branches of the party were

increased and given wide authority. The city and the people were thus watched by many party and regime agencies, while the security agencies were authorized to arrest suspected persons. Residential quarters of important officials—including that of Kishtmand in the Wazir Akbar Khan Maina, close to the presidential palace—were fenced with barbed wire and their walls fortified and raised. Even the city's police headquarters were fortified. Private cars and taxis were searched in various parts of the city, and gasoline purchases limited to ten liters (about two gallons) at a time. Taxis were searched thoroughly, since the mujahideen employed some of them for terroristic activities. Vehicles leaving or entering the city were searched at checkpoints. Also, contingents of troops would surround an area and search houses for draft dodgers and weapons, and groups of security men in plain clothes checked pedestrians in the city to see whether they were fit for military service. Often armed members of the party—including members of the Youth Organization, some of them no more than fourteen years of age—patrolled the streets during the day. Also, for reasons best known to the authorities, groups of armed infantrymen and tanks were posted at strategic points of the city for days on end.

Night curfew was enforced from ten o'clock in the evening until four in the morning, but streets and bazaars emptied of people much earlier, since some sections of the city became dangerous after nightfall. People kept their doors locked and arranged to guard their own neighborhoods. At home people would switch on their radios to hear what foreign news services, especially the BBC, had to say in their Pashto and Dari broadcasts about Afghanistan. Except for news and entertainment programs, people avoided the radio and television services of the regime. Given these security measures, it may be appear that the regime was in control of the situation. It was not. The unusual security measures indicated insecurity and a lack of cooperation between the people and the government. The social contract—the foundation of stability in society—had been broken beyond repair.

The mujahideen had ways of infiltrating the city. They could do so because the people were with them, whereas the regime's men had estranged themselves from them.

MUJAHIDEEN'S PENETRATION OF THE CITY OF KABUL

The city of Kabul was vulnerable from the east, west, and south. With nightfall the mujahideen could enter the periphery of the city from the hilly districts, especially Paghman. They would kidnap party men from their homes, destroy security posts, or fight with patrolling units. After the invasion, shots were heard almost every night. Sometimes the firing was intense, lasting for hours. The shots heard on the night of 8 October 1980 in the suburban towns of Niaz Beg and Fazil Beg were part of an armed engagement between the opposing forces. The first shots of the mujahideen were followed by a two-hour barrage of heavy guns, rockets, and small arms by the Soviet forces. Only when armored units reached the area did the mujahideen leave. During the previous night a group of mujahideen had penetrated as far as Deh Mazang, almost in the center of the city, with the intention of destroying a television installation on top of the Asamaee Hill. They retreated after an engagement with a Soviet unit. A week later shots were exchanged between the mujahideen and a military unit of the regime quartered close to Macroryan, the Soviet-made blocks of apartments where Soviet advisers and top party and government officials lived. In essence, the mujahideen ruled parts of the outskirts of the city; following the invasion, they pasted price lists of commodities in the outskirts of the city, especially Qala-e-Wahid and Bini Hissar. Shopkeepers observed the regulations.

The city's night security deteriorated still further. During the first week of July 1981 the mujahideen began to enter the city in large numbers, although the regime had taken new security measures. The Soviet forces were reluctant to come out at night, and the security forces of the regime merely fired toward the sky, thus avoiding confrontation with the mujahideen while giving a false impression to the regime of their loyalty. At this time the city was disturbed at night more than at any time before. Gunfire was heard not only in the outskirts but also in places such as Chindawal in the center of the city. The cry "Long live Afghanistan!" was also heard. For four hours during the night of 3 July 1981 Soviet troops fired heavy guns, rockets, and light arms over the Qala-e-Wahid section of Mier Wais Maidan and along the road to the Paghman district to oppose the mujahideen, who had appeared there in strength. The firing was so intense that I and my family spent the whole night in our basement. For the next two weeks the western outskirts of the city, including the headquarters of the Qargha Division, which had been reduced to about five hundred soldiers at the time, were under such pressure that people talked of the fall of the regime. It was then that the heaviest operations to date were taken against Paghman.

Despite the operations, the city remained as disturbed as before. Those in charge of the security of Kabul must have been frustrated over the renewed activities of the mujahideen. It was unbelievable. By 23 September 1981 the mujahideen had become more active than ever before. They were particularly bold in Karta-e-Nao in the eastern part of the city; sometimes Soviet tanks were unable to go there at night because of the mujahideen's rockets. The mujahideen were also active in the western outskirts of the city and in places like Khushal Maina, where I then lived. On the night of 18 September 1981 a group of about fifty mujahideen, after announcing their arrival by firing toward the sky, forced their way into a house and took away three government officials, who were said to have been members of the official party. For three hours the mujahideen roamed without encountering any resistance. During the day the regime, as usual, demonstrated its presence in strength. On New Year's Eve, which coincided with the seventeenth anniversary of the founding of the PDPA, the mujahideen demonstrated their strength as they usually did on such occasions. On that night they infiltrated the center of the city as far as Bagh-e-Ali Mardan and Jada-e-Maiwand and distributed antigovernment leaflets. The city in general remained disturbed, and firing at night was heard. However, the mujahideen could not persuade shopkeepers to close their shops as a demonstration of protest in commemoration of the city uprising of February 1980. The regime had anticipated the protest. The cold winter might also have worked in favor of the regime. But more important were the Soviet's major military operations, which by then had relieved the city of the pressure from the mujahideen. This was the situation when the regime arrested me in April 1982.

The security measures taken for the city, as noted, proved insufficient. Given the rate at which party men were lost and the mujahideen's continued disturbances in the city, it was feared that the hostile city population might cause the collapse of the regime. The party's low rate of recruitment was also a matter of concern. In July 1981 the average monthly recruitment in each precinct of the party was about two, and these recruits were government employees. Even within the party-dominated state, the PDPA could recruit very few members, despite the fact that it held the monopoly of access to employment under inflationary conditions. Party members were also lost, although in small numbers, in rural areas where the regime sent its younger members for short periods. The party's main base of recruitment was the Youth Organization, but this source needed time to mature.

There was still no sign that the regime would open a dialogue with the resistance, which it continued to call "bandits." Its view was that the "bandits" must be eliminated if they persisted. Supported by Soviet might, the regime acted on the belief that it would accomplish this in time. One wonders what urge in men and women drives them to suppress others who are unwilling to submit to their rule. When power cannot be obtained through consensus, and when the lives of millions of men and women are at stake, the urge to rule may be pathological. In some instances this urge may reflect a blind faith in the canons of a dogma that may condemn even brilliant minds to ineffectiveness. In such conditions, only people with the strictest moral principles can leave power behind. But in the period under discussion the passion to rule, despite the opposition of the majority, was strong among the Afghan communists. They intended to maintain and extend the power they had already attained. Thus, the PDPA claimed that they wanted to create a Shangri-la for the Afghan people; yet to fulfill that dream, they were willing to inflict terrible violence on those same people.

SECURITY MEASURES FOR THE LAND

During its third plenum, held in August 1980, the PDPA passed a resolution stating that peace and security should be maintained throughout the land. It also stated that, since the reform measures had not been observed, the government felt duty bound to maintain security. This statement confirmed the long-circulated rumors that the Soviets intended to suppress the resistance by the wide use of force after the Olympic games, which were held in Moscow that summer. After the Olympics the Soviets dispatched three fresh divisions of troops to Afghanistan. The troops were composed mainly of commandos who had been trained in conditions similar to those in Afghanistan. At this time party members, low in spirit because of the mujahideen's program of terrorism, needed a boost. In the plenum Karmal informed his comrades of a decision already made by his Soviet comrades in Moscow. The latter had assured its PDPA comrades that, since they were determined to crush the "dark forces of reaction and counterrevolution," they should not lose heart on account of temporary setbacks. The assurance was based on an assessment of the situation by Vladimir Kryuchkov, the head of foreign intelligence in Moscow. Kryuchkov had predicted that "the spring and summer of 1981 will be decisive for the final and complete defeat of the forces of the counterrevolution":[3] hence the program of carrot and stick to pacify the land as quickly as possible.

In August 1980 the authorities divided Afghanistan into eight new "zones," or administrative units, each comprising a number of provinces. The country had twenty-eight provinces in all. A member of the central committee of the party headed each zone; under him was a permanent commission, composed of the provincial governors and a Soviet adviser in command of the military unit stationed there. Although the head of each zone was given special power to resolve administrative, political, and security issues, his real job was that of a social liaison officer. By spending money and exerting pressure, the regime was able to summon community elders to meet with him. The program was a resort to conventions according to which rulers in times of crisis would seek the cooperation of community elders in repairing the broken chains of social order. The heads of the zones would lecture the elders on the goodwill of the regime and the advantages that would be theirs once peace and security were restored. Official propaganda stressed this welfare and peace offensive, while the Soviets undertook military operations.

The permanent commission was more important than its boss, who was not present all the time. Also, since the new arrangement was intended to help pacify the country, security matters dominated the rest of the issues: thus the significance of the military personnel and the Soviet adviser, a general at the head of a thousand commandos. In this sense, the new zones were military rather than civil units. Officially nothing was said about the arrangement except that the head of the unit was described as the "chief of the zone" (*raees-e-zoan*). The Soviet military officers acted on their own, even snubbing the heads of the units when reminded of the excesses they were committing. Whatever social standing the chiefs of zones had, their own Soviet comrades belittled them by their overbearing attitude, their arrogance, and their policy of genocide, which will be described in the last two chapters. Like his predecessor Fayz Mohammad, Sulaiman Laweq, the chief of the Ningrahar zone and the minister of tribal affairs, had established a good relationship with elders of Ningrahar. In response to a request by the elders that he tell the Soviets to withdraw their troops, he jokingly asked them how he could make such a request when the Soviets had refused to comply with the selfsame call from the United Nations.

THE AFGHAN PROBLEM IN INTERNATIONAL FORUMS

After the invasion, the Afghan problem became the concern of the United Nations and some other countries. The concern was, however, expressed in words coupled with actions taken against the Soviet Union for the invasion. Only the United States took any serious measures, canceling grain deliveries ordered by the Soviet Union, prohibiting the sale of high-technology and strategically valuable goods, and boycotting the 1980 Olympic games, which were held in Moscow. Calling the invasion "an extremely serious threat to peace" President Jimmy Carter declared that "this would threaten the security of all nations including, of course, the United States, our allies and our friends." The president then warned the Soviet Union that any move toward the Persian Gulf would be met with force.[4] The French government criticized the Soviet invasion; by contrast, Helmut Schmidt, chancellor of the Federal Republic of Germany, stated that the crisis in Afghanistan was not a "world crisis of dangerous dimensions."[5] Prime Minister Margaret Thatcher of Britain denounced the intervention and asked the Soviet Union to withdraw its forces from Afghanistan. All Western governments froze or suspended their relations with Kabul, leaving only a few personnel in their respective embassies to collect intelligence information. But if the world community did not take stern measures against the invasion, it did bring diplomatic pressure on the Soviet Union to recall its forces.

Starting with a special session on 15 January 1980, every year the General Assembly of the United Nations passed by an overwhelming majority a resolution demanding that foreign forces be unconditionally withdrawn from Afghanistan, that the country's integrity and nonaligned status be maintained, and that the right of self-determination of the Afghan people be observed. In February 1980 the United Nations Human Rights Commission condemned the Soviet aggression against the Afghan people as a flagrant violation of international law and human rights. In 1982 the secretary-general of the United Nations, Kurt Waldheim, on instruction from the General Assembly, appointed a special envoy to seek the withdrawal of foreign troops from Afghanistan, but because of the intransigence of the Soviet Union, no progress could be made. However, the channel was kept open until it finally succeeded in its mission in 1988.[6] Beginning with a special session on 28 January 1980 the Organization of the Islamic Conference, composed of the Muslim countries, annually passed stronger recommendations to the same effect, despite the pro-Soviet stance of some of its members (Syria, Iraq, and Libya).

Similarly, a resolution calling for Soviet withdrawal from Afghanistan was passed by the foreign ministers of the nonaligned countries at a meeting held early in 1981 in New Delhi; this resolution was particularly notable since the number of pro-Soviet countries in the movement was considerable. In summer 1981 the European Economic Community (EEC) used even stronger terms asking that the Soviet Union withdraw its forces from Afghanistan. At the same time, the EEC assured the Soviet Union that Afghanistan would remain neutral after the withdrawal, much like Austria after the Soviet withdrawal in 1955. The proposal was explained to the Soviet authorities in Moscow in July of the same year by a mission of the EEC headed by the British Foreign Minister Lord Carrington; the Soviets called the plan "impractical," although they did not reject it outright. The European Parliament also adopted a similar resolution. In January 1981 President Giscard d'Estaing of France called for an international conference to be held on Afghanistan, but the Soviets rejected that as well. The People's Republic of China was more assertive in its demands. Since it viewed the presence of the Soviet troops in Afghanistan as detrimental to its own security, the Chinese government made the improvement of its relations with the Soviet Union contingent on, among other things, the withdrawal of troops from Afghanistan.

The Soviet Union's invasion of Afghanistan did not create a stir among the people of the world comparable to that aroused by the United States' involvement in Vietnam, but on certain occasions anti-Soviet demonstrations were held. Within Eurocommunist circles there were few defenders of the introduction of Soviet forces into Afghanistan. The French Communist Party was conspicuous among those few who defended the Soviet invasion. The Italian Communist Party, the second biggest communist party in Western Europe after that of France, came out against the invasion, calling it "a mistake." The opposition soon led to an open polemic between the communist parties of Italy and the Soviet Union, but the former did not change its stand. In Eastern Europe dissident groups began to send out protest letters to Western Europe. An eloquent appeal came from Czechoslovakia in January 1980, calling for an international boycott of the Olympic Games in Moscow and even comparing them to the 1936 Olympics, held in the Berlin of Hitler's Third Reich. The letter read in part, "The Soviet intervention in Kabul, deprived of shabby justifications, is an outright and outrageous aggression. Today we can merely guess its continuation, but dread its ultimate objectives. If the Soviet aggression in Afghanistan is merely condemned by words, it will, against our will, become the norm to be repeated on future suitable occasions."[7]

Inside the Soviet empire, although Soviet youths fell in Afghanistan, the voice of opposition to the war could not be heard. The Soviet police state was too strong for Soviet men and women to express their views on the Afghan War as the American people had done on the Vietnam War. The Soviet government had made its involvement in Afghanistan a nonissue. Within the government framework a few military generals, including Chief of General Staff General Ogakov and Major General Zaplatin, adviser to the head of the Afghan chief political directorate, were opposed to the invasion.[8] In the weeks following the invasion, members of the Moscow groups monitoring violations of the Helsinki human rights accords and other dissident groups publicly condemned the invasion.[9] Also, shortly after the invasion "a group of academics, headed by O. Bogomolov, sent to the USSR Central Committee a report in which they reacted sharply to this act and prophesied its failure."[10] Calling the invasion "a fatal error that could cost the country dearly," Edward Shevardnadze stated, "The invasion of that country provided a strong negative reaction that grew daily in our society and abroad, whereas only a few people in the Soviet Union openly protested the sending of troops into Prague in 1968. After 1979 the majority condemned the Afghan adventure, either directly or indirectly."[11] The man who symbolized the Soviet conscience by opposing the war was Andrei Sakharov, the winner of the Nobel peace prize and a human rights activist; for his stand, the Soviet government in January 1980 deported him to the closed city of Gorky, where he spent seven years in isolation. Although Sakharov came to be hailed as the "conscience of the Soviet Union," at the time the Soviet government stifled voices of conscience and as a result lowered its international standing. More serious, the Soviet Union's defiance of the voices of sanity poisoned international trust, an attitude that led to a new phase in international tension and armament programs during the final years of the cold war.

In view of the Soviets' inflexible attitude, the Afghan elders of Ningrahar were almost wildly optimistic in asking Sulaiman Laweq, a mere Soviet proxy, to affect the withdrawal of Soviet troops from Afghanistan. They were carried away by the eloquence of the poet Laweq for making the new plan of rural administration work. To this plan we now return.

THE UNSUCCESSFUL DRIVE FROM CITY TO VILLAGE

Since rural areas were lost to the regime, it adopted new methods to extend control over them from the provincial capitals in a drive called

"From City to Village." In early 1982 Karmal declared that the time had come to "take the revolutionary struggle to the provinces, districts and villages." In this scheme provincial governors continued to function, but their traditionally strong role was reduced. In line with the new central-ized political structure, provincial governors as well as heads of depart-ments acted as heads of administration with limited authority. This was particularly so when they were not at the same time secretaries of their party units. In the new system political and security problems in the various provinces became the concern of party functionaries and KhAD agents, whom the Soviet advisers directed.

The provincial party secretaries (*munshi-e-wilayati*), although only the heads of their provincial committees, were supreme. Their relation-ship to government departments was similar to the relationship of the general secretary of the party to the government in Kabul. Because of the pressures of the continuing war, the absence of administrative statutes delimiting functions, and the long distance between Kabul and many provincial capitals, the new party bosses suddenly found themselves in positions of unlimited authority; they were thus tempted to act like little pharaohs, imposing their power over both the people and their own col-leagues. For example, Ahad Rahnaward, provincial secretary of Mazar and a member of the central committee of the party, was intolerant of criticism; in collaboration with three other members of the committee, he killed Aziem Gowhari and then reported to Kabul that Gowhari had defected to the rebels. However, before his death Gowhari had kept the Soviet adviser informed of the intentions of his rivals; in addition, Gowhari had been a prominent member of a faction of the party known as the Group of Labor (Goroh-e-Kar). Thus, his disappearance was ex-amined, and Rahnaward and his associates were tried and found guilty. In prison Rahnaward continued to act as if he were still in power, advis-ing prison authorities on how to deal with prisoners. Confident that he would not be harmed, Rahnaward admitted to the crime he had commit-ted. He and his accomplices were executed in December 1983.

Less prominent cases were the concern of provincial KhAD agents, who, in the name of security and revolution, felt free to commit ex-cesses. To accomplish their jobs, they had at their disposal money, spies, and the power to arrest, with or without warrants, and to inflict tortures and punishments to the point of killing prisoners by their death squads. To clear the cities of the mujahideen and extend control over the sur-rounding areas, they behaved as if they had been given unlimited author-ity. Many people were imprisoned on the basis of mere suspicion. In the game of survival, such excesses were understandable, though deplorable. What was almost entirely incomprehensible was the intensity of the power struggle that went on among provincial officials. Abdul Basir, a KhAD official of Mazar, shot and killed his rival after he persuaded him to accompany him on a pleasure trip to a nearby spot. Abdul Basir was tried and transferred as a prisoner to Pul-e-Charkhi concentration camp, where he was often heard saying that he was "a son of the party." He was sentenced to twenty years of imprisonment.

More serious was the policy of the regime toward "counterrevolutionaries." General Ghulam Sadiq Mirakai, a former deputy director of KhAD in charge of the three western provinces headquartered in Kandahar, says: "Every night they brought 10 to 15 trucks to the firing range. Each truck would have 50 people. I know the names. I know the people. They are arrested and they are no longer alive." The statement seems unbelievable, and Mirakai is aware of it. He continues, "The Western world can not comprehend what has taken place [in Afghanistan]." He also states that while performing his duty, "I had the Afghan party people on one side and the KGB advisers on the other." [12]

Notwithstanding the new administrative measures and the joint military operations, the drive "From City to Village" failed. But it did bring about a result of a different kind. Because of the unlimited authority that the new party and KhAD officials enjoyed, house searches, imprisonment, torture, embezzlement, licentiousness, and a lifestyle of arrogance became common among them. The known plebeians of yesterday became the hated patricians of the day, and a class of party members emerged from a new power base.

CHAPTER TWELVE

Elimination of Opponents by Nonmilitary Means

One result of the Soviet invasion was the creation of a situation in which the parties involved in the war justified the destruction of life for the slightest of reasons. The Afghans, especially those involved in politics, did not look on life as sacred; indeed, after the communist coup they made the elimination of opponents a part of their policies. Neither side found it difficult to rationalize their stand. The Kabul regime killed in the name of society, the state, the people, and the "revolution"; the mujahideen killed in the name of Islam and the motherland as well as familial and national honor.

In the regime's view, counterrevolutionaries had to be eliminated in order to make society "free of the exploitation of man by man." It did not consider that no one has ever been able to organize such a society. At a public meeting held in the city of Taluqan in the province of Takhar, a Pashtun resident told Deputy Premier Majid Sarbiland that the process of creating such a "just society" might require the death of the people of Taluqan. In the summer of 1981 Sarbiland had gone to Taluqan to address a meeting as part of the campaign to convince people of the good intentions of the regime to create a "just society." The utterances were a masquerade to establish the rule of a group of people whom the Soviets had raised to power. Morality had lost its meaning; those in power acted as if might did indeed make right.

The violence that the Soviets and their compliant Afghans perpetrated could not remain unchallenged by a people whose value system demands that they take revenge. The Afghans also considered it their right to use violence since the Soviets had left no alternative to change the regime they had imposed. The resulting violence brought forth the impulse for destruction "by all sides, on all sides." Hence, the psychology of killing permeated not only the state but the society as well. Human life, that priceless valuable, was cheapened to an unprecedented degree not only on the battlefields but also in ordinary circumstances. It is impossible to absolve those who committed a crime against an unprovoked people by imposing a war on them inside the boundaries of their own fatherland.

"What is fundamental about violence in human affairs is that a person is violated." "A person is violated" when he or she is deprived of rights, "autonomy," dignity, or life.[1] Here we are concerned with the deprivation of life by means other than war for essentially political purposes. Such deprivation was, of course, not something new, since, like so many others, the Afghan society and state were violent even before the invasion. However, the violence perpetrated after the various coups, and particularly after the Soviet invasion, was of such scope, degree, and intensity that it had no parallel in Afghan history. Indeed, the invasion was a violation of Afghans on a national scale.

The first person to lose his life to terrorism was the editor of the weekly *Minhajuddin Gaheez,* killed by a leftist radical in 1972. Until then, in the long reign of the former king Mohammad Zahir, the Afghans lived in an atmosphere free of terrorism, although before the constitutional decade the state had violated human rights, particularly the rights of prisoners. It was after the overthrow of the king that official terrorism took the lives of many people.

Those responsible for official terrorism were the Parchamis who dominated the new republic. Among the victims was the former prime minister Mohammad Hashim Maiwandwal, killed in a prison cell by the Parchamis; specifically, Fayz Mohammad, the minister of the interior, and Samad Azhar, the chief of the Investigation Commission, were said to have been responsible for the killing. Toward the end of the republic, waves of terrorism and counterterrorism went hand in hand, the latter committed by radical Islamists against the leftists and government officials. Among the known victims of these waves were Ali Ahmad Khurram, the minister of planning, and Mier Akbar Khybar, the number two leader and ideologue of the Parchami faction, whose killing triggered the communist coup in 1978. Their deaths, which had far-reaching consequences, were the work of the KGB. Khurram had, on the instruction of President Daoud, started to distance Afghanistan from the Soviet Union; he was soon killed by a member of the PDPA, Marjan. Khybar was killed for his opposition to the PDPA's taking of power; he did not believe that the PDPA would be able to rule the country even if it succeeded in taking power.[2] Thereafter, first the rule of the Khalqis and then that of the Parchamis were reigns of terror, and the number of Afghans killed as counterrevolutionaries is beyond calculation. Counterterrorism likewise became widespread.

The revolutionary method of Stalinesque Russian communism, the overzealousness of Islamists, and the revenge-seeking spirit of Afghans made life in Afghanistan an inferno. It is impossible to detail what happened even in noncombatant places in these turbulent years. Indeed, it was hazardous for a person simply to collect information about it. This means that posterity will not know how the society of the time worked, or failed to work. Rumors will take the place of history, and posterity will have a distorted view of this period. What is described here is an incomplete picture of how the mujahideen eliminated the Soviet Afghan surrogates through terroristic tactics, and how the latter did the same against both the mujahideen and themselves.

After the invasion religious scholars issued fatwas saying that since members of the official party were atheists and the associates of infidels, they were to be killed. Armed with moral and religious justification, the mujahideen and others went on with killing the Parchamis and Khalqis. Even without such an injunction the mujahideen considered it necessary to perpetrate counterterrorism, since they were unable to carry out frontal assaults on the enemy; they were therefore determined to eliminate those whom they called "the internal Russians." This may explain why, following the invasion, the mujahideen soon either killed the Soviet surrogates in the countryside or drove them to cities.

Those who had been associated with both the Khalqi and Parchami regimes also suffered, partly because the distinction between them and the communists was blurred. In addition, the official party had covert members, and KhAD had planted its agents in the ranks of the mujahideen. Solid evidence was not considered essential for acting on such a fundamental point: circumstantial evidence and suspicion were enough for taking life. In addition, the people turned against the regime because of its double face: the repressive one it presented to the Afghans, and the subservient one it presented to the Russians.

ALIENATION OF THE PDPA

In March 1982 I conducted an informal survey of my educated acquaintances in the city of Kabul, concluding that the dominant view was that, since party members were unwilling to abandon their servitude to the Russians, they deserved to be eliminated. The public corroborated this view by their attitude. In the first place, the public excommunicated party members, in particular the Parchamis. People generally would not rent them houses and also refrained from either giving them or accepting from them daughters in marriage. In general, party members were ostracized not only by friends and acquaintances but in some cases even by members of their own families. In the second place, when party members became the target of terroristic attacks, people acted as if nothing had happened. I never heard of any person volunteering information to the police on the subject, although it was the custom to cooperate with the police on other crimes, particularly murder. Terrorists thus could not be caught on the spot. Some were caught later, but only as a result of extensive efforts by KhAD.

When party members or collaborators were killed in provincial cities, notices were served barring mullas or religious functionaries from burying the dead in accord with the rituals of Islam. Such orders were obeyed. So, contrary to custom and the injunction of Islam, the dead bodies of members of the official party as well as of collaborators either lay for days without being buried or were buried without ritual. In Kabul, because of fear of terroristic attacks and because of public pressure, most high-ranking party members and known collaborators lived in the guarded, Soviet-made neighborhoods of Macroryan and Wazir Akbar Khan Maina, where the growing number of Russians also lived. Rents skyrocketed, and the regime undertook to build new prefabricated blocks of residential apartments. Perhaps no other ruling party had become so isolated from its own people in history as the PDPA had.

PARTY MEMBERS TERRORIZED IN PROVINCIAL CITIES

As noted above, professional terror attacks started in the summer of 1980 after religious scholars issued fatwas; until then, party men had been driven from the rural areas, taking refuge in cities where an uncontrollable process of urbanization had started. In the beginning the Khalqis more than the Parchamis were the target of attacks. The brutality of the Khalqis was fresh, and people were harsher with them than with the Parchamis, whose brutality was not yet apparent. Party members were attacked more frequently in big provincial cities than in Kabul. Even in a city like Mazar, which is situated in a flat plain and whose inhabitants are known to be relatively mild, party members were killed in numbers that rivaled and even surpassed those of other cities.

In the city of Kandahar the Khalqis became the target of attacks on a bigger scale. Terrorism also started there much earlier, following the fall of the Khalqi regime. During the course of thirty-four days in January and February 1980, 130 Khalqis were killed in terror attacks in the city of Kandahar and its surrounding districts. This was the work of common people, not professionals. The killings were in revenge for the men the people of Kandahar had lost at the hands of Khalqis when they were in power. Two examples will suffice to make the point clear. During the Khalqi rule about a hundred prisoners from the city and the Helmand area were thrown out of airplanes into the Arghandab reservoir. Also, forty-eight elders from the Karz district were killed in the presence of Engineer Zarif, the Khalqi governor of Kandahar. They were killed because they had protested that government officials should register only the number, not the names, of their female folk when they were taking a census of the population. In the Parchami period, Engineer Zarif and other Khalqis were executed for the crimes they had committed. In any case, following the invasion the Kandahar people killed the Khalqis more in revenge than anything else. They were successful in their revenge because they were more skillful in terror attacks than the people of other cities were.

Many Khalqis were killed in the city of Taluqan following the invasion, but information about them is not available. The story of the fallen Khalqis was more striking in Herat than elsewhere, because Herat had lost more men than any other city or province during the Khalqi rule, as noted earlier. In May 1980, in all Herat only the headquarters of the governor was under the control of the regime, and that was guarded by an armored force. During that time, and for an unknown period thereafter, ten to twelve party men were killed every day. The acts of terrorism in Kabul had many sides, since of all the cities this was the largest and had the highest number of party members.

PARTY MEMBERS TERRORIZED IN KABUL

In Kabul acts of terrorism followed the unsuccessful uprisings in February 1980. By July terrorism had become so common that every day from ten to twelve party members were killed in individual terror attacks. By November the rate had fallen to a lower level; still, on average three party members were killed every day in November 1980. Terrorism had become so common that only when important party members were killed did people talk about them. The fall of the ordinary members of the party was seldom discussed, even though they were killed during the day. The Parchamis accused the Khalqis of being responsible for these attacks in Kabul as well as other cities, calling them Ikhwanis. The accusation was a reflection of the intraparty rifts, and the Khalqis were also unkind to their rivals. By this time the intraparty animosity had reached a new pitch. The Khalqis had been exposed to dangers and were also faced the situation of losing lucrative jobs. By August 1980 about three hundred Khalqis had either been expelled from party membership or demoted for convening separate party meetings, something that had been going on for a long time as if there were two parties.

By January 1981 a new wave of terrorism had become evident. The Soviet army had given up patrolling the city, because it too was losing men to the terrorists. When the regime men took the responsibility of patrolling the city, they were exposed to acts of terrorism more than ever before. By then military officers as well as soldiers, in addition to party men, had become the target of attacks. In mid-January 1981 almost every night acts of terrorism were reported from different parts of the city, especially the crowded sections with narrow lanes such as Qal'a-e-Zaman Khan, Qal'a-e-Nao, and Qal'a-e-Wahid. During twenty-four hours in the second week of February 1981, twenty-five party members lost their lives in terror attacks. It was at the height of such acts that first the political officer of the military KhAD, Akbari, and later the head of KhAD Number Five, Haji Sakhi, also fell victims. Known as the "brain of KhAD" and responsible for the arrest of the SAMA leader Majid Kalakani, Haji Sakhi was killed in daylight on the main road near the Soviet embassy. Also killed were prominent persons who had associated themselves with the regime. A number of others were killed, including a former general, Mier Fatih Mohammad Hazara, who had gone over to the regime and participated in the National Front of the Fatherland.

The National Front of the Fatherland was convened on 15 June 1981 in Kabul with the participation of fewer than a thousand members from the front-line associations and trade unions, including some local dignitaries, members of the party, and those sympathizers who might have been covert members of the party. The front had no specific duties, but the regime hoped to use it to extend its influence. It was said to be consultative, but the consultation was not about political affairs, which could influence national politics. A propagandistic organization, it was set up in imitation of the associations in some East European countries.

By August 1981, however, the number of terror attacks had decreased because the mujahideen had to pay attention to the Soviet force concentrated in Gulbahar in Parwan Province, which was advancing into the valley of Panjsher. In late September, during a time of decreased incidents of terrorism, a Soviet adviser to the Ministry of Mines was kidnapped in a daring daylight abduction and taken through Shewaki toward the east of Kabul city to the mujahideen. In October as well as December the incidents of terrorism once again increased. In the cold season of Kabul the mujahideen preferred to be more active in terrorist acts than in major engagements. At this time a number of Russians were made the targets of terror attacks.

TERRORISM AND INTRAPARTY RIVALRY

In February 1982 Sa'ima Maqsoodi, a television newscaster and one of my former students, fell victim to a terror attack, an incident that raised an uproar among the Khalqis. She was the victim of the Khalq-Parcham rivalry, since in the Dari-dominated atmosphere of television Maqsoodi campaigned for Pashto and criticized the Parchamis on that account. Since the communist coup the problem of propaganda and ideological indoctrination had become significant. When the Khalqis were in power, publication in Pashto was stressed. When the Parchamis came to power, they restricted Pashto publications to such a point that it infuriated the Khalqis, in particular those who worked in the forefront of cultural sectors.

The Parchamis manipulated publications without regard for cultural identity. As part of the Sovietization program, they used the mass media more for the benefit of Russian and Soviet culture than for the benefit of Afghan culture. As part of this policy, they allowed the Tajiks of Soviet Tajikistan and some writers of the Tudeh Communist Party of Iran to influence the Afghan Dari publications. As a matter of policy and also as a result of their ignorance of Pashto, the Russian and Tajik advisers favored the Parchamis and subordinated Afghan cultural values to those of the Russians. For the internationalist Parchamis, this approach was part of their cultural policy, but outside their circles the Afghans, irrespective of the languages they spoke, became furious, since to them the program reeked of cultural exploitation. They began making telephone calls to the personnel of the television, venting their anger in long diatribes, but to no effect. In fact, the television personnel could not have done much about it even if they had wanted to do so, since the Soviet advisers handled the cultural policy of the television and radio stations, and the Parchamis played the role of employees. Besides, since these stations were among the biggest centers of employment, these developments turned them into centers of rivalry, whose effects spilled over to society. Among the results of this rivalry were the murder of Maqsoodi, the killing of Pashto singers such as Qarabaghi and perhaps also Bakhtzamina, and the poisoning on 13 March 1982 of Sa'eedi, the Khalqi rector of Kabul University. Who killed these people is unknown, although the mujahideen had warned Maqsoodi to quit her part-time job as a newscaster.

The loss of the singers, the flight abroad of many others, and the propagandistic program of the broadcast stations reduced their significance. Although the killing happened at a time when terror attacks on party members were common, it was held that KhAD had engineered the killings of both Maqsoodi and Sa'eedi. The Khalqis believed so. Every time a Khalqi was killed, it was said that KhAD was responsible. That was why the Khalqis made the funeral services of Sa'eedi a major event, comparable to the funeral services held for Mier Akbar Khybar. Both events were demonstrations of strength.

My diary entry dated 16 March 1982, just before my arrest, speaks about terrorism:

> These days the killing of party members has increased. Terrorism is widely perpetrated, but only when important members of the party are killed do people talk about it. When members of the ranks of the party are killed, only their own relatives know about them. The public chooses to remain indifferent. Many people seem pleased about the killing. In Kabul it has not been heard that the perpetrator has been arrested. The public does not cooperate with the police.

My last entry on terrorism (22 March 1982) reads: "In the city of Kabul terroristic activities against party members have increased. The opposition has increased their activities with a view to intensifying the animosity between the Khalqis and Parchamis. The Khalqis have been killed in larger numbers as a result of terroristic attacks. It is believed that KhAD agents kill under instruction from Parchamis."

PARTY CONFERENCE OVERSHADOWED BY
TERRORIST ACTIVITIES

Since the foundation of PDPA in 1965, no party congresses had been held, although most communist parties hold a congress of elected members every fourth year or so. Such congresses legitimize party leaders, including the general secretary, and approve guidelines for party programs. As already described, Karmal had failed to obtain legitimacy as head of the state and government. He hoped that legitimacy would follow when he established his rule. He was content with being the de facto ruler of "the exalted, nonaligned, and independent Democratic Republic of Afghanistan."

After two years in office, Karmal hoped that the legitimacy of the party position as general secretary was within his grasp. He also hoped that an assembly of the leading members, under his guidance, would unite the party or at least decrease tension. All along he hoped he would one day become the leader of the united PDPA. But odds stood against the realization of his hope. As noted earlier, Parcham and Khalq were in fact two distinct parties, and the overthrow of the Amin regime had made it impossible for them to reconcile. For these reasons, holding a congress of the elected members of PDPA was out of question. Instead, it was decided that a national conference (*kanfarans-e-sartasari*) of the party should be held, to be attended by members chosen on the basis of consensus. But even this limited congress was fraught with danger.

Clashes occurred in party precincts where members were to be chosen for the conference, and the Parchamis had the worst of them. The new tension that descended on the meetings was converted into violent actions, including the killing of members of the rival groups. In the Chemical Fertilizer Factory in Mazar, for instance, three Parchamis were killed, allegedly by Khalqis. Rival gangs often fired at each other, with Parchamis the most common victims.

It was in this atmosphere that the Khalqis who fell victim to terroristic actions were said to have been killed by KhAD. The Khalqi rector of Kabul University was eliminated in such an atmosphere. One reason for the tension was that fewer Khalqis were chosen, since the Parchamis, who were in the dominant position, manipulated procedures and postponed meetings when they anticipated that the results would be to their disadvantage. For some leaders, particularly Parchamis, the conference became scandalous. To secure a consensus, they had to go to other cities where they were sure they would be chosen, particularly by the military constituencies. The surveys already taken showed that they would be defeated if they stood for election in their own constituencies. Top leaders had lost the confidence of the rank and file, and had free elections been held, most would have been swept away.

On 15 March 1982 the conference was held; it lasted for only one day, during which 830 members attended amid tight security in the Polytechnic Institute. A bomb inside the hall was discovered before it exploded. After two sessions the conference ended. It was announced that decisions were taken "in a free and democratic atmosphere." The issue of membership in the party was the main topic of the agenda. Karmal dealt with the destructive consequences of "factionalism," a criticism pointed at Khalqis. Gulabzoy, the self-styled leader of Khalq, openly accused the Parchamis of factionalism, since it was they who, according to him, regarded the Ministry of the Interior as the "Ministry of Rebels" (de ashraro wizarat).

Meanwhile, contrary to the custom among communists on such occasions, Gulabzoy refrained from holding hands with Karmal in the concluding session. He received more frequent applause from the audience than did Karmal. But for Karmal it was a great moment. For the first time in his life he appeared as the general secretary of PDPA before an assembly of the party, receiving applause and cries of "Hurrah!" But the conference had failed in its purpose. Because of the violence that was committed, the two factions were as much apart as ever, and the unity as unreal as ever.

MURDEROUS SOCIETY

It is impossible to ascertain how many lives were destroyed as a result of terror attacks following the invasion. The highest number killed were party members, most of whom were buried in special graveyards. Every provincial capital had a graveyard of its own, the biggest being in Kabul in Tapa-e-Maranjan, renamed Tapa-e-Shuhada (Martyrs' Hill). The violence that had permeated society, the state, and the ruling party showed the psychology of killing. I commented on this psychology in my diary entry of 21 January 1981:

> The Afghan society may now be regarded a murderous society. The sad thing about it is that there is no investigation of murder cases. Human life has become the life of a sparrow, and the principle that might is right dominates. Time was that a murder case was investigated not only among the people

where the murder had taken place but also among neighbors, who were summoned to the security centers for questioning. In this way social conscience against murder was awakened. But now killing has become so common that only a few people come to know about it. Only they bemoan the fate of the dead. We have become soulless and dry, no longer beings of care and love, but brutal and fierce animals. It is not right to name a society murderous, but the Afghan society may be called so. For now conditions prevail in which the Parchamis kill the Ikhwanis, and the latter kill the Parchamis, the Khalqis, and the Russians. And the Russians kill not only the Ikhwanis but also innocent civilians. They even kill the Parchamis and the Khalqis. The state is the state of killing, not only in the battlefield but also in the lanes and streets of cities where there is no state of war. No one feels secure, and because of this many families have fled abroad.

Because of the frequency of killing, there is now public indifference to it. Onlookers who in the past cooperated with authorities in seizing culprits now gaze impassively, doing nothing. Consider the incident that happened yesterday, on a bright day in the crowded part of Mier Wais Maidan. Three youths fell victim to the bullets of murderers. Two of the victims were killed instantly. One of the murderers drove a short distance with his companions, then returned and fired at close range at the fallen youth who was still alive. After kicking the youth several times and making sure that he was dead, the murderer got into the waiting car and drove away. The spectators just looked at what happened. They did nothing else. It is not known who the murderers were. They got into the same car from which official announcements are made, but whether they were agents of KhAD cannot be said with certainty.

PART FOUR

The Story of Genocide in Afghanistan

CHAPTER THIRTEEN

Genocide Throughout the Country

The claim of the Soviet Union that it dispatched its "limited contingent" to repulse foreign aggression proved groundless after the uprising of February 1980, when its war machine began to kill not only the mujahideen but also defenseless civilians throughout the country. Frustrated by the tough resistance and their inability to suppress it expeditiously, the Soviets embarked on a program of genocide.

Genocide is a term that social scientists have defined in different ways, just as they have defined other social terms differently. This is not surprising, because definitions restrict, encase, and distort concepts. Definitions also change with the passage of time as historical developments add new dimensions to social concepts. Also, social scientists with different backgrounds and outlooks delimit terms by defining them in their own ways. Yet definitions are the necessary conceptual constructions by which people communicate and scientists proceed with the formulation and organization of knowledge. The more precise definitions and generalizations are, the better is the state of knowledge.

People have perpetrated genocide from time immemorial. It was, however, during World War II, when it was committed on a massive scale, that the term *genocide* was coined and became the subject of scholarly study, as F. Chalk and K. Jonassohn have described and evaluated in detail in *The History and Sociology of Genocide* (1990). In a pioneering work, Raphael Lemkin described genocide as the coordinated and planned annihilation of a national, religious, or racial group

by actions aimed at undermining the foundation essential to the survival
of the group as a group.[1] Lemkin's work, composed with a view to illus-
trating the Nazi theory and practice of the extermination of the Jews
and the Gypsies, underlined his statement about genocide. But the Ho-
locaust is unique in history. Lemkin's work partly influenced the United
Nations to consider first in 1946 and then in 1948 the issue of preventing and punishing genocide. Calling genocide a "crime under international law," the United Nations in its Convention on the Prevention
and Punishment of the Crime of Genocide, considered the following acts
punishable: genocide; conspiracy to commit genocide; direct and public
incitement to commit genocide; attempt to commit genocide; and complicity in genocide. But the United Nations, as a "club of sovereign
states" and under pressure from the Communist bloc countries, adopted
as its final resolution a compromise definition that excluded state vic-
timization of groups of people on political grounds. In the United Nations' definition, *genocide* "means any of the following acts committed
with intent to destroy, in whole or in part, a national, ethnical, racial or
religious group."[2] Political groups are excluded from this definition.

Excluding political groups from the definition of genocide is like excluding political history from history. Such a definition excludes activities without which history is incomprehensible, especially in an age of
totalitarian states and nation-states. War can also be understood in
terms of the state, because "war is not a licence to kill, but an obligation
to kill for reasons of state."[3] It is this all-embracing nature of the state
that has made political genocide and, consequently, human rights important aspects of history in modern times, when the perpetrator of
genocide is predominantly the state. That is why, although the United
Nations' definition marked a milestone in international law, and although it is the only internationally accepted one, it is of little use to
scholars.[4] Because not one of the genocidal killings committed since the
adoption of this resolution has been covered by it,[5] "it has never had
any practical effect."[6] It has thus been left to scholars to provide a precise definition of genocide, a full survey of which is to be found in the
Chalk and Jonassohn's work.

Rather than enumerate definitions of genocide, I will describe the em-
pirically based categories about which students of genocide are close to
consensus. These are *retributive genocide,* which is based on the desire
for revenge; *institutional genocide,* which is frequently incidental to military conquest; *utilitarian genocide,* which is motivated by the desire for
material gain; *monopolistic genocide,* which originates in the desire to

monopolize power; and *ideological genocide*, which is motivated by the desire to impose a particular notion of salvation or purification on an entire society.[7] Chalk and Jonassohn have combined these categories into a master definition: "Genocide is a form of one-sided mass killing in which a state or other authority intends to destroy a group, as that group and membership in it are defined by the perpetrator."[8]

For genocide to happen, there must be certain preconditions. Foremost among them is a national culture that does not place a high value on human life. A totalitarian society, with its assumed superior ideology, is also a precondition for genocidal acts.[9] In addition, members of the dominant society must perceive their potential victims as less than fully human: as "pagans," "savages," "uncouth barbarians," "unbelievers," "effete degenerates," "ritual outlaws," "racial inferiors," "class antagonists," "counterrevolutionaries," and so on.[10] In themselves, these conditions are not enough for the perpetrators to commit genocide. To do that—that is, to commit genocide—the perpetrators need a strong, centralized authority and bureaucratic organization as well as pathological individuals and criminals. Also required is a campaign of vilification and dehumanization of the victims by the perpetrators, who are usually new states or new regimes attempting to impose conformity to a new ideology and its model of society.[11]

FEATURES OF GENOCIDE IN AFGHANISTAN

The Afghans are among the latest victims of genocide by a superpower. Large numbers of Afghans were killed to suppress resistance to the army of the Soviet Union, which wished to vindicate its client regime and realize its goal in Afghanistan. Thus, the mass killing was political.

Incidents of the mass killing of noncombatant civilians were observed in the summer of 1980, when the mujahideen frustrated the invaders in their program of speedy conquest. Three considerations prompted the invading army to resort to indiscriminate mass killing outside battle zones. Unable to locate the elusive mujahideen, the wrath of the invading army fell on civilians as well, punishing them for their support of the mujahideen. The mujahideen had to be detached from the people. As guerrilla fighters, they could not be a viable force without the support of local populations. Hence, the Soviets felt it necessary to suppress defenseless civilians by killing them indiscriminately, by compelling them to flee abroad, and by destroying their crops and means of irrigation, the basis of their livelihood.[12] The dropping of booby traps from the air, the planting of mines, and the use of chemical substances, though not on a wide scale, were also meant to serve the same purpose. Also, since the Soviets did not increase the number of their troops above around 120,000 at any one time, they undertook military operations in an effort to ensure speedy submission: hence the wide use of aerial weapons, in particular helicopter gunships or the kind of inaccurate weapons that cannot discriminate between combatants and noncombatants. However, although the total number of the victims of genocide was high, it was not high in each separate incident.

A common feature of the Soviet program of total war was retributive mass killing, which was their means of repaying tough resistance. For example, in revenge for the killing by the mujahideen of three Russian soldiers, the commander brother of the fallen captain led his commando unit into the city of Tashqurghan in April 1982 and razed the city, killing at least two hundred of its defenseless civilians.[13] A third consideration in the mass killing was the necessity of silencing the mujahideen before the Afghan issue attracted too much international support. On the one hand, the authorities prevented the entry into Afghanistan of foreign mass media personnel; on the other, they branded the freedom fighters as "bandits" and "robbers," claiming that they "had sold their body and soul to the American dollars, the Pakistani rupees, and the British pounds." Soldiers of the invading army branded the mujahideen as *dushman* (enemy) as well as *basmachi*s (anti-Russian Muslim freedom fighters of Bukhara). This branding was intended to justify the extermination of the mujahideen because as "robbers" they were the disturbers of peace and social order. Another aspect of the genocide was the killing of civilians while praying in mosques, performing wedding or funeral ceremonies, forming sizable groups for any civil purpose, or engaging in the customs and conventions that constitute the Afghan social fabric. It would appear strange to think that the Soviets were unable to comprehend that these were peaceful and civic gatherings. The frequency of such killing made the Afghans believe that the Russians were barbarians (*wahshi*). The acts of genocide were the work of the Soviets, and as guides or collaborators the Parchamis as well as some Khalqis played the role of accomplices.

Because Afghanistan has long been a crossroads, famous conquerors such as Alexander the Great, Genghis Khan, Timur Lane, Babur, Nadir Shah Afshar, and the British have invaded it, but the Soviet invaders have surpassed all in the systematic killing of its people and the destruction of their land. They did so at a time when nations had never been so loud in support of peace, and never so loud in opposition to war. Among the governments of the world, the Soviet government was the loudest in all this, as well as in its trumpeting of the rights of the toiling people, an instance of truly Orwellian doublespeak. It is thus fitting to cite a few historical facts about the Russians to convey a view of their national culture.

RUSSIA AT A GLANCE

The Russians are latecomers to the fold of civilization. Until the late tenth century they worshiped Mother Earth, but their principal deity was Perun, god of thunder and lightning. The Slavs lived in southern Russia in what is now the Ukraine with its capital city, Kiev, whose Grand Prince Vladmir decided in 988, for reasons both pragmatic and spiritual, to impose the Orthodox form of Christianity on his subjects. According to one chronicle, "He directed that the idols should be overthrown and that some should be cut to pieces and others burned with fire. He thus ordered that Perun should be bound to a horse's tail and dragged . . . to the river. He appointed twelve men to beat the idols with sticks." Vladmir accepted Christianity from the Greek Orthodox empire of Byzantium, not Rome. No split had yet occurred between the two branches of the church, the Latin West and the Greek East. Only much later would it become apparent what a fateful choice Vladmir had made, one partly responsible for cutting Russia off from the dynamics of Western Christendom, in particular from the great Renaissance movement of artistic and intellectual activity. Besides, the Christianity introduced in Russia was a religion of forgiveness, not of tolerance, at least not of other religions. Orthodox Christianity taught Russia that it held the "one truth," for truth, like God, could only be one. The Renaissance of Western Europe eroded a similar doctrine held by the Roman Catholic church, but nothing of the sort took place in Russia.

Russia's political organization, in addition to being of recent origin, was not organized by the Russians themselves but by Scandinavians, who, in the middle of the ninth century, were invited to rule the major Russian city of the north, Novgorod. The very notion of a "Russian state" appeared only in the fifteenth or sixteenth century. The Scandinavian-Slav rule revolved around the combination of war and commerce that was the hallmark of the first few centuries of Russia's history. In the centuries that followed, Russia failed to create a society where order resulted from the self-governing behavior of its own citizens. Russia's rulers were absolute monarchs, particularly after 1547 when Ivan the Terrible was crowned tsar. Ivan's new position corresponded with a belief that Moscow, after the fall of Constantinople to the Ottomans in 1543, was the Third Rome and the last. This belief enabled the tsar to make himself still more absolute by concentrating religious and secular power. In Russia only a few hundred aristocratic families (the boyars), reputedly of foreign origin, dominated the rest of the people, with no middle class in between. Before the advent of the Scandinavians, the Russians were divided into freemen and slaves; After the Scandinavians arrived, the slaves remained as the dregs of society. Slaves were originally prisoners of war; later anyone could become so by birth or voluntary agreement. Warfare was the most important form of commerce, and the principal product was slaves.

The tsar ruled in absolute fashion with the help of his secret police, organized as early as 1565. This period followed the Mongol Yoke, an interim of about two and a half centuries (1240–1480) in which the Golden Horde Mongols mastered Russia after they had ended its flourishing period that had begun after its baptism. Russia's pyramidal society was reformed for the first time in 1861, when about forty million serfs were legally freed from bondage by an edict of the tsar following Russia's defeat in the Crimean War in 1854. The serfs were neither efficient tillers of land nor efficient soldiers in battle. Why should they work hard and die for others? More significant was the reform when the tsar, after Russia's defeat by Japan in 1904–5, introduced a parliamentary democracy that lasted until 1917. In February 1917 the tsar abdicated because of the insurmountable pressures generated by Russia's inability to cope with the problems resulting from her participation in World War I; the liberal government that then assumed power was ousted in October 1917 by the Bolsheviks.[14]

In the period before the end of tsardom, Russia had excelled in cultural, not political, achievements; under the Bolsheviks, it was set on the path toward communism, a new experiment in history. But the idea behind the society's reorganization was old. The communist idea was monolithic (as opposed to pluralist): it emphasized the validity of only one truth, that is, communism. The idea was the same as that of Orthodox Christianity, which Vladmir had chosen for Russia over nine hundred years earlier. However, whereas Russian Orthodox Christianity was a religion of forgiveness, not of tolerance, communism was a creed neither of forgiveness nor of tolerance. Besides, not only the groups ordering the society but every individual in it had to believe in the truth and act on it. The Soviet state, which was the most totalitarian state ever devised, was assigned the task of translating the truth into reality. To achieve this end, this totalitarian state applied all the persuasive and coercive means that it could muster. Among the means was the secret police (first Cheka and later the KGB), which soon became virtually omnipotent and ubiquitous. On the road to the unapproachable goal, it committed many crimes, among which was the genocide of the 1930s; no other state in history has ever perpetrated violence against its own people on such a scale. It also tried to implant abroad by deceit and violence the "truth" of communism, of which Afghanistan is the most recent example.

PROBLEMS RELATING TO GENOCIDE IN AFGHANISTAN

For reasons already stated, it is impossible to give a complete account of the Soviet army's mass killing in Afghanistan. Here I will describe only the tip of the iceberg. Also, I cannot pretend that my descriptions are precise or thorough, because the witnesses whom I interviewed in the course of my inquiry often either had no direct access to the event in question or did not know the whole story in question. In the present case, I have, where possible, compared the observations of various witnesses and other sources to try to arrive at a reasonably accurate account of the events in question. Nonetheless, figures must be understood to be approximate, unless stated otherwise. Despite these qualifications, the information here does indicate the dimensions of the genocide undertaken by the Soviets.

The period under study has not been covered in a substantial way by non-Afghan writers, with the exception of Edward Girardet, a correspondent for the *Christian Science Monitor* who visited certain areas from 1979 to 1982.[15] The most thorough records are the result of joint research by Jerry Laber and Barnet Rubin, but they start with events mainly in 1984. Their works, particularly *A Report from Helsinki Watch* and *A Nation Is Dying,* are monuments of Soviet brutality in Afghanistan. The Russians in particular should read them to know what kind of people their leaders and the military actually are. I have used relevant sections of the final report of the International Afghanistan Hearing. The hearing, held in Oslo in March 1983, is based on the accounts of Afghan witnesses and non-Afghan experts.

Indiscriminate mass killing of the civilians by the Soviet soldiers dates from the invasion, although, as already noted, until the February uprising the Soviets did not initiate military operations. Thereafter they undertook major operations, and in none did they confine themselves to battles with the combatants. Indeed, the Soviet soldiers failed throughout to conduct themselves with proper discipline, showing themselves to be ill trained and unconcerned with observing the laws of war. Since hostilities invoke the instinct to kill, whether for an ulterior motive or in self-defense, combatants often do not confine themselves only to military targets, as recommended by the international conventions agreed to by member countries of the United Nations. But to kill civilians indiscriminately, deliberately, and as a matter of policy; to destroy their sources of livelihood; to force them to flee abroad; to do so without provocation on the part of the civilians, all in an effort to punish them for their support of combatant compatriots in conditions under which the state of war does not officially exist—this constitutes a crime, a crime defined at Nürnberg as "devastation not justified by military necessity."[16] Wars have laws, and as one commentator has put it, the laws of war have as their objective that "the ravages of war should be mitigated as far as possible by prohibiting needless cruelties, and other acts that spread death and destruction and are not reasonably related to the conduct of hostilities."[17] The Soviet soldiers did not observe such laws. On the contrary, they carried on the undeclared war of their rulers in Afghanistan, indiscriminately killing civilians, individually and in groups, and devastating their land for military and nonmilitary reasons alike, visiting on them a terrible variety of unmitigated cruelties.

EARLY INSTANCES OF GENOCIDE

Major operations were underway in the countryside in early June 1980, although they had started much earlier. In late May 1980, during an operation in Ghazni Province, at least thirty villagers were massacred. Because of a battle between the mujahideen and the invading army, these villagers had taken refuge in a subterranean canal (*karez*) in Waghiz near Shilgir. The Soviet army poisoned them with chemical agents of an unknown sort. New operations targeted the districts around Kabul. During the first week of June 1980 heavy guns and mortars were fired from the Begram military base toward villages in Kohdaman, Gul Dara, and Farza valleys. Later, targets as far away as the valleys of Nijrao and Ghorband were shelled from the same base. At the same time, the first-mentioned valleys also became the targets of bombings, followed by operations in which ground forces destroyed houses and orchards and killed "many people." The operations had been undertaken without warning or provocation. During the first two weeks of July 1980, from fifty to sixty villages in districts around Kabul were either wholly or partially destroyed. On 10 July 1980, as a result of a clash between the mujahideen and the invading force in Qarabagh near Kabul, the Soviets killed civilians in such numbers that their bodies lay strewn about the area for days. The remaining inhabitants started to leave for Kabul, but the authorities prevented them from doing so.

During the last week of July 1980 helicopter gunships fired rockets into the town of Islamabad and the villages of Sabrabad, Shamaram, and the small valley of Salao in the upper part of the Alishang Valley in Laghman Province, destroying them either wholly or partly. They were bombed for being considered the hideouts of mujahideen. The massacre in Turani (Nurani?) village and the city of Baghlan in late July 1980 was a case of revenge. A group of Soviet soldiers in tanks was ambushed by the mujahideen after they had searched houses in Turani village close to Baghlan on 28 July 1980. The next day the invading army bombarded the village and, entering the city, killed anyone who happened to be there. About fifty people were killed, and their bodies could be seen scattered about.

In October 1980 Soviet soldiers brought a bigger calamity on the people of Baghlan. Having lost men in fighting with the mujahideen in parts of the provinces of Baghlan and Qunduz, the Soviets turned on the people of the city of Baghlan in revenge. First they searched houses and denuded them of valuables. Then they brought to one place those people whom they had rounded up in the course of the house searches. Having separated out the party members, they shot the rest, dumping their bodies in pits dug with their machines. Some claimed that five hundred people were killed, but this seems an exaggeration. This deliberate massacre was reminiscent of the Keralay tragedy in Kunar Province in 1979 and of the killings in Merv in Turkmenistan 120 years earlier. Following the counsel of a Soviet adviser, the Khalqi governor of Kunar Province massacred more than 620 people of the town of Keralay to intimidate the rest to submit. In Merv the Russians had massacred more than six hundred Turkomen with a view to intimidating the recalcitrants to desist from opposition.

In late July 1980 the Soviets bombarded the Dai Mierdad district in the province of Ghazni so much that the destruction of human and animal lives and property was said to be beyond calculation. Many houses and villages were destroyed, and the survivors found it difficult to dispose of the dead bodies, which lay unburied for days. At about the same time, as many as five hundred people were killed in bombardments in a few villages (names unknown) close to Maidan; the number may be inflated. But at this time helicopter gunships were seen flying almost every minute over the city of Kabul, most of them heading toward the west, where casualties during the two weeks of July and August were said to be beyond calculation. My diary for 3 July 1980 reads in part: "In this way the defenseless, tyrannized people, women, the old, and children alike, fell like leaves in the autumn in their own homes, mosques, hamlets, and villages. The operations were so ruthless that an Afghan regiment in Maidan clashed with the Russians until the regiment was recalled to Kabul."

As a result of these operations, the regime considered Kabul to be safe. It was an illusion. Within the first week of August the city was besieged. The mujahideen wrested Qal'a-e-Qazi, a huge village in the western suburbs of Kabul, from the regime's control and destroyed the military post in the midst of the town of Dasht-e-Barchi. Likewise, the mujahideen destroyed the ancestral house of Karmal along with the houses and property of other party members in Shewaki and Kamari in the eastern suburbs. They also wrested the surrounding villages from the regime's control. On 7 August the villages were bombed and many people killed. The survivors took refuge in Kabul.

In mid-August guns were fired from Mehtarlam, the provincial capital of Laghman, toward villages believed to be hideouts of mujahideen. By now this had become a standard way of dealing with the situation. On 19 August 1980, after tanks were landed by helicopters on some hills in the valley of Ali Shang, villages nearby were shelled. Not much later the trees of Karinj, a hilly area close to the Alishang town from where the mujahideen had fired on the Soviets, were burned with some chemical substances. On 6 September 1980 the mujahideen destroyed two tanks and a number of other vehicles after they had been separated from the convoy and headed toward the village of Shakarman in the Ali Shang valley of Laghman. In revenge, the following night scores of villages, including Deva, Ganjawan, and the town of Maskura, were shelled and a number of people killed or injured. A greater calamity befell the city of Herat when, on 16 August 1980, a part of the city was shelled. Until then, except for the governor's headquarters the rest of the city was out of the regime's control. It was said that three thousand people were killed in the attack. This was the most grievous attack on Herat since the one in March 1979, when approximately 25,000 persons were killed. During the present attack Soviet soldiers looted shops, particularly those selling the gold and silver products for which Herat is famous. The Soviet army then withdrew to its bases in Shindand.

The massacre that the invading army committed in Kandahar at almost the same time as that in Herat was no less atrocious. Guided by Parchamis, Soviet armored units searched houses in villages far from and close to the city of Kandahar. In places clashes occurred with losses to both sides, including the destruction of many tanks. This was more than the Russians could digest, and in revenge they visited a pogrom on the people of the city of Kandahar. This incident began when the invading army, stationing their tanks and other vehicles on high mounds, shelled for hours many villages in the distant Nagahan district. Confident that the opposition had been suppressed, they descended on the villages and orchards to loot goods and pick up fruit. The mujahideen, who had been in their hideouts, fell on them, killing many on the spot and also those fleeing. The remainder of the Soviet soldiers fled to the city, where they, in company with the Soviet force stationed near it, killed many people, including women and children, in revenge for those they had lost in Nagahan. The massacre disturbed party leaders, including Majid Sarbiland (chief of the Kandahar zone), Aslam Watanjar, and Saleh Mohammad Zeray, who were there at the time. They asked the Soviet commander to dissuade the soldiers from committing excesses. The commander replied, in effect, "You do your business, and we will do our business." Zeray and Sarbiland were from Kandahar, and their failure to save the people of their province from their own comrades lowered their standing still further, even among their own relatives; their predicament resembled that of the governor Sher Ali Khan a century earlier, when he, in opposition to his family and his people, served the interests of the British in opposition to the interests of the people of Kandahar.

In mid-October 1980 an armored unit was dispatched to Laghman, where the mujahideen increased their activity in the pleasant weather of the winter. Except for an encounter in the lower part of the valley in Chardihi, no opposition was offered. But near Shamangal in the upper part of Alishang Valley three mujahideen resisted before they were caught. One was doused with gasoline and set afire. The Soviet soldiers, concluding that all people of the area were *dushman* (enemy), began to kill the villagers along both banks of the river. In the course of house searches for weapons and draft dodgers, they also seized valuables. The draft dodgers had already fled to the mountains. The number of casualties was said to be between 350 and 1,200. For days dead bodies lay about the region, and the survivors were unable to cope with the terrible burial problems. The Kaftarmala massacre close to the village of Deva was swift as well as surprising. A number of nomads, arriving at the area in a truck for the purpose of spending the winter, were welcomed by their relatives and locals. All together they formed a big gathering. Soon helicopter gunships were hovering over them; assuming that the nomads were enemies, the Soviets fired into the group, killing eight and wounding scores of others.

MASS KILLINGS IN CIVIC GATHERINGS AND THE KIDNAPPING OF WOMEN

The Soviets considered any gathering of Afghans, no matter for what purpose, potentially hostile. Gatherings of the people, whether for wedding or funeral services or for prayer in mosques, were common features of the Afghan society. Strong social bonds, characteristic of the society, required such functions, which were attended by hundreds of people, whether or not invited. But such gatherings were now fraught with danger. The Russians, brought up in a different social environment, were ignorant of the social conventions or simply intended to terrorize the Afghans. At any rate, helicopter gunships would fire rockets on men, women, and children in groups. They did this so frequently all over the country that it is impossible to describe all of the events. Perhaps the biggest gathering they hit was in the Ganjabad village of the Bala Buluk district of Farah Province. In mid-September 1980 hundreds of villagers were convivially celebrating wedding ceremonies in the village. Suddenly they were hit with rockets fired from a group of helicopter gunships. About 150 were killed and scores of others wounded, some of whom were brought to Kabul for treatment. In August 1981, as a result of a two-hour attack by four helicopter gunships on a wedding party in the village of Jalrez in the upper part of the Maidan Valley, 30 people were killed and 75 wounded.[18]

While military operations in the country were going on, women were abducted. While flying in the country in search of mujahideen, helicopters would land in fields where women were spotted. While Afghan women do mainly domestic chores, they also work in fields assisting their husbands or performing tasks by themselves. The women were now exposed to the Russians, who kidnapped them with helicopters. By

November 1980 a number of such incidents had taken place in various parts of the country, including Laghman and Kama.

In the city of Kabul, too, the Russians kidnapped women, taking them away in tanks and other vehicles, especially after dark. Such incidents happened mainly in the areas of Darul Aman and Khair Khana, near the Soviet garrisons. At times such acts were committed even during the day. KhAD agents also did the same. Small groups of them would pick up young women in the streets, apparently to question them but in reality to satisfy their lust: in the name of security, they had the power to commit excesses. Likewise, in the name of security the security men were involved in creating insecurity, looting shops and stores and breaking into houses while patrolling during the curfew hours at night.

The kidnapping of women disturbed families with young daughters. The incidents were sporadic and infrequent, since the Soviet officers censored the suspected soldiers; nevertheless, the Afghans were still alarmed. In fact, all families with young sons and daughters were alarmed. The former were, as already noted, hunted for military service, and the latter could be stained for life. Of the former, many fled abroad, while the latter became a painful problem for their families. Kabul's inhabitants became conspicuous for a high proportion of children, the elderly, and women. At stake now was their honor, about which the Afghans are sensitive.

KILLING ALONG THE ROADS

One result of the military operations was an increase in the number of military posts, mainly in provincial capitals, their surrounding districts, and along the main roads, which the Soviets manned. For example, by December 1980 about forty posts had been set up along the main Kabul–Jalalabad road. The Kabul–Kandahar road was left unguarded, while the road passing through Salang was guarded very tightly. Obviously, this differential protection demonstrated the Soviet intention to pacify the land by establishing control over the main arteries and also by undertaking military operations. Hoping to reduce the number of attacks on the posts, the Soviets abandoned, although not completely, their practice of unprovoked shelling of the inhabited areas. But if the mujahideen fired at either the military posts or Soviet troops elsewhere, the invading forces adopted scorched-earth tactics. Tanks and helicopter gunships would furiously shell targets in regions from which shots had been fired. Often other areas were also shelled at random. For example, on or about 18 December 1980 a group of mujahideen somewhere near Alishang town in Laghman destroyed a Soviet tank with an officer in it. In retaliation the town of Alishang, the nearby village of Barzay, and the town of Islamabad were bombed. In Barzay alone sixteen persons perished.

The assailants did not bother about who and how many would be killed by their rocket attacks. To deal with the elusive mujahideen, the Soviets intended to frighten the civilians, who would then pressure the mujahideen not to attack the invaders. If the mujahideen disregarded the people's requests, they would be estranged from them. If they accepted their request, the regime would increase the posts, which, along with other measures, would lead to the pacification of the country. On requests from the locals the mujahideen often desisted from attacking the invaders, but the Soviets still massacred civilians. Apparently, their mission was to loot and kill in order to establish the regime.

The Soviet strategy made the mujahideen cautious, but it was impossible for them to remain spectators. This would have been the end of their mission. Encounters were still common, and retaliations, whether by the Russians or the regime's forces, became widespread. The mobile mujahideen could anticipate retaliation and escape. It is impossible to give even an estimate of the number of civilians killed in the clashes, which were sporadic and irregular. The frequency of notes on the subject in my diary is depressing to read.

As a by-product of the policy of guarding the main roads, a disaster of a different kind befell the people. Of the main roads, the roads of Kabul–Jalalabad, Kabul–Gardez (via Logar), and Kabul–Hairatan (via Salang) were especially important, since the first two lead to Pakistan and the latter to the Soviet Union. Among other things, control over the first two meant some control over the movements of the mujahideen as well as the materiel and weapons they brought from Pakistan; control over the last meant the maintenance of undisturbed transportation between Kabul and the Soviet border. As already noted, along the Kabul–Jalalabad road about forty military posts had been manned by the Soviets. To control the roads, the Soviets had to ensure that the districts through which they passed were clear of mujahideen. The two roads leading to Salang and Gardez passed through densely populated districts. It was hazardous to set up military posts along these roads like those along the Kabul–Jalalabad road. Instead, the Soviets chose either to bomb villages close to the roads or shell them by guns and submachine guns from tanks stationed on mounds. The bombing of these villages was comparable to the bombing of the districts around cities, particularly Kabul. The attacks on Logar, which suffered more than any other district, will be described in the next chapter. An unknown number of men, women, and children either perished or moved out of their homes because they lived near roads, the outward symbol of civilization.

This was, however, not the end of the plight of the inhabitants of the areas. Even before the major operations had begun, the plan for making the main roads safe was on the agenda. For some time in July 1980 a major military force destroyed houses, orchards, and other constructions as well as trees along both sides of the Logar road. Helicopter gunships hovered over the ground force. Whatever lay within about 150 meters on both flanks of the road was scheduled to be destroyed. The idea was to make the military convoys on the roads safe from rocket attacks by the mujahideen, who often concealed themselves in nearby villages. How precisely the order was carried out is difficult to determine. The setting up of permanent posts along the Logar road was risky; instead, expeditions were undertaken frequently. The destruction must have been tremendous, since in some places the road passed close to main villages. In mid-December groups of tanks were stationed here and there along the road, and the nearby villages were searched. The plight of the people affected by this act can be guessed from the reaction of an old man who lost an apple tree near his home in Mohammad Agha. After his pleas with the regime men failed to be effective, the old man leaned on a wall, looked to the heavens, and cried, "Oh God, where are you? Do you not see?" For a devout old Muslim to utter such words, he must have been at the height of despair. But he was lucky to have lost only his tree, not his life. Many others in his district lost their lives. On one day alone, 9 October 1980, the Russians killed forty pedestrians along the Logar road in an effort to make the road safe for their convoys.

Similar measures were taken to secure the road going through Shamali. The bazaars of Qarabagh and Saray Khoja through which the road passed were burned, and houses and villages near the road were destroyed. Huge trees on both sides of the road, which had pleasantly distinguished it from those in the rest of the country, were felled. But the manning of roads by groups of Russian soldiers created new sorts of problems that were staggering to the Afghans.

The incidents happened along the Salang and Jalalabad roads, which were, unlike all other roads, manned by Soviet soldiers. Instead of maintaining the security of the road for which they had been commissioned, the Russians began looting passengers and even killing them. For a brief time they looted consignments from trucks passing along these two roads, the busiest in the country; they would then sell the stolen goods, as well as a wide variety of state goods in their possession, to other drivers at low prices at gunpoint. They would also force the drivers to sell them marijuana (*chars*). Most drivers provided the soldiers with the drug with a view to making them addicts. Judging from the frequency of exchange, the number of the addicts must have been considerable. But at times this trade led to violence. A group of Soviet soldiers had been taking marijuana somewhere near the Wood Factory in Samarkhel to the east of Jalalabad. In August 1980 a soldier intended to enter a house near the factory to steal either marijuana or money. When stopped at the door, he suspected a trap and began firing at random at the inhabitants. All but one member of the family died in the initial assault, and the sole survivor died later in the hospital. It was said that to hush up the story the authorities arranged to do away with him. Party activists gave out that the tragedy was the work of the "rebels."

More serious were the incidents when Soviet soldiers fired at passenger buses without provocation. Apparently they were killing human beings for the fun of it or for revenge on innocent passengers for the men they might have lost elsewhere. Such tragedies were many. In December 1980 eleven persons died and many others wounded in an attack along the Jalalabad road; drivers refused to drive on the road for two days thereafter. Earlier (8 November 1980) two bus drivers close to the Salang Tunnel were killed for no apparent reason. Drivers protested to the Ministry of the Interior and refused to drive for days. In Ounduz, Soviet soldiers walked across the flat rooftops of the houses at night and fired through the openings at the people inside for no apparent reason. The common Afghans called the Russians barbarians (*wahshi*).

Despite all the killings, the Soviets failed to establish control over the roads. Frequently the roads leading to Kabul were closed. On such occasions the city was deprived of the essentials of life, food and fuel. Along these as well as along other roads, armed mujahideen also checked transport vehicles. In certain places they operated within sight of the Soviets without being molested. Close to Kabul beyond Khair Khana the mujahideen checked transport vehicles. The Soviets and the mujahideen had accepted a modus vivendi.

It is now time to survey the Soviet operations in areas visited by foreigners during the period covered by this work. Pal Hougen, chair of the Norwegian Committee for Afghanistan, states that three of his fellow countrymen who had visited Afghanistan in the summer of 1980 "brought home pictorial documentation of bombarded farms, destroyed villages and the destruction of Kamdesh, the central town in Nuristan. Much of what I had heard and read was not to be believed, even [though they] were reliable persons and journalists." He then made two trips himself in the summer of 1981 and 1982, the first to the upper part of the Kunar Valley, and the second to the town of Bashgul in the same valley.

> During my two visits, I had to admit that the reports were true. I did not only see ruined dwellings, observe terror bombing myself, but I found a society where all ordinary functions were disturbed, even the basic ones: the production of food, the supplies from outside of salt, sugar and tea—other items of trade as I mentioned. The infrastructure in this society was broken down, not [torn] into pieces, for no single piece of the former modest modernization was [left] intact, there was no trade, no school, no medical care, the water supplies were disturbed, the irrigation system severely harmed.[19]

Hougen states that the people of Bashgul "were still living in the mountains, unable to go back to their farm and cultivate their soil. . . . It was dangerous for men and cattle to stroll around the passes, and passes as well as the forests had every day and every week to be systematically examined for small booby-traps-butterflies [small antipersonnel bombs shaped somewhat like butterflies]." If these people returned to their homes, they were bombed without provocation. Hougen writes, "Two days after, when part of the population had returned, the town was attacked from the air and set on fire. The result was that the entire population of the town and of the neighboring districts emigrated to Pakistan, a total of 3,000 people."[20]

Hougen describes a fellow Norwegian's experience in Kandahar Province in 1981: "In the autumn [of] that year, he stayed in the outskirts of Kandahar where he daily experienced air attacks, bombing and mining of civilian dwellings." The situation in the province of Paktia was no better. Hougen comments on the experience of a nurse who stayed in a village in Paktia for three weeks in September 1982: "She reported about air attacks a year earlier which had ruined 50 percent of the houses, how the villages on the plains had been attacked by tanks— in units with 200 and 400 tanks—and the houses had been destroyed. According to her accounts, the attacks were entirely directed against the civilian population."[21] The people of the Jaghori district of the Ghazni province had dug bunkers to save themselves from the hazards of bom-

bardment. According to Tone A. Odegaard and Jame Reitan, two Norwegian women who stayed with them for a week in September 1982:

> They [the Hazara inhabitants of the Jaghori district] are accustomed to air
> attacks and every family had their own shelters—one for each person—dug
> as small holes outside the house, as they [Vietnamese] did it in Vietnam. All
> children were instructed how to behave when the next attack would come
> and how they should escape for the mountains after [the] attack. There can
> be no doubt that the air attacks were aimed at the civilian population and
> took place regularly.[22]

One of the most striking descriptions comes from Nicolas Danziger,
a British lecturer in art history and one of the authors of *A Report from
Helsinki Watch*. In describing "this image of Hiroshima in Herat," Danziger writes:

> We went along the asphalt road from Iran to Herat. The desert on the Iranian
> side was absolutely covered in track marks, the hooves of horses, of camels,
> footmarks, bicycle marks,—you name it. By the time it was about nine
> o'clock in the morning, there were people in droves, a man with a camel; he
> had lost all his family, and all his possessions were on top of the camel. There
> were some young boys who had been orphaned. Then there were some nu-
> merous donkeys with women riding on them with their husbands next to
> them. All of these people were on their way to Iran. I stayed in a village where
> they claimed there had been 5,000 inhabitants. There remained one building
> intact in the whole village. I did not see more than ten inhabitants there. To
> destroy this place the bombers came from Russia. And there were craters
> everywhere, even where there were no buildings, so there was no pretense
> about, "we are trying to hit the mujahideen." It was a complete blitz. All the
> way from there on into Herat there was no one living there, absolutely no
> one. The town that I stayed in, Hauz Karbas, looks like Hiroshima. And there
> had been tremendous amounts of vineyards there, and they were just reduced
> to gray dust. It really sums up everything that exists in Afghanistan to-day.[23]

CHAPTER FOURTEEN

Genocide in Districts Around Kabul

As already noted, the immediate purpose of the invading army was to enable the regime to establish control over cities and the main roads. The countryside was to be pacified afterward. The mujahideen had to be made incapable of disturbing the cities, especially Kabul. The regime then had to extend control over the immediate surrounding districts as well: hence the intensification of operations there and the killing of civilians inside their homes and villages. This chapter highlights the massacres that resulted from the operations in districts around Kabul.

For Kabul, Logar and Shamali (districts south and north of Kabul, respectively) are important strategic regions. From Logar the mujahideen can infiltrate the city more easily. Through Logar, Kabul is connected to Paktia, the frontier region bordering Pakistan. The shortest route from Kabul to the border passes through Logar (in Dobandi), Zazay, and Tiramangal (in Kurram) beyond the Durand Line. Of all the major conduits, Logar was the most important one for weapons and logistics as well as combatants for almost the whole country, as Pakistan was the most important conduit for weapons for the whole of Afghanistan. Also, Afghans from many other areas, including those from the central and northern regions, could flee to Pakistan through Logar. Thus, it was primarily through Logar that the Peshawar-based organizations kept in touch with mujahideen throughout most of Afghanistan. It was also through Logar that Kabul received its main supplies of fuel from Paktia. But while Shamali enjoys an abundance of water for agricultural purposes, Logar is not as fortunate, although it has both open water canals and underground canals (*karez*). Both regions are among the most fertile in the country, and their inhabitants live mainly in relatively large villages with attached mud houses.

MASSACRE IN LOGAR

Following the invasion, the mujahideen expelled party members and government officials from Logar and extended control over the road passing through it. Only Pul-e-Alam, the headquarters of the province, remained in the government's hands. When the Soviets undertook their first military operation there is unknown. Units of their army had clashed with the mujahideen a number of times, and civilians had been among the victims. After the mujahideen defeated a unit of the invading army along the Logar road on 2 October 1980, the Soviets responded strongly. My diary entry for 10 October 1980 reads, "The recent operations of the Russians in the region were barbarous. On 5 October a Russian armored unit on the way to Logar killed or wounded anyone who happened to be on the road or within range of it from Beni Hissar up to Pul-e-Alam"—that is, from the southern outskirt of the city to the provincial capital, a distance of eighty-six kilometers. After the incident a delegation of elders from Logar raised the matter in Kabul with two members of the politburo, Saleh Mohammad Zeray and Nur Ahmad Nur. An elder of the delegation from the Surkhab Valley of Logar said to them, "Since you are no longer able to govern, you should either quit or join us so that together we can expel the Russians from our fatherland." It might seem incredible that anyone would dare make such a bold statement in a police regime whose KhAD agents could not tolerate outspoken critics; nevertheless, on such occasions Afghan elders become bolder than usual. In another instance, an elderly man from Logar, Haji Sharif, had been imprisoned in Pul-e-Charkhi because one of his sons was a successful commander. The government offered to release him if he dissuaded his son from opposing the government, but Haji Sharif replied, "While you have a superpower behind you, and the mujahideen have no such supporter, let my son be with them." In any case, the delegation failed in its purpose. Its mission was tactical, a reflection of the view among the Islamic Revolutionary Movement commanders that while carrying on the jehad they intended to maintain at least the façade of a relationship with the government.[1]

After the meeting, greater calamities befell not only the people of Logar but the people in most parts of the country. In November Karmal returned to Kabul from his first state visit to Moscow; thereafter, the government adopted a tougher stand. In late November, Karmal announced that the government had planned to hold military exercises in the provinces of Kabul, Parwan, and Ningrahar. These "military exercises" were in fact major military operations intended to suppress the resistance before Ronald Reagan took office as president of the United States on 20 January 1981 so that his rumored assistance in weapons to the mujahideen could not materialize. The winter season favored the well-protected mechanized army units over the poorly supplied mujahideen. As already noted, the KGB had predicted that "the spring and summer of 1981 will be decisive for the final and complete defeat of the forces of the counterrevolutionaries." The operations that the Soviets undertook in Logar afterward were the biggest and widest in the area.

A typical pattern of military operations developed. A slow-flying reconnaissance plane would precede the operations. Afterwards, helicopter gunships would fire rockets into certain places and villages where the mujahideen were suspected to be. Sometimes as many as thirty helicopter gunships would bombard targets. Targets would also be hit by rocket launchers mounted on tanks. Then units of tanks would surround a village or a group of villages. During major operations armored units would appear in Logar from four directions: from Kabul, from Gardez (provincial capital of Paktia), from the Maidan area in the west, and from Pul-i-Alam, the only place in the province under the government's control. After an area was thus encircled and believed cleared of the defenders, armed groups of the invading army, accompanied by KhAD guides, would descend on it and search houses for weapons, draft dodgers, and persons suspected as mujahideen or antiregime activists. Soon, though, the intruders exerted themselves more in looting valuables and Western and Japanese gadgets than they did in performing their assigned job. With nightfall they would assemble in a distant desert or return to their headquarters.

In military operations the civilians were the main victims, although the Russians also lost many men. The casualties of the mujahideen were the least in number. In spite of the severity of the operations the invading army and their Afghan henchmen failed to suppress the resistance. However, they did succeed in keeping the road from Kabul to Gardez open at least temporarily, but they had to guard it with units of tanks stationed along the way for the 125 kilometers to Kabul. They also vandalized Logar and denuded a considerable area of it. My diary entry for 21 November reads: "The actual number of the casualties is unknown. It is said that they were beyond calculation. In many places dead bodies lay here and there. No one dared to bury them. Dogs have consumed many. They have decomposed and have an offensive odor. Some houses have been destroyed while others are closed because of the destruction of their inhabitants." The people were unable to cope with the enormous problems relating to casualties, and many left their homes to take refuge in Pakistan.

For a long time no major operation was reported to have taken place in Logar, although sporadic bombing was routine. On 7 May 1981 a caravan of the invaders, as a result of encounters with the mujahideen in Mohammad Agha and Mosayee, lost about thirty tanks and a large number of Parchamis as well as KhAD agents. Usually the mujahideen, particularly in the Mohammad Agha district, would destroy around twenty tanks of a convoy on the Logar road. It is estimated that on this road alone the invaders lost about one thousand tanks during the occupation. This front, particularly its Bini Sharafgan locality, was the toughest in the province. The invaders also lost men in large numbers after they ascended a mound where they were shelled simultaneously by the mujahideen and the outraged Afghan soldiers. The aftermath was terrible. My diary entry for 14 May 1981 reads: "Following the incident, when the Soviets assaulted many villages with their armored units they showed no mercy to any human being."

The massacre that the invaders committed in an underground irrigation canal came to be known in the West through an American anthropologist, Mike Barry, who visited the area in September 1982. Such canals are wide and deep enough to accommodate many people. In my diary I noted that an unknown number of people perished somewhere in a cave where they had taken refuge; informed by a proregime villager, Soviet soldiers burned petroleum products in its entrance. The "cave" was the underground irrigation canal Karez-e-Baba, which passes through the Padkhab-e-Shana village in Logar. Mike Barry writes:

> According to eyewitness reports, . . . villagers who fled spoke of soldiers wearing gas masks, pouring mysterious things into an underground irrigation canal where villagers including children were hiding. Our investigation showed that the soldiers had actually used gasoline, diesel fuel and an incendiary white powder, an evil-smelling [substance] designed to ensure that the gasoline would properly burn in a tunnel with little oxygen. After the 105

people including the little children were burned to death, the population in a panic decided to run away to Pakistan.[2]

In the second week of August 1981 the Soviets massacred people in the village of Dadokhel in Logar. This event happened when a unit of the Soviet army was forced to retreat after trying to enter the small village of Babus. In revenge for the loss of four drunken Soviet and Cuban officers who had separated from the main convoy in the region of Kulangar, the village of Dadokhel was razed by attacks from the air and ground; about forty-five villagers perished.[3] In the third week of October 1981 a Soviet army unit of about three hundred tanks and other vehicles again visited Logar, accompanied as usual by helicopter gunships. At this time the main road was under the control of the mujahideen, and the invading army had to go instead through the deserts of Babus and Kulangar, after they spread rumors that a huge force was about to visit Logar. The mujahid commanders, who at the time were more disunited than before, desisted from opposing the enemy. The army surrounded many villages where children, women, and old people had remained. The draft dodgers had escaped. The mujahid commanders complained to their leaders in Peshawar of the inadequacy of their weapons when pitted against the superior weapons of their adversaries. They demanded anti-aircraft weapons, but their leaders were unable to supply them at the time.

Before winter set in, when the well-protected units of the invading army had the upper hand, a delegation of about ninety elders of Logar visited Sulaiman Laweq, minister of tribal affairs, in Kabul to plead for the suspension of military operations. They told the minister, "Instead of being supplied with clothes, houses, and food, as promised, now the things in our possession are destroyed and our people are killed indiscriminately." The Khalqi government, when Laweq was a member, had promised to provide the people with clothes, food, and homes. But Laweq now told the elders, "You are to blame for your own misfortune: you support the rebels, you do not want to pay taxes, and you are unwilling to cooperate with the government." He told them further, "In defending our land against the United States of America, China, and Pakistan, we had to ask for Soviet military assistance. But," added the minister, "if you really want to live in peace, cooperate with us, expel the rebels from your region, and pay your taxes, for which you will be granted local autonomy."[4] The elders returned disappointed.

Earlier, a progovernment mulla had preached the same things to a gathering of the people of Logar whom the government had summoned.

When the mulla promised that the Soviet forces would withdraw if the people cooperated with the government, an elderly man answered, "Unless the Soviet forces are withdrawn, we would not be willing to do anything of the sort."[5] The Soviets were, of course, unwilling to withdraw, and in June 1982, in the course of an unprovoked and unopposed operation that lasted for two days, their forces massacred 240 people of the district of Baraki Barak. In addition, of the 900 people whom they took with them, some they killed in a camp in the Kulangar region; others they imprisoned, and still others they pressed into the army. The perpetrators were all Russians. Zahir Ghazi Alam, who along with others had in the course of the operation taken refuge in an underground canal, writes:

> This is written at a time when the dust of the bloody Soviet operation in the district of Baraki Barak is still unsettled. In every house there is wailing and weeping. In common graveyards new graves are dug, the dead are buried, and new flags are hoisted over the martyred. Barefoot and pale, mothers and sisters, men and women, are looking for their disappeared ones, hurrying through vineyards, streams, and fields. The Russians have perpetrated their most barbarous operation in the region. The eyes of the people of the world are closed, their ears deaf, and their tongues mute to this unprecedented crime of the Russians. Worse still is the fact that even in this third year of the war the Peshawar-based Islamic organizations are still astray from the path of jehad and distant from the Afghan spirit and values. They have let themselves be seized by the disease of disunity, personal interest, and ambition.[6]

The effect of these operations on Logar has been described by Borge Almqvist and Mike Barry, who visited the province in late summer and early fall 1982. The Swedish journalist Almqvist notes:

> I entered into a country where every village has been bombed at least once since the war started or fired at by Soviet land forces. Many villages are deserted, there are whole areas where the entire population have run away to the camps in Pakistan out of fear of being killed in further air bombardments. These areas are so-called helicopter territories. When you move in them and you hear a helicopter you have 60 seconds to go. These areas have turned into the age before stone age. Civilization has gone back. This is before man entered Afghanistan in the very old times.[7]

Barry's comments are even more sobering:

> In our trip to Logar province, . . . we crossed 12 villages including Dobandi, 8 of these villages, including Dobandi, were completely uninhabited. One further village we saw destroyed virtually before our eyes. We were told that we should visit a village called Altamor, and in the fog, we saw a great flash in the distance. . . . And that evening and early the next morning the first

wounded came into where we were from Altamor, telling us there is no more Altamor.[8]

As a result of these battles, the fertile Logar had become a place of ruins and graves, just as Herat had become after the conquest of Genghis Khan in the early thirteenth century. Almqvist continues:

> Everywhere in the Logar province the most common sight except for ruins are graves. [At] the first sight you see when you enter the village, huge grave-yards or a small one, and you can see which graves are new and which are [old, that is] before the war, because nowadays they [the people of Logar] have started like in the old days to put up flags like they did for holy men before, because the ones killed by the Russians are considered as holy people and according to Afghan Islamic belief they go to paradise if they were killed by the Karmal troops or the Russian troops.[9]

Again, in his words, "The Logar province in many areas looks like an archaeological site."[10]

Almqvist provides frightening evidence about the frequency of the bombing. In one passage he describes seeking a shelter in the company of villagers, all of them in great panic from the danger of an imminent bombing:

> We got to the village shelter which was a small grove of trees, the only shelter available for hundreds of people. After these bombardments within a week I saw two other bombardments. . . . Every morning the helicopters come from Kabul to the airbase and headquarters for the Soviet and Karmal troops in the Logar province, where they get the orders which village in the valley to bomb. That morning [when] they were bombing a village for thirty minutes, only 5 people died.[11]

In such a helpless situation people still lived, perhaps unable or unwilling to move out, hoping that the carnage would end. No one, however, was sure, and the fear of being killed in one's own home haunted the inhabitants. Almqvist writes, "In the villages in the Logar province where people [still] live, they live under a constant fear, if next morning will be the last, if they will wake up to the sound of helicopter[s] zooming in over the rooftops, heavy machine gun fire, rockets and bombs exploding in the village."[12]

Farms, too, were unsafe. Almqvist observed that "farmers working on in the fields were shot down by their helicopter gunships. They had no time to run away for shelter and guns, they were just gunned down unarmed." Here Almqvist refers to a particular incident that happened in the village of Baraki Rajan in Logar on 19 June 1982, before Almqvist arrived in the area. In that locality, after a brief encounter with a group of retreating mujahideen, the army of "internationalist solidarity" embarked on a spate of "burning and looting and killing." Looting was not an individual but a group act, common among the Russians in Logar. Almqvist writes, "I went to quite a few villages where people told me how the Russians had taken everything out of the houses, like radios, carpets, food, all sorts of household tools. These houses were completely empty."[13] Even individuals had been robbed. During the winter of 1982 I met a number of inmates in the prison each of whom had been looted simultaneously by a number of Russian soldiers in Logar. According to the victims, the soldiers acted as if they were competing with one another in robbing the same person.

Mike Barry describes how the Russian soldiers denuded the "enormous" village of Aochakan of its wealth. The invaders had apparently undertaken the whole operation for that purpose:

> On August 30th 1982, the whole village was surrounded in the classical way by tanks, helicopters flying above. Young men of military age had been able to run away into the mountains on time, so all the people who were collected by the Soviet troops were elderly villagers, farmers' women and children. The soldiers did not kill anybody this time, they simply stripped every single person in the village that they could lay their hands on of anything valuable he had on, whether jewelry or wrist watches. Houses were searched, and all transistor radios were confiscated. The granaries were emptied, all sacks of grain reloaded on to the lorry vehicles, and finally all the sheep, all the goats, and all the cattle were loaded on to the military lorries and taken away.[14]

The village was also emptied of its inhabitants since there was nothing left for them to live on. Barry continues, "I saw an enormous village by moonlight which had not been bombed, and yet there [was] not a single human being left alive in it. It was already snowing, and you could tell that there were no footsteps in the snow. It was a freezing night, and with my companions I explored the village, and all we found living in the village was a single dog."[15]

The villagers had fled to Pakistan, but flight abroad in the cold winter could be deadly, especially for families with children. It was so for the people of Dehsabz, a cluster of villages northeast of Kabul. Again in Mike Barry's words:

> The villagers ... were told by Parcham communist officials, "Get up, go away"—"Where are we supposed to go?"—"We do not care, go away, we are going to kill you, go away." And the people then were subjected to bombardment. All during the succeeding days bombs fell on the village, and the

population began to run away at night. 450 families reached Pakistan after 7 or 8 days; . . . 50 children froze to death on the march over the mountains, and 150 people had to be amputated for frost-bitten limbs in Peshawar hospitals. The population has collapsed on a mud field under the rain, no tents, no shelter. They are told they must now go towards the Indian border, they do not want to go, they are obstinate, they want to stay, but are getting desperate, and it seems that now we are reaching the breaking point.[16]

Almqvist has also noted the accounts of local witnesses about genocide committed by the Soviets. In one incident the Russians first looted then set fire to shops; when the shops were ablaze, they threw a number of old people into them. They burned the shops after they had looted them. Quoting a witness, Almqvist writes, "At Ghulam Raza's house in Baraki Rajan they [the Soviet soldiers] forced nine people out and killed them."[17] This was probably the end of the whole family. The account of another witness is more revealing: "I was on the roof of my house on watch. The Russian forces were attacking the village of Baraki Rajan. The attack was both from the air and the ground. . . . The Russian forces and their allies started to search the houses. Men, women and children were forced out of their homes and shot. [I] myself did see 8 people being murdered. I did see myself from the roof how the Russian soldiers threw mines out into the wheatfields." According to the same witness, the Soviet soldiers forced some locals to go in front of their tanks so that the mujahideen would not fire on them. During the three days of operations in the village of Baraki Rajan, 298 people were killed, 25 of whom were children, and 203 resistance men.[18] The latter were caught unaware while working in the fields. This was a big loss to the mujahideen, since usually their casualties were not so high.

The Soviets also poisoned drinking water to make the civilians sick or do away with them. According to one witness, "They put medicine in the well and we cannot drink the water, because it is poisoned. We turn sick." Many villagers told Almqvist that the Soviets had poisoned their food in the course of searching houses. That the Soviets would destroy heaps of ready crops in fields was common. When the crops were ready, the mujahideen would refrain from opposing the invaders, saying, "We cannot defend this village now, because if we do, we will have our food burnt. They shoot with machine guns, with Kalashnikovs or Kalakovs at the heaps of wheat or whatever on the fields so that they catch fire."[19] Small butterfly mines were also thrown here and there in Logar, but not in as large numbers as in other isolated areas.

These operations made the people of Logar believe that "it is a normal way of fighting when a European occupation force comes into the country to shoot and kill people in many, many different ways." Since the Soviet soldiers felt free to kill as they pleased, common Afghans called them with the awe-inspiring names of "Rus" and "barbarians." Even children held this opinion. They would scream at the sight of the blond Swedish Almqvist, who looked like the Russians. Parents apologized to him, saying, "Very sorry, but you have blond hair you know, you look like a Russian. And they have never seen a camera before. They have seen so many new guns in this area, they are small kids, they do not understand that it is a camera, they think it is a new gun and that you want to kill them." Almqvist wrote in conclusion: "When I left Afghanistan I felt like a traitor leaving all these people behind."[20]

MASSACRE IN SHAMALI

The region toward the north of Kabul up to the Hindu Kush is called by the traditional name of Shamali. This region comprises the two provinces of Parwan and Kapisa. The latter, lying as it does to the south of the Hindu Kush, includes a number of long, narrow, and tortuous river valleys, among them the famous district (*wuluswali*) of Panjsher. Like Logar, this region is significant to Kabul, particularly in times of disturbance. In the present war it became even more important. The shortest road from Kabul to the Soviet border passes through this region. For the Soviets, it was important to keep this road open to supply its forces and the regime. To the north of the Salang Tunnel in Kelagai the Soviets had stationed the bulk of their troops, while to the south of it was the Bagram military air base. Significant also was the location of Panjsher, which links Shamali with northeastern Afghanistan. The Soviets thus treated Shamali as a special region.

As mentioned above, Soviets killed many villagers in Shamali and fired on the villages from their bases in Khair Khana in the city and from Bagram in Parwan Province. In addition, they undertook several expeditions in the course of which they killed many civilians. The intensity of the operations, here as elsewhere, was such that cows ceased to give milk and some children died of shock. Both sides of the main road for a considerable distance were flattened to ensure its safety. The invaders still failed to pacify the region, although the mujahideen here were far from united. Besides the two unfriendly Islamist groups of Hizb (led by Hekmatyar) and Jam'iyyat, the leftist SAMA was also active in the region. Despite the disunity, because of grass-roots support the resistance here, as in many rural areas, was strong.

As in Logar so in Parwan the Soviets, descending in groups of tanks, searched houses for weapons and draft dodgers. When not allowed to do so, they would attack the village or residential forts. For example, the fort of Dade Khuda Hussain Khel close to the village of Musa near Qarabagh was hit so much by rockets in early February 1981 that of its ten inmates and a number of cattle, only one child survived for a few days. While searching houses, the Soviet soldiers would denude them of valuables, as they did in other places. In an attempt to make the Bagram air base safe from attacks from the surrounding districts, they looted Parwan even more scandalously. For the same reason they hit villages at random with rockets and guns from the south of the city of Charikar and Bagram. They were still unsafe from the ambushes of the mujahideen, who attacked them from trenches in the walled orchards, where they could hide and escape retaliatory fire. The Soviets were more frustrated in Parwan than elsewhere, although KhAD had recruited many persons from the area. Many senior officials of KhAD were from the various districts of Parwan, but the locals had ostracized them. When the mujahideen fired at them, and particularly when they inflicted casualties on them, the Soviets would do what they could to take revenge. Then they would fire at anything and anyone whom they wished to destroy. On one such occasion in early May 1981 they killed a number of children in the village of Kalakan, the stronghold of SAMA. The Russian soldiers were stated to have said, "When the children grow up they take up arms against us"; much later, Russians in Baghlan said, "We do not need the people; we need the land."

In May 1981 the Soviet soldiers flattened the village of Mahigiran close to Raig-i-Rawan. They also killed nearly all of its residents to take revenge for a defeat the mujahideen had inflicted on them elsewhere. Their massacre of the Kushkeen (or Kuchkeen) villagers close to Mazeena was without provocation. When Soviet tanks appeared, the mujahideen, acting on the request of the villagers, withdrew without firing at the invaders. The Soviets were nevertheless unsatisfied: they killed thirty-one villagers, slaying them inside mosques, in lanes, or inside their homes. This they did on the second day of Eid, a religious festival. The invaders inflicted incredible cruelty on some people in a village near the town of Jabalus Siraj in August 1981. After they had been fired on, the Soviets entered the village. By then the young people had escaped, and only women, children, and elderly men remained. The Soviets wrapped thirteen of the elderly people in bedsheets and blankets and set fire to them.

MASSACRE IN PANJSHER

The regime still had only precarious control from Kabul to Charikar, the capital of Parwan Province, which they controlled through terror. In August 1981 KhAD arrested about six hundred men of the city, accusing them of having cooperated with the mujahideen. To pacify the region, the Soviets undertook a regionwide operation (*'amalyat-e-sartasari*). But before that operation is described, it is necessary to note their operations in the valley of Panjsher. A long, tortuous river valley, Panjsher is inhabited by Tajiks and a number of Sunni Hazaras. The valley is flanked by high mountains, pierced here and there with habitable caves; indeed, the caves are so spacious that people sometimes use them as summer quarters. A combination of circumstances made Panjsher famous as a resistance front. Mujahideen, taking cover in the caves or other protected places in the mountains, could be safe from rockets and bombs. In an emergency whole populations could take refuge in the rugged hills. From the start of the jehad only one resistance organization, Jam'iyyat, operated in Panjsher; Jam'iyyat was, moreover, under the leadership of a local commander, Ahmad Shah Mas'ud. Emeralds, rubies, and other precious gems, taken from twenty-five mines in the crags of the Siah Qullah in Khinj above the valley, gave the resistance an income from eight to nine million dollars a year with which to buy weapons and meet other expenses.[21] Unlike the mujahideen in other areas, who pressured the locals for taxes and other necessities of life, the Panjsher mujahideen did not. Hence, the solidarity between them and the locals was unstrained. This solidarity proved significant, since the Panjsheris who worked in Kabul as technicians, drivers, shopkeepers, and government employees provided the resistance with necessary intelligence. Since Panjsher, like many areas, was not self-sufficient, the enterprising Panjsheris worked and lived in Kabul, particularly after the development programs begun in the late 1950s. Some owned transport companies.

The district of Panjsher and Ahmad Shah Mas'ud did not at first attract the attention of the Soviets. When, however, Parwan and Kapisa became disturbed and when the mujahideen of Panjsher also took part in the disturbances, the Soviets directed their war machine at it. They did this to dry up one source of mujahideen and to guard the Salang

road, which runs close and parallel to the Panjsher Valley. The road from
the south of the tunnel to the town of Jabalus Siraj is vulnerable to attacks from the Panjsher side. In early January 1981, after the mujahideen had repulsed some Soviet military operations and inflicted losses
on them, the Soviets blockaded the valley of Panjsher. At the foot of the
valley, near Unaba, they erected a wall, a miniature version of the Berlin
Wall, and intensified the bombardment. The French medical doctor
Lawrence Laumonier, who visited Panjsher for the second time in the
summer of 1981, states:

> For three months I did not see any bombings in Panjsher when I was there
> [in 1980], but this time I saw [bombardment] every day. . . . It was practically
> every day [that] the civilian population, especially women and children, at
> five o'clock in the morning, left the villages, went up into the mountains to
> find refuge in grottoes and caves, and they only came back at five or six
> o'clock in the evening. And it is only during the nights that the women can
> do the house work and the men can irrigate the fields and do the normal
> agricultural work.[22]

But the bombing destroyed their houses and killed their cattle. Dorr Mohammad, a native of Panjsher, states: "In villages they [the Soviets] managed to destroy our fruit trees like walnuts, almonds, things that we live
on. When they come to a village they even destroy or kill our cattle . . .
like cows, sheep and even our donkeys. In our villages there are not
many houses left for the people . . . to live in. Consequently, they have
to move from their villages which are totally deserted now [1983]."[23]
The blockade failed, and grain was imported to Panjsher, although with
difficulty, from other regions, notably Andarab. In September 1981 the
Soviets undertook their fifth operation against Panjsher; it, too, was repulsed by the mujahideen. By this time the Panjsher front had become
famous, and in order to raise the morale of its forces the regime lied that
it had pacified it. Addressing the Polytechnic students, Saleh Mohammad Zeray, a member of the politburo, said, "After the USA and the
USSR, the Panjsher front is the strongest in the world, and our forces
are now stationed there."[24] On 22 September 1981 the regime announced that Panjsher had fallen to it, but it was untrue.

Against this background, in February 1982 the Soviets undertook a
regionwide operation in Parwan and Kohistan that resulted in the massacre of civilians. The Soviets had started the operations in December
1981, but until the following February they were small and sporadic;
moreover, the Soviet forces had fared badly, and their casualties in men
and weapons had alarmed them. For example, on 11 February 1982 a

group of seventy-one members of SAMA destroyed thirty-three enemy tanks. Ten days earlier SAMA had defeated another Soviet unit. Having acquired weapons from the Soviets and the regime forces, and being composed of daring men, SAMA fought the Islamic Party as well as the Soviets at the same time. Frustrated at their failure, on 14 February the Soviets undertook the largest operation to date in the region; it continued for five days.

Military units of the Soviet and of the regime, supported by approximately five thousand tanks, took positions in certain areas surrounding Parwan and Kapisa while helicopter gunships hovered over them to block exits of the mujahideen. At the request of the locals, the mujahideen refrained from opposing the invaders, and many withdrew under cover of night. Some Soviet army units from the opposite points in Bagram and Jabalus Siraj spread throughout the region unopposed. In the course of house searches, the invaders did what men with consideration for life would not do. My diary entry for 26 February 1982 reads:

> Although not fired at, the Soviet army showed barbarity, especially in the villages where female folk threw certain things over them from rooftops. The invaders killed women, children, and the elderly. They killed anyone who was sighted. They were also said to have used gas. Every family lost some members. The dead bodies lay in fields, mosques, lanes, homes, everywhere. The total number of casualties was estimated to be between one thousand and two thousand. The Parchamis gave out that the backbone of the resistance was broken. Throughout the region military posts were set up, but when the troops withdrew the mujahideen destroyed them. The mujahideen, as before, spread throughout the region, and assisted the bereaved in burying their dead.

But before withdrawing, the Soviet forces brought another calamity on the locals. To mark the triumph, the regime assembled thousands of the locals at a rally led by Dastagir Panjsheri, an eccentric member of the central committee. When the televised fanfare and the cries of "Hurrah!" were over, the people found themselves prisoners. Led into waiting buses, they were taken to Kabul, where some were said to have been executed for being suspected as mujahideen. Others were enlisted in the army, some were later released, and the greater number imprisoned in the Zone Ward of Pul-e-Charkhi, where I, along with about three hundred other inmates, was transferred from block two in 1984.

MASSACRE IN PAGHMAN

As already noted, Paghman, a region of several valleys lying only a few miles west of Kabul, was also hazardous to the regime. In peaceful times Paghman was a most pleasant summer resort for almost all Kabulis, just Jalalabad was a winter resort for many. Paghman is famous for its private villas, public parks, and orchards; here streams, flowers, fruits, trees and cool shadows abound in the summer, when Kabul becomes dry and hot. In the last century Amir Abdur Rahman Khan chose Paghman as a summer resort, and later King Amanullah conducted public affairs and built the Arc of Triumph there; since then, down to the Soviet invasion, Paghman has increasingly attracted the public. But if it was so in peaceful times, after the invasion Paghman, and especially its densely populated valley of Pashaee, became a tough resistance front, despite being so close to Kabul.

Since Paghman has rocky caves and paths leading to the mountains beyond it, the Soviets found it difficult to overcome the mujahideen of the area, despite the many expeditions they took against them. The Soviets bombarded it almost daily, as I could see from Khushal Maina. A result of the bombing was a continuous exodus of its inhabitants toward Kabul with their belongings on their backs. While the mujahideen had established control over the district in July 1981, later they occupied its headquarters. Protected by MIGs and helicopter gunships, a large Soviet force was dispatched to the area. When it spread in groups into glens, the mujahideen descended on them from their hideouts, inflicting casualties before retreating. Led by their officers, groups of the invading army searched houses for weapons, draft dodgers, and valuables. They also embarked on a novel program of homicide. When the officers suspected the locals as mujahideen or collaborators, they would hand them over to the regime officers and the KhAD personnel to kill them. The KhAD men had no choice but to carry out the order, which was said to be a military order. The following example is an eyewitness account.

During the course of a house search, eight boys were taken out. The Soviet officer singled out four and handed them over to the regime officer to kill them somewhere. The latter demurred, arguing that their guilt had not been established. The Soviet officer warned him that if he did not carry out the order, then he would be killed instead. Accompanied by, among others, two Russian soldiers and the condemned boys, the officer set out for a place to carry out the order. Along the way the officer, speaking in the Pashto language, told the boys to drop down as if dead on hearing the shots, which would not be fired directly at them. The scheme worked as arranged, but as the boys ran homeward, they were killed by another group of Soviets, who took them for mujahideen. The place and time of the event is unknown, but it did happen. It confirms a statement by a former Soviet army sergeant: "We did not take any prisoners of war. None. Generally we killed them on the spot. As soon as we caught them, the officers ordered us to slaughter them."[25]

Paghman was still not pacified. After the withdrawal of the forces. the mujahideen spread out in the district and pressured the military posts that the invaders had set up in Peer-e-Biland (the district headquarters) and other places. The Soviets sent occasional expeditions into the region and continued their frequent bombardments. The destruction of houses, the killing of civilians, and the almost continuous flight of refugees to Kabul and elsewhere was the outcome. The Soviets must have been frustrated at their inability to pacify a district so close to Kabul. The mujahid commanders Abdul Haq, Bilal Nairam, and Jagran Sayyed Hassan became well-known for their resistance.

CHEMICAL WARFARE

The term *chemical warfare* comprises a variety of chemical substances, such as irritating agents, lethal gases, chemical warfare agents, blister gases, nerve gases, and toxins, the latter designating both biological and chemical agents. Used massively, any of these substances can incapacitate and even kill thousands of people. Since World War I the subject of chemical warfare has caused fear and horror. The international community outlawed it. The 1925 Geneva Protocol, one of the oldest arms control agreements still in force, forbade the use of chemical and biological weapons in war. The 1972 Biological and Toxic Weapons Convention prohibited the possession of toxic weapons. The question at issue here is what kinds of these substances the Soviets used in Afghanistan.

The Soviets used chemical agents in inaccessible areas so that others might not know about it. For this reason, the Soviets and the regime wreaked havoc by helicopter gunships on areas where the presence of foreigners was suspected. Apart from other considerations, the Soviets feared the foreigners would inform the world about their use of chemical agents in Afghanistan. They bombed a few health centers set up in certain areas by French and other physicians. The symbol of the International Committee of the Red Cross was anathema to the Soviets. Although in the spring of 1982 they allowed a team of the Red Cross to visit Kabul in connection with the exchange of prisoners of war, they soon obliged the team to leave the city. The Soviets were unwilling to allow other international bodies to visit the suspected areas about which certain countries, particularly the United States, voiced concern. The Afghans were inexperienced in rushing their victims of chemical warfare or items contaminated by chemical agents to international bodies in Pakistan. Hence, it is difficult to verify the use of chemical substances in Afghanistan during the period covered by this study. Nevertheless, an unspecified number of people in a number of places did fall victim to substances other than conventional weapons. A manifestation of these substances was the peculiar decomposition of bodies.

I have noted two cases of peculiar decomposition. On 7 February 1982 the Soviets disposed of thirty-one elders in a pit somewhere between the villages of Ayamak and Rabat in the province of Ghazni. The Soviets had taken the elders to present them to the governor of the province in Ghazni to cooperate on matters relating to the Fatherland Front. A few days afterwards, the people of the area found their bodies, already decomposed despite the short time. The elders were killed because the Soviets were met sourly by the people of a village where the Soviets had shot dead a small boy after he had protested to them for their burning the fuel of the village mosque. In autumn 1980 some people were killed by chemical substances after they had entered an underground canal in the district of Shilgir in Ghazni. Their bodies had also been decomposed, apparently by injection of some chemical substance. A Panjsheri from the Malekat village of Kapisa Province describes such rapid decomposition thus: "The injured Afghans were injected with chemicals and within 20 minutes [their bodies were] practically decomposed." He adds, "When they [the Soviets] use gas bombs the victims' bodies decompose quickly." [26]

A Norwegian narrator of a film shot in Afghanistan comments on the subject of chemical warfare near the village of Charpur in Paktia in June 1980:

In the morning we were woken up by helicopters [which] were flying around. Hurriedly we left the village, but left one man behind us; he was wounded and we could not carry him out. The helicopters dropped a couple of what we thought at that moment were bombs. The only thing which we saw was a kind of explosion and a yellow cloud. Then, the second wave of helicopters came in and bombed with chemical rockets. So, everything in the village was bombed. Then a [villager?] told me that the first wave was a gas tank. Well, at that moment I did not believe it, because it [was] rather unbelievable that they [the Soviets] were doing [this] and a lot of Afghans [had] been claiming it before and I never saw any evidence of it. We came [back to] the village a couple of hours later. We found the man we [had] left behind dead. His face was swollen. We took him out and brought him to another place and came back the next morning and then the face was completely swollen, physically like what would have been dead for three or four weeks. It was really strange, and everybody in the group who was in the village was having blisters on his head, his face, [while] the face was swollen. Seemingly, a wide variety of [chemical] agen[ts] have been used from the old classic, if you will, nerve agents to a number of agents we do not fully understand yet. Mycotoxins which have been found in south-east Asia, apparently are also being used in Afghanistan. That is a new kind of agent, rather hideous and extremely lethal. Riot control agents are apparently also being used, and there are some agents that have been reported and which have symptoms that are not fully understood which cause sudden onset of death without any prior symptoms.[27]

Mycotoxins such as yellow rain, sleeping death, and Blue X seem to have been used in Afghanistan. Yellow rain causes burning sensations, vomiting, headaches, spasms, and convulsions. Internal bleeding follows, followed by the destruction of the bone marrow. The skin then turns black as necrosis sets in. The time from exposure to physical decomposition may be a matter of hours. Sleeping death kills the victim instantly. Victims have been found in fighting position, holding their rifles, eyes open, fingers on their triggers, with no apparent cause of death. Blue X, a nonlethal agent dispensed in aerosol form and dropped from aircraft, renders the victim unconscious for eight to twelve hours.[28]

George Shultz, the former American secretary of state, has dealt with the subject of chemical warfare in Afghanistan in detail. According to Shultz, "Reports of chemical attacks from February through October 1982 indicate that the Soviet forces continue their selective use of chemicals and toxins against the resistance in Afghanistan." In twelve provinces yellow, black, red, and white substances, along with nerve gas, were released from aircraft and assault helicopters as well as pumped from armored vehicles. The chemicals were stored at Kandahar Airport, which was an important staging area for Soviet military operations. Until late 1982 many observers suspected the Soviets of using chemical substances, which were said to have been deployed as early as 1979. Shultz comments, "Our suspicions that mycotoxins have been used in Afghanistan have now been confirmed." He also states that "reports during 1980 and 1981 described a yellow-brown mist being delivered in attacks which caused blistering, vomiting and other symptoms similar to those described by 'yellow rain' victims in Southeast Asia." He then goes on to state that "new evidence collected in 1982 on Soviet and Afghan Government forces' use of chemical weapons from 1979 through 1981 reinforces the previous judgement that lethal chemical agents were used on the Afghan resistance."[29]

Ricardo Fraile, a French legal expert on chemical warfare, visited Logar for a week in December 1982. Unlike the narrator of the film mentioned above, he did not see the use of chemical agents. He collected information about chemical warfare from sources in Afghanistan and also from diplomatic sources abroad. Being cautious by profession and by nature, and being well aware of the implications of his professional views on such a matter, he took the stance of a scholar-philosopher in his statement to the Oslo hearings on Afghanistan. In this statement he says:

> I personally can not say, "Yes, I can with great certainty say that there is chemical warfare [going on in Afghanistan]," but for some years now, since south-east Asia and since Afghanistan, I can say that there is an ever-growing bulk of evidence which is growing every time, and which is becoming clear. We have been shown masks, we have been shown protective clothing, we hear witnesses—people who have come from different parts of the country. Thus we create a composite of a mosaic. How can Afghan witnesses who describe something—they could never have been in contact with people in south-east Asia or in Eritrea and describe the same fact?[30]

In fact, Fraile was too cautious, at least at this phase, to express a view on the subject, despite the "evidence," which he described as "fairly well supported." For he said, "On one hand we have an ever-growing number of facts and evidence which are fairly well supported, and we are far closer to being convinced that chemical warfare is in fact taking place [in Afghanistan]. And then we have the attitude of the incriminated countries, which do nothing to prove their good faith or to actually re-move suspicion."[31]

Although the scholar-philosopher summed up the "well-supported evidence" as "indications," "clues," and "elements," and although in his views "the Russians [were] using the Asians as . . . guineapigs for . . . [testing] military hardware and . . . chemical weapons," he was still un-willing to take a position until he was asked to do so. Then in categorical terms he said, "In the past I was not necessarily convinced that chemical warfare was being carried out in Afghanistan. Today I am convinced that such chemical weapons are being used."[32]

A United Nations Commission of Enquiry set up in December 1980

had concluded, in Fraile's words, that "at least for one case in Afghanistan it would seem that it is almost certain that chemical agents, very
specially of the irritant type, had been used." This was in the early stage
of the war. Besides, the commission had not visited Afghanistan, where
these agents had allegedly been used as early as 1979. Dr. Fraile writes,
"The first alleged use of chemical warfare [is] from the summer of
1979, when it was suspected that the Afghan army with the help of
Soviet advisers was using chemical warfare in Badakhshan and in
Parwan . . . and in Bamiyan, the center of the country." By the time the
hearing was held, the number of cases of the use of chemical agents
had increased, according to Dr. Fraile, to approximately one hundred
instances, resulting in the deaths of about three thousand people.[33] But
in Afghanistan the Soviets caused more destruction through conventional warfare than through chemical warfare. Edward Girardet, who
visited a number of areas in Afghanistan from 1979 to 1982, holds that
"there is a form of chemical warfare carried out at least on a sporadic
basis." But in his view conventional bombing had been more destructive,
a subject that has not been made the focus of attention. He says, "I
think the conventional bombing has taken such a toll on civilian lives in
Afghanistan, that I think it is really an academic question to pursue the
so-called issue of chemical warfare."[34] The "sporadic basis" and the relatively small number of victims—three thousand—as a result of about
a hundred cases of the use of chemical agents in the period under discussion tend to support Fraile's suggestion that the Soviet Union had used
Afghanistan as a guinea pig for its experiments with chemical warfare.

The mining of certain areas and the spread of booby traps also led,
and will continue to lead, to the indiscriminate killing of people.[35] I have
already commented on the fact that areas surrounding military garrisons
and military posts had been mined. Also mined were certain routes in
the frontier areas leading to Pakistan. Both sides of the war mined their
opponents' routes. This mining was limited to war zones, but areas in
the countryside with no military significance were also mined with plastic mines. In mid-March 1982 large numbers of plastic bombs were
dropped from helicopters along the Shonkaray road and the surrounding areas in Kunar Province.[36] In spring 1981, while dropping
"heavy bombs" from air on villages, the Soviets also dropped plastic
bombs and antipersonnel bombs on fields and pathways in Dehshaykh
in the district of Baraki Barak.[37] The Soviets also used poisonous bullets
in many places. One foreign observer described plastic bombs "camouflaged to look like stones or leaves":

Soviet helicopters scatter them by the thousands in the fields and on mountain pass[es]. They are desired to maim not kill and these tiny booby traps have been responsible for the maiming of hundreds of men, women and children. The use of camouflaged mines in civilian areas was outlawed by an international convention signed by the Soviet Union in April 1981. At the time of the signing Russian helicopters were dropping the mines. They are still [1983] dropping them. For those [who] opposed the Soviets there is little medical care. The International Red Cross is not allowed to work in Afghanistan. Since the invasion a handful of French [medical] doctors make secret trips to Afghanistan and provide medical care to the people. This hospital was marked with a cross, but the Soviets still strafed it. It is estimated that half a million civilians have died, and no one knows how many have been wounded. But still, the Afghans resist.[38]

Conclusion

This work, as noted in the Introduction, deals with actual, living, dynamic men who fought against each other in a brutal struggle for domination and survival. As such, this is a historical work describing the group actions of men in the actual theater of life. Since they struggled in a matter of life and death, they were compelled by the force of circumstances to reveal their true selves, something that they would not have done in ordinary circumstances. It is therefore a study of people who have provided us the opportunity to understand them from their actual deeds. Also, since the combatants belonged to different nations, they may be considered as samples of their cultures. This is, then, a work of international as well as a national and local political history.

On the one side were men predominantly from the Slav republics of the Soviet Union and their communist Afghan allies; on the other were patriotic Muslim Afghans and their distant, external supporters. They warred against each other for opposite reasons. The former believed—or, rather, their prophetic ideologues and absolute state had made them believe—that the tide of time had commissioned them to clear the Afghan land of weeds, to create a paradise in this world where its people could live in happiness forever. They also believed that since the reactionaries had misled the warring Afghans, preventing them from realizing the truth, they had no alternative but to make them accept what was good for them. This belief justified their paternalism and the violence they directed against those Afghans whom they thought had gone astray. In short, the Soviets and their Afghan allies believed that they knew what was good for the Afghans, and the Afghans themselves were incapable of comprehending it.

The patriotic Afghans held the opposite view. They believed that what the Soviets and their Afghan allies preached was a smoke screen covering their designs on the Afghans' possessions and souls. Further, they held that what the Soviets and their Afghan comrades preached was false, that they themselves were misled, and that in any case it was not the Soviets' business to organize the Afghans' lives for them. Hence, the patriotic Afghans opposed the invasion, willingly sacrificing what they possessed to emancipate themselves and to safeguard their value system and mode of life. And they persisted in their resistance despite the odds, despite the pundits' gloomy predictions that against the Red Army the Afghans, like the people of the East European countries, had no alternative but to submit.

There was then no common ground that could constitute a basis for accommodation. The issue was left to be settled by the sword. As a result, many thousands of Afghans perished, and their centuries of accomplishment were destroyed. Common sense should have persuaded the Kremlin decision makers to stop the destruction and let the Afghans live the way they pleased, but they did so only in 1989, after almost ten years of war. By that time every ninth Afghan had died, every seventh (or eighth) had been disabled, and every third had fled abroad. Afghanistan lay in ruins, and the Soviets had still not accomplished their war objective. This, then, was the longest, costliest, most destructive, and most indecisive war a superpower (with 280 million people) has ever fought against a small country (with 15.5 million people). If there were a grain of truth in what the Soviet decision makers preached, they would not have let this happen. Why they let this happen; why they were long unwilling to stop the destruction; and, above all, why they intervened in the first place—this is a subject beyond the scope of this discussion. But, as this study shows, they were unable to motivate their men to break the Afghan resolve to resist, and thus they were unable, superpower though they were, to accomplish their war objective.

An explanation for this failure may be found in the unworkability of the Soviets' convictions and, conversely, in the potency of the Afghan's convictions.

The Soviets' convictions failed to motivate their fighting men to action except when they were under direct discipline or under the impulse of revenge. In the latter case, they were indifferent to the lives of men, women, and children. "The average Soviet had no motivation to fight in Afghanistan, other than to survive and go home. He was not defending his homeland, he was the invader detested by most Afghans, allies or enemy, and badly trained, fed and accommodated."[1] The Soviet fighting men expected to fight foreign enemies on Afghan soil, but instead they encountered as adversaries the very men and women for whose protection their leaders claimed to have sent them. The contradiction in what the Soviet fighting men were to believe and what they were to do was bewildering enough to shake their resolve to fight. To finance the war the Soviet authorities sold billions of dollars worth of gold and diamonds,[2] but they were unable to convince their fighting men that those who encountered them were not Afghans, despite their Pavlovian indoctrination.

The Afghan adventure was not the Soviets' only adventure, but it was their last. And, although they did not succeed at their stated purpose, they did succeed in destroying an independent government without being able to replace it by a viable one. Their failure caused a surge of ethnocentric and destructive tendencies in war-torn Afghanistan and helped speed the break-up of the Soviet Union itself. In late December 1991 the Soviet Union ceased to exist, fracturing into a number of smaller nation-states. A state that war had produced, war reduced. A state that by its rise had divided the world, by its demise reunited it. In this gratifying end, the Afghans played a part. The world owes them not only recognition but also appreciation, since in the course of their struggle for emancipation the Afghans also served the world in emancipating itself from the scourge of one of the leading totalitarian states of our time. Happily, after more than seventy years of its mischievous existence, this state is now a part of history, as is the German fascist totalitarian state. Both were rooted in wars; both brought on wars; both committed genocide; and both perished as a result of wars.

In contrast to the Soviet fighting men were the mujahideen, whose will to fight inside their own country in the defense of their faith, their homeland, their independence, and their honor was unshakable. As already noted, they believed that in the fight against the intruding infidels, "The weapons of faith are the strongest and most effective weapons in the world." Because of this faith and their other values, the Afghans have fought many wars in the past against foreign intruders, so much so

that, as I have commented elsewhere, probably every settled square me-
ter of the Afghan soil has cost the lives of Afghans, and is therefore
priceless to them.[3]

Any other explanation would be less than satisfactory.

Epilogue, 1982–1994

The period from 1982 to the present was marked by the replacement in 1986 of Karmal by Najibullah, the withdrawal in 1989 of Soviet troops after the conclusion in 1988 of the Geneva Accords, and the replacement in 1992 of the Parchami regime by the Islamic state.

From 1982 to 1986, when Najibullah (Najib Allah) replaced Karmal, the situation in the country remained basically unchanged. During this period the Soviets followed first an "enclave strategy" and later a "scorched earth policy." Under the former policy the Soviets undertook less ambitious campaigns, restricting themselves to the defense of military bases, military installations, key cities, major roads, and communications, avoiding as far as possible countrywide pacification campaigns. But throughout 1983 and 1984 repeated military operations across the country were undertaken, sometimes as large as the one in Panjsher involving between fifteen thousand and twenty thousand troops.[1] To cut off weapon supplies to the mujahideen, the Soviets littered the frontier provinces bordering Pakistan with mines. Described as "migratory genocide," the Soviet campaigns were "massive reprisals against towns and villages harboring mujahideen." The campaigns were undertaken "with a view to uprooting the local population, hurting the mujahideen and curtailing their mobility."[2]

Still, the Soviets scored no success in pacifying the country; only during the winter months were they able to extend their defenses, push their perimeter outwards, and capture mujahideen bases and arms in the hills surrounding Kabul.[3] Beginning in 1985, though, the mujahideen were supplied with thick jackets, snow boots, and ski tents, which enabled them to remain in the field in large numbers during the winter months.[4] More important, they began to receive heavy equipment, such as bazookas and heavy machine guns;[5] they were also supplied some relatively primitive SAM-7 missiles.[6] Their old Lee Enfield rifles had already been replaced with Kalashnikovs. During this time, too, the Reagan administration raised the level of funding for weapons to the mujahideen from $280 million in 1985 to $470 million in 1986 and to $630 million in 1987.[7] From 1984 on, Chinese assistance and the flow of Saudi funds to the resistance also stabilized at a substantial scale.[8] "With the network of logistical supplies and coordination development through the seven-party alliance, the Afghan Resistance became a highly efficient force by 1986."[9]

But the regime scored some successes among the city population by repairing mosques, promoting the Islamic Affairs Department to the status of ministry, increasing subsidies to religious persons, holding jirgas, promoting trade facilities with the Soviet Union, adopting local languages as the medium of instruction in primary schools, and undertaking publications in those languages. Nevertheless, even with these measures the Karmal regime remained a city regime.

With the rise in March 1985 of Mikhail Gorbachev as the general secretary of the Soviet Communist Party, the scene was set for changes: in the Soviet Union by the inauguration of *glasnost* (openness) and *perestroika* (economic restructuring); in Afghanistan by the gradual disengagement of the Soviet Union; and in the world by the relaxation of tensions.

In Afghanistan the change was marked by the replacement in May 1986 of Karmal by Najibullah, first as general secretary of the PDPA and then as president of the Revolutionary Council. This replacement occurred after Gorbachev described the Soviet war in Afghanistan as a "bleeding wound." The change reflected the Soviet policy of pulling out its troops after a settlement had been worked out.

As early as 1983 Yuri Andropov, general secretary of the Communist Party, had told Karmal that "he should not count on [an] indefinite and protracted stay of the Soviet troops in Afghanistan; that it was his obligation to expand the social base of his government by political means."[10] But Andropov died shortly afterward, and during the brief reign of his successor, Konstantin Chernenko, the issue was not pursued, and "Karmal did not draw the required conclusion."[11] In 1985 Gorbachev told Karmal that "we must think together" about the issue; Karmal, after his face "darkened," replied, "If you leave now, you will have to send in a million soldiers next time."[12] Karmal, who had brought the calamity of Soviet troops on the Afghans, found it impossible to "expand the social base of his government by political means." Still, early in November 1985 he unveiled his so-called ten-point thesis to achieve, among other things, "conciliation" and "compromise." He also showed willingness to include non-PDPA members in the State Council and to promote a mixed economy. But his "conciliation" proposal was addressed only to those who had not raised arms against the regime. At the time neither the Soviet Union nor Kabul was willing to expand the social base of the regime by including the Islamic groups. Instead, calling these groups "counterrevolutionaries," they aimed at their destruction. Karmal wanted his Soviet comrades, out of their internationalist duty, to seal the border with Pakistan with an additional 500,000 soldiers; he would then approach the Islamic groups for negotiations.[13]. The Soviet Union was, of course, unwilling to embark on such a policy. Karmal therefore had to go, and Najibullah, who did not share his view, was promoted to his position.

But the Soviet leaders did not agree on how Najibullah should proceed to form a coalition government. Marshal S. F. Akhromenyev, chief of general staff, and G. M. Kornienko, a member of the committee on Afghanistan, argued that the PDPA should "forgo the major share of power in order to establish a coalition government." "This government" they said, "had to represent the interest of various sections of Afghan society." By contrast, Foreign Minister Edward A. Shevardnadze and V. A. Krutchkov, the chairman of the KGB, held "a conviction that even after the Soviet troops' withdrawal the PDPA could retain . . . a determining and a 'leading' role in the new regime."[14] Tilting toward the latter view, Gorbachev in December 1986 informed Najibullah of the Soviet leaders' decision "to withdraw the troops within one and a half to two years." He also "urged an intense pursuit of the national reconciliation policy," emphasizing at the same time "the necessity to extend the reconciliation policy not only to include the conservative forces, but also those who had been fighting with arms against the authorities."[15] But Shevardnadze, during a conversation with Najibullah, "emasculated" this proposal, telling him that half of the ministerial portfolios, and not the main ones, in the coalition government could be assigned to the opposition.[16] Najibullah, however, was given to understand that the president in the new order should be someone like the former King Mohammad Zahir, who could be acceptable to all sides, and that "the whole range of political forces of the country [was] to be represented in [a] loya jirga, which was scheduled to elect a President by the end of November [1987]."[17]

After these discussions two series of events dominated the scene: the intensification of military operations and the pursuit of a policy that the regime called "national reconciliation." As R. M. Khan correctly notes, "Soviet military activity appeared to have intensified following the rise of Gorbachev and the appointment of General Mikhail Zaitsev as the new commander of the Soviet forces in Afghanistan."[18] According to a rumor circulated at the time, Gorbachev had given a span of one year to the military to suppress the resistance. If it failed, so the rumor went, he would then try to resolve the issue through diplomacy. Whatever the truth, for about a year after Gorbachev's rise the Soviets carried out the severest operations they had ever undertaken in Afghanistan. In this series was the battle for the base of Zhawara near Khost in Paktia in April 1986, in which they and their Afghan allies lost thirteen helicopters and aircraft. Also, more than 100 soldiers of the regime were captured, and more than 1,500 either killed or wounded. The loss in the mujahideen camp exceeded 300. The Soviets occupied the base, but they retreated within hours of its destruction.[19] Incidental to these operations was the detonation of explosive devices inside Pakistan, killing or wounding hundreds of people. This was probably the work of KhAD agents.

But if the Soviets escalated the war, so did the United States and Pakistan. They heightened the defense capability of the mujahideen by providing them with the Stinger, a sophisticated shoulder-fired, antiaircraft missile which America had recently made operable. This was the most effective defensive weapon which the mujahideen received. At 3:00 P.M. on 25 September 1986, Engineer Abdul Ghaffar of the Islamic Party (Hekmatyar) successfully fired the first Stinger against a helicopter landing at the Jalalabad airfield. It became "a turning point of the campaign."[20] From then on Stingers partly neutralized Soviet aerial offensives. According to the estimates of Pakistan's Intelligence Service (ISI), "During the summer of 1987 the mujahideen hit an average of 1.5 aircraft of varied description every day." By the end of 1987 the military situation had deteriorated to the extent that even Najibullah admitted that "80 percent of the countryside and 40 percent of towns were outside the control of his government."[21]

On 15 January 1987, while inaugurating the policy of "national reconciliation," Najibullah invited political groups for a dialogue about the
formation of a coalition government. He also invited leaders of the Islamic groups, but in reply they reiterated their view: "the continuation
of armed jehad until the unconditional withdrawal of Soviet troops, the
overthrow of the atheistic regime, and the establishment of an independent, free and Islamic Afghanistan."[22] The former king Mohammad
Zahir also rejected the call.

Even within the PDPA opposition was felt.[23] The followers of Karmal,
who numbered more than the followers of Najibullah, set up a separate
faction, SNMA (Organization for the National Liberation of Afghanistan). They held a rally and voiced their discontent, but they were dispersed. Their leaders were dismissed or demoted from government and
party positions, and Karmal was sent to Moscow against his will. The
pro-Taraki Khalqis, although seemingly on good terms with Najibullah,
were, like the pro-Karmal Parchamis, unwilling to follow him for a variety of reasons. Nevertheless, confident of the support of his Moscow
mentors, Najibullah went on with the program of "national reconciliation," trying to persuade the noncommitted individuals and groups to
serve under him even before the Soviet troops had left.

The splinter group of the PDPA led by Zahir Ofuq reunited with it
after years of separation. The Sitami factions of SAZA and SZA (formerly SAFRA) declared their support for the policy of "national reconciliation," and their leaders joined the government. Led by Sufi Shina, a
new faction, KAJA (Young Workers of Afghanistan), made up mainly
of the disillusioned Parchamis and Khalqis, also broadly supported the
policy of "national reconciliation." Later, three separate factions
emerged, representing the interests of peasants, religious groups, and the
business community, all of which supported the new policy. Only leaders of the Afghan Millat who had recently been released from prison
declined the offer of joining the government. Except for the latter, the
factions were made up mainly of pro-Moscow leftists and opportunists
whom KhAD had encouraged to organize with a view to creating a mul-
tiparty system. In addition, many prominent former bureaucrats outside
political groupings, including community and tribal elders, joined Najibullah in his efforts to effect national reconciliation.

Najibullah's accomplishments were more pronounced in his efforts
to reform himself and the state he had inherited. He now claimed he
was a Muslim, whereas following the April coup of 1978 the PDPA leaders had said they were the sons of Muslim fathers. An eloquent speaker

in Pashto and Persian, he backed up his stand with passages from the Quran. On Fridays he prayed in the mosque of Pul-e-Khishti. An Islamic center was set up for research in Islamic studies, and the government spent still more lavishly on the 'ulama and religious centers.

The night curfew that had been imposed following the uprising in Kabul in 1980 was lifted. The regime began to release groups of prisoners in intervals; some time passed before most prisoners were released. Our group of professors was released in early 1987 before we had completed our terms of imprisonment. Peace commissions were set up and were granted authority in administrative and welfare affairs. I was invited to attend the National Peace Commission; had I done so, the rights that I had lost during my stay in prison would have been restored, but I declined. The National Front, led by Abdur Rahim Hatif, was authorized to play a major role in the implementation of the program of "national reconciliation."

To change the state structure, on 30 November 1987 Najibullah convened a loya jirga composed of men and women selected by the authorities from among members of social organizations, the National Front, government officials, and members of the PDPA. The two-day session of the loya jirga was marred by violent incidents. While Najibullah was delivering his opening statement, four rockets launched from the hills of Paghman hit the area of the Polytechnic building where the jirga was held. Members of the jirga were alarmed, but Najibullah kept on reading his statement. The next day, General Asmat Muslim, commander of the Achakzay tribal militia, was barred from entering the hall with his armed guards; they clashed with the security men outside, in the course of which several men, including two senior officials, were killed or wounded. Muslim was responsible for keeping the road from Kandahar to Speen Boldak open.

Despite these difficulties, the loya jirga succeeded in its mission. It passed a new constitution and elected Najibullah president for seven years—not surprisingly, since he was the only candidate for the position. The constitution devised a presidential system with an elective bicameral parliament to which the executive was made accountable. The constitution declared "the sacred religion of Islam" the official religion, and it stated that the state power belongs to the people, who exercise it through their representatives. It guaranteed the democratic rights of the individual and made it legal to form "political parties," a provision allowed for the first time in an Afghan constitution. It declared the society "multi-nationalities" and charged the state with pursuing the develop-

ment of all "tribes and nationalities" to ensure equality.[24] To appease
the nationalists, photos of Afghan heroes of the past were posted in the
city. The word "democratic" was dropped from the name of the republic
because of its communistic connotation;it was now called the Republic
of Afghanistan. Later in 1990 the PDPA was renamed the Fatherland
Party (Hizb-e-Watan), a party whose published aims claimed that it
"fights for democracy based on a multi-party system" and loya jirga, as
well as "national reconciliation whose contents it would develop on the
basis of Islamic beliefs, patriotism, the chosen customs of the people,
and the experience of practical politics."[25]

Despite these changes, Afghans not connected with the party or the
regime held that President Najibullah was so committed to the ideals of
PDPA and so loyal to the Soviet Union that he would not transform. In
particular, they distrusted the PDPA and KhAD. The latter, though now
called WAD (Ministry of State Security), was dominated by the same
Parchamis, who still called themselves "khadists, the true sons of comrade Dzerzhinsky,"[26] the bloodthirsty prophet of the leftist revolutionaries. The Afghans viewed the regime to be unviable and the "national
reconciliation" policy a ploy, especially since the Soviet troops were still
present; however, rumors were afloat that the troops would leave as soon
as a coalition government was in place. But President Najibullah had
started a move that even the Islamic groups could not ignore. They could
not do so because the regime, among other measures, doubled its efforts
at neutralizing the resistance commanders and building up militias.

As explained in chapter 10, through Premier Kishtmand the regime
promoted in effect a policy of fragmentation by promising autonomy to
localities, in particular in the north and to the Hazaras. Now President
Najibullah, who also headed the Supreme Council for the Defense of
the Fatherland, approached the commanders about running their territories in an autonomous manner with the assistance of the regime, provided that they refrained from fighting and negotiated.[27] Among the approximately four thousand commanders throughout the country,[28] a
considerable number went along with the proposal; however, Mohammad Hassan Sharq, who headed the government as prime minister from
1988 to 1989 and who abrogated the special political arrangement of
an autonomous nature that had been devised for northern Afghanistan,
notes, "Until the end of my office no known commander submitted, nor
any known refugee was willing to negotiate. If a known commander
received a government emissary it was to tell him that they were unwilling to negotiate but willing to fight to the end."[29]

On 10 February 1988 Yuli Vorontsov, the ace Soviet diplomat, told President Zia al-Haq in Islamabad that "the Soviet troops would be withdrawn, with or without national reconciliation and with or without the Geneva settlement."[30] The Geneva talks that had been going on at intervals since 1982 under the supervision of the UN secretary general's personal envoy, Diego Cordovez, were expedited. On 14 April 1988 the accords, known as the Geneva Accords, were signed by representatives of the governments of Pakistan and Kabul. The U.S. Secretary of State George Shultz and the Soviet Union's Foreign Minister Edward Shevardnadze were present as the coguarantors of the accords. The Soviets undertook to withdraw their troops in nine months, completing it on 15 February 1989.

Since the basic parameters and structure of the agreements had been completed at a time when Moscow enjoyed a position of strength militarily, "The Geneva Accords accomplished little more than providing a respectable exit for the Soviet troops."[31] The "respectable exit" and the nonexistence of a national government helped the Soviets avoid paying war indemnities. More to the point, the accords—from which the resistance leaders had been excluded—had no provision to stop the war. "Specifically, they failed to address the question of self-determination, an issue critical for any restoration of peace in the country."[32] On the contrary, by accepting the principle of "positive symmetry," whereby the coguarantors would provide weapons as they pleased to their respective Afghan sides, the accords in effect increased the chances of war and the destruction of an already battered Afghanistan.

The Soviet Union took full advantage of this situation by supplying abundant arms to Kabul and raising its fighting capability several times.[33] The Soviet Union, until its dissolution in December 1991, is believed to have continued its delivery of weapons to Kabul at the same pace. It did so with "a conviction that even after the Soviet troops' withdrawal the PDPA could retain, if not the complete control of power, then a determining and a 'leading' role in the new regime."[34] But this "conviction" was ill founded, and Mikhail Gorbachev knew it. In separate meetings in the Kremlin, Afghan Premier Mohammad Hassan Sharq, Minister of the Interior Sayyed Mohammad Gulabzoy, and Minister of Defense Shahnawaz Tanay had told Gorbachev and others that "the mujahideen and the people of Afghanistan would neither negotiate nor reconcile themselves with Dr. Najibullah."[35]

Unlike the Soviet Union, the United States, having achieved its goal of forcing the withdrawal of Soviet troops,[36] gradually disengaged itself.

To meet its goal, the United States even "allow[ed] the Soviet Union to leave Afghanistan without losing face."[37] Although as of 1990 the United States "appeared to be pushing for an understanding with the Soviets on an effective transitional arrangement that could lead to UN-supervised elections,"[38] in effect it left regional powers, in particular Pakistan, free to devise a government for Afghanistan.

But Pakistan, like the Soviet Union, had a view of its own on the subject that was well known until the death of President Zia al-Haq and General Akhtar Abdur Rahman in a mysterious plane crash in August 1988. Specifically, Pakistan wanted "an outright military victory and the establishment of an Islamic government in Kabul," and this view was promoted in the ISI.[39] The man who fought hardest for this end was General Akhtar, who, as chief of ISI from 1979 to 1987, was second in command only to President Zia while the office he was heading "was considered all-powerful" in Pakistan and "the most effective intelligence agency in the third word."[40] Akhtar opposed the alternative view put forward by Foreign Minister Sahibzada Ya'qub Khan. "Yakub Khan wanted to push the [Islamic] Alliance to take political initiatives and felt that it did not receive support from the ISI for this purpose."[41] The same was true of Prime Minister Mohammad Khan Junejo, who "lacked control over the ISI setup and had little rapport with the Alliance leaders."[42] President Zia al-Haq, who did not pursue "a single clear line of policy," allowed "the hard-line leadership to stall on the Foreign Office efforts."[43] That was why the ISI had allotted 67 to 73 percent of weapons it received from the donor countries to the four fundamentalist groups.[44] These groups effectively opposed the "broad-based" formula that Diego Cordovez proposed shortly after the Geneva Accords had been concluded. Thus, settlement of the issue was left to the sword. Most believed that after the withdrawal of the Soviet army the mujahideen would soon oust the Kabul regime from power. But like the Soviet conviction that its army would suppress the resistance within weeks or months, this conviction, too, proved simplistic.

As the withdrawal date (15 February 1989) approached, the Kabul regime rearranged its forces and evacuated the headquarters of the outlying province of Kunar. The mujahideen occupied it on 11 October 1988. They behaved not as liberators but as pillagers and set up a dual system of administration for the province, one run by men of the seven group, and the other by the followers of Jamil ur Rahman, leader of the Salaffiya group known as Wahhabi. The inhabitants of the plain fled. In late 1988, seventy-four officers and soldiers of the regime submitted to the border authorities of Pakistan in Torkham, but they were said to have delivered them to a commander of the Hizb-e-Islami of Khalis. Later they were found dead on the Afghan side of the border. Visiting the area in January 1989, I saw the remains of some of them. Also, in early January, when the mujahideen overran the military post of Shewa, some Arabs of the Salafiyya group slaughtered two officers of the post who had submitted and possessed as war booty sixteen women, while members of two Islamic groups possessed five women. The incidents began to shake the conviction about the mujahideen as saviors, especially when the regime publicized the Torkham incident in its mass media after it had reoccupied the region for a short while in late November. The jehad had begun to degenerate into a war for spoil and revenge.

In this atmosphere efforts were made to convene a shura to form an interim government to replace the Kabul regime after the Soviets left. However, the shura was restricted to the seven Peshawar-based Islamic Sunni groups, the Islamic Unity of Afghanistan's Mujahideen (IUAM). It was a loose structure, and the leader of each of the seven groups became its spokesperson for three months. The IUAM also had a leadership council, composed of leading members of the groups. In June 1988 Engineer Ahmad Shah was chosen head of the interim government, but a more effective interim government was required. In January 1989 the ISI chief, General Hameed Gul, persuaded leaders of the IUAM in a joint meeting to set up such a government.[45]

But the IUAM leaders were disunited about the basis on which to set up the shura. Hekmatyar proposed that the shura be elected, but Mohammad Nabi Mohammadi called elections un-Islamic. Mohammad Yunus Khalis held that only the pious, the intelligent, and the learned were entitled to elect an amir. The suggestion that the council should be elected by the refugees was brushed aside, because in 1987 a survey of them had given a higher rating to the former king Mohammad Zahir than to the IUAM. The IUAM then devised a formula according to which each Islamic group, including the Tehran-based Shi'ite group of the Islamic Alliance Council (IAC), was to nominate sixty members to the shura. The IAC, however, held out for a hundred members. The IUAM increased the number to sixty-five, but no more. Mojaddidi, who was the spokesman of IUAM at the time, came out in favor of the IAC's demand but backed away after he found that he was being isolated on the subject. The efforts of Iran's diplomats, including Foreign Minister Akbar Velayati, who argued the IAC's case with the government of Pakistan, bore no fruit, and the Tehran-based Shi'as were excluded from the shura.

The IUAM leaders also had to battle with tribal and community elders. More than eighty elders and mullas from various parts of Afghanistan, among them Azizullah Wasifi, Abdul Ahad Karzay, and Abdul Quddus, arrived in Peshawar and on 2 February 1989 held a rally there along with other Afghans; similar demonstrations were held in Quetta. In a communiqué the spokespersons for the Peshawar demonstrators stated, "The time has come to constitute a united leadership and a united government. Not a few leaders, but the whole of mujahid, muhajir [émigré], and Muslim people of Afghanistan have the right and the discretion to institute them." The demonstrators suggested that a coalition government be formed with equal numbers of representatives from the mujahideen, the refugees, and the Kabul regime; this proposal was similar to the one-third formula which President Zia al-Haq had held until the previous January. Expressing support for the former king and denouncing the IUAM, the leaders of the rally reiterated the view that in the present circumstances only a loya jirga could achieve this goal. Some circulated the view, now widespread, that the Islamic groups were the creation of Pakistan. But as in 1980, so now too the latter reacted swiftly. While the police watched, followers of the Islamists disrupted the meeting and condemned the loya jirga. Hekmatyar said, "It was not our traditional system, but a deception of our nation by the tyrannical and absolutist governments," and later stated, "Henceforth, without the mujahideen no one else can rule over Afghanistan."[46] By this time the schism between the Islamic fundamentalists and secularists had widened, and a number of prominent figures from the latter group, including Aziz al-Rahman Ulfat, Jannat Khan Gharwal, and the activist philosopher Sayd Bahauddin Majruh, had been killed by terrorists. Among those killed later were two physicians, Sa'adat Shigaywal and Naseem Ludin. Fearful for their lives, others, including the author of this book, took refuge in the West. In Peshawar the controversy raged, and division surfaced everywhere. Community and tribal elders worked for the view that King Mohammad Zahir was the only person under whom the nation could unite and the war be ended. The fundamentalists, though, reiterated the conviction that during his rule the former king had allowed the communists to penetrate the state and society and that he had taken no part in the resistance. In fact, the controversy was part of the wider division between those who stood for a theocratic order in which they would steer the state and society and those who stood for a secular order governed by elected representatives.

On 10 February 1989 the shura, made up of 439 members from among the seven groups and a few smaller ones including the Unity Council of Hazarajat, met with Mohammadi as chairman and Sayyaf as spokesperson. With 420 members, the seven Sunni groups dominated the shura, but a rift occurred between the traditionalists and the fundamentalists. While the latter wished to ratify the existing interim government, the traditionalists wanted a new one. They opposed the interim government of Engineer Ahmad Shah because he was known to be a Wahhabi. At the time the dispute over the quota for the IAC had not been settled. The traditionalists made it known that they would boycott the shura if the fundamentalists persisted in their demand. For three days the shura was adjourned to give time for consultation. When it was reconvened on February 13, it opted for a new interim government with a president and a prime minister. To establish this new government, first a seventy-member commission and then a fourteen-member subcommission were set up to lay down electoral procedures. Commander Jalaluddin Haqqani, a veteran in mediation and settlement, presided over both.

Inasmuch as many agents of the ISI were also present in the shura, the subcommission met secretly in an unknown place where it formulated electoral procedure. Each member of the shura was entitled to two votes, one for his own group and the other for the group of his choice. The position of the head of state was to go to the group that obtained the highest number of votes, and the position of the prime minister to the next in order. Each group was assigned two ministerial posts. On 23 February votes were cast and the result declared: 174 votes were cast for the National Liberation Front, led by Mojaddidi; 173 for the Islamic Union, led by Sayyaf; 139 for the Islamic Revolutionary Movement, led by Mohammadi; 126 for the Islamic Party led by Hekmatyar; 102 for the Islamic Party led by Khalis; 99 for the Jam'iyyat, led by Rabbani; and 86 for the National Islamic Front, led by Pir Gailani. Thus, Sibgatullah Mojaddidi became president and Abdur Rab Rasul Sayyaf prime minister of the Afghan Interim Government (AIG). The purpose of the state was declared to be the establishment of an Islamic order in accord with the Quran. One month after its inception the government was to be transferred into Afghanistan, and a year afterward it would obtain a vote of confidence from a shura to be devised.

The outcome surprised many observers, who had expected victory to go to the major groups, not the smaller ones such as the fundamentalist Islamic Union and the traditionalist National Liberation Front. The votes were, however, cast more for persons than groups. Although a strict and orthodox scholar, Sayyaf had the exceptional ability of simplifying complex issues and winning adherents. It was mainly this attribute that in 1980 won for him the leadership of the Islamic Union. Besides, Arabs were said to have won him votes by offering gratuities to members of the shura. Sayyaf was popular with Arabs, in particularly with the Wahhabis. By contrast, Mojaddidi, though mercurial, was a moderate traditionalist, not an Islamist; he also had a longer anticommunist and antiabsolutist stand. No one feared either him or his group. These attributes, and Pir Gailani's decision not to seek a high position for himself, helped Mojaddidi stand with head high on that day among his peers in the shura. More than anything else, Mojaddidi's victory was a response to the rigidity of the fundamentalists and a reflection of opposition to the ISI's manipulation of the affairs of the resistance groups.

Despite Mojaddidi's selection, the AIG was inherently weak: because nationalists, tribal elders, and the PDPA had been excluded, the new government rested on a narrow basis. The Sunni Afghans who stood for a theocratic order dominated it. The field commanders, who were more pragmatic than the personnel of the groups, were not part of it. They had even been underrepresented in the shura by the failure of each group to send, in accord with the quota formula, 50 percent of its members from among its commanders. More serious was the unwillingness of the constituent groups to subordinate their military structures to the AIG. In addition, like the groups the new government was dependent on the ISI for money and other support.

The AIG needed to establish itself inside Afghanistan as a prelude to overcoming the Kabul regime. For that purpose, on 6 March 1989, after the Soviet troops had left on time (15 February 1989), between five thousand and seven thousand mujahideen under the leadership of eight senior commanders advanced on the frontier city of Jalalabad, but without a coordinated plan of action.[47] After a speedy advance from the east, their advance was halted close to the city by the defenders, who were better armed and who were, moreover, in commanding positions. They had either to defend with determination or face slaughter, as the Torkham tragedy had warned them. Besides, from Kabul "over 400 Scud missiles thumped down among the hills around Jalalabad during the siege," which lasted for four months.[48] After having sustained more than three thousand casualties, the mujahideen lifted the siege; thus, the mujahideen failed in their first frontal attack in a conventional war, and the AIG failed in its bid to find a seat inside Afghanistan. The "catastrophe" of Jalalabad raised the morale of the regime's army, which had warded off the assault without the support of the Soviet army. While the regime rewarded Manokay Mangal, the commander of Jalalabad, for his successful defense, Pakistan replaced the ISI director, General Hameed Gul, with Shamsur Rahman Kallu, a general whom President Zia had earlier pensioned off.

More serious for AIG was the unwillingness of Pakistan and the United States to officially recognize it. Not long afterward the Islamic Party boycotted the AIG when Hekmatyar resigned as foreign minister. His resignation showed that the existing rivalry between the two major constituent groups of AIG—the Jam'iyyat and the Islamic Party—had turned into a vendetta. The feuding intensified after Sayyed Jamal, a commander of the latter group, ambushed and killed in the gorge of Farkhar in Takhar Province thirty-six men of the Jam'iyyat, including seven of its commanders who were close to Ahmad Shah Mas'ud, the commander of Jam'iyyat and the head of its special unit, the Supervisory Council. Subsequently, Sayyed Jamal and three other commanders were caught and in December 1989 hanged before the public by court order.[49] All this happened after Takhar had been nearly completely liberated and divided between the two groups, and "a truce had been arranged and sealed by the reading aloud to each other of the Commanders [Ahmad Shah Mas'ud, and Sayyed Jamal] of passages from the Holy Koran."[50] The event further weakened the AIG, widened the schism between the Jam'iyyat and the Islamic Party, and turned Hekmatyar and Mas'ud into undeclared enemies. It was rumored that Sayyed Jamal had acted on Hekmatyar's instructions. The episode showed that taking revenge is a practice of ambitious Afghan politicians. Thereafter the AIG became ineffective, and Hekmatyar concentrated on subverting the Kabul regime from within.

As noted in chapter 2, in late 1979 Hekmatyar had reached an agreement with the Khalqi leader, Hafizullah Amin, to share power with him in a coalition government. Now that the Soviet forces were out, Hekmatyar began to persuade the Khalqis to work for the downfall of President Najibullah. At that time the Khalqis had decided to win the trust of the people and for that purpose were prepared to make sacrifices[51]—hence their cooperation with Hekmatyar. However, the Khalqis were unable to escape the watchful eyes of the KhAD agents, who arrested many of their military officers for attempting a coup in December 1989.[52]

While Gulabzoy, the self-styled leader of the Khalqis, served as ambassador in Moscow, the Khalqi minister of defense, General Shahnawaz Tanay, showed signs of rebellion; but before he could strike, the Soviet deputy minister of foreign affairs, Yuli Vorontsov, persuaded him to accept his mediation. Vorontsov, who also served as the Soviet ambassador in Kabul, assured him that Najibullah would meet his demands: that is, he would release all Khalqi prisoners and subordinate all militias to the Ministry of Defense. President Najibullah had made the militias part of his own office, which he had lately expanded. Vorontsov and the Soviet advisers were trying apparently to reconcile the Parcham and Khalq factions, but they were in reality working for clashes between them: hence the delaying tactics of President Najibullah in meeting the demands.[53] The outcome was Tanay's coup effort on 6 March 1990, the fifth since the withdrawal of the Soviet army. Tanay was still unprepared for it, but President Najibullah forced him to embark on it prematurely. After a one-day clash in which parts of Kabul were destroyed and scores of people killed and wounded, Tanay and a number of senior officers flew to Pakistan. There, in separate statements Tanay and Hekmatyar declared that the Islamic Party and the Khalqis had made a coalition to oust President Najibullah, whom they called a Soviet man.

A coalition between the pro-Tanay Khalqis and the Islamic Party, who were polar opposites, bewildered observers. Many senior members of the Islamic Party resigned in protest, and leaders of other Islamic groups ridiculed the idea of uniting with the Khalqis to oust the Parchamis. They saw no difference between Najibullah and Tanay. Hekmatyar had never been so isolated by his peers.[54] Some believed that the coalition had been made under ethnic impulse, but this view overlooks the fact that President Najibullah was also a Pashtun and, like Tanay, came from the same province of Paktia. The core consideration of the alignment was for its designers to snatch state power from President Najibullah. In the context of Parcham-Khalq rivalry after the Soviet army had departed, Tanay represented the ambition of the Khalqis to regain the leading position they had lost.

In Kabul the regime rounded up three thousand Khalqis in the military and civilian departments. "The incident changed the balance of power [in the army] in favor of the followers of Karmal and the people of the north."[55] Instructed by the Soviets, the Kabul regime concentrated on building up tribal militias, especially in provinces bordering the Soviet Union. "After the clearance from the army of the Khalqis for being pro-Tanay, the tribal commanders of the provinces of Herat and the north were armed to the teeth and drowned in money."[56] Among the militia commanders was Abdur Rashid Dostum, whom the regime groomed to build up his Jawzjan Uzbek militias, known for their looting as *gilam jam* (total pillagers). Numbering about forty thousand, they were used as storm troopers against the enemies of the regime.

President Najibullah was, however, unable to enjoy the fruits of victory for long. His troubles resurfaced the next year. On 31 March 1991 the city and garrison of Khost in Paktia, and on 21 June the garrison of Khoja Ghar in Takhar, fell to the mujahideen. These losses were in addition to many others the regime had already sustained. But in Khost and Khoja Ghar it lost about eight thousand soldiers and huge quantities of military hardware. It was, however, still receiving weapons, foodstuffs, and fuel from the Soviet Union worth between $250 and $300 million a month, an assistance that helped it remain in place. But this lifeline was to be cut: on 13 September 1991, following the failed coup attempt by hard-liners in Moscow in August 1991, Soviet Foreign Minister Boris Pankin and U.S. Secretary of State James Baker agreed that effective the beginning of the new year, their countries would cease to deliver "lethal materials and supplies" to the warring parties in Afghanistan.[57] More serious, the regime lost its patron when, in December 1991, the Soviet Union broke up into fifteen constituent republics. The new Russian Republic, headed by Boris Yeltsin, was unwilling to help the Kabul regime. Although by then President Najibullah had extensively reformed the government in line with the new liberal constitution and given high state positions to many prominent Afghans outside the PDPA, he had still failed to persuade any leader of the armed Islamic groups, as well as the former king, to negotiate with him.[58] Even though his patron was now gone, Najibullah's record as KhAD's boss and a Soviet surrogate was the stumbling block.

Among the nearly one hundred thousand Afghans living in the West, those who were active in the issue put forward agendas for the convening of a loya jirga and the institution of an interim government to be made up of nonaffiliated technocrats, statesmen, and others without the participation of leaders of the Islamic groups or the PDPA in the transitional period. For this purpose, some had in 1990 set up an association, the Movement for a Representative Government in Afghanistan. But they all failed to develop a common front to work for this scheme. They stood behind the "broad-based" plan which the United Nations had devised for Afghanistan. In November 1989 the United Nations General Assembly had instructed Secretary General Javier Perez de Cuellar to work for the realization of "a comprehensive political settlement in Afghanistan." On 21 May 1991 Perez de Cuellar put forward a plan that called for "an intra-Afghan dialogue" to work for "a broad-based government" in a "transition period" before a national government could be set up through "free and fair elections."[59] The plan required consultation with and the concurrence of the principal sides in Afghan politics. The secretary general commissioned Benon Sevan as his special envoy for this purpose.

Unlike the "broad-based" formula that Diego Cordovez had put forward in the summer of 1988, this plan came out in a more favorable climate. The breakup of the Soviet Union and the opening of Central Asia had made Afghanistan once again significant in linking the latter region with South Asia. Hence, Pakistan was interested in a stable Afghanistan primarily for economic reasons, hoping to reach through it to Central Asia.[60] On 27 January 1992, after the ISI's reservations had been overcome, the foreign minister of Pakistan announced that his government had decided "to support the UN Secretary-General's efforts to convene an assembly of Afghan leaders to decide on an interim government."[61] Before its dissolution, even the Soviet Union had, in a joint communiqué with a delegation from the major parties of the Afghan resistance, agreed on the need to "pass all power in Afghanistan to an Islamic interim government."[62] Similarly, the United States softened its stand on the PDPA: as early as February 1990 Secretary of State James Baker had announced that "it would not be a precondition that Mr. Najibullah step down in advance of beginning discussions on a political settlement or transitional government."[63]

Nearly all the Afghan power groups came out gradually in favor of the plan. Hekmatyar, who initially called it "complicated, ambiguous and impractical," modified his position in early April 1992, "swinging behind the United Nations plan and warning that any delay in accepting it would have serious consequences."[64] A gathering of more than five hundred commanders in Paktia in early February 1992 supported the proposal in principle, stating that if the plan, after clarification, was "not against the expectations of our jehad, and national interest and results in the establishment of Islamic government, it will not be opposed."[65] While Sayyaf rejected the plan, the three traditionalist Islamic groups and the former king endorsed it in categorical terms. Echoing the voice of the Jam'iyyat, Commander Ahmad Shah Mas'ud accepted the plan but stated that "as long as Najib is in power or has a share of power, in one form or another, UN efforts will not succeed."[66] Thus, the prospects for the plan seemed good. At the urging of Benon Sevan, on 18 March 1992 President Najibullah, who was the first to support the plan, declared that he was ready to step down from office and cooperate in the transfer of power to a commission of nonaffiliated Afghans. By then Sevan, who had met with all the parties concerned, had arranged for the transfer of power on 28 April 1992. First a fifteen-member commission composed of nonaffiliated persons would transfer power to itself; after forty-five days from that date it would, under the supervision of the United Nations, convene either in Geneva or Ankara a 150-member jirga of the mujahideen, commanders, and influential Afghans to set up an interim government.[67] But before the plan was set in motion, an alignment known as the Coalition of the North (*Ittilaf-e-Shamal*) emerged, and it undid what Sevan had accomplished.

When the Coalition of the North (CN) was established is unknown, but it became active in March 1992 in Mazar after Abdur Rashid Dostum, commander of the Uzbek militias, rebelled.[68] He did so because Kabul could no longer grant him money and weapons. President Najibullah dispatched a force by air under General Mohammad Nabi Azimi, deputy minister of defense, to silence the rebellion, but Azimi secretly joined Dostum instead. More serious, on 22 March Ahmad Shah Mas'ud, Dostum, Azad Beg Khan, Abdul Ali Mazari, and Azimi decided in a meeting to overthrow President Najibullah and set up a new government with Mas'ud as the head of state, Mazari as prime minister, and Dostum as minister of defense. Mazari was head of the Islamic Unity Party of the Tehran-based Afghan Shi'as; Azad Beg Khan was an Uzbek émigré from Uzbekistan whose agenda was to work for the unity of all Uzbeks. Sayyed Ja'far Nadiri, commander of the Sayyed-e-Kayan militias and spiritual leader of the Isma'ili Shi'as of Kayan, also joined the CN. Dostum claimed that he had headed the National and Islamic Movement ever since he entered the service of the regime, and now he joined the Karmal faction against his patron. Babrak Karmal, who had returned home before the unsuccessful Moscow coup of August 1991, schemed behind the scene, while his followers in the army and the PDPA put his plans into motion. But the CN was made under ethnic impulse, as none among those who devised it spoke Pashto. It originated from the regime's "nationalities" policy and reflected the "national oppression" which Tahir Badakhshi had advanced (see chapters 3 and 10).

At 2:00 P.M. on 14 April 1992, the militias of Dostum, which had been brought to Kabul by air, took positions in the city. Surprised, President Najibullah, in a hastily convened session of the Supreme Council of Defense, asked for an explanation. Azimi and other Parchami leaders told him that the militias had been brought to protect Kabul against the threats posed by Hekmatyar, who had concentrated his men at the city's southern limits. They also asked Najibullah to announce this on the mass media and apologize to the nation for having invited the Soviet army in 1979. Giving the impression that he would do so, Najibullah instead went straight to the headquarters of the United Nations; from there he asked Benon Sevan, who was in Islamabad at the time, to come immediately to Kabul. After Sevan arrived, Najibullah arranged to fly with him abroad, but Dostum's militia controlled the airport and refused to let him go. He escaped death in the coup, but his chief of WAD (the former KhAD) was killed. Najibullah took asylum in the headquarters of the United Nations, where he still remains (June 1994). Azimi declared him "a national traitor," and Abdur Rahim Hatif, the first vice-president, took his place. The event opened a Pandora's box, which, among other things, killed the United Nations plan, which Sevan had brought to the threshold of success.

Kabul was no longer immune to hostile armed groups. On 16 April Foreign Minister Abdul Wakeel, an architect of the coup, met Mas'ud in Parwan; afterward Mas'ud's men, who had already occupied the Bagram military base and the nearby town of Charikar, took positions in the northern part of the city and in some military installations. The Parchami officers turned over the arsenals to them, to the men of Dostum, and, to a lesser degree, to those of Mazari. Because the lion's share went to Mas'ud, he surpassed his rivals in modern weapons. The Parchamis did so with the understanding that with Mas'ud they would be safe. Hekmatyar's men had entered Kabul from the south, and on 20 April the Khalqis and the pro-Najibullah Parchamis helped them occupy the building of the Ministry of the Interior. On 22 April Vice-President Mohammad Rafi' met Hekmatyar in Logar, afterward stating, "I obtained his agreement with regard to the transfer of power to the mujahideen." By 24 April nearly twenty thousand armed mujahideen had entered Kabul under the cover of darkness. The situation in Kabul became explosive, and as Benon Sevan said, "Kabul belonged to every one, but no one controlled it."[69]

On 23 April, after cautioning heads of the Afghan factions against armed clashes, Benon Sevan informed Premier Nawaz Sharif of Pakistan of the dangerous situation in Afghanistan. On the next evening (24 April) Premier Sharif summoned heads of the Islamic groups to the official Governor's House in Peshawar. Only Hekmatyar refused to attend, saying that "his presence was needed inside Afghanistan." Qutbuddin Helal represented him in the meeting but soon left because of disagreements principally over the assignment of the Ministry of Defense in the interim government to the Jam'iyyat, that is, Commander Ahmad Shah Mas'ud. Soon a formula was devised for an "interim government of the Islamic state of Afghanistan." A fifty-one-member commission, headed by Sibgatullah Mojaddidi, was to transfer power to itself from the Kabul regime. Mojaddidi was to represent the state as its president for two months, after which time he was to hand it over to Burhanuddin Rabbani. The latter was to hold the office for four months; a shura was then to devise a new interim government, which would remain in power for two years. The post of prime minister was assigned to the Islamic Party of Hekmatyar and ministerial portfolios to other Islamic groups, but not to their leaders. The latter constituted the leadership council (*shura-e-qiyadi*), which Rabbani was to preside over for four months. The arrangements came to be known as the Peshawar Accords.

The Peshawar Accords were agreed on in a meeting whose non-Afghan participants outnumbered their Afghan counterparts, although Afghan self-rule was the subject for decision.[70] Some of these foreign dignitaries had, during the course of resistance, granted the Afghan leaders weapons, logistics, and millions of dollars in cash, thus making them susceptible to their influence. As compelling evidence of this influence, all except for Hekmatyar accepted the summons to an official headquarters of a foreign government and agreed to accords initiated by its premier. Setting aside the foreign pedigree of the Accords, they were unrealistic. Even some Afghan participants called them "impracticable," "hastily drawn and monopolistic," and not devised "in line with the will of the [Afghan] nation." However, these critics lacked the courage to stand by their views.[71] The accords were drawn to meet the requirements of Pakistan with respect to the new Central Asian republics. That was why Pakistan took their wishes into account in the accords. For "Pakistan has been told in unequivocal terms that its support of the establishment of an extreme right-wing government in Afghanistan would impede friendly relations with Central Asia"[72]—hence the virtual dismissal of Hekmatyar's Islamic Party, the preponderance of the Jam'iyyat, and the assignment of the key post of defense minister to Ahmad Shah Mas'ud before someone had been assigned the post of prime minister. Besisdes, either in collusion with the CN or by themselves, the framers of the accords devised a government of minorities to make it amenable to the interests of its eastern neighbor.

Abdullah Shiniwari even goes so far as to hold that, through a "grand conspiracy agrainst Afghanistan," foreigners "forced a[n] alliance of the minorities and the Communists to trigger an internecine war between the majority Pashtuns and the minority represented by Ahmad Shah Mas'ud." Shiniwari also maintains that these foreigners schemed to embroil the Afghans among themselves with a view to exhuasting the huge stockpiles of the Scud, Oregon, Luna-I, and Luna-II missiles, as well as the huge stockpiles of conventional weapons Afghanistan had acquired during Najibullah's rule—weapons that not many countries in the region possessed.[73] Indeed, the external influence was considered so important that the AIG, which a shura had elected, was discarded, and the setting up of another AIG by another shura or by heads of the Islamic groups themselves was not attempted; and, of course, other political forces outside the Islamic Sunni groups should have been consulted but were not. The Peshawar Accords showed that the Afghans had now more than one "Soviet Union" to deal with, and that, like Big Brothers in Islamic garb, the new Soviet Unions were bent on patronizing them as well.

2

On 28 April 1992 / 8 Saur 1371 Sibgatullah Mojaddidi arrived by road in Kabul and formally received power from a vice-president of the defunct regime in the presence of Afghan dignitaries and foreign diplomats. As president of the Islamic state and the Jehad Council (the Commission of the Peshawar Accords), Mojaddidi appointed ministers and other senior officials to the departments which the previous regime had set up. Among Mojaddidi's first acts was to declare a general amnesty. Mojaddidi had no prime minister; Ahmad Shah Mas'ud, the minister of defense and chairman of the security commission, acted as the second in command. After 14 April, when Mas'ud had approached Kabul more closely, some felt that he might advance on it, but he halted and called on the leaders of the Islamic groups to set up an Islamic government in unison. He also said that "he [did] not wish a position for himself, and that, as a soldier of Islam, he was ready to serve Islam and the people of Afghanistan." He had apparently changed his mind and cooperated in the implementation of the accords.[74] Soon more than twenty governments officially recognized the new government, and Benon Sevan promised UN assistance provided that security was maintained. Premier Sharif of Pakistan paid a brief visit to Mojaddidi, granting him $10 million and promising to provide foodstuffs; the Islamic Republic of Iran followed suit. These measures, and the fact that the people of Kabul accorded Mojaddidi and his entourage a joyous welcome, made the government look legitimate. Indeed, the Kabulis, who were overwhelmingly anti-Parchami, accepted the government, assuming that it would provide essential goods, restore basic services, and maintain law and order. But it failed to fulfill these expectations. From the beginning, problems emanating from group politics, personal ambitions, the desire to loot, and ethnic and religious prejudices paralyzed this Peshawar-made importation.

It soon became apparent that the Leadership Council (LC), of which Mojaddidi was also a member, was the chief decision-making body. In line with the Peshawar Accords, Burhanuddin Rabbani, as head of the council, was to activate it after Mojaddidi's term had ended, but he did so only a week after the advent of the new government. A semiofficial journal wrote, "The opportunists, instead of observing the Peshawar Accords, . . . started opposing the president of the state whom they themselves had elected."[75] The journal also stated that "the Leadership Council . . . by issuing contradictory decrees surpassed all, even the president."[76] This complaint was made after the LC abolished the Ministry for State Security; Mojaddidi had earlier appointed General Yahya Naoroz, a veteran mujahid military officer, to head it. Similarly, General Mohammad Rahim Wardak, also a professional mujahid officer whom Mojaddidi had appointed chief of staff, was demoted and the office given to its former Parchami holder, General Asif Delawar. This switch was made because Defense Minister Mas'ud believed that "all those generals and militias who helped in the overthrow of the Najib regime should be praised rather than abused."[77] Thus hamstrung, Mojaddidi was unable to perform his real task, that is, to transfer power from officials of the defunct regime.

The first few decrees issued by the LC indicate the features of the new Islamic state. It declared Islamic law (shari'a), to be the law of the land. Among the existing laws, those considered to be contrary to Islamic law were declared null and void. The LC confirmed the general amnesty which Mojaddidi had already declared, but only as far as it concerned the right of society, not of private individuals. Meanwhile, it decreed that the state should set up a special court "against traitors and transgressors and for their trial and for maintenance of general security." This court was, however, directed against violators of laws, not the former communists. Nevertheless, the former PDPA was declared illegal and its property confiscated.[78] Later, when Rabbani had succeeded Mojaddidi, the court ordered three men to be hanged, and the order was publicly carried out. Mohammad Siddiq Chakari, the minister of information and culture, proclaimed, "Our people have no need for music"; in line with this attitude, cinemas were closed. Alcoholic drinks were banned, and the liquor stock of the government-run Ariana Hotel was burned. The LC declared that "all officials and workers of Government and private organizations shall pray collectively at fixed times." It also directed the Ministry of Information and Culture "to collect all anti-religion books from libraries and other places and keep them in a sealed place." A commission was set up "for Islamic preaching and publicity," and women were instructed "to cover their heads, legs, and arms"—that is, to observe the law regarding the Islamic veil.[79] Presumably this order was not fully enforced: in September 1993 the Supreme Court issued a fatwa complaining that "women as before work in schools as well as radio and television, and wander about in the streets unveiled." Holding that the "admixture of women with men in offices, cities and [their] learning and teaching in modern schools are unlawful, and are an imitation of the West, and of atheistic orders," the fatwa forbade such mingling. The fatwa also demanded that the government "immediately enforce all the commands of Allah, especially that concerning the veil, and drive women out of offices, and close schools for girls."[80]

The decrees were not fully implemented, since shortly afterward Kabul was divided among the former mujahid groups and the militias, whose overriding concern became short-term personal and group gains instead of those of society. The government represented the country, but it was unable to extend direct rule over it. After Kabul fell, all of the garrisons and provincial capitals submitted one after the other with the cooperation of the military and the civilians of the defunct regime. More provincial capitals submitted to Mohammadi's Islamic Revolutionary Movement than any other single Islamic group. In Herat the well-known commander Mohammad Isma'il predominated; he soon disarmed other groups, expelled the militias from Herat, and maintained law and order throughout the province. Also, as the guardian of an important frontier province, he showed vigilance about the intrigues of Iran. (Isma'il Khan is now more popular and effective in Herat than any other governor is in his own province.)

Dostum dominated the northwest provinces around Mazar. But as parts of many of these provinces also were in the hands of various Islamic groups, and because Dostum, as the commander of the Uzbek militias during the resistance period, had fought the mujahideen, the potential for clashes there was great. In the major provinces of Kandahar, Ningrahar, and Ghazni, local notables and Islamic groups set up joint councils. Gul Agha Sherzoy, Abdul Qadeer, and Qari Baba headed these councils, respectively. Essentially, each maintained peace in its region, and the country remained quiet. Kabul maintained educational, financial, and other links with these local governments, each of which began to assert its authority over its own domain in its own fashion with empty coffers and small income but abundant weapons. Kabul also sent them money when it received it from Moscow, where it was still printed. But to establish real authority over the provinces, Kabul needed an effective government, a steady source of income, and international help. Before it could procure these, the government had to assert its authority over the city itself, which had been the bone of contention among the armed groups almost from the start.

In the confusion that followed the fall of the regime, eleven armed groups entered Kabul and its immediate environs.[81] These included the seven Peshawar-based groups; the Islamic Movement, led by Shaykh Asif Muhsini; the Islamic Unity, led by Abdul Ali Mazari; and two militia groups, the Jawzjan militia led by Abdur Rashid Dostum, and the Kayan militia led by Sayyed Ja'far Madiri. Khair Khana and the central part up to Dehmazang were controlled by the Jam'iyyat and the Supervisory Council; from the International Airport up to Bala Hissar was the domain of the Jawzjan militia; the eastern and southern parts were dominated by the Islamic Party of Hekmatyar; the western part (Karta-e-Char, Meer Wais Maidan, and beyond) was controlled by the Islamic Unity; and Khushal Maina and beyond were the fiefdom of the Islamic Union, led by Sayyaf. Each group hoisted its own flag in the area under its control; Arabs, Punjabis, and Iranians wandered about with their Afghan groups inside their own domains.[82] As an observer writes, "Neither the state nor any group is able to guarantee security. This is because none has the power to order anyone beyond its own domain."[83]

The major groups were responsible for guaranteeing peace and promoting the effectiveness of the government, but instead of cooperating with the government, they fought among themselves with an intensity that Kabul had never seen before. Within days of their arrival the three groups of the CN—that is, the Supervisory Council, the Jawzjan militia, and the Islamic Unity—had ejected the Islamic Party of Hekmatyar from the city and forced it to retreat to Tangi-e-Waghjan in Logar. Shortly afterward the Islamic Unity and the Islamic Union fought each other in and around Mier Wais Maidan in the western part of the city. During this fighting the Hazara Islamists of the Islamic Unity captured, tortured, and slaughtered innocent Pashtuns, while the Pashtun followers of the Islamic Union did the same to the ordinary Hazaras. The victims were tortured singly and in groups in newer, more brutal ways. Nearly two weeks later the Supervisory Council and the Islamic Union fought the Islamic Unity in Chindawal and Khushal Maina, from which the latter was forced to retreat. In this round of fighting ordinary Panjsheris and Hazaras were the main victims. They were treated as brutally as the others already had been. A few weeks later the Islamic Party of Hekmatyar, the Supervisory Council, and the Jam'iyyat fought each other. While the Islamic Party launched rockets on the positions of its opponents in the city, the Supervisory Council and the Jam'iyyat bombed the Islamic Party's positions in Char Asia and Bagrami. Afterward the Jam'iyyat and the Jawzjan militia fought in the old Macroriyan district, from which the former was ejected and the area looted.

In the majority of cases fighting began when the armed men of one group incited the men of another and then their respective leaders stood by their own men. The rich city was too tempting for warriors to be restrained. They went about looting property, raping women, and kidnapping persons for money. State property, including government offices, was thoroughly looted. "From the beginning of their entry into Kabul these forces [armed groups] took to their headquarters in Panjsher, Char Asia, Paghman and Jawzjan whatever they could lay hands on including light and heavy weapons, war materials and public properties."[84] The Islamic Unity did the same. The groups treated Kabul as if it was the capital city of the land of war (*dar al-harb*). This thievery set the warriors at loggerheads against each other. The CN fought the Islamic Party because Hekmatyar demanded that the Jawzjan militia should leave Kabul and that the Parchamis should be cleared from the government. After the ejection of the Islamic Party from the city, the CN members fought each other. The temptation noted earlier inclined them to do so. The men of the former KhAD, in the guise of mujahideen, also played a role in creating anarchy. But the underlying cause of all of this turmoil was the disintegration of the standing army of the former regime. The government lacked the power, the means, especially monetary, and the vision to integrate the warriors of the groups into a national army. The CN became irrelevant, and a new group alignment began to emerge. The association of the Jam'iyyat with the Islamic Union estranged it from its allies, especially the Islamic Unity. More serious, the latter's unacceptable demand for a share of 25 percent of the seats in the government caused clashes.

Outmaneuvered by Rabbani and handicapped by Mas'ud, Mojaddidi looked to Dostum and the Islamic Unity as his allies. He promoted the former to the position of senior general and great mujahid when he visited him in his stronghold in Mazar in late May. With one stroke Mojaddidi transformed the mercenary of yesterday into a hero. Mojaddidi also accorded a few seats in the Jehad Council to the representatives of Dostum and of the Islamic Unity. He also offered a few ministerial posts to the latter. As a spiritual leader more at home with followers than with bureaucrats and the intricacies of governmental affairs, Mojaddidi often met with notables and promoted the idea of convening a loya jirga, hoping thereby to extend his term. However, even on 26 June—that is, before his term formally ended—he was refused entry to his office. On 28 June 1992 Burhanuddin Rabbani succeeded him.[85]

When Rabbani took over, the foundation of the Islamic state had been laid down. He tried to broaden and solidify it. He persuaded Hekmatyar to let a member of his party become prime minister, as the Peshawar Accords stipulated; thus, Abdul Sabur Farid became the first prime minister of the Islamic state. He remained in office, however, for only a few months. Efforts were also made to broaden the basis on which the army was to be built. Four persons of various mujahid and ethnic groups, including General Dostum, were named deputies to the minister of defense; however, Dostum declined the offer. General Mohammad Rahim Wardak, member of the National Islamic Front, was again given the post of chief of staff after General Asif Delawar, the Parchami chief of staff, had narrowly escaped death in a terroristic attack. General Wardak tried to make the army professional, but the meager financial resources and the outstanding political issues were virtually insurmountable obstacles. The issues were the presence in Kabul of the Jawzjan militia and in the army of the Parchami officers, with whose cooperation Defense Minister Mas'ud had advanced on Kabul and expelled from it the forces of the Islamic Party. President Rabbani officially recognized the Islamic and National Movement headed by Dostum. The latter had stated that the movement, "in solidarity with the Supervisory Council and the Islamic Unity, had played a decisive role in the conquest of Kabul and the institution of the Islamic state."[86] In a meeting with

Hekmatyar on 25 May 1992, Mas'ud had agreed to dismiss the militia in return for Hekmatyar's willingness to dismiss the Khalqis and cooperate with the government; however, he not only did not do so but even let Dostum increase the size of his militia, explaining that the militia had been integrated into the army. Hekmatyar, though, was adamant, arguing that the presence of Jawzjan militia in Kabul and of Parchami officers and officials in the army and the Ministry of National Security constituted a danger to the Islamic Party and was unpopular with the people.[87] In an undated statement the Islamic Party demanded that the communist army contingents be disbanded, the militias withdrawn, and the security of the city made the responsibility of the LC; otherwise, the Islamic Party would have no alternative but to fight. The scene was thus set for conflicts between the two sides. The Islamic Unity and the Islamic Union also sporadically clashed with each other in the western parts of Kabul. Other Islamic groups stayed away from the conflict.

The main features of the conflict were rocket attacks by the Islamic Party and aerial bombardment by the Islamic state and its allies. Rockets were aimed at the military installations and centers, but since they were guided imprecisely, they also hit civilian centers and men, women, and children. Likewise, since men of the Islamic Party had penetrated into the eastern and southern parts of the city, the men of the Islamic state also bombed and shelled these areas. The positions of the Islamic Party in Char Asia, Logar, Bagrami, and Shewaki were likewise bombed. Whatever the exact tale of who did what and to whom, the result was the further destruction of Kabul, the death and wounding of its residents by the thousands, and their displacement by the hundreds of thousands; Kabul had not experienced such a calamity before in a struggle for political ascendancy among rival Afghans. The conflict continued off and on, and in the intervals that followed the Kabulis came out from inside their shelters, haggling in crowded bazaars and open-air markets for foodstuffs and other necessities which, though available, were expensive.

At the end of his four-month term Rabbani was unable to arrange for an elected shura to set up a new government, as the Peshawar Accords had stipulated; thus, he persuaded the LC to extend his term for one and a half months (until 12 December 1992), despite the fact that the accords prohibited extension. On 29 December, when he was not legally the head of state, Rabbani summoned a thirteen-hundred-member council of resolution and settlement (*shura-e-ahl-e-hal wa 'aqd*). Under the conditions of war the convening of such an assembly seemed impressive, but most of its members had been won by money. Most leaders of the Islamic groups, including Dostum, boycotted it. Rabbani was the only candidate for president, and the shura elected him for the position for two years by 737 votes in favor, with 380 abstentions; 60 members walked out in protest. The boycotts, the rigging, and the novelty made the shura controversial, incredible, and ineffective.[88] The sporadic war of rockets and bombs continued; in February 1993 the worst round of it took place in Afshar and other neighborhoods in Kabul between the Supervisory Council and the Islamic Union on the one hand and the Islamic Unity on the other. Hundreds of civilians were wounded, taken prisoner, or killed. Among them, eighty abducted women were said to have been offered for sale.[89] As a consequence, the animosity of the Shi'-ite followers of Islamic Unity toward the followers of the Islamic Union, known as Wahhabis, and toward the Panjsheris, became still more intense.

Until now Commander Jalaluddin Haqqani, head of the council of commanders, and Shaykh Asif Muhsini, head of the Islamic Movement, had tried to reconcile the two sides, but except for occasional short-term truces, nothing had come of their efforts. Now Qazi Hussain Ahmad, leader of the Jama'at-e-Islami of Pakistan, and General Hameed Gul, the former chief of the ISI, who dreamed of "turning Afghanistan into the base for Islamic revivalism,"[90] separately tried to do the same. The outcome was the Islamabad Accords, concluded on 7 March 1993 by the leaders of eight Islamic groups, including the Islamic Unity and the Islamic Movement; the new accords were signed in the residence of Prime Minister Nawaz Sharif, with representatives of the governments of Iran and Saudi Arabia also present. Mohammad Yunus Khalis and General Dostum were conspicuous by their absence. The Islamabad Accords spelled out in detail the jurisdictions of the offices of president and prime minister and laid down procedures for the formation of the future government through an elected shura. In consultation with the president and leaders of the mujahid parties, the prime minister was to form a ministerial cabinet. The accords shortened President Rabbani's present term of office from two to one and a half years and assigned the post of prime minister to Hekmatyar or anyone else from his party.

The Islamabad Accords were an improvement on the Peshawar Accords. My evaluation of the latter accords, therefore, applies broadly to the former.[91] Here it is sufficient to note that by shortening the term of the president the Islamabad forum showed that it was above the council of settlement and resolution. Even the leaders of the groups tacitly admitted this by attending the forum. Otherwise, they would have boycotted a forum that was scheduled to deliberate on an issue which was the exclusive prerogative of the people of Afghanistan. In particular, if the council of settlement and resolution was legitimate, President Rabbani should have refrained from taking part in the forum, let alone accepting its decisions.

To honor the new accords, the leaders paid visits to the president of Iran and the king of Saudi Arabia; in the Ka'ba (the House of Allah) they renewed their pledges to abide by the accords. Nevertheless, they took their pledges lightly. Back home President Rabbani and Hekmatyar disagreed on the ministerial cabinet. While Rabbani wanted Mas'ud as the minister of defense, Hekmatyar, as prime minister–designate, did not. The war dragged on.

To iron out the differences, leaders and representatives of the eight Islamic groups assembled on 30 April 1993 in the city of Jalalabad under the supervision of the Ningrahar shura and Governor Abdul Qadeer. After long negotiations, on 20 May they concluded an agreement known as the Jalalabad Accords. Among other things, these accords agreed on the implementation of the Islamabad Accords; the formation of a supreme council to be composed of leaders of the Islamic groups, commanders, the 'ulama, and others; the implementation of a cease-fire; the deliverance by the groups of their heavy weapons to the Ministry of Defense; the setting up of a national and Islamic army; and the formation of a commission composed of two commanders from each province to select in the course of two months the ministers of defense and home affairs. Until then Rabbani was to head a commission for the Ministry of Defense and Hekmatyar a commission for the Ministry of Home Affairs.[92]

The immediate outcome of the Jalalabad Accords was the official resignation of Defense Minister Mas'ud. This was a significant change: Rabbani wanted the ministry under him, but Hekmatyar wanted it to go to an unaffiliated person who had not taken part in the fighting. Mas'ud took his headquarters and the heavy weapons to Jabalus Siraj in Parwan just north of Kabul. Although Mas'ud had no official position, he "still control[led] the government forces of some 20,000 men who patrol[led] the capital's streets."[93] This situation made Hekmatyar wary of entering Kabul, just as Mas'ud had felt insecure about going to Jalalabad to take part in the meeting. Both distrusted each other to a degree that made accommodation between them impossible. Thus, the other clauses of the accords could not be implemented, although some steps were taken. The Jalalabad Accords were orchestrated partly to silence the general outcry that accused the leaders of being overly malleable under foreign influence, as the Peshawar and Islamabad accords had demonstrated. "Every day thousands of people held rallies in front of the Ningrahar Palace where the meetings were held, and vehemently denounced the leaders. They also shouted that these pseudo-leaders including Mas'ud and Dostum (who were not there), should be killed . . . so that the nation is freed from them."[94] To calm the mobs, the hosts did not let diplomats and foreign journalists visit the participants and created hope among Afghans by giving out that the leaders had been warned of being "imprisoned" unless they came out with a settlement.

In mid-June 1993 Hekmatyar and his cabinet were sworn in by President Rabbani in Paghman, which was under the control of Sayyaf. As noted, since Hekmatyar felt insecure in Kabul, he kept his office in Darul Aman and chaired cabinet meetings in his stronghold in Char Asia just south of Kabul. But his ministers were unable to commute freely, and once they were abducted near Pul-e-Charkhi when they were on their way to hold a cabinet meeting. This was hardly an effective way of governing. Hekmatyar and Mas'ud then took long-term views of their positions and looked for alternatives. The immediate result was a lull in the fighting. For months Kabul and the areas under the influence of the Islamic Party remained relatively free of rockets, siege, and bombing. Some embassies were reopened in Kabul, and about a million refugees from Pakistan returned. In November, though, the alternative policy of Mas'ud became known; as before, it was military.

On 1 November 1993 Mas'ud attacked the positions of the Islamic Party in the valley of Tagab about forty miles northeast of Kabul. From Tagab, Mas'ud intended to grab Sarobi, a region linking the strongholds of the Islamic Party east of Kabul. Situated on the road between Kabul and Jalalabad and supplying hydroelectric power to Kabul, Sarobi was an important region. Had he taken it, Mas'ud would have split the domains of the Islamic Party and weakened it. But he failed in his design. Tagab changed hands about ten times between the contenders before one of them dominated one part of it and the other dominated the rest. The local Safay Pashtuns refrained from taking sides. About forty-five hundred men, among them a few hundred Arabs and Punjabis, fought on the side of the Islamic Party, led by Commander Zardad Khan under the supervision of Hekmatyar. By contrast, Mas'ud's men, who were fewer, fought with less determination, but the Parchami pilots on his side wreaked havoc by bombing the positions of the Islamic Party in

Tagab, Sarobi, Lataband, and Laghman. General Dostum took a neutral position.[95] In this round of fighting about eight hundred were killed and fifteen hundred injured.[96] Subsequently, Mas'ud's men were driven out from Tagab altogether.

On Saturday, 1 January 1994, Mas'ud's opponents struck in what came to be the fiercest round of fighting after the establishment of the Islamic state. After the Supervisory Council clashed with the forces of the Islamic and National Movement led by General Dostum in Mazar on 31 December 1993, Dostum's tanks and artillery units in Kabul advanced on the airport, the radio and television stations, and the presidential palace at 5:00 A.M. on 1 January 1994 under the command of General Raofi. Rabbani's forces retreated but soon recovered part of the airport after Sayyaf, leader of the Islamic Union, supported them with his warriors. While Rabbani's warplanes, stationed at the Bagram airport, bombed the strongholds of Dostum in Tapa-e-Maranjan, Bala Hissar, and the airport, Dostum's planes from Mazar started bombing the presidential palace, the Ministry of Defense, the radio and television stations, and other places considered to be militarily significant. At the same time, rockets hit the city from many directions. On 3 January 1994 rockets and shells rained on the city "at the rate of about six or seven a minute for much of the day."[97] During the first few days the fighting was so severe that people could not come out of their homes, and many injured persons died because they could not be transferred to hospitals. The dead were buried inside homes or in places nearby. According to an observer "alone during the first day of the fighting perhaps about 2,000 civilians had died."[98] "A survey of the city's hospitals put the number of casualties admitted in the 36 hours since the start of the battle at more than 670."[99] Throughout the month of January fighting was intense. By 21 January, 9,593 casualties had been admitted to the ten functioning hospitals, with an estimated 700 to 800 killed.[100] After the outset, the warriors of the Islamic Party penetrated as far as Jada-e-Maiwand in the central part of the city, but the assailants failed to overthrow Rabbani. After January the war gradually slackened. Probably about 12,000 recruits of the so-called state are now in positions to the left side of the Kabul River dividing the city. "But the warriors of no group wish to endanger their lives. On the other hand, no side is willing to accept the advance of the other. That is why each side pressures the other by rockets and bombs. The armed recruittees and their commanders prefer their own interests to those of the warlords. In addition to the huge allowances they receive, the warriors and their commanders sell war supplies and private and public properties. They make themselves increasingly prosperous."[101]

As of this writing (20 June 1994) the bombing, rocketing, and shelling have continued on an intermittent basis. The part of the city that Rabbani's forces control is under siege, although not for essential foodstuffs. The Rabbani government has ceased functioning, as it has no offices and no employees. Four groups—the Islamic Party, Islamic Unity, the National and Islamic Movement, and the Islamic Liberation Front—have come out against Rabbani. They have made a coalition and set up a coordination council that has asked him as well as Hekmatyar to resign and transfer power immediately to an interim government to be set up by all of the forces (that is, the Islamic groups). The council also states that leaders of the groups should not take part in the interim government, and that the latter, in consultation with a shura, should prepare the ground for general elections.[102] Rabbani, by contrast, states that he is ready to transfer power but only to a representative shura (*shura-e-mumassil*) to be convened by a nongovernment commission under the supervision either of the United Nations or the Conference of Islamic States.[103] Under this proposal, Rabbani would remain in his position until the representative shura has been convened, an arrangement which would take considerable time; thus, his opponents are unwilling to accept his offer. In their view this is a ploy by which he intends to extend his rule, as he had done before, when he extended his term of office until 12 December 1992. His opponents suspect that now, too, he wants to prolong his term until 29 December 1994, whereas the Islamabad Accords had stipulated that he should step down on 28 June 1994. They therefore distrust him as well as Mas'ud, and the latter two distrust Hekmatyar. The distrust is indeed the crux of the crisis. Hekmatyar and others are adamant in their demands, the more so because now Khalis, Mohammadi, Pir Gailani, and Muhsini have also for the first time abandoned Rabbani and Mas'ud because of their delaying tactics. Only Sayyaf has remained in alliance with them.

The distrust is also evident from the nature of the coalition itself. The core of the coalition consists of the groups of Hekmatyar and Dostum, whose warriors fight against Rabbani's forces; other groups support Hekmatyar and Dostum morally and diplomatically. The coalition is fundamentally negative, having arisen from opposition to Rabbani and Mas'ud rather than from an affirmative program of action. It originated in the Islamic state, and specifically in the policies established by Rabbani, first as head of the LC and later as head of state, and by Mas'ud as the all-powerful figure in the state. As I have already described, although Mojaddidi was the head of state, Rabbani and Mas'ud administered it. Since he headed a small group and lacked the support of leaders of other groups, Mojaddidi could not do much vis-à-vis Mas'ud and Rabbani. As a counterpoise to them, Mojaddidi raised the moral and military stature of Dostum. Mojaddidi left the office a frustrated man, alienated by the machinations of Rabbani and Mas'ud.

President Rabbani's efforts at extending his terms of office, his reliance on the shura of resolution and settlement, and his equivocations have raised questions about his integrity. Mas'ud's refusal to enlist the cooperation of Commanders Haqqani and Abdul Haq and Generals Yahya Naoroz, Rahim Wardak, Abdur Rauf Safay, and Rahmatullah Safay in maintaining peace made clear his intentions, which were to monopolize power in the pursuit of a private agenda. He proved himself "unwilling to ease his grip on power,"[104] preferring instead to perpetuate the "Tajik-dominated government in Kabul."[105] Part of this agenda involved blocking the entry of Prime Minister Hekmatyar into Kabul (here, though, other considerations also played a role). The successful blockage discredited Hekmatyar. Mas'ud also alienated his erstwhile ally, General Dostum, by refusing to give him his share of the billions of afghanis he received from Moscow and with which he tried to win influential commanders. Dostum, who had played the key role in ousting the communist regime and who later protected Mojaddidi and Rabbani against Hekmatyar, felt betrayed.[106] More serious was Mas'ud's "ambitious bid to wrest control of certain areas [in Kunduz, Hairatan, and Mazar] in the northern part of the country and his refusal to reach a settlement with Dostum."[107]

The repercussions of Mas'ud's activities in the north were felt in Central Asia as well. Because of his successful role in the resistance and the overthrow of the Kabul regime, Mas'ud was looked on there as a leader capable of unifying all Tajiks in a "greater Tajikistan."[108] Although only a dream, the idea troubled President Islam Karimov of Uzbekistan because a "greater Tajikistan" would mean destabilization in the region and the disruption of the existing borders. Since a million Tajiks live in Uzbekistan and a similar number of Uzbeks live in Tajikistan, and since the two countries have had ethnic problems between themselves, President Karimov became still firmer in his conviction in the sanctity of the existing borders and took measures aimed at curbing disrupting activities.[109] Among the measures was Uzbekistan's backing of Dostum, who was supported in his stand against the Islamic radicals in creating troubles in Central Asia.[110] It is unknown whether Uzbekistan has advised Dostum to join with Hekmatyar, but Rabbani and his spokesman have alleged that "we found Uzbekistan participating in the confrontations"[111] to overthrow the state.[112]

Let us turn now to the internal aspect of the coalition. Many of Dostum's officers, especially the Khalqis, pressured him to draw closer to Hekmatyar. Similarly, Hekmatyar's commanders in the north urged him to join forces with Dostum. Sibgatullah Mojaddidi had been a major influence in effecting the coalition.[113] The pressure explains why, in forging the alliance with Dostum, Hekmatyar did not face a revolt from his colleagues as he did in 1990 when he made a similar deal with the Khalqis. The alliance, however, was a political expedient born out of opposition to a common enemy rather than of unity in a cause. For its builders the overriding concern was power politics, not ethnic, sectarian, or ideological politics. Since they had until then played out conflicting policies among themselves, they could not do otherwise. By making the alliance, Hekmatyar came out of isolation and instead isolated his archrival, a significant achievement considering the fact that Mojaddidi was against him and that Mazari and Dostum were Mas'ud's allies. Dostum's apparent change of views made the alliance easier. Whereas before Dostum stood for federalism, which many thought might endanger the integrity of the country, he now said, "I am for a prosperous and non-federal Afghanistan complete with its boundaries, and willing to serve it as a soldier of the minority." As before, he still stood for equal rights for minorities.[114] Dostum and some of his nearest relatives are related to Pashtuns by marriage (indeed, his wife is a Popalzay Pashtun), and this fact might have influenced him to change his views. His participation in the alliance showed that, like his counterparts, he was also concerned with national rather than provincial politics. At one time widely considered to be an unscrupulous militia commander, Dostum probably has transformed; but his warriors in recent fighting in Qunduz have treated the innocent civilians as brutally as before, for which they were called *gilam jam*. An alliance with such people is nothing but politics without morality. But ever since the fall of the monarchy, politics without morality has been the profession of all the ideologically committed groups in Afghanistan. That is why Commander Rahmatulla Safay holds that the "activities of Dostum as well as Mas'ud in the region are pregnant with danger."[115] Indeed, by resorting to violence as a means of resolving the crisis, leaders of the coalition as well as their opponents did not help Afghanistan "to prosper." On the contrary, the war policy of the leaders of the coalition destroyed Kabul, as did the impracticable agenda and the belligerency of their opponents. Originally the destruction was the dream of General Akhtar Abdur Rahman of the ISI, who had proclaimed that "Kabul must burn."[116] But he had uttered those words when Kabul was in the grip of the Russians; now leaders of the Islamic groups and their warriors made his dream come true when they themselves controlled it.

Kabul has indeed suffered widespread destruction. The modern parts of the city—Macroriyan, Wazir Akbar Khan Maina, the city center, Sher Shah Maina, Mier Wais Maidan, Khushal Maina—have been largely destroyed, and the rest partly. While the northern part of the city, that is, Khair Khana, has suffered the least, the eastern parts lie in total ruin. Factories, workshops, stores, and shops have been looted and destroyed. Now vendors offer the necessities of life for sale in mobile stalls. The city has no running water, no public transport, no electricity, no postal service. Educational institutes, including Kabul University and Polytechnic, are closed, and professors and teachers have either fled to the provinces or abroad, mainly to Pakistan. Those who have remained sell produce to make a living. Thus, after the former professors were sent back to Kabul to govern, the incumbent professors and the students were not allowed to teach and learn. Instead, armed men were let loose on the university campus, where they destroyed, killed, and burned. Most public and private libraries, including mine, have been looted, and their contents burned or sold in Pakistan. Hit by a rocket (or rockets), Kabul Museum caught fire, and its countless artifacts, some of which were the unique relics of remote ages, have been destroyed, looted, or smuggled out of the country. The whereabouts of the golden artifacts of Tilla Tapa, the fascinating crown of the Kabul Museum's rich contents, are unknown. Of about three million inhabitants who lived in Kabul before 1992, how many still breathe there no one knows for sure. Thousands of homeless families now live in public buildings, mosques, and schools. A larger number have found accommmodation with relatives and friends. Probably about 50 percent of the population has fled to the countryside whence they or their fathers had come.[117] Even Khalqis and Parchamis who had been expelled from the countryside and who had no known criminal record have gone to the places of their birth, and there relatives and villagers have accepted them back. About two hundred thousand of the inhabitants of Kabul have escaped to Jalalabad and Peshawar. In Jalalabad they live in tents provided by the United Nations in the nearby desert of Sarshahi amidst snakes, scorpions, and insects. In Peshawar the destitute women among them beg and prostitute themselves for subsistence. Those killed since April 1992 are said to number ten thousand, but the actual number is *many times higher*, as this figure is based only on hospital reports. Uncounted numbers of people have been injured. Many families have been split, and their members' separate destinies have taken them to different places, where they do not know each other's whereabouts.[118] The people who live in Kabul now are those who either do not want to leave, come what may, or those who are without the means to do so. All this was allowed to happen to a people who were the first to rise en masse against the Soviet occupiers and their puppets, as has been described.

Afghanistan will long feel the effects of the destruction of Kabul as the nation's main political, industrial, commercial, administrative, and cultural center—the place where people from all over the country had mingled and begun the move earlier in the century toward detribalization, secularization, national solidarity, and modern ways of life. For the moment, as one observer states, "Nowhere in Kabul is life safe; everyone is afraid of everyone else."[119] There are reasons for this state of mind. A woman was forced to give birth on a street. Female inmates of a mental asylum (*mrastun*) were repeatedly raped. To protect her honor, Miss Naheeda gave her life, when, chased by the sex maniacs of an armed band, she threw herself from the sixth floor of her apartment in the sixteenth block in the Macroriyan district. In early November 1993, by the order of a commander, no fewer than fourteen men were thrown from the second floor of a mosque in the Qarabagh district for not praying. Two of them died on the spot. Political terrorism, the kidnapping of wealthy persons for money and of women for sexual abuse, and burglary are now features of life in Kabul. The warriors of the Islamic groups, especially the warriors of Dostum, have commited all these acts. An analyst notes, "Since there is no effective legal authority in the country, those who possess guns, money, and fighters call the shots."[120]

As described, in the resistance period rural Afghanistan was severely damaged, the agricultural system disrupted, and millions of mines placed throughout the land, while more than five million Afghans fled abroad. Conversely, in this period the city of Kabul swelled;when the Islamic state was set up there, it was the dwelling place for about three million people. The destruction that it has suffered since then is bound to adversely affect the future of Afghanistan as an independent nation-state. But the subject is here considered from the human perspective. So here are some speculations as to why this happened and whither Afghanistan is now bound.

The immediate cause of the destruction was the entry into Kabul of more than twenty thousand armed men belonging to eleven groups, some of which totally opposed each other. These men entered the city even before the new government had taken its seat there, while the former regime lay prostrate. The groups clashed almost immediately. After the expulsion of the Islamic Party from the city, intergroup clashes ceased for a while, but the militias as well as the Islamic warriors engaged in looting, burglary, kidnapping, and rape. The jehad had changed them, making them unsuited to ordinary life. They had led lives of deprivation. The Islamic warriors "lived on stale bread and tea. They slept on stones in the mountains. And they drove the Soviets out."[121] Besides, they as well as the militias were used to destroying and killing. Thus, they could not be restrained, especially when the rich city lay helpless before their eyes. The Islamic Party alone exhibited restraint; others— that is, the militias of Dostum, the Supervisory Council, the Islamic Unity, and the Islamic Union—played havoc with the helpless people of Kabul. But each of these five groups had its share in the destruction of the city and the killing and displacement of hundreds of thousands of its inhabitants. I know of no other groups of people in history who have, in the course of their struggle for power, destroyed the capital city of their own country the way these groups have. Evidently, their leaders cared more for securing state power than for their city and its inhabitants. Had it not been so, once the Soviet invaders had been expelled and the regime of their puppets overthrown, they should have opted for a modus vivendi at least among themselves. After the destruction they had wrought by their policies they should have given up politics, as men and women who respect moral values would. They would then have immortalized the heroism which they had shown in frustrating the designs of a superpower on their country. But it was not to be.

Much depended on Ahmad Shah Mas'ud as the key military figure in the new state, but in the complicated environment of Kabul this internationally known commander of the resistance period found himself embroiled with conflicting groups and interests; thus taxed, he failed to establish law and order. Consequently, the Islamic government failed to bring peace to the city. The government failed because it failed to restrain the unruly armed bands in the first place. It failed because, strictly speaking, it was not a government: it was actually a commission established principally by foreigners, to transfer power in the course of two

months, a short period for such a difficult task. It failed because the
groups constituting it did not cooperate with it. They could not even
restrain their own warriors. The Islamic state thus failed in its early critical stage.

The failure was the result primarily of the absence of an alternative
government, which should have been set up during the resistance period.
Of course, leaders of the Afghan jehad groups were divided on this issue
for various reasons; as a leader of one faction said, "[The leadership] of
every group tries to grab power by force, and then use it as it pleases." [122]
However, the host government of Pakistan did not seriously work toward establishing an alternative government, particularly at a time when
the Soviet Union had disappeared and the situation seemed ripe for the
setting up of such a government. At no time did Pakistan exert influence
on Afghan leaders to work for an alternative *national government.* On
the contrary, it discouraged Afghan nationalists, royalists, and community and tribal elders when they worked for such a government. Pakistan
instead concentrated on the Sunni Islamic groups, and even then it pursued a policy of favoritism by distributing among them weapons, logistics, and cash that it received from donor countries. The absence of an
alternative national government to replace the crumbling regime, one
strong enough to ensure order and security in the initial critical stage,
was the underlying cause of the destruction of the city and of the mo-
mentous failure of the Islamic state.

The destruction and the failure can properly be understood when the
scene where it was played out is considered. By 1992 Kabul had assumed
the features of a cosmopolitan city whose three million inhabitants had
adopted different lifestyles and held various ideologies and beliefs. Although the secular rule of the communists, especially the relatively lax
rule of Najibullah, had in theory followed a policy of conformity, it had
in fact encouraged this trend toward diversity. Kabul was largely a modern city with liberated women working side by side with men. Females
outnumbered males in Kabul. It differed in many respects from the
tradition-bound countryside. The latter was medieval in features, and
the difference between the two, the result of uneven development, became still sharper during the resistance period. Kabul had been run by
urban and urbanized persons, most of whom were communists, while
the countryside was in the grip of the Islamic groups whose leaders opposed secularism and imposed the puritanical ways of Islam in their domains. The two had become worlds apart. The warriors entered Kabul
as the Germanic warriors had entered Rome. They treated the Kabulis

as if they were beings from a different planet, an attitude that led to the destruction of Kabul.

Whither Afghanistan is a subject of speculation for futurologists. However, I wish to venture a few words about it, even though the subject is yet to become history, my particular field. To expect Afghanistan to be a country with a government constituted by the participation of its own citizens, capable of extending its rule throughout the land and conducting its domestic and foreign policy independently remains a dream for the present. The changed correlation of forces of society, the absence of a national government, the disjointedness of the country, the bickering among the contenders for power, foreign interference in Afghan affairs—all these militate against the reemergence of an independent nation-state. The educated and bureaucratic middle class, many of whose members have fled abroad, has become insignificant. The secular-minded community and tribal elders likewise have been weakened. "In present-day Afghanistan the groups of clergy, community elders, intelligentsia, and the military cannot be seen."[123] The laity, the commanders, and the Islamic fundamentalist groups—or, to put it differently, bearded men, veiled women, and armed warriors—now constitute the principal characters of Afghan society.

In particular, the young generation has changed. The fifteen years of war "have almost totally changed the culture of the Afghans under the age of thirty, who [now] know nothing but war, its ravages, and the power of the gun." With no education and no career to pursue, the Kabul youth are, like mercenaries, sitting idly in military posts "addicted to hashish (chars), heroine, homosexuality, sadism, and other kinds of moral degradation."[124] Also, as a result of the prevailing anarchy in Kabul, the value the Afghans cherish most has been hurt beyond imagination: Because the *gilam jam* have injured people's dignity and honor, adults wish not to have new babies, and when they want them they pray God to give them ugly ones. Women hate themselves for being attractive.[125] Most provincial officials are illiterate. After the advent of the Islamic state, unprofessional and illiterate persons in the Samangan province headed all departments except the judiciary department, which was headed by a professional one. Even the head of the education department was illiterate.[126] As commanders of the resistance period, they distributed the posts among themselves on the strength of the sword.

The economic deterioration is still more phenomenal. The extremely low rate of productivity and the super rate of inflation (in 1977 one U.S.

dollar equalled 35 afghanis; in 1992 the ratio was 1 to 1,200; now it is 1 to 3,000) are hurting all. Those who can grab feel free to do so. "Because of the absence of the central government, commanders, heads of political parties, and tribal elders [of the frontiers areas], backed up by external powers, derive abundant incomes from opium, custom dues, smuggling, and the theft of natural resources."[127]

The commanders and the heads of the groups are now the main actors in Afghan politics. But since they follow conflicting and unattainable goals, and since they are prone to following foreign advice, their politics is anything but compromise. They agree to disagree; when persuaded by others, they may agree on a formula, but then they soon undo it. Besides, as opposition leaders they have all along pursued policies the essence of which was to contradict, defeat, and destroy in order to dominate. With these policies they succeeded over the communists and the Soviet invaders, but it is unlikely they will triumph over each other. None is strong enough by itself to come out on top. Likewise, personal ambitions, the Islamism of some, and the ethnic nationalism and religious sectarianism of others have put them at loggerheads not only with each other but also with the bulk of Afghans. In this they resemble the communists, whose revolutionary ideology turned them into intolerant creatures. As ideological politics failed the latter, it may also frustrate the former. The politics of coalitionism is a sign of this trend. It may be the beginning of a new culture of pluralistic politics. The trend can be understood when it is borne in mind that Afghanistan had no theocratic order in the past, to say nothing of radical Islamism, which is only a new current. Also, Afghanistan's political structure, although far from perfect, was not exclusive to a particular ethnic group. On the contrary, in modern Afghanistan an ethnic dynasty ruled principally with the help of persons drawn from various ethnic groups. In fact, as mentioned in the introduction, because of the extensive practice of intergroup marriages, the spread of bilingualism, the recent emphasis on Islamic values, and the introduction of communistic values, ethnicity has lost much of its traditional sharpness, although it is still a dominant force.

The present armed groups are still strong, deriving strength from their organizations, the vast arsenal of modern weapons at their disposal, and the backing of their foreign patrons. But their manpower has thinned, as noted. Many of those who now fight for them are mercenaries, some even foreign mercenaries. The continuation of war politics is bound to weaken the groups further, discredit them further with their compatriots, and make them still more receptive to their foreign patrons. Already they have become unpopular. For "during their time Afghanistan has been looted more than when the British and the Soviets had occupied it. Besides, these armed groups have injured the dignity and honor of a nation."[128] It is a proof of their unpopularity that even "though it is shameful people everywhere long for the days of Najibullah and Russia."[129] The people have become so tired of the war that they now hate even iron. Still, the armed groups remain adamant in their stands, and this rigidity is likely to perpetuate the crisis. The reverend Mawlawi of Tarakhel even holds that "as long as they [the leaders of the groups] are on the scene, the Afghan crisis will not be resolved."[130] The danger to Afghanistan's national sovereignty lies here, and it is real in view of its encirclement by self-serving neighbors.

Still, all this is not cause for despair. Afghanistan has experienced many critical periods in the past. The nineteenth century witnessed the transition of rule from the Sadozay to the Mohammadzay dynasty, as well as the two Anglo-Afghan wars. Although each crisis lasted a long time, in every case Afghanistan finally emerged as a nation-state. In the present crisis, if wars abound, so do peace efforts. Because of widespread opposition to the war and to foreign interference, this peace movement is gaining momentum. Even the ill-disposed neighbors approach the Afghan problem in the name of peace, whatever their real intentions. Although they still promote their intentions through their Afghan surrogates, their intelligence services know well the maxim: "You can hire an Afghan but you cannot buy him." So far the efforts of these neighbors have been aimed at setting up an Afghan government amenable to them. The multiplicity of neighbors hinders efforts to monopolize the Afghan issue and tends to promote the state of equilibrium among them that is likely to ensure Afghan statehood. This in part explains why, despite the prolongation of the crisis and the schemes of the Russians with respect to northern Afghanistan, no group has emerged to advocate separatism. The rise of such a movement, particularly if incited by outsiders, is likely to become more menacing to the integrity of Afghanistan's major Muslim neighbors. A stable, independent, nonaligned, and friendly Afghanistan is to their advantage. After the breakup of the Soviet Union, Afghanistan has become once again the most important link between South and Central Asia. It and Pakistan have become as interdependent as they were in pre-Soviet times. Now, as much as Afghanistan needs Pakistan to reach the sea and the world beyond it, the latter needs the former to have access to Central Asia and Russia. These considerations and the fact that despite the recent odds the Afghans have remained loyal to their fatherland are signs that a nation-state is going to be instituted in Afghanistan. Most important, unlike the nineteenth century, the current era is marked by the presence of the United Nations. This organization has been especially concerned with the territorial integrity, national sovereignty, and nonaligned status of Afghanistan from the time the Soviet Union invaded it.

The United Nations for the third time has addressed the Afghan problem, or what Secretary-General Boutros Boutros-Ghali has called this "human tragedy." On the recommendation of the General Assembly, on 11 February 1994 he commissioned Mehmoud Mestiri as his special envoy "to canvas a broad spectrum of Afghanistan's leaders to solicit their views on how the UN can best assist Afghanistan in facilitating national rapprochement and reconstruction." Mestiri has concluded the first phase of his mission, and the United Nations is now expected to adopt measures to help Afghans end the tragedy. Mestiri met Afghan leaders in Quetta, Peshawar, Kandahar, Khost, Mazar, Herat, and Bamian, where they expressed support for the UN efforts. In Peshawar, Kandahar, and Quetta, they held rallies for this purpose and also spoke out against the war and its perpetrators, for a loya jirga, and for the former king Mohammad Zahir. Undoubtedly, these rallies reflected the sentiments of the greatest number of Afghans. Mestiri was so impressed by this sentiment that in a rally in Peshawar he said, "We hear there is war in Kabul. Let them make war; we will make peace." Ambassador Mestiri has made an optimistic statement the like of which his predecessors, Diego Cordovez and Benon Sevan had not made. It seems that this time the United Nations or, more correctly, Boutros-Ghali and Mestiri, are serious about helping the Afghans to cut their Gordian knot.

Supporters have also urged the former king to come out of Rome. Mohammad Aziz Na'eem, his son-in-law and nephew of the former president Mohammad Daoud, has summed up the sentiment well: "The time has come for the former king to put forward his platform and personally supervise its implementation to its logical conclusion." Na'eem adds that this end cannot be achieved by the mere issuance of messages.[131] The former king has issued statements suggesting that an interim government be set up by an emergency loya jirga under the supervision of the United Nations. This delaying policy has led to speculation, as these words from Rahimullah Yusufzai indicate. "The former king is keen on winning the support of Western powers, led by the United States as well as Russia, before making up his mind whether or not to play a role in forming a broad-based government in Afghanistan. He is seeking guarantees of their support to be channeled through the United Nations not only to ensure his personal safety but also to sustain his government in power in the face of threats by some of the radical Islamist elements."[132] If so, the former king is waiting for a political miracle.

It is doubtful whether the United States and other major powers will effectively back the UN plan. Robert Oakley, the former U.S. ambassador to Pakistan who was also concerned with Afghan affairs, holds that "the political future of Afghanistan is no longer of interest to the U.S."[133] This may or may not be the official line, but since the dissolution of the Soviet Union the U.S. administrations have shown no evidence to the contrary. The United States and other powers have even forgotten about the part that Afghanistan played in the dissolution of the "evil empire" and the end of the cold war, events that made it possible for world governments to improve their economies for the first time in four decades.[134] Their Afghanologists as well as men and women of the mass media have turned their backs on Afghanistan. They all have left a former friendly people in their vulnerable moment to the mercy of their scheming neighbors. Feeling betrayed, the disillusioned Afghans have become bitter about them, particularly about the U.S. administrations, whereas during the resistance they lauded them for their support.

The neglect is bound to endanger the lives of the innocent people of the world, especially those of the United States. Since the Soviet withdrawal, Afghanistan has become connected to drug trafficking and the training of terrorists. Because of the absence of a central government and the openness of its borders, "thousands of Islamic radicals, outcasts, visionaries and gunmen from some 40 countries have come to Afghanistan to learn the lessons of jehad, . . . to train for armed insurrection, to bring the struggle back home."[135] Also, Afghanistan is now the source of "roughly a third of the heroin reaching the United States."[136] Afghan farmers have long grown opium poppies, which require only small landholdings and offer high monetary returns; the absence of suitable substitute crops and the lack of other sources of livelihood have also led farmers to the cultivation of poppies. Now, though, these traditional compulsions have been exacerbated by the presence of millions of mines in the country, which has greatly reduced the amount of arable land and thereby forced Afghan farmers to grow more opium poppies than at any time before; the opium is then sold to dealers who process it into hard drugs for sale abroad.

Thus, the legacy of the Soviet war and the Western response to it is not only a ravaged Afghanistan without a functioning national government but also a culture of guns, drugs, and terrorism that is as poisonous to others as it is to Afghans. The world governments have a moral responsibility to the Afghans, and it is now time for them to assist in transforming the poisonous culture into a healthy one by permitting the Afghans to institute a national government. They can do so if regional powers are persuaded to keep their hands off Afghan affairs. Specifically, if world governments discourage Russia from printing unsupported banknotes for Kabul and encourage Pakistan, Iran, Saudi Arabia, and Uzbekistan to cease supporting their Afghan surrogates illegally, before long the war in Afghanistan likely will end. The Afghans then will be able to set up a government for themselves in accordance with their conventions, preferably under UN supervision. By helping to establish such a government, the world governments, among other things, would secure millions of men and women throughout the world from the dangers of the poisonous culture. "A lawful, massive and coordinated law enforcement response" to the culture, as FBI Director Louis Freeh, has suggested in another context,[137] will be possible only when Afghanistan has a stable, broad-based government. Conversely, the continued absence of an actual government will allow the poisonous culture to flourish more rankly. In the end, the problem may grow too great to ignore. Then, as Commander Abdul Haq predicts, "Maybe one day they will have to send hundreds of thousands of troops to deal with that. And if they step in they will be stuck. We have a British grave[yard] in Afghanistan. We have a Soviet grave[yard]. And then we will have an American grave[yard]."[138]

Political Organizations, Factions, and Unions

English	Dari	Pashto
Afghan Social Democratic Party (Afghan Millat)	Hizb-e-sosyal demokratik-e-afgan	De afgan tolinpal woleswak gund
Akhgar (Organization for the Liberation of the Working Class)	Sazman-e-mubariza bara-e-azadi-e-tabaqa-e-kargar	De Kargaro de tabaqi de azade de para de mubarizay sazman
Association of Mohammad's 'Ulama	Jam'iyyat-e-'ulama-e-Mohammadi	
Awakened Youth	Jawanan-e-baidar	Weesh (Weekh) zalmyan
Banner	Parcham	
Council of the Revolutionary Youth of the University	Shura-e-jawanan-e-inqilabi-e-pohantun	De pohantun de-inqilabi zwanano shura
Eternal Flame	Shu'la-e-jawed	
Fatherland	Watan	
General Union of Professors and Students of Afghanistan	Ittehadiyya-e-'umumi ustadan wa muhassilan-e-afganistan	De afganistan de ustadano and muhssilano 'umumi ittehadiyya
Group of Labor	Goroh-e-Kar	De kar dala
Industrious Youth	Jawanan-e-zahmaytkash	Khwarikisha zwanan
Islamic Association of Afghanistan	Jam'iyyat-e-islami-e-afganistan	De afganistan islami jam'iyyat

English	*Dari*	*Pashto*
Islamic Movement	Harakat-e-islami	Islami harakat
Islamic National Revolutionary Council	Jirga-e-inqilabi-e-milli-e-islami	Islami milli inqilabi jirga
Islamic National United Front	Jabha-e-muttahid-e-milli-e-islami	Islami milli muttahida jabha
Islamic Party of Afghanistan	Hizb-e-islami-e-afganistan	De afganistan islami gund
Islamic Revolution	Inqilab-e-Islami	Islami inqilab
Islamic Uprising	Qiyam-e-islami	Islami pawczun
Khurasan	Khurasan	
Movement of Islamic Revolution	Harakat-e-inqilab-e-islami	Inqilabi islami harakat
Nation	Ulus	
National Islamic Front of Afghanistan	Mahaz-e-milli-e-islami-e-afganistan	De afganistan islami milli mahaz
National Liberation Front of Afghanistan	Jabha-e-nejat-e-milli-e-Afganistan	De Afganistan de-milli nejat jabha
National Oppression	Sitam-e-milli	Milli sitam
National Unity	Ittehad-e-milli	Milli ittehad
New Generation of Hazaras	Nasl-e-nao-e-hazara	De hazara neway nasl
NUFA (National United Front of Afghanistan)	Jabha-e-muttahid-e-milli-e-afganistan	De afganistan milli muttahida jabha
Organization of Islamic Victory	Sazman-e-islami-e-nasr	De nasr islami sazman
Organization of the Toiling People	Sazman-e-mardum-e-zahamatkash	De khwarikisho khalko sazman
Party of God	Hizbullah	
PDPA (Peoples Democratic Party of Afghanistan)	Hizb-e-demokratik-e-khalq-e-afganistan	De afganistan de khalko demokratik gund
People	Khalq	Khalk
Peoples New Democratic	Demokratik-e-naween-e-khalq	De khalko neway demokratik
Progressive Democratic Party	Hizb-e-muttaraqi-e-demokratik	Muttaraqi demokratik gund
Rihaye. *See* Surkha		
SAMA (Organization for the Liberation of the People of Afghanistan)	Sazman-e-azadibakhsh-e-mardum-e-afganistan	De afganistan de khalko azadigushtunkay sazman
SARFA (Commando Organization for the Liberation of Afghanistan)	Sazman-e-rihayeebakhsh-e-fedayee-e-afganistan	De afganistan de azadigushatunko fedayee sazman

English	*Dari*	*Pashto*
SAWO (Organization of the Real Patriots of Afghanistan)	Sazman watanparastan-e-waqiye-e-afganistan	De afganistan de re-shteeno hewadpalo sazman
SAZA (Organization of the Toilers of Afghanistan)	Sazman-e-zahmatkashan-e-afganistan	De afganistan de khwar-ikisho sazman
Servants of the Quran	Khuddam ulfurqan	
Spark	Angar	
Strength	Nairo	
Struggle	Paikar	
Surkha (Rihaye) (Organization for the Liberation of the People of Afghanistan)	Sazman-e-rihaebakhsh-e-khalqha-e-afganistan	De afganistan de khalko de azadigush-tunko sazman
Thunder	Ra'd	Tander
Union for the Independence of Pashtunistan	Ittehadiyya baray-e-azadi-e-pashtunistan	De pashtunistan de azadi de para itteha-diyya
Union of the Liberationists	Ittehadiyya-e-istiqlal ta-laban	De khpelwaki ghush-tunko ittehadiyya
United Islamic Council	Shura-e-ittifaq-e-islami	De islami ittefaq shura
Unity for the Liberation of Afghanistan	Ittehad baraye azadi-e-afganistan	De afganistan de azadi de para ittehad
Voice of the People	Saday-e-'awam	De khalko gag
Voice of the People	Nida-e-khalq	De khalko awaz

Selected Biographical Sketches

For additional biographical sketches, see J. B. Amstutz, *Afghanistan, The First Five Years of Soviet Occupation* (Washington, D.C.: National Defense University, 1986); A. Arnold, *Afghanistan's Two-Party Communism* (Stanford: Hoover Institute, Stanford University, 1983); R. Klass, *Afghanistan: The Great Game Revisited* (New York: Freedom House, 1987).

AMIN, HAFIZULLAH (1929–79)

Hafizullah Amin received a B.Sc. from the Kabul University and an M.A. in education from Columbia University in New York. In the early 1960s he returned to Columbia to work for a Ph.D degree. After having passed the general examination, he was about to begin work on a dissertation when he was called home. He also failed in his efforts to enroll in England, where I tried to help him in his efforts. While in the United States, Amin had tried to politicize the Afghan student association after he was elected its president. Back home he joined the PDPA, concentrated on politics, and recruited his Pashtun students in the government-run boarding high schools of Teachers Training and Ibn-e-Sena, which he served as a teacher and principal respectively for several years.

A rural Pashtun himself, Amin succeeded in influencing the rural Pashtun students of the schools, many of whom became military officers after completing the military academy in Kabul. Amin was the only Khalqi member of the PDPA to be elected to parliament (1969). After the fall of the monarchy, when the PDPA had already split into the Parcham and Khalqi factions, the latter decided to recruit army officers, and Amin was commissioned to do the job.

After the two factions reunited in 1977 Amin still went on with his job. His opponents, especially Babrak Karmal, unsuccessfully asked Taraki to relieve him of this work. On the eve of the communist coup Amin was a member of the central committee. The police did not single him out for immediate imprisonment, as it did politburo members of the PDPA on 25 April 1978. He was the last person to be arrested, and even then the police officer, who was a secret member of the Parcham faction of the PDPA, postponed his imprisonment for five and a half hours (3:00–8:30 A.M., 26 April 1978) during which time Amin, without having the authority and while the politburo members were in prison, instructed the Khalqi army officers to overthrow the government.

President Daoud was still in the besieged palace when Amin took command of the coup after he and his comrades were released from the prison. During the first night of the coup he alone remained in the radio station directing the coup. The other leaders of the PDPA, uncertain about their success, spent the night at the Kabul airfield ready to fly to safety if the situation warranted it. In the first week or so of the coup, Amin worked twenty-three hours a day to make the coup a success. Mainly because of the army support and the support of his associates in the party, Amin overcame both his Parchami and Khalqi opponents and reached the highest position in the party and the state, after the government had suppressed major civilian and military rebellions. During the 104 days of his own rule, except for one failed military rebellion, no major uprising took place. The Soviets killed him during their invasion of Afghanistan after Amin had effected the suffocation of pro-Soviet Taraki and had tried to govern as an independent ruler.

BADAKHSHI, TAHIR

A native of Fayzabad in the province of Badakhshan and the son of an Uzbek father, Tahir Badakhshi graduated from the Habibiyya High School in Kabul and entered the College of Law and Political Sciences of Kabul University. He joined the PDPA at its inception in 1865, but quit it in 1968 to set up an organization of his own, the Sitam-e-Milli (Against National Oppression). The main emphases of his organization were "a Maoist-type revolution, in which the peasants would be given local power in the countryside, and on countrywide mobilization of minority population to combat internal colonialism by the Pashtuns. . . . Badakhshi considered that the Soviets were aiding Pashtun dominance and exploitation of the non-Pashtuns; hence his dislike of the Soviets" (Shahrani, "Saur Revolution," 157). Badakhshi also attempted to unite Tajiks, Uzbeks, and others in an autonomous region against the Pashtun "domination." In the late 1950s Badakhshi, who then lived in Kabul, expressed his ethnic and regional identity by wearing clothing made only in Badakhshan. But he lost credit and followers after he divorced his Badakhshani wife and married a Kabuli girl, a sister of Kishtmand. He was moderate and cooperated with the Khalqi government by joining it as the head of the Publications Department in the Ministry of Education. Badakhshi was imprisoned in 1978 and eliminated by prison authorities during Amin's rule. In 1979 his faction was named the

Organization of the Toilers of Afghanistan (SAZA), and its few leaders cooperated with the Soviets and the Kabul regime, forming some militia contingents
and serving in various administrative capacities.

BARYALAY, MAHMUD

An eccentric younger full-brother of Karmal, Mahmud Baryalay received a B.A.
from the University of Kabul and an M.A. in political economy from Moscow
State University in 1977. In the same year he became a full member of the Parcham central committee. After the communist coup he was appointed Afghan
ambassador to Pakistan and then dismissed and deprived of Afghan citizenship
after the conspiracy of the Parchamis against the Khalqi government. Following
the Soviet invasion, he became a member of the central committee of the PDPA,
president of its International Relations Commission, and editor of its daily,
Haqiqat-e-Inqilab-e-Saur. In 1981 he became an alternate member of the politburo. He is married to the daughter of Anahita Ratebzad.

BAW'ESS, ABHARUDDIN

A Tajik from the Darwaz district in the province of Badakhshan, Abharuddin
Baw'ess studied for three years in the College of Theology of the University of
Kabul without completing his studies. Like Tahir Badakhshi, Baw'ess believed
in national struggle instead of class struggle. By "national struggle" he meant a
struggle of the ethnic minorities against Pashtun "domination." Baw'ess advo-
cated violence in attaining this goal. With the help of his followers he occupied
the district of Darwaz for a while in 1975. Afterward he lived in hiding until the
Khalqis eliminated him in 1978. Later in the year his followers kidnapped the
U.S. ambassador Adolph Dubs. Under the instruction of Soviet advisers, the police killed all in storming the hotel where they had been. In 1979 Baw'ess's radical faction was called SARFA. Pressured by the mujahideen, this small faction,
known as Sitam-e-Milli or "national oppression," cooperated with the Karmal
regime by serving it with contingents of militias in the provinces of Badakhshan
and Takhar. Its leaders also entered the regime.

DAOUD (DA'UD), MOHAMMAD (1910–78)

No other Afghan in the twentieth century has influenced Afghan politics as
much as Daoud. Except for the constitutional decade—when, as a prince, he
was constitutionally barred from conducting politics—he was involved in the
government from an early age, often exerting virtually unrestricted authority.
An ambitious person, Daoud was first cousin and brother-in-law of the former
King Zahir as well as the eldest son of Mohammad Aziz, the eldest brother of
the ruling Musahiban family (the late king Mohammad Nadir, the late premiers
Mohammad Hashim and Shah Mahmud, and the late ambassador Shah Wali).
Daoud held a number of high military posts before he ruled as prime minister
for a decade (1953–63), when he introduced reforms and established closer ties
with Russia. In the constitutional decade he stayed home but proved an irreconcilable dissident. Finally, with the cooperation of communists, he overthrew the

monarchy and set up a republic in 1973. He had established ties with Karmal and other Parchami leaders but had declined to do so with Taraki, although Abdur Raof Benawa had asked him to. When along with Habibullah Tegy I met him in 1976 I found him overweight and unlively, but he showed interest in conversation. In 1978 Khalqi officers overthrew him in a coup that resulted in his death and the death of eighteen members of his and his brother's families.

GAILANI, PIR SAYYED AHMAD (1932–)

Sayyed Ahmad Gailani is leader of the moderate Islamic resistance organization, the National Islamic Front of Afghanistan. As *pir* or leader of the Islamic mystic order Qadiriyya with a significant number of followers among the Pashtuns, and with a modern view of life, the soft-spoken Gailani made his organization a sanctuary for liberal, nationalist, and democrat intellectuals as well as tribal and community elders and commanders. His organization favors "a basically secular government incorporating Islamic law and Afghan tradition, preferably with a parliament based on free elections" (Klass, *Afghanistan,* 394).

GULABZOY, SAYYED MOHAMMAD (1951–)

A Zadran Pashtun from Paktia, Sayyed Mohammad Gulabzoy graduated from the Air Force College. A recruit of Amin to the PDPA, Gulabzoy was his close associate and his liaison member in the army. During the communist coup he was wounded and could not perform his assignment. Gulabzoy served as minister of communication in the Khalqi period, siding with Taraki when relations between Taraki and Amin became strained. After the failure of the anti-Amin conspiracy, Gulabzoy and others took refuge in the Soviet embassy. He served as a guide with the invading forces. Afterward he was appointed the minister of interior and a member of the central committee. With Soviet support and his own Sarindoy (the police force), this enterprising pro-Taraki Khalqi made the ministry more a stronghold of his own than a coordinated department of the Parchami government. Many disgruntled Khalqis joined him in various capacities. He aspired to leadership of the Khalqis, with an eye to the top state position, but Amin's followers thought little of him. Gulabzoy is barely literate.

HEKMATYAR, GULBUDDIN (1948–)

A Kharotay Ghilzay Pashtun from the district of Imam Sahib in the Qunduz province, Gulbuddin Hekmatyar graduated from the Sher Khan high school. His family had migrated there in 1948 from Ghazni, where, like the rest of the Kharotays, they had lived as nomads. Before graduating from high school, Hekmatyar studied for two years in the military high school in Kabul. He entered the College of Engineering of the University of Kabul but left it before completing his studies. In the late 1960s he became active in the campus Islamic Movement, in particular its Muslim Youth branch. He was among its twelve student founders. He made his reputation opposing the communists; in particular, he allegedly killed a Maoist opponent, for which he was jailed. After release from prison in the early 1970s, he fled to Peshawar, where, along with other Afghan Islamists, he became active with the support of Pakistan against the Afghan Republic. In 1975, after the Islamist-instigated uprising against the republic failed, Hekmatyar broke off from the Afghan Islamic Association and formed a separate organization of his own, the Islamic Party. Hekmatyar has made this centralized organization a vehicle for realizing the views of the radical Islamist thinkers in a bid to acquire power and set up an Islamic state. After the Soviet invasion of Afghanistan, the support of Pakistan, of the Islamist Jama'at-e-Islami of Pakistan, and of other distant patrons helped Hekmatyar's party become a major resistance organization. It holds an uncompromising attitude toward internal and external opponents of different shades of opinion, in particular the communists and their Soviet supporters during the jehad.

KARMAL, BABRAK (1929–)

Although born into a wealthy Tajikized family of Kashmir origin in the village of Kamari east of Kabul, Babrak Karmal lived in hardship following the death of his mother. After graduation from the Nejat High School, Karmal enrolled at the College of Law and Political Sciences in 1951. The next year he was arrested for holding rallies in support of Abdul Rahman Mahmudi, the well-known revolutionary figure of the 1950s. In prison Karmal was befriended by a fellow inmate, Mier Akbar Khybar. A third inmate, Mier Mohammad Siddiq Farhang, initiated both to pro-Moscow leftist views. Karmal then broke off relations with the imprisoned Mahmudi because the latter had turned pro-Beijing. Following his release in 1955, Karmal resumed his studies at the university. After graduation he entered the Ministry of Planning, keeping in close touch with those who had special knowledge on communism, among them Mier Mohammad Siddiq Farhang and Ali Mohammad Zahma, a professor at Kabul University; in the 1960s Karmal addressed Farhang as *ustad* (master). Farhang then introduced him to the royal court. Both played a leading role in influencing the youth in adhering to communism (Sharq, *Memoirs,* 234). After he was raised to power, Karmal appointed Farhang as his adviser, promising him that the Soviet troops would leave Afghanistan within months and that "as economic adviser Farhang would have real power" (Hyman, *Afghanistan under Soviet Domination,* 194).

On 1 January 1965 the PDPA was founded in Kabul, with Karmal serving as one of its twenty-eight founding members in its founding congress. Karmal was appointed its secretary. In 1967, when the PDPA split into the rival Parcham and Khalq factions, Karmal headed the smaller, and more cosmopolitan, Parcham faction. When Daoud overthrew the monarchy and instituted a republic, Karmal's faction shared power with him, although Karmal himself did not hold an official position. But the honeymoon did not last long. After he felt secure in his position, President Daoud dismissed Parchamis from the presidential cabinet and tried to distance Afghanistan from the Soviet Union. Under pressure from Moscow the Parcham and Khalq factions reunited in 1977, but the alliance was superficial. After the PDPA usurped power, Karmal held the posts of vice president of the Revolutionary Council and deputy premier, but he had no real power. Soon he was demoted to the post of ambassador to Czechoslovakia. Afterward the Khalqi government implicated him in a conspiracy, expelling him and his associates (who were at the time abroad as ambassadors from the PDPA) and depriving them of Afghan citizenship. The outcasts took refuge in Czechoslovakia and the Soviet Union. The Soviets resurrected them after the invasion of Afghanistan and promoted Karmal to the posts of president of the Revolutionary Council, prime minister, supreme commander of the armed forces of Afghanistan, and general secretary of the PDPA. The Soviets let him assume the lofty titles but denied him the power that went with them. They let him serve only as a figurehead.

KHALIS, MAWLAWI MOHAMMAD YUNUS (1919–)

A Khugianay Pashtun from Ningrahar Province, Mawlawi Mohammad Yunus Khalis is a traditional scholar in Islamic studies and a specialist in formal logic. He served the precommunist governments as an official in the departments connected with the promotion of Islamic studies. He was the editor of *Payam-e-Haqq*, a journal of the Ministry of Justice. When he joined the Islamic Movement is unknown, but from an early date he argued with those whom he considered to be holding un-Islamic views. Tolerant of opposing arguments, he holds that "you should continue your jehad with the available means without hoping to become a state ruler. Obey anyone whom the Council for Resolution and Settlement chooses on the basis of qualification and competence." After the failure of the Islamists in 1975, Khalis, Hekmatyar, and others set up the Islamic Party. Khalis was chosen to lead it, perhaps because of his status as an elder. The unity did not last long. Differences arose over whether the jehad was for the conquest of state power or the liberation of Afghanistan. Khalis stood for the latter view and set up a party of his own under the same name. Although over sixty years of age, he personally took part in jehad; famous commanders emerged in his organization, which soon became a major resistance party of the Islamist type.

KHYBAR, MIER AKBAR (1925–78)

A Hussaynkhel Ghilzay Pashtun from the province of Logar, Mier Akbar Khybar along with two others was arrested after he graduated from the Military Academy in 1951. According to one source, he was arrested for having turned communist; according to another, he was arrested for having plotted to assassinate the prime minister. Neither story seems convincing. In prison Khybar met leftist inmates, including Babrak Karmal. After release from the prison in 1953, he and Karmal were stated to have found "the common faith and the only way toward the leadership of the people of Afghanistan" (Sharq, *Memoirs,* 234). Khybar could not trace his wife and children after he was released from the prison; the Intelligence Department was said to have kidnapped them. Khybar then married a sister of Sulaiman Laweq and taught at the Police Academy. Afterward he held other posts as a police officer in the Ministry of Interior. Reading Marxist literature in the English language, he also contributed articles to journals. Among the growing circle of his educated followers from different ethnic and linguistic groups, he came to be known as master (*ustad*) for his knowledge of Marxism as well as his unpretentious and guileless personality.

Khybar did not participate in the founding congress of the PDPA in 1965: because he was a police officer, the future Khalqis did not trust him. Afterward he resigned his official post to work full-time in promoting party activities and editing its newspaper, *Parcham*. Among his major contribution was the recruitment of police officers, who became an asset to the Parcham faction. In the second half of the 1960s, when the university campus was in turmoil and the probability of confrontation between the police and students was always there, Khybar—mainly through Najibullah, a student of the College of Medicine skillful in oratory—forestalled clashes without at the same time discouraging Parchami activists. Opposed to violence, he once told me that he wanted to prove that educated Afghan youth were capable of conducting politics without resort to force.

What role Khybar played during the coalition of the Parchamis with President Daoud is unclear, but he was one of those who urged Karmal to fuse with the Khalq faction in 1977. Karmal was reluctant to do so, insisting that the Khalqis accept Khybar in the joint politburo; Khybar considered Karmal's insistence on this point to be insincere. By this time differences had crystallized between them. On the one hand, Khybar considered Karmal's licentious behavior harmful, and once he even slapped him for seducing the unwilling wife of a party comrade, as noted in chapter 3. On the other hand, Karmal considered Khybar a threat to his leadership. More important, Khybar did not think the reunited PDPA would be able to rule the country even if it took power. At this time he confided in one of his friends that he was "first and foremost an Afghan, and then what you may think." In this atmosphere, in the late afternoon of 17 April 1978, he was shot dead from a passing jeep while strolling along the street near the Printing Press in Kabul.

Some Muslim fundamentalists claimed responsibility for the incident. The PDPA leaders accused certain "circles" of the government, while some Parchami leaders claimed that Hafizullah Amin had engineered the killing. The first Parchami minister of the interior, Nur Ahmad Nur, has been quoted as saying that Khybar's assassins were members of the Islamic Party of Hekmatyar, who were executed. From circumstantial and other evidence, I have concluded that the KGB directed the killing, which was carried out through agents of Karmal and Nur. (See also Sharq, *Memoirs,* 161.) The incident provoked the PDPA to stage a rally that led ultimately to the overthrow of the government and the coming to power of the PDPA.

KISHTMAND, SULTAN ALI (1936–)

A Gadee Isma'ili Shi'a from Chardi, Sultan Ali Kishtmand graduated from the College of Economics and worked in the Ministry of Planning from 1960 to 1972. In 1965 he ran for parliament but was defeated. He was a founding member of the PDPA and sided with Karmal when it split in 1967. When the PDPA reunited in 1977, Kishtmand entered the politburo. After the communist coup

Kishtmand headed the Ministry of Planning but was soon arrested for his alleged part in a plot against the government. In prison the head of AGSA, Asadullah Sarwari, tortured him. After the invasion, Kishtmand was appointed deputy premier and minister of planning. In June 1981 he was appointed president of the Council of Ministers. The Soviets found him a willing figure in aligning the minorities against the Pashtun majority in an effort to weaken national solidarity against the invaders and the regime. He had composed a booklet, *Fruit of Friendship* (*Samara-e-Dosti*) on the subject for the benefit of party comrades (Sharq, *Memoirs*, 215).

LAWEQ, SULAIMAN

A Sulaimankhel Ghilzay Pashtun, Sulaiman Laweq, initially a student of the College of Theology, graduated from the College of Literature in 1957. His father was a representative (*khalifa*) of the Mojaddidi family; hence, Ghulam Mojaddidi (Slave of Mojaddidi) was Laweq's original name. His family was also related to the Mojaddidi family by marriage. An excellent poet and a writer in Pashto and Dari, Laweq held various posts in the government-controlled mass media from the time he graduated until 1968, when he began editing *Parcham*. By this time he had become a member of the central committee of the Parcham faction of the PDPA and a close associate of Khybar, his brother-in-law. After the communist coup he became the minister of radio and television and for a time was admitted to membership of the politburo after the government had expelled the Parchamis. Then he was imprisoned for being pro-Karmal, but the authorities treated him mildly. Following the invasion, Laweq held some unimportant posts until 1981, when he was promoted to membership in the central committee and appointed president of the Academy of Sciences and minister of tribes and nationalities.

MEESAQ, KARIM

A Jaghuri Hazara, Karim Meesaq has no formal education, but he is a writer and a man of wide knowledge. Under Taraki and Amin, Meesaq served as the minister of finance and a member of the central committee and politburo. Meesaq was one of the few Khalqi ministers to stay at home after a few days of imprisonment following the invasion. Although guarded closely, Meesaq received his Khalqi followers and visitors in his apartment.

MOHAMMADI, MAWLAWI MOHAMMAD NABI (1920–)

An Andar Ghilzay Pashtun from the Sherkhel village of the province of Logar, Mawlawi Mohammad Nabi Mohammadi is the leader of the centrist traditionalist Islamic resistance organization, the Islamic Revolutionary Movement. Mohammadi studied in the Mulla Lawang madrasa in Ghazni and after graduation served as a mulla in various villages, including villages in northern Afghanistan. Mullas and *mawlawi*s (religious scholars), among them Mawlawi Mughalkhel, formed the widest circle of his acquaintances. He also served as a representative (*khalifa*) of the Mojaddidi family. Mainly because of the support of the family, he won a seat in the National Assembly in the constitutional period. There he once physically beat Babrak Karmal for making pro-Soviet remarks. Mullas and mawlawis mainly from the Logar, Ghazni, and Helmand provinces, as distinct from the educated Islamists, form the bulk of support for Mohammadi's organization, which is one of the major resistance organizations. Its original rapid progress was curbed by the Islamist organizations of Islamic Association and the Islamic Party of Hekmatyar (Z. G. Alam, personal communication, San Diego, 1993).

MOJADDIDI, SIBGATULLAH (1929–)

Sibgatullah Mojaddidi is a member of the well-established religious family of the Mojaddidis, known also as the Hazrats of Shorebazaar or the Hazrats of Qala-e-Jawad. As *pirs* (leaders of religious order) of the Naqshbandiyya mystic order, the Mojaddidis are respected and have followers mainly among the Pashtuns. The Khalqi government executed more than thirty Mojaddidis. Because of their conservative role in politics, the Mojaddidis had been at odds with the liberal intelligentsia and nationalists since the 1950s. Sibgatullah Mojaddidi taught at Habibiyya High school after he graduated from the University of al-Azhar in Cairo. In the early 1960s he spent three years in prison for his opposition to the government's pro-Soviet stand. In 1979 he founded the National Front for the Rescue of Afghanistan, a small and moderate traditionalist resistance organization.

MUHSINI, AYATULLAH SHAYKH MOHAMMAD ASIF (1935–)

Born in Kandahar, Mohammad Asif Muhsini studied in Najaf in Iraq and was accorded the highest position of the religious hierarchy (ayatullah) of the Shi'ite denomination of Islam. He is the author of twenty books on moral, social, and religious subjects, particularly the Shi'a jurisprudence (Ja'fari) of Islam in the Dari language. Muhsini set up his resistance group, the Islamic Revolutionary Movement, in 1978 and has followers among the Shi'as in Kandahar as well as Kabul. His followers played a conspicuous role in the uprising in Kabul in 1980. Unlike many Shi'as, Muhsini follows the Iran-based ayatullah of the Shi'a denomination only in religious affairs, not in secular affairs: hence the expulsion of his organization from Iran and his willingness to cooperate with the Afghan Sunni resistance organizations in Peshawar (N. Shahabzada, personal communication, San Diego, 1993).

NAJIBULLAH (1947–)

An Ahmadzay Ghilzay Pashtun from Paktia, Najibullah graduated from the College of Medicine in 1975. It took him ten years to complete his studies because of political activity and imprisonment as a party activist. He was known on the campus for his skill in oratory, in particular for reciting poetry that enchanted the audience. For his athletic activity he was known as Najib the Bull (Najib-e-Gao). He was under the spell of Khybar at the same time that he was loyal to Karmal. In 1977 he joined the central committee and in 1978 the Revolutionary Council. After the Khalqis pressured the Parchamis, the former banished him to Iran as ambassador. Soon it dismissed him and deprived him of Afghan citizenship. Najibullah took away "about $300,000 of the embassy cash in addition to other valuables" (Sharq, *Memoirs*, 165). After the invasion he was made the head of KhAD; in 1981 he was promoted to membership in the politburo. At the same time that KhAD brutalized inmates, Najibullah, its director, embraced youngsters in kindergartens or gave sermons to elders summoned to his presence.

NIAZI, GHULAM MOHAMMAD (1932–1978)

Niazi was the founder of the Islamic Movement of Afghanistan. The son of Abdul Nabi, Niazi came from the village of Raheem Khel in the district of Andar in Ghazni Province. He received his early education at the local Hajwiri school and later joined Madrasa-e-Abu Haneefa at Kabul; in 1957 he earned a master's degree from the University of al-Azhar in Cairo. There Niazi was influenced by the teachings of Sayyed Qutb and the organizational structure and underground activities of the Islamic Brethren, founded by Hassan-al-Bannan in 1929. "Niazi returned to Afghanistan a firm believer in reorganizing the Afghan society in conformity with the requirement of Islam." In 1957 he established cells first at Abu Haneefa and then at Paghman, enlisting a group of devout teachers. The meetings continued uninterrupted and the number of participants increased, especially after the fall of Premier Mohammad Daoud in 1963.

After expansion, the organization was divided into five levels: cell (*hasta*), circle (*halqa*), precinct (*houza*), provincial shura (*shura-e-vilayati*), and central shura (*shura-e-markazi*). Meanwhile, Niazi had attained the status of professor and headed the Faculty of Islamic Studies at Kabul University. Until 1972 the organization still had no specific title; it was probably then that it was named the Islamic Association of Afghanistan (Jam'iyyat-e-Islame-e-Afghanistan). By then Niazi had succeeded in developing three distinct cells: (1) a thinker's cell through which religious scholars were to plan the future course of action; (2) a worker's cell to carry its messages to the public; (3) a link cell to establish contacts in the government with a view to influence policymakers.

In 1972 Professor Niazi was arrested and later released; he was arrested again in April 1974 and killed in 1978. (For details, see M. A. Khan, "Emergence of Religious Parties.")

PANJSHERI, DASTAGIR (1933–)

An eccentric Tajik from the district of Panjsher, Panjsheri obtained a B.A. from the College of Literature of Kabul University. He worked as a minor official in various capacities in the Ministry of Information and Culture. In 1965 he participated in the first congress of the PDPA and became a member of its central committee. After the PDPA split in 1967, he went first with Karmal and then with Taraki. He agreed with neither, though, and led a subgroup of his own, the Labor Group (Goroh-e-Kar). His belief in the notion of class struggle was total. From 1969 to 1972 he was in prison. Under the Khalqi government he served first as the minister of education and then as the minister of public works. In August 1979 he went for medical treatment to the Soviet Union, where he stayed for a long time. On his return he participated in the poisoned luncheon in the presidential palace on 27 December 1979, but he was the only one who was not poisoned. Also, he was one of the few ministers of the Khalqi government not imprisoned, and he served the Karmal regime in various capacities of the second rank.

RABBANI, BURHANUDDIN (1940–)

A Tajikized ethnic Yaftal from the Yaftal district of the province of Badakhshan, Burhanuddin Rabbani received a B.A. from the College of Theology in Kabul in 1963 and an M.A. in Islamic philosophy (1966–68) from the University of al-Azhar in Cairo. In Cairo he was influenced by the teachings of the Ikhwan al-Muslimin. There he undertook to translate some works of Sayyed Qutb. On returning to Kabul, he resumed teaching at the university. He worked with Ghulam Mohammad Niazi and others in founding the Islamic Association, a mother organization of the Islamic Movement of the Islamist type. In 1972 he succeeded Ghulam M. Niazi as its amir. The following year he fled Kabul after the government began a crackdown of the Islamists. At the time he was an associate professor (Pohanwal). After the failed uprising of the Islamists against the government in 1975, the more radical Islamists seceded from the association; Rabbani, though, stuck to it and remained its amir. Afterward the Tajiks dominated the association. Following the Soviet invasion and the intensification of resistance, the association became a major resistance organization throughout the country, in particular the Tajik-dominated regions.

RAFI, MOHAMMAD (1946–)

Major General Mohammad Rafi became known after the communist coup in 1978. After the coup he held the post of minister of public works. Shortly afterward the government imprisoned him for his alleged part in the attempted coup. After the Soviet invasion he was named minister of defense and was sent to Moscow for special training, 1981–82.

RATEBZAD, ANAHITA (1931–)

A graduate of the Medical College of the University of Kabul, Anahita Ratebzad, known by her given name, entered politics by working among the educated and professional Afghan women. Connected to the Mohammadzay and other families with a liberal outlook, Anahita set an example of liberation by organizing her female followers around leftist ideas and a promiscuous lifestyle. Cultural activities and literacy courses also formed part of her program. She dissociated herself from her husband after she had a daughter and a son by him. In 1965 she participated in the founding congress of the PDPA; at the same time she also set up the Democratic Organization of the Women of Afghanistan, the first left-ist woman organization of its kind in the patriarchal Afghan society. But the organization's association with the pro-Moscow PDPA made it suspect from the start. Anahita's association with Karmal as his mistress helped her to win a seat in parliament in 1965. She cemented this alliance by marrying her daughter to Baryalay, Karmal's brother. In 1976 she entered the central committee. After the communist coup Anahita was appointed minister of social affairs, an insignifi-cant post. Afterward the government sent her as ambassador to Yugoslavia, and soon it dismissed her as it dismissed other Parchami ambassadors. After Karmal was raised to power, Anahita became a member of the politburo, a member of the Revolutionary Council, and minister of education. But Anahita was unable to match her work as a stateswoman with her work as an organization woman. By making the women's organization a political tool in the service of the Par-cham faction and ultimately of the Soviet Union, Anahita dealt the Afghan women's movement a setback from which it is unlikely to recover in the near future.

SARWARI, ASADULLAH

A Pashtun from the city of Ghazni, Asadullah Sarwari had been trained as a helicopter pilot in the Soviet Union. As a radical Khalqi, Sarwari was for action against the government of President Daoud even before it was overthrown. After the coup he headed the Intelligence Department, AGSA. For him, AGSA was an agency meant to suppress any person or any group that he considered to be antigovernment. He himself used to torture the accused. The Afghans dreaded no other Khalqi official as much as they dreaded Sarwari. Siding with President Taraki, he turned against First Minister Amin and hatched plots to do away with him. After his last plot failed on 14 September 1979, Sarwari, along with Gulabzoy and Watanjar, took refuge in the Soviet embassy. Later they served as guides for the invading Soviet army. Sarwari was afterward appointed vice presi-dent of the Revolutionary Council and deputy premier. Sarwari intended to overthrow the Parchami regime by a coup, but in June 1980, before his plan could reach fruition, he was sent to Mongolia as Afghan ambassador.

SAYYAF, ABD AL-RAB RASUL (1947–)

A Cholizay Ibrahimkhel Ghilzay Pashtun from the district of Paghman, Abd al-Rab Rasul Sayyaf obtained a B.A. from the College of Theology in Kabul and an M.A. from the University of al-Azhar in Cairo. There he joined the Islamic Brethren. After graduation from al-Azhar he taught at the College of Theology of Kabul University until the government of President Daoud arrested him in 1975. While the Khalqi government executed other Islamist inmates, it spared him, since he was a cousin of Hafizullah Amin. After release from prison he fled to Peshawar, where he was chosen as "a non-partisan independent to help unify the alliance formed in 1980" under the name the Islamic Union for the Liberation of Af-ghanistan (Klass, *Afghanistan,* 401). Soon the constituent members seceded from the Islamic Union, but Sayyaf used the name as an organization under his own leadership. An eloquent speaker in Arabic, Sayyaf invoked the name of jehad to obtain contributions from rich individuals, particularly Wahhabis, in the Arab world. The contributions helped him consolidate his organization as a resistance group, albeit a small one. To please his Wahhabi donors, Sayyaf also changed his name from Abd al-Rasul Sayyaf to Abd al-Rub Rasul Sayyaf. He is even said to have become a Wahhabi.

TARAKI, NUR MOHAMMAD (1917–79)

Nur Mohammad Taraki was a Shabikhel Taraki Ghilzay Pashtun from the Sur Kelay village in the Nawa Valley in the Muqur District of Ghazni Province. In 1965, Taraki was elected general secretary of the PDPA in its founding congress. Thirteen years later, in 1978, he became the president and prime minister of Afghanistan after a coup that toppled the centuries-old Durrani rule. It is therefore necessary to describe his biography in detail, particularly because of incorrect but widely reported information about him.

Taraki had no formal education except for a few classes he attended in a school in Quetta in British India, where he learned English. It was customary for members of his family to go there for work. When he returned home, his knowledge of English brought him a job as clerk with the Pashtun Trading Company of Musa Jan (Tokhay), first in Kandahar and later in its Bombay branch. On arrival in Kabul in 1937 Taraki was appointed a member of the editorial board of a periodical of the Ministry of Finance, a post that helped him learn the art of writing. An influential patron, Mohammad Zaman Taraki, helped him get the job (A. M. Karzay, personal communication, March 1993). During World War II Abdul Majid Zabuli (Taraki), an influential businessman and president of the National Bank, appointed him director general in the State Monopoly Department. Zabuli also commissioned Taraki to supervise the construction of his house. But Taraki misappropriated construction material as well as money to build a house for himself; for this he was tried and dismissed (Zabuli, personal communication, Boston, 1975).

Afterward Abdur Raof Benawa, director general of the Pashto Academy, helped Taraki find a job in the Press Department, where in 1952 he became assistant director of the Bakhtar News Agency. This was during the democratic interlude, when a free press and political parties had emerged and the government had become impatient with them. Among the parties was the Awakened Youth (Weesh Zalmyan), founded in 1945 in Kabul by known nationalist contitutionalists—Qazi Bahram, Abdul Hadi Tokhay, Mohammad Rasul Pashtun, Fayz Mohammad Angar, Gul Pacha Ulfat, Qiamuddin Khadem, Ghulam Hassan Safay, Ghulam Mohayuddin Zurmulwal, Abur Raof Benawa, Nur Mohammad Taraki, and others. This was the major political party of the time (Zurmulwal, "Weesh Zalmyan," 17).

Fearful of being arrested, Taraki and Benawa resigned from the party and followed the government line; for this service, in 1953 Premier Shah Mahmud appointed them press attachés to Washington and Delhi, respectively. Taraki remained at his new Washington post only a short time, however. Mohammad

Na'eem, foreign minister in the new government of Premier Mohammad Daoud, recalled Taraki because of his poor knowledge of English (G. M. Zurmulwal, personal communication, 1993). Taraki declined to obey the order, and instead tried to claim political asylum in the United States. When this was denied him, he held a press conference in which he declared his opposition to Daoud. . . . Five weeks later, in Karachi, he disavowed his press conference and said he was returning to Afghanistan" (A. Arnold, *Afghanistan's Two-Party Communism,* 17). His return was made possible by the intercession of Benawa and Mohammad Akbar Parwani with Premier Daoud. The former was then a press attaché in the Afghan embassy in New Delhi (Karzay, personal communication, March 1993). In Kabul, Taraki was unemployed, and toward the end of the premiership of Mohammad Daoud, he made a trip to the Soviet Union, where the KGB is believed to have recruited him. In the early 1960s he applied to the American embassy in Kabul to work as a translator but failed to get the job. When asked why he was not there, Taraki replied, "I was not employed because I have eyes as green as those of Khruschev" (Haroun, "Daoud Khan," 183). He then opened the Noor Translation House, apparently to make a living but, in fact, to organize like-minded Afghans into a political organization. His command of English did not enable him to do the difficult translation work. His clients were few, but the house served as an avenue of contact, especially with the Soviet agents (Karzay, personal communication, March 1993). Later Taraki gave up the translation work to devote his full time to organizational activities. On 1 January 1965 he was able to assemble twenty-eight young, educated Afghans in a secret meeting in his residence in Karta-e-Char in the city of Kabul. There they founded the PDPA.

On returning from the United States, Taraki read Marxist literature in both English and Persian, the latter the work of the writers of the Tudeh communist party of Iran. Before his departure to the United States, Taraki showed no sign of being a Marxist (Karzay, personal communication, March 1993). In 1957, though, he published his first novel, *The Journey of Bang,* an imitation in Pashto of the works of the Soviet novelist Maxim Gorky (Zurmulwal, personal communication, May 1993). Though a mediocre piece of literary work, *The Journey of Bang* is the first novel of its kind in Pashto that paints issues in rural society in terms of the Marxist notion of the exploitation of agrarian laborers by landlords, spiritual leaders, and government officials. This means that some time before 1957 Taraki had turned communist. A year or two earlier, when Taraki and I held a discusssion, he did not give me the impression of being a communist. Rather, he sounded like a discontented leftist. When in power, Taraki published two more novels similar to *The Journey of Bang,* but the book published under his new surname, Nazarzad, is a standard Marxist sociological and philosophical treatise that his comrades in the Soviet Union wrote for him.

Although Taraki took part with others in compiling the first English-Pashto Dictionary, which the Pashto Academy published in 1975, he was neither a historian nor a sociologist but an orthodox Marxist-Leninist. He was also unsophisticated, and friends used to make fun of him. The more he believed in communism, the more dogmatic he became. In 1968 I returned home from higher studies in England and told Taraki of my research thesis; he replied, "Any work based on the sources of imperialism we reject." Yet this Taraki organized hundreds of educated men around socialism, and after the April coup he allayed the fears of his countrymen with the simple words of the country folk, lecturing group after group of their elders that those who had overthrown the rule of the Mohammadzay tyrants were their sons, determined to do them good by providing them "home, clothes, and food," the epitome of Bang's dreams. But the ephemeral allaying of fear was the only service of note he rendered his "revolution." When he was rejected by the peasants for whose emancipation he claimed he was toiling, Taraki did not hesitate to ask the then unwilling Soviet Union to suppress them by the army. When in the game of power politics his own "loyal disciple," Hafizullah Amin, asserted himself, Taraki did not hesitate to suppress him either. On 9 October 1979 Amin managed to suffocate Taraki after removing him from power on 14 September. His other opponents then blew up his grave with dynamite. All this prompted the Kremlin decision makers to order their army to invade Afghanistan. So ended the life of "the genius of the East" and "the soul and body of the party" who was without issue and often drunk, but affable with a good sence of humor. During his short rule Taraki, in imitation of the Mughal emperors of India, watched dancing girls and enjoyed a good life (Haroun, "Daoud Khan," 186).

WATANJAR, ASLAM (1946–)

An Andar Ghilzay Pashtun from Zurmula in Paktia, Aslam Watanjar was trained as a tank officer in the Soviet Union after he had graduated from the Military Academy in Kabul. He was almost illiterate. He took part in the overthrow of the monarchy in 1973, but his role in the communist coup of 1978 was more conspicuous. Instructed by Amin, he initiated the march of tank forces from the motorized forces of numbers 4 and 15 near Pul-e-Charkhi against the government. He was in charge of the operation until Amin took over from him in the evening. Following the coup, Watanjar was appointed deputy prime minister and minister of communications. Later he served successively as minister of the interior, of defense, and again of the interior until he joined others in a plot against Amin. When the plot failed, he took refuge in the Soviet embassy along with Sarwari and Gulabzoy. Along with them, he served as a guide for the invading army. After the invasion he was promoted to membership in the central committee and the Revolutionary Council and was appointed minister of communications. In June 1981 he was added to the politburo.

Afghan Refugees in Pakistan

The following table was compiled by the Chief Commissionerate for Afghan Refugees, Islamabad, from figures received from the provincial commissioners.

According to Zia al-Din Mojaddidi, Afghan refugees in Pakistan, registered and unregistered, totaled approximately 0.5 million in Baluchistan and 1.8 million in the rest of the country. In Iran there were approximately 1 million. Thus, the total number of Afghan refugees in Pakistan and Iran was approximately 3.3 million, much less than the official figures given by these two countries and noted in this book on p. 344 n. 12. Also according to Mojaddidi, internally displaced Afghans numbered approximately 5 million. Further, he believes that the CIA handed over approximately 900 shoulder-fired Stinger missiles to the ISI and that the latter delivered only 300 of them to the mujahideen.

A former junior professor at Kabul University, Mojaddidi was the correspondent for the Voice of America in Quetta, Baluchistan, during the entire resistance period. He now lives with his family in San Diego. (Personal communication, September 1994, San Diego.)

	No. of Camps	Total Population	Male	Female	Children	Total Familie
FRONTIER PROVINCE (NWFP)						
Settled Districts						
Abbotabad	18	143,459	22,095	32,854	88,510	23,83
Bannu	7	73,418	15,381	19,480	38,557	10,54
Chitral	3	38,530	8,784	11,953	17,793	6,62
Dir	10	89,654	16,731	25,546	47,377	15,73
D. I. Khan	11	88,082	18,144	24,379	45,559	13,01
Kohat	18	232,604	58,225	65,608	108,771	32,24
Mansehra	9	71,965	9,088	14,252	48,625	10,19
Mardan	17	106,578	22,610	28,318	55,650	17,99
Peshawar (1)	31	280,921	65,686	73,876	141,359	57,64
Peshawar (2)	29	225,518	56,279	53,423	115,816	41,69
Swat	2	14,334	2,564	4,194	7,576	2,57
Total	155	1,365,063	295,587	353,883	715,593	232,11
Tribal Agencies						
Bajaur	25	197,646	49,426	58,867	89,353	28,42
Kurram	34	347,790	99,759	96,983	151,048	50,75
Malakand	3	54,966	7,615	14,392	32,959	7,90
Mohmand	2	15,807	4,525	5,006	6,276	2,64
N/Waziristan	24	184,528	48,496	43,356	92,676	26,25
Orakzai	2	13,356	2,685	4,922	5,749	1,97
S/Waziristan	6	56,423	11,611	13,725	31,087	8,95
Total	96	870,516	224,177	237,251	409,148	126,91
Total NWFP	251	2,235,579	519,704	591,134	1,124,741	359,02
BALUCHISTAN						
Chagai	21	171,980	41,275	48,154	82,550	28,57
Gulistan	12	171,556	41,173	48,036	82,347	26,47
Loralai	10	105,041	25,210	29,411	50,420	16,94
Pishin	19	168,534	40,448	47,190	80,896	25,58
Quetta	5	121,365	29,128	33,982	58,255	20,45
Zhob	5	55,267	13,264	15,475	26,528	9,11
Chaman Sub Division	5	41,638	9,993	11,659	19,986	6,06
Total BALUCHISTAN	77	835,381	200,491	233,907	400,982	133,21
PUNJAB						
Kot Chandna	16	180,428	29,550	40,630	110,308	31,84
SIND						
Karachi	1	18,674	4,481	5,229	8,964	2,99
Grand Total	345	3,270,122	754,226	870,900	1,644,995	527,07

Notes
[1]Approximately 300,000 unregistered and scattered refugees in Baluchistan and NWFP are awaiting registration.
[2]Fresh registration during the fortnight: 34,883.
[3]Refugee influx continues at the average monthly rate of between 6,000 to 8,000.
[4]Percentage of Men:Women:Children: 24:28:48.
[5]163,225 unregistered refugees who have been provided provisional ration cards by CCAR, Quetta, are included in the tot

Telephone Conversation Between Kosygin and Taraki

For more than a week beginning 15 March 1979, the people of the city of Herat and its environs, joined by the military division stationed there, rose in rebellion. About twenty-five thousand of them were killed before the Khalqi government was able to suppress their uprising, principally with the assistance of the Soviet warplanes that bombed the city from bases across the border in the Soviet Union. Of the many antigovernment uprisings this was the biggest, and the government felt a danger to its survival. To avert the danger, Premier Nur Mohammad Taraki first held a telephone conversation with A. N. Kosygin, the Soviet premier, and then flew in secret to Moscow to persuade his comrades there to suppress the uprising with their own military men from the Central Asian republics disguised as Afghans.

The telephone conversation between Taraki and Kosygin, which occurred on 18 March 1979 and is transcribed here, shows how desperate Premier Taraki had become. He was desperate because he believed that "the power of the people is the power of God." Now the full weight of this power had been turned against his government. The text also throws light on the sociopolitical situation of the country, a situation that is in contrast with what the government was depicting in its propaganda. The text is here reproduced in full with the permission of the *Journal of South Asian and Middle Eastern Studies*, which published this and other documents related to the Soviet invasion of Afghanistan in vol. 17, no. 2 (winter 1994). The conversation was carried on through the Soviet interpreter in Kabul, an assistant to the chief military adviser, General-Lieutenant Gorelov, and written down by someone named Batsanov.

KOSYGIN.   Tell comrade Taraki that I want to give him warm regards from Leonid Ilyich [Brezhnev] and from members of the Political Bureau.

TARAKI.   Thank you very much.

KOSYGIN.   How is comrade Taraki; he does not get too tired, does he?

TARAKI.   I do not get tired. Today we have had a meeting of the Revolutionary Council.

KOSYGIN.   That's good, I am very glad. Ask comrade Taraki whether he can describe the situation in Afghanistan.

TARAKI.   The situation is not good, it is getting worse. During the last month and a half from the Iran side four thousand servicemen in civil[ian] clothes penetrated into the city of Herat and into military units. At present all the 17th infantry division is in their hands, including the artillery regiment and anti-aircraft battalion which is firing at our planes. Fighting continues in the city.

KOSYGIN.   How many people are there in the division?

TARAKI.   About five thousand men. All ammunition and store houses and depots are in their hands. Foods and ammunition are carried by planes from Kandahar to our comrades who are fighting there against them.

KOSYGIN.   How many of your people have remained there?

TARAKI.   Five hundred men. They are on the Herat airfield and the division commander is with them. As a reinforcement, we sent there by planes from Kabul an operation group. This group is on the Herat airfield since early morning.

KOSYGIN.   And what about the officers of the division? Have they become traitors or [are] some of them . . . together with [the] division commander on the airfield[?]

TARAKI.   A small part of the officers have remained faithful, the rest of them are with the enemy.

KOSYGIN.   Are some of the workers, citizens and office workers in Herat on your side? Or anyone else?

TARAKI.   We do not have active support of the population. Almost all of the population is under the Shi'ite slogans. "Do not believe the atheists, follow us"—their propaganda is based on this slogan.

KOSYGIN.   How large is [the] Herat population?

TARAKI.   200 or 250 thousand people. Their behavior depends upon the situation. They go to where they are led. At present they are on the side of the enemy.

KOSYGIN.   Are there many workers there?

TARAKI.   Very few; only one or two thousand people.

KOSYGIN.   What do you think is the situation in Herat?

TARAKI.   We think that either this evening or tomorrow morning Herat will fall and be in hands of the enemy.

KOSYGIN.   And what are further perspectives?

TARAKI.   We are sure that the enemy will form new units and will continue the offensive.

KOSYGIN.   Do you have armed forces to defeat them?

TARAKI.   If only we had them . . .

KOSYGIN.   What are your suggestions concerning this situation?

TARAKI.   We ask you to render practical and technical assistance with men and armament.

KOSYGIN.   This is a very complicated problem.

TARAKI.   Otherwise the rebels will go to Kandahar and then to Kabul. They will bring half of Iran into Afghanistan under the flag of [the] Herat division. Afghans who have run away to Pakistan will come back. Iran and Pakistan have a common plan against us. Therefore if you inflict a blow on Herat now the revolution may be saved.

KOSYGIN.   The whole world will learn about this immediately. The rebels have radio sets and they will inform the world right away.

TARAKI.   I ask you to help us.

KOSYGIN.   We must take counsel about this.

TARAKI.   While you will be taking counsel Herat will fall and both the Soviet Union and Afghanistan will have still greater difficulties.

KOSYGIN.   Maybe you may tell me now what assessments you can offer concerning Pakistan and then Iran? Do you have connections with progressive-minded people in Iran? Can you tell them that at present your chief enemy is the United States[?] Iranians are very embittered against the United States and probably this can be used for propaganda purposes.

TARAKI.   Today we have broadcast a statement to the Iranian government pointing out that Iran interferes in our home affairs in the Herat region.

KOSYGIN.   And what about Pakistan? Don't you consider it necessary to make a statement to it?

TARAKI.   Tomorrow or the day after tomorrow we shall make the same [kind] of statement to Pakistan.

KOSYGIN.   Can you rely upon your army? Is it trustworthy? Maybe you can assemble your troops to deliver a blow on Herat?

TARAKI.   We believe our army is trustworthy. But it is impossible to withdraw troops from other cities in order to send them to Herat because this will weaken our positions in the cities.

KOSYGIN.   But if we give you quickly additional planes and arms will you be able to raise new units?

TARAKI.   This will take much time and meanwhile Herat will fall.

KOSYGIN.   Do you believe that if Herat falls Pakistan will act the same way as Iran does?

TARAKI.   The possibility of this is very great. The spirit of Pakistani people will stiffen after that. Americans lend them adequate support. After Herat falls Pakistanis will also send soldiers in civil[ian] clothes who will begin to capture towns and the Iranians will interfere actively. Success in Herat is the key to all other problems connected with the struggle.

KOSYGIN.   What political actions or statements would you like us to make? Have you got any consideration [suggestions] in this respect?

TARAKI.   It is necessary to combine propagandistic and practical assistance. I suggest that you mark your tanks and planes with Afghan signs[,] then nobody will know anything. Your troops could move from Kushka and from Kabul.

KOSYGIN.   To reach Kabul will also take time.

TARAKI.   Kushka is very near to Herat. As for Kabul troops can be brought there by planes. If you bring troops to Kabul and they will move from there to Herat we think that nobody will know the truth. People will think that they are government troops.

KOSYGIN.   I don't want to distress you but such a fact is impossible to conceal. It will become known to the whole world in two hours. Everybody will shout that the Soviet Union has started intervention in Afghanistan. Tell me, comrade Taraki, if we bring arms and tanks to Kabul by planes will you you be able to provide tank-men?

TARAKI.   Very few of them.

KOSYGIN.   But how many?

TARAKI.   I don't have exact data about this.

KOSYGIN.   If we send you tanks, necessary ammunition and mortars by planes immediately will you find specialists who could use them?

TARAKI.   I can't answer this question. Soviet advisers can answer it.

KOSYGIN.   As I understand you have no well-trained military personnel at all or very few of them.
            Hundreds of Afghan officers have been trained in the Soviet Union. Where are they?

TARAKI.   Most of them are Muslim reactionaries or they are also called Muslim Brothers. We can't rely on them, we are not sure of them.

KOSYGIN.   How many people live in Kabul now?

TARAKI.   About one million men.

KOSYGIN.   Can you recruit fifty thousand soldiers if we send you arms by planes immediately? How many soldiers can you recruit?

TARAKI.   We can recruit some men, first of all young men, but it will take much time to train them.

KOSYGIN.   Can you recruit students?

TARAKI.   It is possible to recruit students and pupils of the 11th or 12th grades of the Lyceums.

KOSYGIN.   Can't you recruit workers?

TARAKI.   There are very few workers in Afghanistan.

KOSYGIN.   And what about the poorest peasants?

TARAKI.   We can recruit only students of the Lyceums, pupils of the eldest forms and a small number of workers. But to train them will take much time. When it is necessary we are ready to do anything.

KOSYGIN.   We have taken a decision to send you urgently military equipment, to take upon ourselves the repair of planes and helicopters free of charge. We have also decided to send you 100,000 [*sic*] tons of grain and to raise the cost of gas from 21 US dollars per thousand cubic meters up to 37.82 US dollars.

TARAKI.   That is good, but let us talk about Herat.

KOSYGIN.   All right. Can you now form several divisions in Kabul of progressive people upon whom you may rely? Can you do that in other places too? We would give you necessary arms.

TARAKI.   We have no officers. Iran sends service men in civil[ian] clothes to Afghanistan. Pakistan also sends soldiers and officers in Afghan clothes. Why can't the Soviet Union send Uzbeks, Tajiks, Turkmen in civil[ian] clothes? Nobody will recognize who they are.

KOSYGIN.   What else can you say concerning Herat?

TARAKI.   We want Tajiks, Uzbeks, and Turkmen to be sent to us because they can drive tanks and besides all these peoples live in Afghanistan too. Let them wear Afghan clothes, Afghan badges and then nobody will recognize them as foreigners. We think this is very easily done. Judging by the example of Iran and Pakistan we see that it is easy to do.

KOSYGIN.   But you oversimplify the problem, while this is a complex political, international problem. Yet despite all this we shall have consultations and then give you our answer. I think that you should try to form new units. You can't rely only upon people who come from elsewhere. [The] Iranian revolution is an example: the people threw out all Americans and all other peoples too who tried to show themselves as defenders of Iran.

                 Let us make an agreement: we shall take counsel and then give you our answer. And you on your side counsel your military men and our advisers. Certainly there are forces in Afghanistan who will support you at the risk of their lives and will fight for you. These forces are to be given arms immediately.

TARAKI.   Send us fighting infantry machines [armored personnel-carriers] by planes.

KOSYGIN.   And do you have men who can drive them?

TARAKI.   We have 30 or 35 men who can drive them.

KOSYGIN.   Are they reliable? Will they not go over to the enemy together with the machines? Our drivers do not know the language.

TARAKI.   But you send machines and drivers who know our language— Tajiks, Uzbeks.

KOSYGIN.   I expected you to give such an answer. We are comrades and are fighting [a] common fight, therefore we must not feel shy before each other. Everything is to be subordinated to the fight. We shall call you and tell you our opinion.

TARAKI.   Please give our regards and best wishes to comrade Brezhnev and to members of the Political Bureau.

KOSYGIN.   Thanks. Remember me to all your comrades. I wish you firmness in solving problems, assurances and well-being. Good bye.

Notes

INTRODUCTION

1. For details see Kakar, *Government and Society;* Kakar, *Afghanistan.*
2. Kakar, "Trends in Modern Afghan History," 24, 25.
3. Gregorian, *Modern Afghanistan* 352; Farhang, *Afghanistan* 1:426.
4. Gregorian, *Modern Afghanistan,* 363.
5. Ibid., 381.
6. Ibid., 380–89.
7. Farhang, *Afghanistan* 1:446–58; Dupree, *Afghanistan,* 494–98.
8. Ghaus, *Fall of Afghanistan,* 65–79.
9. Noorzoy, "Economic Policies," 378; Ludin, "Economic Conditions."
10. Ghaus, *Fall of Afghanistan,* 90.
11. Poullada, "Road to Crisis," 43.
12. Fayzzad, *National Loya Jirgas,* 232–96. I am grateful to Habibullah Rafi for giving me this along with a number of other books recently published on Afghanistan. Farhang, *Afghanistan* 1:485–93.
13. For details see Kushkaki, *Constitutional Decade;* Farhang, *Afghanistan;* Dupree, *Afghanistan;* Fletcher, *Afghanistan;* Kakar, "Fall of the Afghan Monarchy"; Magnus, "Constitution of 1964."
14. Ghaus, *Fall of Afghanistan,* 147.
15. Ibid., 173, 179.

1. THE SOVIET INVASION OF AFGHANISTAN

1. For a background to the Soviet invasion of Afghanistan and its wider implications for the region and the world, see Bradsher, *Afghanistan.*
2. Andrew and Gordiesky, *KGB,* 574.

3. Deac, "Sky Train Invasion," 22.
4. Ibid., 23
5. Andrew and Gordiesky, *KGB*, 574.
6. Quoted in Reshtia, *Price of Liberty,* 54.
7. Zurmulwal, *Russia's Armed Aggression*, 27.
8. Andrew and Gordiesky, *KGB*, 575.
9. Anwar, *Tragedy of Afghanistan*, 190.
10. Dobbs, "Secret Memos."
11. Ibid.
12. Deac, "Sky Train Invasion," 24.
13. Arnold, *Afghanistan's Two-Party Communism*, 186.

2. WHY DID THE SOVIET UNION INVADE?

1. A. Morozov, "Between Amin and Karmal," 37. Morozov was the KGB deputy chief in Afghanistan from 1975 to 1979. I am grateful to Mr. Alam Katawazay for providing me copies of the three articles by Morozov. Quoting from Morozov, Arnold states that "[President] Da'ud delegated to him [Amin] the military-recruitment program and introduced him to the K.G.B." ("Communism in Afghanistan," 114). If not a printing mistake, this wild statement should be rejected outright.
2. Morozov, "Night Visit," 32.
3. Morozov, "Between Amin and Karmal," 39.
4. Morozov, "Night Visit," 30.
5. Roy, "Origin," 53.
6. Arnold, "Communism in Afghanistan," 53.
7. Safi, *Just Uprising;* Anonymous, *Uprising of the Twenty-fourth;* Yusufi, *Uprising;* Khairkhwah, *Commemorating the Martyrs.*
8. Deac, "Sky Train Invasion," 23.
9. Dobbs, "Secret Memos." This article is based on the newly disclosed Soviet archives containing the minutes of the decision the Soviet leaders had made about invading Afghanistan. I am pleased to note that the article confirmed my findings. I am grateful to Dr. Zamin Mohmand for providing me the clipping of the article.
10. Wakman, *Afghanistan,* 119.
11. Anwar, *Tragedy,* 162.
12. Ibid., 162, 165.
13. Ibid., 168.
14. A photographer of the Afghan delegation quoted by Daoud Malikyar, personal communication, San Diego, June 1991.
15. Morozov, "Shots Fired," 32.
16. Anwar, *Tragedy,* 168.
17. Ibid., 170, 171.
18. Morozov, "Shots Fired," 34.
19. G. Povlovsky, the Soviet chief adviser in Afghanistan in 1979, quoted in Sharq, *Memoirs,* 159. Dr. Mohammad Hassan Sharq held high state positions

when Mohammad Daoud was prime minister and president of Afghanistan. A medical physician by profession, Dr. Sharq was Mohammad Daoud's associate. From 1988 to 1989 he himself was prime minister of Afghanistan. His book, which describes mainly the events in high circles, is very informative. Sharq is the first prime minister of Afghanistan to publish his memoirs.

20. A former government official, personal communication, Los Angeles, February 1991. The official said that he was present at the occasion.

21. Quoted in Morozov, "Shots Fired," 34.

22. Bradsher, *Afghanistan*, 117.

23. Ibid.

24. Ibid.

25. Shroder and Assifi, "Afghan Mineral Resources," 112. According to the authors, the Soviet exploitation of Afghan resources can be understood from the further facts that Afghan-Soviet agreements called for the average annual export of 2.5 billion cubic meters of gas to the Soviet Union up to 1985. The revenues from the sale of gas were not, however, to be paid to the Afghan government: they were to be applied as repayment for Soviet loans and the interest on those loans, including funds spent by the Soviets for Soviet-assisted projects. In addition, in 1980 the Soviets took the step of crediting its imports of Afghan natural gas against the cost of maintaining the "friendly fraternal assistance" of its "limited military contingent" in Afghanistan. In other words, after 1980 the Afghans were forced to pay with their natural resources for the invasion and occupation of their own country and the destruction of their own people. Also, in early 1980 Soviet experts began to increase gas production by 65 percent. Afghan gas fields at a place near Shiberghan were (as of 1977) estimated to have reserves in excess of 500 trillion cubic feet. In 1979 Soviet experts discovered another gas-bearing zone in northern Afghanistan capable of producing one-quarter million cubic meters per day. See also Assifi, "Russian Rope."

26. A former official of the Afghan Ministry of Finance, personal communication, Pul-e-Charkhi concentration camp, 1983.

27. A former senior official, personal communication, Kabul, 1987.

28. Mansur Hashemi, the former Khalqi minister of water and power, personal communication, Sadarat prison, 1982.

29. A former junior professor of Kabul University, personal communication, Peshawar, 1988.

30. A senior official of the Ministry of Foreign Affairs of the Khalqi Government, personal communication, Kabul, 1987.

31. Bradsher, *Afghanistan*, 118.

32. S. Harrison, quoted in Wakman, *Afghanistan*, 121.

33. For details of how the United States and other noncommunist governments stopped financial aid to the Khalqi government, see Bradsher, *Afghanistan*, 99.

34. Ibid., 118.

35. Ibid., 117.

36. Ibid., 122. In July 1979 Amin took an unusual step to establish a personal relationship with the U.S. administration. According to a former government official, he carried a personal message from Hafizullah Amin to Zbigniew

Brzezinski, President Carter's national security adviser. The official said that he personally handed over the letter to Mr. Brzezinski but received no reply.

37. Bradsher, *Afghanistan,* 179.

38. Nasrat, "Bitter Facts," 97. According to Nasrat,"If the country's situation had not taken a different turn, Gulbuddin Hekmatyar, on his own request, would have been appointed minister of tribal affairs." According to rumors in circulation in Kabul at the time, Hekmatyar was assigned the post of prime minister in the envisaged Khalqi-dominated coalition government.

39. "Abstract, Politburo, Central Committee, USSR," *Journal of South Asian and Middle Eastern Studies,* Vol. XVII, winter 1994, 54–55.

40. "Conversation between Kosygin and Taraki," source above, 30.

41. G. M. Noorzoy, personal communication, Kabul, February 1980.

42. Ivanov, "Revelations," 20.

43. Bradsher, *Afghanistan,* 176. According to Abdul Hakeem Hakeemi, commander of the Bagram airbase at the time, the number was much smaller, and they arrived only weeks before the invasion. Personal communication, San Diego, March 1995.

44. A former Afghan official, personal communication, Los Angeles, 1991.

45. Roy, *Islam and Resistance,* 121, 76.

46. Bradsher, *Afghanistan,* 173–75; see also Arnold, *Afghanistan's Two-Party Communism,* 96.

47. Bradsher, *Afghanistan,* 185.

48. In 1989 the Soviet Supreme Council denounced the invasion by a vote of 1,678–18, with 19 abstentions (*Honolulu Advertiser,* 25 December 1989, C1).

49. Bradsher, *Afghanistan,* 155.

50. Dobbs, "Secret Memos."

51. Ibid.

3. UNDER THE SOVIET SHADOW

1. Ivanov, "Revelations," 18.

2. Bradsher, *Afghanistan,* 181.

3. An Afghan cabinet minister, personal communication, Kabul, August 1968.

4. Kakar, *Afghans in the Spring of 1987,* 91.

5. Roy, "Origin," 41.

6. Zaki-Ullah, *Russo-Afghan Friendship,* 44. Haqshinas, *Russia's Intrigues and Crimes,* 311.

7. Zurmulwal, "Khalqi and Parchami Factions," 3.

8. Zaki-Ullah Khan, *Russo-Afghan Friendship,* 40.

9. A. R. Safay (former member of parliament), personal communication, Los Angeles, April 1991.

10. Farhang, *Afghanistan* 1:514.

11. Zurmulwal, "Khalqi and Parchami Factions," 3.

12. Bradsher, *Afghanistan,* 99.

13. Sharq, *Memoirs,* 216.

14. For details about the PDPA, see Arnold, *Afghanistan's Two-Party Communism;* Arnold and Klass, "Afghanistan's Divided Communist Party"; Kushkaki, *Constitutional Decade;* Haqshinas, *Russia's Intrigues and Crimes;* Roy, "Origin"; Rubin, "Political Elites."

15. Kushkaki, *Constitutional Decade,* 147; Morozov, "Between Amin and Karmal," 36–38.

16. Kushkaki, *Constitutional Decade,* 58, 141, 149; Farhang, *Afghanistan* 1:514.

17. Zurmulwal, "Khalqi and Parchami Factions," 4; Farhang, *Afghanistan* 2:8.

18. Morozov, "Between Amin and Karmal," 39.

19. Kushkaki, *Constitutional Decade,* 149.

20. Mansur Hashemi, the former Khalqi minister of water and power, personal communication, Sadarat prison, July 1982.

21. Morozov, "Night Visit," 32.

22. Morozov, "Betweeen Amin and Karmal," 39.

23. Ibid.

24. A former Khalqi cabinet minister, personal communication, Pul-e-Charkhi prison, July 1986; Sharq, *Memoirs,* 164.

25. Morozov, "Night Visit," 33.

26. Zahir Ghazi Alam, personal communication, San Diego, 1991.

27. Baha, "Cruel Executions," 79, 81. Baha's source of information was N. Dooryankov, a Soviet specialist on Afghanistan whom she met in Moscow when she was sent there by the party for medical treatment.

28. Gharzay, *Memoirs,* 89.

29. A former senior government official, personal communication, Kabul, August 1987.

30. Farhang, *Afghanistan* 1:498.

31. A. Tufan, a former Khalqi governor, personal communication, Sadarat prison, Kabul, August 1982.

32. Arnold, *Afghanistan's Two-Party Communism,* 101.

33. Ivanov, "Revelations," 19.

34. Fazili, *Days as Dark as Nights,* 72.

35. Arnold, *Afghanistan's Two-Party Communism,* 99.

36. Zadran, *History of Afghanistan,* 808.

37. Quoted in Sharq, *Memoirs,* 239.

38. Ibid., 240.

39. Arnold, *Afghanistan's Two-Party Communism,* 99; Anwar, *Tragedy,* 223.

40. Girardet, *Afghanistan,* 136.

41. Ibid., 138.

42. Sharq, *Memoirs,* 236.

43. Ibid., 236.

44. Ibid., 235, 237.

45. A former cabinet minister, personal communication, Kabul, July, 1987.

46. Arnold, *Afghanistan's Two-Party Communism,* 108.

47. The appointment of these well-known Afghans—Abd al-Hay Habibi; a

prolific author, writer, poet, and former member of parliament; Abdur Raof
Benawa, a poet, former cabinet minister, and former member of parliament;
Mier Mohammad Siddiq Farhang, an author, former member of parliament,
and cofounder of the Fatherland Party; and Rawan Farhadi, a scholar and diplomat—was a shock to many. They had good reputations, particularly among the
intellectuals who expected them at least to stay away from the client regime. But
they entered its service without being able to influence its policy. They cooperated with it at a time when the Soviets had occupied their homeland and were
killing Afghans by the thousands.

Except for Habibi, who died later in Kabul, I met the others and raised the
subject of their accepting the posts. Abdur Raof Benawa said that he was in the
hospital when he heard the news of his appointment. When I suggested to him
that he had then an excuse to decline the offer, he cautioned me to be careful in
these critical times. Subsequently, the efforts of his more intimate friends to
achieve the same end also failed. In 1980 the regime appointed him ambassador
to Libya. Later he developed bone cancer and went to the United States for
treatment; he died there in 1985.

Mier Mohammad Siddiq Farhang had accepted the post as a matter of policy.
Karmal had, he said, assured him that he wanted to honor the promises that he
had made, while serving in parliament, to set up a national democratic government. Farhang argued that since politics is the art of the possible, he accepted
the post to pave the way for the return home of the Soviet troops. Apparently
he was sympathetic to the regime. Over the years, together with Mohammad
Omar the Pilot, Karim Nazihi, and Asif Ahang he had worked to promote the
leftist views of the Moscow line. While in prison in the 1950s he introduced
Karmal and Khybar, who were also in prison at the time, to these views. (A.,
personal communication, United States, 1990.)

When Farhang served as an adviser in the Ministry of Mines and Industry,
he also introduced Karmal to the royal court. Encouraged by it, Farhang, along
with Karmal, played a role in spreading communism among the youth (Sharq,
Memoirs, 234). I told Farhang that the Soviets had introduced their troops into
Afghanistan not for the sake of Karmal or against Amin but for their own purposes, and that the introduction of the troops was likely to result in disasters;
he remained silent. Disillusioned, Farhang later left for the United States, where
he became mildly critical of Karmal. Nevertheless, Karmal arranged that Farhang's valuable antiques, which he had left in his home in Kabul, be safeguarded. He gave instructions in this regard to the Parchami who was then resid-
ing in Farhang's home; later, though, after Najibullah replaced Karmal, another
Parchami who lived in Farhang's home took possession of the artifacts. (A.,
personal communication, United States, 1990.) Farhang died of a heart attack
in 1990.

Although a devout Muslim and probably opposed to the regime from the
start, Rawan Farhadi accepted Karmal's offer of a job. Farhadi was fond of
official positions, and Karmal had just released him from the Khalqi prison under the terms of the general amnesty. Besides, Farhadi was pessimistic, arguing
that the equation was incomparably in favor of the Soviets. By this he meant
that the Soviets were too powerful for the Afghans. When I said to him that the

Soviets had made themselves morally weaker by waging war against the Afghans inside their own country, he changed the topic. Farhadi served the regime for about two years and made two trips to the Soviet Union; he even called the invasion "a positive development in Soviet-Afghan relations" (A. T. Wahhab, *Peace,* 18 Apr. 1994, 2). Farhadi then absconded. In 1993 he was appointed head of the Afghan delegation of the Islamic State of Afghanistan to the United Nations.

48. Arnold, *Afghanistan's Two-Party Communism,* 106.
49. Dobbs, "Dramatic Politburo Meeting."
50. Ivanov, "Revelations," 19.
51. Ibid., 18.
52. Dobbs, "Dramatic Politburo Meeting."
53. Bradsher, *Afghanistan,* 227.

4. ISLAMIC RESISTANCE ORGANIZATIONS

1. Ministry of Planning, *General Statistics,* 113–22. I am grateful to Amanullah Mansury, a minister of the interior during the constitutional decade, for giving me his only copy of the book. Farhang, *Afghanistan* 2:41. Barnet Rubin writes about the expansion of modern education in Afghanistan: "In the last eight years of Daoud's premiership . . . the number of primary and secondary school students nearly tripled, and the number of post-secondary students . . . increased more than fourfold; and in the period of political liberalization known as New Democracy (1963–73), the number of primary school students doubled, and secondary students increased more than sixfold, growing an average of one-fifth per year. University enrollment was 3.4 times larger at the end of the decade than it had been at the beginning; there were 11,000 students in Afghanistan and 1,500 per year sent abroad by 1974" ("Political Elites," 80). On the eve of the communist coup in 1978 Kabul University and Polytechnic had a total of more than 13,000 mixed students, and 1,000 professors. Polytechnic had about 1,000 students and a small number of Afghan junior professors. The Soviet professors outnumbered the latter. Kabul University had more than 800 professors. A. S. Aziemi, personal communication, Peshawar, February 1989. Mr. Aziemi was chancellor of Kabul University before the communists took over.

2. Newell and Newell, *Struggle for Afghanistan,* 45.

3. The Front of Afghanistan's Militant Mujahideen, *Watan;* M. N. Majruh, personal communication, Los Angeles, January 1991. About the resistance groups which the Afghans set up in Peshawar in 1980, an observer writes, "Anyone who entertained the idea of becoming the Afghan amir or king would rent a garage, a shop, or a house, and would distribute membership cards with his party's name and his photo boldly engraved on them. In this way over 60 small and big Afghan parties were set up" (Zadran, *History of Afghanistan,* 795).

4. *Fundamentalism,* in the words of Professor Bernard Lewis, refers to the maintenance, in opposition to modernism, of traditional orthodox beliefs, such as the inerrancy of Scripture and literal acceptance of the creeds as fundamentals of Protestant Christianity. It is thus essentially a Christian term. The term *fundamentalist* is now also applied to a number of Islamic radical and militant groups.

Muslim fundamentalists, however, base themselves not only on the Quran but also on the Traditions of the Prophet and on the corpus of transmitted theological and legal learning. Their aim is nothing less than the abrogation of all the imported and modernized legal codes and social norms and the installation in their place of the full panoply of the Shari'a—its rules and penalties, its jurisdiction, and its prescribed form of government. For details, see Lewis, *Political Language of Islam,* 118.

5. Hekmatyar, *Interview,* 10; Haqshinas, *Russia's Intrigues and Crimes,* 330.

6. For details see, Choueirei, *Islamic Fundamentalism,* 94; Shepard, "Islam as a System," 37.

7. Choueiri, *Islamic Fundamentalism,* 94, 123.

8. Shepard, "Islam as a System," 32.

9. Mawdudi, *Political Theory of Islam,* 31. I am grateful to Rahmat Zirakyar for giving me this and another book.

10. Hyman, *Muslim Fundamentalism,* 20.

11. Choueiri, *Muslim Fundamentlism,* 110.

12. Mawdudi, *Political Theory of Islam,* 22.

13. Choueiri, *Muslim Fundamentalism,* 111.

14. Ibid., 127.

15. Kakar, *Government and Society,* 177. Choueiri, *Muslim Fundamentalism,* 137.

16. Choueiri, *Muslim Fundamentalism,* 138.

17. Ibid., 135.

18. Ibid., 136.

19. Shepard, "Islam as a System," 33.

20. Professor M. E. Yapp has described the terms *modernization, traditional society,* and *modern society* as follows: "The attributes of a traditional society are: politically, a minimal role for government; economically, the predominance of agriculture or pastoralism, with little industry and the great bulk of the population living in the countryside; and socially, a system of organization based on birth, compartmentalized rather than hierarchic, with low mobility and little literacy, and in which the family, tribe, village, guild and religious community form the the principal units of social life, providing educational, legal and social services for their members and, frequently, economic organization and defence as well. The attributes of a modern society are the opposite of these: politically, there is a large role for the state; economically, it is predominantly industrial and urban; and socially, it is based upon contract, arranged horizontally with a high degree of mobility, and the older units of social life play a much reduced role, their major functions having been usurped by the state or other public organizations. Modernization denotes the passage from the first to the second" (Yapp, "Contemporary Islamic Revivalism," 180).

21. Newell and Newell, *Struggle for Afghanistan,* 45.

22. Nangyal, *Political Parties,* 10; Haqshinas, *Russia's Intrigues and Crimes,* 332–39; Naeem, *Russian Program,* 71; Khan, "Emergence of Religious Parties."

23. The founding students of the Islamic Movement, besides Hekmatyar, were Mawlawi Abdur Rahman, Engineer Habibur Rahman, Abdur Rahim Ni-

azi, Engineer Sayfuddin Nasratyar, Abd al-Qadir Tawana, Ghulam Rabbani 'Ateesh, Sayyed Abdur Rahman, Abdul Habib, and Gul Mohammad. Except for Hekmatyar, all are now dead (Hekmatyar, *Interview*, 20).

24. Ibid., 23.

25. Ibid.

26. Shahrani, "Saur Revolution," 158.

27. Ibid.

28. Khan, "Emergence of Religious Parties,"; Hekmatyar, *Interview*, 24.

29. Rubin, "Political Elites," 81.

30. Hekmatyar, *Interview*, 21

31. Quoted in Hyman, *Muslim Fundamentalism*, 4.

32. Zadran, *History of Afghanistan*, 610.

33. Ibid., 510.

34. On rejecting general elections, the foundation of democracy, Khalis is categorical and uncompromising. He states: "General elections are the outcome of the ignorance of the East and West. That is why, as they are contrary to the Islamic justice, they are rejected and are unacceptable to us. The advocates of this voice can't go with us along the same road." Khalis, *Message to the Mujahid Nation*, 5, 12, 26; Khalis, *Two Articles*, 12, 13.

35. The fundamentalists are not only opposed to those who have exercised political domination in the past in Afghanistan but are equally vehement in their denunciations of the traditional elite, who are, in their view, to be blamed for the moral degeneration that led to the present tragedy. See Ghani, "Afghanistan," 92.

36. Haqshinas, *Russia's Intrigues and Crimes*, 331.

37. Before his arrest in 1973, Mawlawi Habib al-Rahman Fayzani (Kakar), known as Mawlana Fayzani, dominated the soul and body of his followers, first as a schoolteacher and principal in Herat and later as a reformer, pir, and political leader. He gave up teaching to combat communism and create an Islamic movement. For this purpose he composed a number of books and traveled in the country before taking up residence in Kabul, where he opened a library and set up Madrasa-e-Quran, a seminary for the teaching of Quran; this program took on an active political dimension among his followers of traditional mullas and artisans. His teachings transcended the communal line of Sunni and Shi'a. To his followers of both sects he appeared as a messianic personality. He played a leading role in the anticommunist agitations of the traditional mullas in 1970. By the time of the Daoud coup in 1973 he had united a number of secret Islamic associations under the name of the School of Monotheism (Maktab-e-Tawheed), of which he was elected amir. Shortly after the coup he was arrested on a charge of plotting to overthrow the regime. During the Khalqi rule Fayzani along with more than one hundred Ikhwanis, including Professor Niazi, were executed. For details, see Edwards, "Shi'i Political Dissent," 217–20; Haqshinas, *Russia's Intrigues and Crimes*, 336; Gharzay, *Memoirs*, 49.

38. Hekmatyar, *Interview*, 25.

39. For details on organizational structure of the Islamic Association, see Roy, *Islam and Resistance*, 73.

40. Hekmatyar, *Interview*, 20.

41. Brigot and Roy, *War in Afghanistan,* 27.

42. Roy, *Islam and Resistance,* 75.

43. Ibid.

44. Wolasmal, "Foreign Interference," 3.

45. Dupree, *Afghanistan,* 762; Haqshinas, *Political Changes,* 26–32; Roy, *Islam and Resistance,* 74–76.

46. Haqshinas, *Political Changes,* 30.

47. Edwards, "Shi'i Political Dissent," 221.

48. For details, see Jamiat-e-Islami, *Aims and Goals;* Hezb-e-Islami, *Aims.* I am grateful to Dr. Nazif Shahrani for providing me with both texts.

49. Brigot and Roy, *War in Afghanistan,* 109.

50. Khalis, *Message,* 2.

51. For details, see Ghaus, *Fall of Afghanistan.*

52. Roy, *Islam and Resistance,* 77.

53. Alam, "Memoirs of Jehad," 108–11.

54. Nangyal, *Political Parties,* 30–36. The first coalition, the Covenant of the Islamic Unity, comprising Jam'iyyat, Harakat, Nejat, Mahaz, and Hizb (Khalis), was set up in August 1979, but it was no more than a name. Na'eem, *Russian Program,* 93–103; Roy, *Islam and Resistance,* 122–24.

55. A senior official of the Ministry of Foreign Affairs, personal communication, Islamabad, December 1988.

56. Roy, *Islam and Resistance,* 122. Bradsher may have been the first to observe Pakistan's concern about a strong Afghan leadership. He states that Pakistan "had reason to be concerned that a strong single organization based on its territory might become the voice of a new form of Pashtunistan movement or comparable to the Palestine Liberation Organization in periods when the P.L.O. had defiantly extraterritorial power in Jordan and later Lebanon" (*Afghanistan,* 295).

57. Hekmatyar, *Interview,* 59.

58. Charliand, *Report from Afghanistan,* 47.

59. Quoted in Wassil, "Opinion," 26.

60. Haqshinas, *Political Changes,* 36.

61. Quoted in Emadi, *State, Society, and Superpowers,* 102.

62. Shah Mohammad Nadir Alami, leader of the Islamic Unity of Central Afghanistan, personal communication, 1991.

63. Edwards, "Shi'i Political Dissent," 201–29; Haqshinas, *Political Changes,* 35–36; Roy, *Islam and Resistance,* 139–48.

5. NATIONALIST RESISTANCE ORGANIZATIONS

1. Wajdi, *Traditional Jirgas,* 222. This is an important book on the Afghan jirga system. Wajdi is particularly commendable on the jehad jirgas held in Peshawar, where he worked as chief of the Publication Department of the Islamic and National Revolutionary Councils. I am grateful to Masood Majruh for lending me his copy of the book. See also Hyman, "Afghan Politics of Exile."

2. Wajdi, *Traditional Jirgas,* 220.

3. Zamani, "Jirga in Peshawar," 17, 22, 23.

4. Wajdi, *Traditional Jirgas,* 225.

5. Ibid., 229–37.

6. Ibid., 226.

7. Ibid., 236.

8. Ibid., 237.

9. Ibid., 243.

10. Ibid., 249.

11. Ibid., 241.

12. Ibid., 246.

13. Ibid., 247.

14. Ibid., 248.

15. Ibid., 251.

16. Alam, "Memoirs of Jehad," 110.

17. Zamani, "Jirga in Peshawar," 31, 35.

18. Ibid., 14. The Consultative Board had the following as its members: three senior military officers, Shahnawaz Khan of the Ministry of Foreign Affairs, and the leader of the Jama'at-e-Islami of Pakistan. The latter was not a government official.

19. Ibid., 14.

20. Alam, "Memoirs of Jehad," 111; Wajdi, *Traditional Jirgas,* 251.

21. Wajdi, *Traditional Jirgas,* 264–67.

22. Ibid., 268.

23. A. Wasifi, personal communication, Los Angeles, May 1991.

24. Wajdi, *Traditional Jirgas,* 269.

25. Ibid., 270–71.

26. For details, see Mohammad Zahir, *Messages,* 21. I am grateful to Ibrahim Majid Seraj and Sultan Mahmud Ghazi for providing me with this rare book.

27. Adamec, *Afghanistan's Foreign Affairs,* 81.

28. Mohammad Zahir, *Messages,* 47, 22, 34.

29. Ibid., 46, 47.

30. Amin, "Future of Afghan Society," 13. The authoritative biography of the former king states that "it was due to his statesmanship that on several critical occasions collisions between the two Muslim countries were averted" (Mohammad Zahir, *Messages,* 3).

31. Mohammad Zahir, *Messages,* 142.

32. A. Wasifi, personal communication, Los Angeles, May 1991.

33. S. M. Ghazi, personal communication, Orange County, Calif., January 1991.

34. Roy, *Islam and Resistance,* 124.

35. Mohammad Zahir, *Messages,* 151.

36. S. M. Ghazi, personal communication, January 1991.

37. Mohammad Zahir, *Messages,* 151.

38. Emadi, *State, Society, and Superpowers,* 104.

39. Ibid.

40. Surkha: Sazman-e-Rihayeebakhsh-e-Khalq-e-Afghanistan, (Organization for Liberation of the People of Afghanistan).

SAMA: Sazman-e-Azadibakhsh-e-Mardum-e-Afghanistan (Peoples Liberation Organization of Afghanistan).

Akhgar: Sazman-e-Mubariza baraye Azadi-e-Tabaqa-e-Kargar (Organization for the Liberation of the Working Class).

SAWO: Sazman-e-Watanparastan-e-Waqi'ee-e-Afghanistan (Organization of the Real Patriots of Afghanistan).

Paikar (Struggle).

'Ayyar-e-Khurasan (the 'Ayyar of Khurasan).

41. Duran, "Setback for Peace," 15.

42. Kalakani's father and grandfather also lost their lives for social causes. For details, see Anonymous, "Two Martyred and the Same Fate."

6. URBAN UPRISINGS AND THEIR SUPPRESSION

1. Farr and Merriam, *Afghan Resistance*, 2.

2. Hyman, *Afghanistan*, 179.

3. Zadran, *History of Afghanistan* 1:671.

4. Haqshinas, *Russia's Crimes and Intrigues*, 404.

5. Anonymous, *Uprising of the Muslims of Kabul*, 17. I am grateful to Professor Sayyed Yusuf Ilmi for giving me this and a number of other pamphlets. See also Zadran, *History of Afghanistan*, 673.

6. Anonymous, *Uprising of the Muslims of Kabul*, 22.

7. Hyman, *Afghanistan*, 180.

8. Ibid., 179.

9. Zadran, *History of Afghanistan*, 671.

10. A. S. Aziemi, personal communication, Peshawar, February 1989. Mr. Aziemi was chancellor of Kabul University before the communists took over.

11. S. Sh. Ayyar, personal communication, San Diego, 1993. Ayyar and Mahfuz (Baryalay) Kakar were among the seven founding members of the Council of Students.

12. Hyman, *Afghanistan*, 181.

13. Ibid.

14. S. Sh. Ayyar, personal communication, San Diego, 1993.

15. For details see, Ilmi, *Afghanistan*; Ilmi and Majruh, *Sovietization of Afghanistan*; Shah, "Soviet Interferences."

7. BEGINNING OF THE COUNTRYWIDE ARMED CLASHES

1. Ruiz, *Left Out in the Cold*, 3.

2. At the end of the war, Wendy Batson, a consultant of the United Nations High Commissioner for Refugees stated, "Even those [Afghan] villages not directly affected by the conflict are often as devastated as those that were. The long years of war have left houses collapsed, roads and irrigation systems deteriorated to the point of uselessness, and fields long overgrown. The scale of destruction is enormous" (quoted in ibid., 5).

3. Sahari, *Jehad in the Kunars*, 22.

4. Not every village had as many Parchamis as Deva had. Deva was the

only village throughout the land that had many Parchamis in proportion to the number of its educated elements of both sexes. School dropouts, high school graduates, and some college graduates had turned Parchami, while those holding higher degrees had not. (I myself am from Deva.)

8. A NEW TYPE OF WAR LEADER

1. Alam, "Memoirs of Jehad," 170. Originally from Logar, Zahir Ghazi Alam has spent about twenty months in his home province during four trips that he made there from Peshawar, where he had been a refugee. A medical physician, he made the trips to treat patients. His memoirs cover many aspects of life of the people of Logar in the period under discussion. Dr. Alam and other Afghan refugee physicians—Pashtunyar, Farouq Mairanay, Asadullah, Abdur Rahman Zamani, Ahmad Sher Zamani, Farid Safi, and others—had started the Afghan Doctors Association, which operated at one time with approximately 170 members both in Afghanistan and among the refugees in Pakistan before pressure from the resistance organizations led to its dissolution. Dr. Alam now lives in the United States. For details on the association and the role of the Afghan educated middle class in the resistance, see Farr, "Afghan Middle Class."

2. Alam, "Memoirs of Jehad," 168.

3. Ibid., 170. Among Zadrans of the province of Paktia even during the reign of King Mohammad Zahir the 'ulama preached that when renegades persist in "rejecting the fundamentals of Islam," it behooves their relatives to do away with them, even if they be their own sons or close relations. Zadran, *History of Afghanistan*, 15.

4. Alam, "Memoirs of Jehad," 168.

5. Ibid., 146.

6. Quoted in Alam, "Jehad of Afghanistan," 31.

7. Barth, "Cultural Wellsprings," 198. For patterns of local political leadership in Afghanistan, see Kakar, *Government and Society*.

8. Commander Mati'ullah Safi of the Pech Valley of Kunar Province is a good example in this connection. A son of the famous Sultan Mohammad Khan, Mati'ullah Safi, with the assistance of his brothers, first waged jehad independently as a member of the leading family of his community, but subsequently he had to join the Mahaz organization.

9. 'Izzatullah Safi, personal communication, Chak Darra refugee camp, Deer, Northwest Frontier Province, 4 November 1988. For a general description of religious groups in Afghanistan, see Kakar, *Government and Society*. The term *mulla* or *molla* is derived from the Arabic term *mawla*, which may mean "master," "trustee," or "helper." *Mawla* frequently appears in titles—for instance, *mawlawi* and *mulla*—in several parts of the Muslim world, especially India, and in connection with scholars and saints (*Encyclopedia of Islam* 3:417).

10. Majruh, "Past and Present Education," 79.

11. Alam, "Memoirs of Jehad," 148. *Akhund*, a title given to scholars, has been current since the Timurid times in the sense of "schoolmaster" and "tutor." The word derives from Persian *khwand*, from *khudawand* (*Encyclopedia of Islam* 3:331).

12. Alam, "Memoirs of Jehad," 136.

13. Ibid., 147.

14. Ibid., 175.

15. In places the intergroup clashes were so bloody that a group would disarm and kill followers of the rival group. When victorious, a group would massacre followers of the rival group. Sometimes the groups robbed people on roads (Zadran, *History of Afghanistan*, 817). The district of Maidan to the west of Kabul provides us with an extreme example of intergroup clashes. According to one source, up to 1988 Commander Amanullah had lost about forty thousand men in intergroup clashes; by contrast, only forty men had been lost fighting the common enemy, the Soviets and the regime. Although clashes were frequent, this figure is surely an exaggeration.

16. Alam, "Memoirs of Jehad," 173. It was not only in Logar that people were executed on a suspicion of being Khalqis or collaborators; such killing was common throughout the land. In reply to an accusation that some people executed by his orders were not Khalqis, Mawlawi Abd al-Hay said: "I again reiterate that if I order that 150 Khalqis be executed, the act is permissible even though 50 among them be non-Khalqis." The mawlawi was general amir (*amir-e 'umomi*) of the Harakat-e-Inqilab-e-Islami of the provinces of Takhar, Badakhshan, Kunduz, Baghlan, Samangan, Joazjan, Faryab, and Badghis. (See Nasrat, "Bitter Facts," 37, 38, 39.) A commander-mulla in Wardak claimed that he recognized Khalqis from their smell. From among the suspicious passengers who were picked up from buses along the Kabul-Kandahar road, some were executed on that account. Another commander of Char Asia, south of Kabul city, instructed his followers in Peshawar to do away with any suspicious person found in their locality: if he were a Muslim he would go to heaven, and if not he would have been accorded the punishment he deserved (Alam, "Violation of Human Rights," 7).

17. Alam, "Memoirs of Jehad," 135.

18. Ibid., 161.

19. Ibid., 136.

20. Ibid., 141.

21. Ibid., 147.

22. On the religious impact of jehad on the society, see Cultural Council of Afghanistan Resistance, *Future of Islamic Afghanistan*.

23. Alam, "Memoirs of Jehad," 141–44; personal communication with a commander, Germany, August 1988. For a general description of the commanders, see Kakar, *Afghans in the Spring of 1987*.

24. Alam, "Memoirs of Jehad," 139.

25. For institutionalized forces behind the Afghan resistance movement, see Barth, "Cultural Wellsprings," 187; Canfield, "Ethnic, Regional, and Sectarian Alignments."

26. Canfield, "Islamic Sources," 69.

27. Alam, "Memoirs of Jehad," 139.

28. Z. G. Alam, personal communication, San Diego, December 1990.

29. Alam, "Memoirs of Jehad," 174.

30. Emad, "Impact of Jehad."

31. Alam, "Memoirs of Jehad," 153.

32. Kakar, *Afghans in the Spring of 1987,* 37.

33. Goodwin, *Caught in the Crossfire,* 46.

34. Bradsher, *Afghanistan,* 205.

35. Ibid., 272.

36. Quoted in ibid., 278.

37. Alam, "Memoirs of Jehad," 183.

38. Ibid., 182.

39. Ibid., 175.

40. Ibid., 139.

41. Ibid., 172.

42. Ibid., 175.

9. KhAD AS AN AGENCY OF SUPPRESSION

1. Amnesty International, *Afghanistan,* 2, 6.

2. Quoted in Bullock, *Hitler and Stalin,* 59.

3. Mackenzie, "Brutal Force," 15.

4. Sharq, *Memoirs,* 230.

5. Rasul Bie, son of Haji Barat Bie, personal communication, Pul-e-Charkhi, 1983. Rasul Bie said that his efforts to get the gold back failed because the Soviet advisers had a share in it. For details about KhAD, see Kakar, *Afghans in the Spring of 1987,* 55–64.

6. Sharq, *Memoirs,* 230.

7. B. Rubin, quoted in Mackenzie, "Brutal Force," 10.

8. KhAD officials had told the imprisoned members of Afghan Millat that on Karmal's order they were going to be released. For a list of the names of members of the imprisoned Afghan Millat, see Amnesty International, *Democratic Republic of Afghanistan,* 8.

9. Personal communication, Pul-e-Charkhi prison, 1985.

10. M. Nabi, formerly director of interrogation, personal communication, Pul-e-Charkhi prison, 1986. About twenty elders from Laghman Province, led by Abdul Aziz Kakar, twice met Najibullah as well as Prime Minister Kishtmand to discuss my release. But the officials declined their request, stating that Kakar did not want to budge from his opposition to the Soviets. If they could have released me, they probably would have done so to make the elders grateful.

11. Mackenzie, "Brutal Force," 14. According to Yves Heller from the Agence France Presse, "KhAD has become not just a state within a state, but the state itself" (quoted in Laber and Rubin, *A Nation Is Dying,* 77).

12. Mackenzie, "Brutal Force," 14; Rustar, *Pul-e-Charkhi Prison,* 9.

13. Sharq, *Memoirs,* 230.

14. Ibid.

15. Laber and Rubin, *A Nation Is Dying,* 77.

16. K. Matiuddin, quoted in Mackenzie, "Brutal Force," 14.

17. Fahima, quoted in Mackenzie, "Brutal Force," 9.

18. M. Rasuli, personal communication, San Diego, 1991.

19. Barnet Rubin, quoted in Mackenzie, "Brutal Force," 15.

20. "Torture in Afghanistan," *Amnesty International Newsletter* (London), December 1983, 1.

21. Amnesty International, *Afghanistan*, 1.

22. Bilolavo, "One Man's Sentence," 13.

23. Mackenzie, "Brutal Force," 15.

24. Bilolavo, "One Man's Sentence," 12.

25. Sharq, *Memoirs*, 231.

26. I arrived at the approximate figure of thirty thousand with the help of inmates who had been to all the cellblocks in Pul-e-Charkhi. It is satisfying to note that another inmate, Mohammad Jan Werr, formerly press director in Baghlan Province, had arrived at almost the same figure by a separate approximation. The difference between our figures was 400, the number of criminal inmates in cellblock number 4. Shafi Ayyar notes that the number of inmates for the cellblocks number 1, 2, and 3 alone was 20,000. Shafi Ayyar was also a prisoner; see Ayyar, *Bloody Fists*, 7.

27. In the Sadarat detention center, women were confined to separate cells in a separate block, adjacent to the block where I had been. Women with babies were also imprisoned. Once the authorities punished them for tying the names of cabinet ministers to the tails of mice—a form of insult. Saliha and Tajwar Kakar were known inmates in 1982. T. Kakar, personal communication, Peshawar, 1988.

28. Ayyar, *Bloody Fists*, 12.

29. Ibid., 16.

30. Ibid., 20–43. Ayyar had also taken part in the hunger strike.

31. A *bashi*, or head, of cellblock number two, personal communication, Pul-e-Charkhi prison, February 1987.

32. A former director of operation of KhAD number five, quoted by an inmate, Pul-e-Charkhi prison, February 1987.

33. Homosexuality is, of course, viewed differently in different cultures. Although it is practised among the Afghans, they condemn it on moral and religious grounds. The act is liable to punishment and viewed seriously when it becomes a scandal. For how KhAD abused this ruling and blackmailed a former junior university professor in prison to spy for it, see Rustar *Pul-e-Charkhi Prison*, 96. Conversely, KhAD condoned the homosexual activity of one of its former agents, who also worked for it in the prison. On homosexual acts in the Pul-e-Charkhi prison, see Ayyar, *Bloody Fists*, 13, 23.

10. MILITARY AND ADMINISTRATIVE MEASURES FOR CONSOLIDATION OF THE GOVERNMENT

1. Wajdi, *Traditional Jirgas*, 263.

2. Ibid., 93, 98, 146, 151, 159.

3. For details, see Sharq, *Memoirs*, 211–19. To make sure that the scheme was real, on 3 March 1993 I held a telephone conversation with the author, Dr. Mohammad Hassan Sharq, who now lives in Laguna Hills, California. He stuck to the words in his book on the subject and, further, disclosed for the first time

the names of those "who, to defeat the mujahideen, split Afghanistan, and consolidate the Soviet order in Afghanistan, had undertaken to implement the scheme." He named the following:

Najibullah and Sulaiman Laweq, for the Pashtun "nationality";
Babrak Karmal, Najmuddin Kawyani, and Farid Mazdak, for the Tajik "nationality";
Sultan Ali Kishtmand and Nabi Zadah, for the Hazara "nationality";
Sayyed Ikram Paigeer and Abdur Rashid Dostum, for the Uzbek and Turkomen "nationality";
Sattar Purduli, for the Baluch "nationality."

Under the Ministry of Tribes, Ministry of Nationalities, and later under a separate administration for northern Afghanistan, the Central Council for the Hazara Nationality, and the Central Council for Nomads, these men spent billions of afghanis free of state audit "to embroil the Pashtuns with the Tajiks, and the Uzbeks and the Hazaras with the Pashtuns." They had a similar program for embroiling the Sunnis with the Shi'as. Sharq, *Memoirs,* 212.

4. E. B. Taylor, quoted in Schusky and Culbert, *Understanding Culture,* 35.

5. Sharq, *Memoirs,* 233. This reference is in the errata to the volume.

6. Seeing no foreign soldiers fighting them but only the Afghans defending their land, the Central Asian soldiers of the Soviet Union not only did not war with the mujahideen but joined them. A group that had done so told them, "Since you fight well, go on fighting. We are with you. You should be grateful that you are free. Our fathers were also free. The Russians who invaded your land, had also invaded our fatherland. If you didn't fight, your fatherland would become like our fatherland, and you would become as slaves as we have become. The Russians are in great difficulty; don't shun resisting them" (Zadran, *History of Afghanistan,* 709–12).

11. VICTORY AT ANY COST

1. Quoted in Champagne et al., *Afghanistan,* 4. Victor V. Grishin, a politburo member, was specific about the dispatch of troops to Afghanistan: "Socialist internationalism obliged us to help the Afghan people defend the April Revolution's gains"; see Payand, "Soviet-Afghan Relations," 122.

2. Quoted in Bradsher, *Afghanistan,* 208.

3. Quoted in Dobbs, "Dramatic Politburo Meeting."

4. Champagne et al., *Afghanistan,* 20, 21.

5. Ibid., 21.

6. For a detailed study of the negotiations under the auspices of the United Nations that led to the conclusion of the Geneva agreements on the basis of which the Soviets withdrew their forces from Afghanistan, see Khan, *Untying the Afghan Knot.* As a Pakistani diplomat, Riaz M. Khan had attended all the meetings covering the negotiations. See also Kakar, *Geneva Compromise on Afghanistan.*

7. Quoted in Hyman, "Afghan Crisis," 18.
8. Ivanov, "Revelations," 20.
9. Hyman, "Afghan Crisis," 18.
10. Ivanov, "Revelations," 20.
11. Shevardnadze, *Future*, 121.
12. Quoted in Mackenzie, "Brutal Force," 9, 14.

12. ELIMINATION OF OPPONENTS BY NONMILITARY MEANS

1. Garver, "What Violence Is."
2. For details of the assassination of Ali Ahmad Khurram as well as his assassin, Marjan, see Popal, "Ali Ahmad Khurram," 33, 43.

13. GENOCIDE THROUGHOUT THE COUNTRY

1. Quoted in Chalk and Jonassohn, *Genocide*, 8.
2. Ibid., 10. For the text of the Convention and Punishment of the Crime of Genocide adopted by the United Nations General Assembly on 29 December 1948, see ibid., 44–49.
3. T. Taylor, quoted in Wasserstrom, "Laws of War," 495.
4. Chalk and Jonassohn, *Genocide*, 10.
5. Ibid., 11.
6. Ibid.
7. R. Smith, quoted in Chalk and Jonassohn, *Genocide*, 22.
8. Ibid., 23.
9. Horowitz, quoted in Chalk and Jonassohn, *Genocide*, 14.
10. For details, see Carlton, *War and Ideology*.
11. Horowitz, quoted in Chalk and Jonassohn, *Genocide*, 13.
12. The intensity of the Soviet military operations is suggested by the number of Afghans who fled abroad. By the middle of 1981 about 2 million Afghans had fled to Pakistan alone. By the end of 1984 the figure had exceeded 3 million. In 1991 the total number of Afghan refugees abroad was estimated to be 5,670,000. (See Azari, "Afghan Refugees": *Humanitarian Assistance Program*, 4.) A more recent study indicates that by the end of 1981, 2.3 million Afghans had fled to Pakistan alone. The total number of refugees is calculated to be "more than 3 million in Pakistan and as many as 3 million others in Iran" (Ruiz, *Left Out in the Cold*, 2, 3). More Afghans fled to Pakistan than to Iran. Afghans fled to Iran from the three western provinces of Herat, Farah, and Nimroz; Afghans from the rest of the country, especially the eastern frontier provinces, took refuge in Pakistan. This explains why the Pashtuns constitute the highest percentage (85 percent) of the refugee population in Pakistan (Sliwinski, "Afghanistan 1978–87," 18). The total figure for Afghan refugees in Pakistan and Iran are official and therefore cannot be considered accurate; still, Afghan refugees are clearly the world's largest group in absolute terms as well as in proportion to the total number of Afghans, who numbered 15.5 million before the invasion.

Period	To Pakistan	To Iran	To other destinations
Through 1978	18,000	?	?
Through 1979	389,000	?	?
Through 1980	1,232,000	250,000	?
Through 1981	2,500,000	?	?
Through 1982	2,700,000	500,000	?
Through 1983	2,900,000	650,000	?
Through 1984	3,200,000	850,000	70,000

Source: Amstutz, *Afghanistan,* 224.

For a table of the numbers of refugees in various refugee camps in Pakistan, see appendix C.

13. A Soviet Tajik deserter quoted in Laber and Rubin, *A Nation Is Dying,* 18. According to the soldier, "When the drunk commander found out that his brother and three soldiers were killed by mujahideen, he took the whole commando unit at night. He went to the village and butchered, slaughtered all the village[rs]. They cut off the heads and killed perhaps 2,000 people." To terrorize the people, the officers of the invading army also ordered the brutal killing of individuals. In 1983 they assembled the people of the village of Babyan in Logar; they then singled out Qazi Fatih, a retired judge who looked like a mulla. They tied him to a tank, then dragged him behind it at high speed. The Qazi was smashed to pieces in front of the villagers. See Alam, "Violation of Human Rights," 7.

14. Carmichael, *History of Russia;* Lourie, *Predicting Russia's Future.*

15. Girardet, *Afghanistan.*

16. Wasserstrom, "Laws of War," 484.

17. T. Taylor, quoted in Wasserstrom, "Laws of War," 484.

18. Laber and Rubin, *Helsinki Watch,* 53.

19. For details, see *International Afghanistan Hearing,* 173.

20. Ibid., 174.

21. Ibid., 175.

22. Ibid., 176.

23. Laber and Rubin, *Helsinki Watch,* 23.

14. GENOCIDE IN DISTRICTS AROUND KABUL

1. Alam, "Memoirs of Jehad," 139.

2. For details, see *International Afghanistan Hearing* (hereafter *IAH*), 186–212. The date and the number of casualties in the canal are not the same in all sources. According to Z. G. Alam, between seventy-one and eighty persons perished in the canal (personal communication, San Diego, 1991). The incident occurred in spring 1982, but the precise date is uncertain.

3. Alam, "Memoirs of Jehad," 178.

4. Quoted in ibid., 186–89.

5. Quoted in ibid., 161.

6. Ibid., 209–19.

7. *IAH,* 186.

8. Ibid., 198.

9. Ibid., 190.

10. Ibid., 191.

11. Ibid., 187.

12. Ibid., 186.

13. Ibid., 190.

14. Ibid., 195.

15. Ibid.

16. Ibid., 196.

17. Ibid., 188.

18. Ibid., 189.

19. Ibid., 191.

20. Ibid., 192.

21. Ten miners work in each of the twenty-five mines, using primitive techniques. Around twenty-five miners are killed each year from the collapse of tunnels and gas from the explosives. Annual yield varies from $80 to $90 million. Led by Ahmad Shah Mas'ud, the supervisory council oversees the extraction. The gems have brought prosperity to the region. The houses in Khinj are solidly built, and the latest Japanese vehicles crowd the narrow streets. (*Asian Journal* [Southern California], 11 September 1992.)

22. *IAH*, 26.

23. Ibid., 1.

24. From my journal.

25. Laber and Rubin, *Helsinki Watch*, 173.

26. *IAH*, 77, 78.

27. Ibid., 106.

28. Cordsman and Wagner, *Lessons of Modern War* 3:216.

29. For details, see Shultz, *Chemical Warfare*.

30. *IAH*, 84.

31. Ibid., 85.

32. Ibid., 100.

33. Ibid., 88.

34. *IAH*, 65.

35. How many mines the Soviets and (to a much lesser degree) the mujahideen planted throughout the war in Afghanistan will never be known. According to a Soviet engineer, the invading army planted two thousand minefields (Kakar, *Geneva Compromise on Afghanistan,* 232). Other sources have put the number up to fifteen million mines. The United Nations survey of November 1991 has this to say: "About 10 million mines are thought to have been laid in Afghanistan. They have been dropped randomly from the air, laid in concentrated clusters and minefields, laid singly and as booby-traps. Often they are washed down by floods on to previously cleared land. In some areas, they are everywhere: in villages, gardens, tracks, fields. In others, they may be only on access roads. There are large quantities of unexploded ordinance in almost all the areas where intensive fighting has taken place. Information on locations, concentrations, and types of mines is acquired slowly and often tragically. The problem tends to be worst in provinces bordering Pakistan, and in areas where fighting was heaviest"

(Ruiz, *Left Out in the Cold,* 12). "The consequences of all this mining are only too visible. Two million people, or one in seven or eight, are disabled in Afghanistan. Of these, 20 percent or 400,000 people, have been maimed by mines or unexploded ordinance. A recent U. N. survey found that 10 percent of villagers in Afghanistan, and 60,000 refugees in camps in Pakistan are disabled. In four camps surveyed, 2 percent of all men were amputees. At least 50,000 have been provided with artificial limbs" (Girard, "Afghanistan," 23).

36. Alam, "Memoirs of Jehad," 264.

37. Ibid., 180.

38. *IAH,* 107.

CONCLUSION

1. Yousaf and Adkin, *Bear Trap,* 54.

2. M. Poltoranin, Russia's minister of information, quoted in Dobbs, "Secret Memos," A1. The Soviet foreign minister, Edward Shevardnadze, put the cost of war to the Soviets at sixty billion rubles (Shevardnadze, *Future,* 58).

3. Kakar, *Second Anglo-Afghan War,* 146.

EPILOGUE, 1982–1994

1. Khan, *Untying the Afghan Knot,* 86–87.

2. Ibid., 84–86.

3. Yousaf and Adkin, *Bear Trap,* 154.

4. Ibid.

5. Ibid.

6. Saikal and Miley, *Soviet Withdrawal from Afghanistan,* 16.

7. McClintock, *Instruments of Statecraft,* 32.

8. Khan, *Untying the Afghan Knot,* 88.

9. Ibid., 89.

10. Kornienko, "Afghan Endeavor," 10.

11. Ibid.

12. Najibullah, quoted in Khan, *Untying the Afghan Knot,* 178.

13. "A." Personal communication, Kabul, 1987.

14. Kornienko, "Afghan Endeavor," 11.

15. Ibid., 12.

16. Ibid.

17. Ibid., 13.

18. Khan, *Untying the Afghan Knot,* 89.

19. Yousaf and Adkin, *Bear Trap,* 166–73.

20. Ibid., 174–79.

21. Khan, *Untying the Afghan Knot,* 89, 90.

22. Kakar, *Geneva Compromise on Afghanistan,* 138; Kakar, *Afghans in the Spring of 1987,* 13.

23. Kakar, "Afghanistan on the Eve of Soviet Withdrawal."

24. To effect equality among Afghan ethnic groups, Kishtmand, a politburo

member of PDPA, wrote that the state was to carve out "autonomous administrative units" on the basis of "national characteristics" within a "federal structure." "The Constitution and the National Problem in the Republic of Afghanistan," *The Truth about the Saur Revolution* (PDPA newspaper), 9 Qaus 1367
(30 November 1987), page unknown. Kishtmand's view was a replica of the
Soviet model, which is impracticable in Afghanistan because of its highly
mixed population.

25. Resolution of the Second Congress of the Party, Aims of the Fatherland
Party (Maramnama-e-hizb-e-watan), Kabul, 1990.

26. Sharq, *Memoirs*, 282.

27. Ibid., 256.

28. Yousaf and Adkin, *Bear Trap*, 42.

29. Sharq, *Memoirs*, 272.

30. Khan, *Untying the Afghan Knot*, 255.

31. Ibid., 285, 294.

32. Rais, "Afghanistan and Regional Security," 82.

33. The departing Soviet army handed over all of its heavy weapons and
food supplies to the Kabul regime; in addition, it is believed that during the six
months of 1989 the Soviets delivered $1.5 billion worth of weapons, including
five hundred Scud surface-to-surface missiles. Every day from fifteen to eighty
huge planes would bring weapons of all kinds to Kabul. Sharq, *Memoirs*, 292;
Yousaf and Adkin, *Bear Trap*, 227; Khan, *Untying the Afghan Knot*, 297.
"Moreover in significant areas of military advice and intelligence support Moscow's direct invlovement in Afghanistan's internal affairs did not end with the
formal withdrawal of Soviet troops"; Rais, "Afghanistan and Regional Security," 82.

34. Kornienko, "Afghan Endeavor," 11.

35. Sharq, *Memoirs*, 260, 257.

36. Khan, *Untying the Afghan Knot*, 296.

37. Kornienko, "Afghan Endeavor," 14; Yousaf and Adkin, *Bear Trap*, 234.

38. Khan, *Untying the Afghan Knot*, 297.

39. According to the CIA, General Akhtar of the ISI promoted the idea of
outright military victory for Afghan Islamists. Yousaf and Adkin, *Bear Trap*,
234.

40. Ibid., 1, 22, 234.

41. Khan, *Untying the Afghan Knot*, 200.

42. Ibid., 201.

43. Ibid.

44. In 1987 the following broad percentages were allowed to the Islamic
groups: to Hekmatyar, 18–20 percent; to Rabbani, 18–19 percent; to Sayyaf
17–18 percent; to Khalis, 13–15 percent; to Mohammadi, 13–15 percent; to
Gailani, 10–11 percent; and to Mojaddidi, 3–5 percent. Yousaf and Adkin, *Bear
Trap*, 105.

45. Kakar, "Afghanistan on the Eve of Soviet Withdrawal." The information on the shura held in February 1989 are drawn from this source. I lived in
Peshawar at the time. I am grateful to Mohammad Qasim Laghmani for giving
me valuable information and some documents on the shura. Laghmani was a

member of the commissions of the shura that laid down electoral procedures for it. See also Khalilzad, *Prospects for Afghan Interim Government;* Maley and Saikal, *Political Order in Post-Communist Afghanistan.*

46. Quoted in *Shahadat,* Newspaper of the Islamic Party (Peshawar), 2 Sunbula 1367/1988, 1.

47. Yousaf and Adkin, *Bear Trap,* 226–32.

48. Ibid., 230.

49. Ibid., 129, 231.

50. Ibid., 129.

51. Sharq, *Memoirs,* 301.

52. Ibid. Kakar, "Failed Coup," 112.

53. Sharq, *Memoirs,* 301.

54. Kakar, "Failed Coup," 113.

55. Bisharat, "Stormy Developments," 12.

56. Sharq, *Memoirs,* 302.

57. Maley and Saikal, *Political Order in Post-Communist Afghanistan,* 27.

58. Ibid., 28.

59. Ibid., 24.

60. Kakar, "Central Asia."

61. Maley and Saikal, *Political Order in Post-Communist Afghanistan,* 27.

62. Ibid., 26.

63. Ibid.

64. Ibid.

65. Ibid.

66. Ibid.

67. Kakar, "The Policy of Intrigues," 12.

68. Kakar, "The Policy of Intrigues," 12; Yusufzai, "Dostum."

69. Kakar, "The Policy of Intrigues," 17.

70. Along with Nawaz Sharif, other foreign dignitaries who participated in the Peshawar meeting were the governor of the Northwest Frontier Province; Siddiq Kanju, minister of state without portfolio; General Asif Nawaz, Pakistan's chief of staff; General Javid Nassir, chief of the ISI; Mehr Mosawi, Iran's roving ambassador; the ambassdors of Iran and Saudi Arabia in Islamabad; Turkey al Faisal, chief of the intelligence service of Saudi Arabia; and Benon Sevan. After Helal, Hekmatyar's representative, walked out of the meeting, the Afghan leaders present were Khalis, Sayyaf, Mohammadi, Rabbani, Gailani, and Mojaddidi.

71. Kakar, "The Success of the Failed Babrak Karmal," *Mujahid Wolas* (newspaper), June 1992, 4.

72. Rais, "Afghanistan and Regional Security," 82.

73. A. Shinwari, "Afghanistan—two years of mujahideen's rule," *Afghanistan Forum,* July 1994, 7. The article first appeared in *The Frontier Posts,* 10 May 1994. Marwat even holds that not only the Peshawar Accords but "all accords proved to be the license given by vested interests to the mujahideen leaders for killing and [destroying] their own people and country." F. R. Marwat, "Waiting for the U.N.," *Writers' Union of Free Afghanistan,* July–August 1994, 48.

74. Kakar, "Success of Babrak Karmal," 2.

75. Anonymous, "From Peshawar to Kabul," *Rastgoyan, Journal of the National Salvation Front* 4, no. 4 (1992): 3.

76. Ibid.

77. S. M. Maiwand, *The Maiwand Trust* (New Delhi), 10 May 1992, 4. I have drawn throughout on this informative and trustworthy weekly newsletter for the Mojaddidi period.

78. Ibid.

79. *Maiwand Trust,* 17 May 1992, 6.

80. Supreme Court of the Islamic State of Afghanistan, "Fatwa on Veil," Kabul, 1993, 36.

81. BEBT, "Note on Events in Kabul" (in Pashto), December 1993. A manuscript by an insider, 7, 8.

82. *Maiwand Trust,* 17 May 1992, 5.

83. BEBT, "Note on Events in Kabul," 8.

84. H. Azizi, "Guardianship or Looting of a City?" *Afghanistan [Journal]* (Peshawar), April 1994, 66.

85. For details, see S. Kh. Hashemyan, "The End of Two Months of Blood, and the Start of Four Months of Troubles," *Afghanistan Mirror,* special bulletin, 29 June 1992.

86. A. R. Dostum, statement in the Constituent Assembly of the National and Islamic Movement, Mazar, 31 May 1992, 2.

87. Bisharat, "Stormy Developments," 10. For a list of senior Parchami officers in the army of the Islamic State, see *Peace* (monthly newspaper), December 1993, 4.

88. Interview with Mawlawi M. Zarif, *Mujahid Wolas* (newspaper), November–December 1993, 1.

89. Ermacora, "Human Rights in Afghanistan," 32.

90. Rashid, "Green Revolutionary," 19.

91. For comments on the Islamabad Accords, see Kakar, "Time for Choice," 2–9.

92. For details, see Gh. Parwani, "The Jalalabad Accords," *Writers' Union of Free Afghanistan,* May 1993, 7; "New Peace Accords Concluded in Jalalabad," *Afghanistan Forum,* July 1993, 6.

93. "Strange Calm in Kabul," *Afghanistan Forum,* November 1993, 10.

94. M. K. Momand, "My Observations," *Sabawoon [Journal]* (California), July 1994, 21. In a letter sent in January 1994 from Kabul the writer states: "To the people of Kabul there no longer exists either a lion [Mas'ud] or an amir or a hero. They are all thieves and violators of people's honor and property. Mas'ud's men are illiterate Panjsheri youth who do not even know how to pray and observe the commands of Islam. They know nothing else but to engage in homosexuality and make the boys and girls dance for them. They steal people's property and kidnap their children. Hekmatyar's men, who are older than Mas'ud's men, respect people's honor, but their rockets have destroyed much of Kabul. In fact, their rockets and the aircraft and bombs of Mas'ud have ravaged Kabul. Dostum's men are all addicted to hashish (*chars*); they are all homosexuals, burglars, and criminals. Even their officers cannot control them. Just like

Mas'ud's men, they also do as they please." Qari Abdullah in *Peace* (monthly newspaper), 15 March 1994, 4.

95. A. Safi, former member of parliament from Tagab, personal comunication, December 1993. In the Tagab round of fighting Mas'ud paid 100,000 afghanis, and Hekmatyar paid from 1,200 to 2,000 Pakistani rupees a month to each of their recruits. One rupee equalled 95 afghanis. Mas'ud had advantages over his rivals in money matters. According to a commander of Mas'ud, "I would spend 20 million afghanis on each of the military posts per week." Also, according to him, "once, shortly after 20 billion afghanis had arrived from Moscow, these were all taken out of the bank for military purposes." Anonymous, "Why and How the War in Kabul Started," *Afghanistan Journal,* April 1994, 10.

96. D. Sahari, "Afghanistan and the Islamic World," *Mujahid Wolas* (newspaper), January–February 1994, 2.

97. *Afghanistan Forum,* January 1994, 7.

98. "Why and How the War Started," 72.

99. Ibid.

100. *Afghanistan Forum,* March 1994, 13.

101. "Why and How the War Started," 72.

102. Interview with Hekmatyar, *Shafaq* (newspaper), May 1994, 3. For details see A. H. Ahady, "An Evaluation of the Four Main Peace Plans for Afghanistan," *Afghan Millat* (newspaper), Peshawar (21 July 1994).

103. Statement by Rabbani, *Jam'iyyat* (newspaper), May 1994, 3.

104. S. Coll, "The Agony of Victory," *Afghanistan Forum,* March 1994, 16.

105. Z. Abbas, "The Battle for Kabul", *Afghanistan Forum,* May 1994, 9. According to S. Mojaddidi, "Mas'ud has gathered around him a number of companions who hold that the Pashtuns have ruled over us for years, and now it was time we ruled over them"; *Shafaq* (newspaper), May 1994, 3.

106. Abbas, "Battle for Kabul," *Afghanistan Forum,* 9.

107. Ibid. In particular, the loss in November 1993 to Dostum of the Sher Khan Post on the Oxus at the instigation of Mas'ud by a commander of the Islamic Union became the last straw in the coalition between Dostum and Mas'ud. See "Why and How the War Started," 9.

108. B. Rumer and E. Rumer, "Who Will Stop the Next Yugoslavia?" *World Monitor,* November 1992, 38; Malik, "Contemporary South and Central Asian Politics," *Asian Survey,* October 1992, 901. Masu'd, who "dreams of a panTajik constituency for himself," is backing Tajik rebels against the Moscowinstalled government in Doshanbay, the capital of Tajikistan. A. Rashid, "Battle for the North," *Far Eastern Economic Review,* 31 March 1994, 23.

109. Anonymous, "Central Asia: The Silk Road Catches Fire," *Far Eastern Economic Review,* 26 December 1992, 45, 46.

110. D. Sahari, "Afghanistan and the Islamic World," *Mujahid Wolas* (newspaper), no. 11–12 (January–February 1994), 2.

111. Interview with Rabbani, *Afghanistan Forum,* March 1994, 26.

112. In Kabul an official spokesman claimed, "We have clear-cut evidence about direct interference by Uzbekistan in the Kabul fighting"; ibid., 20.

113. A. R. Safi, former member of parliament from Shiberghan, personal communication, February 1994.

114. Ibid.

115. "Message to the Kunduz Commanders," *Writers' Union of Free Afghanistan,* 4 May 1994, 1.

116. Yousaf and Adkin, *Bear Trap,* 142.

117. N. Majruh, personal communication, June 1994.

118. Interview with Q. M. A. Wiqad, *Writers' Union of Free Afghanistan,* 30 March 1994, 8.

119. BEBT, "Note on Events in Kabul," 9.

120. R. Yusufzai, *International News* (Peshawar), 3 November 1993, 21.

121. T. Weiner, "Blowback from the Afghan Battlefield," *New York Times Magazine,* 13 March 1994, 53.

122. Interview with Q. M. A. Wiqad, *Writers' Union of Free Afghanistan,* 30 March 94, 8.

123. Sahari, "Afghanistan and the Islamic World," 2.

124. S. Yarzay, "Problems and Fighting in Kabul," *Writers' Union of Free Afghanistan,* 20 July 1994, 6; Z. Durani, "What is Going on in Kabul?" *Writers' Union of Free Afghanistan,* 2 August 1994, 7.

125. Momand, "My Observations," 21.

126. M. Shindanday, "The Tyrannized and Powerless Afghans," *Writers' Union of Free Afghanistan,* 20 July 1994, 6.

127. Sahari, "Afghanistan and the Islamic World," 2. "From the city of Mazar to the frontier post in Torkham the Islamic groups have set up customs posts (*pataks*). In each of these posts each group levies tolls on a loaded truck, ranging from twenty thousand to over a million afghanis. Because of insecurity trucks now go in caravans as the caravans of men, camels, and horses went in the Middle Ages. It now takes about twenty days for a caravan to reach Torkham from Mazar, whereas before the communist coup in 1978 it took only a day for a truck to make the journey. From Mahipar, east of Kabul, to Torkham twenty-eight such posts are in place. This part, which is the worst, is called the Looting Highway (*Shahrah-e-Choor*). A man who had made the journey from Mazar to Torkham with a caravan has been quoted as saying 'The situation of the highway from the hydroelectric dam of Mahipar to Sarobi is totally disappointing. In each bend of the road one and even two customs posts operate. In these posts rusty, ruthless, and tyrannical men, seen often with wild and long hair and beards, have come together. To them it is useless to plead and implore. Instead of God, the Prophet, the Quran, and the love of parents they recognize money. For them it is ordinary to curse, insult, and beat a passenger and bring down his belongings and food. An ordinary man of them can stop a truck and even a caravan with impunity for days and beat a passenger whom he dislikes to the limit of death. Most of these posts belong to major groups.' Some among them are, of course, pious, but the majority are such as described. It is because of the heavy tolls that in Kabul a sack of wheat flour [70 kilograms] is sold for one hundred thousand afghanis, a staggering amount. The pious muslims now say that Doomsday is near." Shahbaz, "Mazar-e-Sharif—Torkham," *Writers Union of Free Afghanistan,* 7 September 1994, 6.

128. "Interview with the Mawlawi of Tarakhel," *Afghanistan (Journal),* April

1994, 41. The bickering among the Islamic groups is harming Afghanistan. Internally, it acts as a divisive force, subverting the process of reunification and reconstruction. Abroad, it is looked on as a symbol of Islamic fundamentalism, terrorism, intolerance, and radicalism. This is why Afghanistan has plummeted from a global flash point to a local affair. From a major catalyst that initiated the disintegration of the Soviet Union, it has developed into a "self-destructive inter-Afghan affair, threatening to split Afghanistan." Marwat, "Waiting for the U.N.," 48.

129. Momand, "My Observations," 24.

130. Quoted in Sahari, "Afghanistan and the Islamic World," 2.

131. Statement by M. A. Nae'em, *Writers' Union of Free Afghanistan,* 24 April 1994, 2.

132. R. Yusufzai, "Zahir Shah Option Resurfaces in Search for Afghan Peace," *The Breeze of Freedom* (journal), no. 4 (Mar.–Apr. 1994): 38.

133. H. Naweed, interview with R. Oakley, *Writers' Union of Free Afghanistan,* nos. 22–23 (8 June 1994), 7.

134. N. M. Kamrany, personal communication, June 1994. Kamrany is a professor of economics at the University of California, Los Angeles.

135. Weiner, "Blowback," 53.

136. Ibid. According to a U.S. satellite survey, 19,470 hectares were cultivated in poppies during the 1991–92 season in Afghanistan. *The Breeze of Freedom* (journal), no. 4 (Mar.–Apr. 1994): 63.

137. Quoted in the *San Diego Union-Tribune,* 5 July 1994, A12.

138. Quoted in Weiner, "Blowback," 53.

Glossary

AKHUND Traditional teacher or master.

AMIR Originally "commander," as part of *amir al-mu'minin* (commander of the faithful); in Afghanistan, the title of Mohammadzay rulers down to Amanullah (1919–29); in the jehad period, title of leaders of the Islamic groups.

AROBAKI Tribal police force among the Paktia tribes.

'AYYARI Exemplary boldness and chivalry; a social morality of a high degree.

AZAN Call for prayer.

BASMACHI Anti-Soviet freedom fighters of Bukhara in Central Asia.

FATWA Ruling or opinion on legal issues issued by head of the Islamic community, and in his absence by the *'ulama*.

IMAM Leader in prayer; chief of the Muslim community. Originally the imam was the Prophet himself, and his successor filled the office. According to the Shi'as, an imam must be descended from the Prophet through his daughter, Fatima; the Sunnis hold that an imam must be elected.

ISMA'ILI Follower of a Shi'ite sect that holds the imamate passed from 'Ali, the fourth caliph, to his descendants through a seventh imam, Isma'il.

JAHILIYYA The state of religious ignorance before the rise of Islam; adjective form, *jahili*.

JEHAD Extreme exertion of self and property in the cause of God.

JIRGA Council or assembly held for the settlement of a dispute in a locality.

JIRGAMAWR Specialist of jirga regulations and codes.

KAHOLE Main family; household.

KAREZ Underground irrigation canal.

KHAN Originally a Mongol term signifying prince or ruler; now, head of a tribe or community with many chiefs working under him; also, an honory title by which a man is addressed by others. In earlier periods, the khan was usually a big landowner and enjoyed feudal privileges.

KHANI The institution of tribal or tribal eldership.

KUFR State of unbelief; anti-Islamic belief.

LOYA JIRGA Ad hoc grand assembly or grand council, usually called by a setting ruler for the settlement of a national problem, especially in times of emergency.

MADRASA Center for higher studies in Sunni Islam.

MARAKCHI Specialist of jirga regulations and codes; plural, *marakchiyan*.

MAWLAWI Traditional religious scholar.

MUJAHID One who makes jehad; plural, *mujahideen*.

MUJTAHID One who has attained such preeminence in religious scholarship that he may issue opinions on matters of faith.

MULLA Leader of prayer.

NAGHA Compensation, especially for something socially significant.

NAMOAS Honor with social significance, referring especially to the womenfolk of one's own and of one's father's household.

NAQSHBANDIYYA A Muslim mystic order.

NINAWATAY The act of seeking admittance or asylum; a part of *pashtunwali*.

NIRKH Disciplinary and punitive aspects of *pashtunwali*; also, prices of commodities.

PASHTUNWALI Social and legal codes of the Pashtuns.

PIR Head of a mystic order; a religious person with profound influence over his followers.

QADIRIYYA An Islamic mystic order.

SAYYED A real or assumed descendant of the Prophet Mohammad through his daughter, Fatima.

SHABNAMA Literally, "night letter"; clandestine antiopponent and usually antigovernment leaflet.

SHARI'A Literally, "path"; the path of Islam; Islamic laws comprising the four major codified schools of Hanafi, Shafi'i, Maliki, and Hanbali; the first is applied in Afghanistan.

SHURA Council.

TURBOOR Literally, "cousin"; rival; peer rival.

TURBOORI Literally, "cousinhood"; rivalry; rivalry among peers, especially cousins among the Pashtuns.

'ULAMA Religious scholars of Sunni Muslims; singular, *'alim*.

'USHR The Islamic rate of revenue on land; tithe.

WAHHABI Disciple of Mohammad bin 'Abd al-Wahhab (1703–87), whose aim was to do away with all innovations later than the third century of Islam.

Select Bibliography

MANUSCRIPTS

Note: All manuscripts are in the possession of the author.

Alam, Z. G. "The Jehad of Afghanistan: Observations, Views, and Evaluations." (In Pashto.)
——. "The Memoirs of Jehad, 1979–85." (In Pashto.)
Duran, Kh. "Setback for Peace in Afghanistan." (In English.)
Haroun. "Daoud Khan in the KGB Trap." (In Pashto.)
Hyman, A. "The Afghan Crisis and the European Response."
Kakar, M. H. "Afghanistan on the Eve of Soviet Withdrawal." (In Pashto.)
——. "Journal of Political Developments, 1979–1982." (In Pashto.)
Nasrat, Gh. R. "Bitter Facts on the War in Afghanistan." (In Dari.)
Zamani, M. H. "Note on a Jirga in Peshawar in 1980." (In Pashto.)
Zurmulwal, G. M. "Weesh Zalmyan or Jawanan-e-Baidar." (In Dari.)

BOOKS AND BOOKLETS

Adamec, L. *Afghanistan's Foreign Affairs to the Mid-Twentieth Century.* Tucson: University of Arizona Press, 1974.
Afghan Cartographic Institute. *The Atlas of the Provinces of Afghanistan.* (In Dari.) Kabul: Afghan Cartographic Institute, 1970.
Amnesty International. *Afghanistan: Torture of Political Prisoners.* London: Amnesty International Publications, 1986.
——. *Democratic Republic of Afghanistan.* London: Amnesty International Publications, 1983.

357

Amstutz, J. B. *Afghanistan: The First Five Years of Soviet Occupation.* Washington, D.C.: National Defense University, 1986.

Anderson, E., and N. Dupree, eds. *The Cultural Basis of Afghan Nationalism.* London and New York: Pinter Publishers, 1990.

Andrew, C., and O. Gordiesky. *KGB: The Inside Story.* New York: Harper Perennial, 1991.

Anonymous. *The Uprising of the Muslims of Kabul, Third [of the Month of] Hoot 1358.* (In Dari.) Peshawar: Cultural Council of Afghanistan Resistance, 1984.

Anonymous. *The Uprising of the Twenty-fourth [of the Month of] Hoot of Herat.* (In Dari.) Peshawar: Cultural Council of Afghanistan Resistance, 1984.

Anwar, Raja. *The Tragedy of Afghanistan.* London: Verso, 1988.

Arnold, A. *Afghanistan's Two-Party Communism.* Stanford: Hoover Institution, Stanford University Press, 1983.

Ayyar, S. *The Bloody Fists.* (In Dari.) Washington State: privately published, 1984.

Bradsher, B. *Afghanistan and the Soviet Union.* Durham: Duke University Press, 1985.

Brigot, A., and O. Roy. *The War in Afghanistan.* New York and London: Harvester, 1988.

Bullock, A. *Hitler and Stalin: Parallel Lives.* New York, Vintage, 1993.

Carlton, E. *War and Ideology.* London: Routledge, 1990.

Carmichael, J. *A History of Russia.* New York: Hippocrene Books, 1990.

Chaliand, G. *Report from Afghanistan.* New York: Viking, 1982.

Chalk, F., and K. Jonassohn, eds. *The History and Sociology of Genocide: Analysis and Case Studies.* New Haven: Yale University Press, 1990.

Champagne, D. C., et al. *Afghanistan: Background and Status of the Global Crisis.* Omaha: Center for Afghanistan Studies, University of Nebraska, 1980.

Choueiri, Y. *Islamic Fundamentalism.* Boston: Twayne Publishers, 1990.

Cordsman, A. H., and A. R. Wagner. *The Lessons of Modern War.* Vol. 3, *The Afghan and Falkland Conflicts.* Boulder: Westview, 1991.

Cultural Council of Afghanistan Resistance. *The Future of Islamic Afghanistan.* (In Pashto and Dari.) 4 vols. Islamabad: Cultural Council of Afghanistan Resistance, 1980.

Dupree, L. *Afghanistan.* Princeton: Princeton University Press, 1980.

Emadi, H. *State, Society, and Superpowers in Afghanistan.* New York: Praeger, 1990.

Farhang, M. S. *Afghanistan During the Last Five Centuries.* (In Dari.) [Vol. 1.] Peshawar: Mayar Publisher, 1988.

―――. *Afghanistan During the Last Five Centuries.* (In Dari). Vol. 2. Herenden, Va.: privately published, 1990.

Farr, G., and J. G. Merriam, eds. *Afghan Resistance: The Politics of Survival.* Lahore: Vanguard, 1988.

Fayzzad, M. A. *The National Loya Jirgas of Afghanistan.* (In Dari.) Peshawar: privately published, 1989.

Fazili, M. Q. *Days as Dark as Nights*. (In Dari.) Paris: privately published, 1989.

Fletcher, A. *Afghanistan: The Highway of Conquest*. Ithaca: Cornell University Press, 1966.

Gharzay, R. *The Memoirs from the Pul-e-Charkhi Prison*. (In Dari.) Peshawar: privately published, 1988.

Ghaus, A. S. *The Fall of Afghanistan*. Washington, D.C.: Pergamon Brassey's, 1988.

Girardet, E. *Afghanistan: The Soviet War*. London: Croom Helm, 1985.

Goodwin, J. *Caught in the Crossfire*. New York: Dutton, 1987.

Gregorian, V. *The Emergence of Modern Afghanistan*. Stanford: Stanford University Press, 1968.

Haqshinas, N. *Political Changes of Jehad in Afghanistan*. (In Dari.) Germany: Islamic and Refugee Association of Afghan Students, 1986.

————. *Russia's Intrigues and Crimes in Afghanistan*. (In Dari.) Tehran: Cultural Committee, Islamic Association of Afghanistan, 1984.

Hekmatyar, G. *Interview of Brother Hekmatyar with a Turkish Journalist*. (In Dari.) Peshawar: Islamic Party of Afghanistan, 1988.

Hezb-e-Islami of Afghanistan. *Aims of Hezb-e-Islami of Afghanistan*. Peshawar: Hezb-e-Islami, n.d.

Humanitarian Assistance Program for Afghan Refugees in Pakistan. Islamabad: Chief Commissionerate for Afghan Refugees, 1984.

Hyman, A. *Afghanistan under Soviet Domination*. London: Macmillan, 1984.

————. *Muslim Fundamentalism*. London: Institute for the Study of Conflict, n.d.

Ilmi, M. Y., ed. *Afghanistan: A Decade of Sovietization*. Peshawar: Afghan Jehad Works Translation Center, 1988.

Ilmi, M. Y., and S. B. Majruh, eds. *The Sovietization of Afghanistan*. Peshawar: Afghan Information Center, 1986.

International Afghanistan Hearing. Edited by the Committee for International Afghanistan Hearing. Oslo: Committee for International Afghanistan Hearing, 1984.

Jamiat-e-Islami of Afghanistan. *Aims and Goals of Jamiat-e-Islami of Afghanistan*. Peshawar: Jamiat-e-Islami, 1981.

Kakar, M. H. *Afghan, Afghanistan, and the Afghans and the Organization of the State in India, Persia, and Afghanistan*. (In Dari.) Peshawar: Writers' Union of Free Afghanistan, 1988.

————. *Afghanistan: A Study in Internal Political Developments, 1880–1896*. Lahore: Panjab Educational Press, 1971.

————. *The Afghans in the Spring of 1987 in War with the Russians*. (In Pashto.) Nürnberg: Spinghar Publication Union, 1990.

————. *The Geneva Compromise on Afghanistan*. (In Pashto.) Peshawar: Writers' Union of Free Afghanistan, 1988.

————. *Government and Society in Afghanistan: The Reign of Amir Abd al-Rahman Khan, 1880–1901*. Austin: University of Texas Press, 1979.

————. *The Second Anglo-Afghan War*. (In Dari.) Peshawar: National Islamic Front of Afghanistan, 1989.

Khairkhwa, S. M. *Commemorating the Martyrs of the Twenty-fourth [of the Month of] Hoot of Herat*. (In Dari.) Tehran: Cultural Committee of the Islamic Association of Afghanistan, 1987.

Khalilzad, Z. *Prospects for the Afghan Interim Government*. Santa Monica: Rand, 1991.

Khalis, M. Y. *A Message to the Mujahid Nation of Afghanistan*. (In Pashto.) Peshawar: Islamic Party Publications, 1988.

———. *Two Articles*. (In Pashto.) Peshawar: Islamic Party Publications, 1988.

Khan, R. M. *Untying the Afghan Knot: Negotiating Soviet Withdrawal*. Durham: Duke University Press, 1991.

Khan, Zaki Ullah. *The Story of Russo-Afghan Friendship*. (In Pashto.) Peshawar: Writers' Union of Free Afghanistan, 1989.

Klass, R., ed. *Afghanistan: The Great Game Revisited*. New York: Freedom House, 1987.

Kushkaki, S. *The Constitutional Decade*. (In Dari.) Islamabad: Cultural Council of Afghanistan Resistance, 1986.

Laber, J., and B. Rubin. *A Nation Is Dying, 1979–87*. Evanston: Northwestern University Press, 1988.

———, eds. *A Report from Helsinki Watch, 1979–1984*. New York: U.S. Helsinki Watch Committee, 1984.

Lewis, B. *The Political Language of Islam*. Chicago: University of Chicago Press, 1988.

Lourie, R. *Predicting Russia's Future*. N.p.: Whittle Direct Books, 1991.

McClintock, M. *Instruments of Statecraft: U.S. Guerilla Warfare, Counterinsurgency, Counter-Terrorism, 1940–1990*. New York: Pantheon, 1992.

Maley, W., and F. S. Saikal. *Political Order in Post-Communist Afghanistan*. Boulder and London: Lynne Reinner Publishers, 1992.

Mawdudi, A. A. *Political Theory of Islam*. Lahore: Islamic Publication, n.d.

Ministry of Planning. *General Statistics*. (In Dari.) Kabul: Ministry of Planning, 1971.

Mohammad Zahir. *His Messages, Interviews, and Statements During the Decade of Jehad*. (In Pashto and Dari.) Edited by A. R. Ashraf. Bonn: privately published, 1990.

Na'eem, H. *The Russian Program and the Beacon of Uprisings in Central Asia, 1784–1984*. (In Pashto.) Peshawar: Peshawar University Press, 1985.

Nangyal, Sh. *The Political Parties of Afghanistan*. (In Pashto.) Peshawar: privately published, 1984.

Newell, N. P., and R. Newell. *The Struggle for Afghanistan*. Ithaca: Cornell University Press, 1981.

Pakistan, Government of. *Handbook on Management of Afghan Refugees in Pakistan*. Islamabad, 1984.

Rishtia, S. Q. *The Price of Liberty: The Tragedy of Afghanistan*. Rome: Bard Editore, privately published, 1984.

Roy, O. *Islam and Resistance in Afghanistan*. London and New York: Cambridge University Press, 1986.

Ruiz, H. A. *Left Out in the Cold: The Perilous Homecoming of Afghan Refugees*. Washington, D.C.: U.S. Committee for Refugees, 1992.

Rustar, M. O. *The Pul-e-Charkhi Prison, or the Inferno of Soviet Imperialism in Afghanistan.* (In Dari.) Peshawar: Writers' Union of Free Afghanistan, 1990.

Safi, M. A. *The Just Uprising of the Military Division of Herat.* (In Pashto.) Peshawar: privately published, n.d.

Sahari, D. *Jehad in the Kunars.* (In Dari.) Peshawar: Writers' Union of Free Afghanistan, 1989.

Saikal, A., and W. Miley, eds. *The Soviet Withdrawal from Afghanistan.* Cambridge: Cambridge University Press, 1989.

Schusky, E., and T. P. Culbert. *Understanding Culture.* Englewood Cliffs, N.J.: Prentice-Hall, 1967.

Sharq, M. H. *The Barefooted Coarse Cotton Wearers; or, Memoirs of Dr. Mohammad Hassan Sharq, 1931–1991.* (In Dari.) Delhi, India: privately printed at Army Computer Point, 1991.

Shevardnadze, E. *The Future Belongs to Freedom.* New York: Free Press, 1991.

Shultz, G. *Chemical Warfare in Southeast Asia and Afghanistan.* U.S. Department of State Special Report no. 104, 1982.

Tapper, N. *Bartered Brides.* Cambridge and New York: Cambridge University Press, 1991.

Wajdi, A. J. *The Present and Future of Traditional Jirgas of Afghanistan.* (In Pashto.) Peshawar: Aman Publication House, 1986.

Wakman, M. A, *Afghanistan, Nonalignment, and the Superpowers.* New Delhi: Radiant Publishers, 1985.

Yousaf, M., and M. Adkin. *The Bear Trap: Afghanistan's Untold Story.* Lahore: Jang Publishers, 1992.

Yusufi, S. Sh.. *The Uprising of the Twenty-fourth [of the Month of] Hoot of Herat.* (In Dari.) Peshawar, 1984.

Zadran, G. *History of Afghanistan from 1747 up to 1982 A.D..* Vol. 1, *From the Memoirs of History: Lessons and Warnings.* (In Pashto.) 1983. Rev. and enlarged. ed. Peshawar: privately published, 1989.

————. *Paktia in Uprising Waves.* (In Pashto.) Peshawar: privately published, 1983.

Zurmulwal, G. M. *Russia's Armed Aggression on Afghanistan.* (In Pashto.) Peshawar: Writers' Union of Free Afghanistan, 1990.

ARTICLES

Alam, Z. G. "Violation of Human Rights of the Afghans." (In Pashto.) *Mujahid Wolas* (newspaper), May–June 1991, 1.

Amin, R. "The Future of Afghan Society after Settlement of the Conflict." *Writers' Union of Free Afghanistan Journal* (Peshawar), January–February 1991, 1–20.

Amnesty International. "Torture in Afghanistan." *Amnesty International Newsletter* (London), December 1983.

Anonymous. "Two Martyred and the Same Fate." *Voice of Freedom* 4, no. 9 (September 1990): 35–43.

Arnold, A. "Communism in Afghanistan." In *Encyclopaedia Iranica*, 111–18. Costa Mesa, Calif.: Mazda Publishers, 1992.

Arnold, A., and R. Klass. "Afghanistan's Divided Communist Party." In R. Klass, *Afghanistan: The Great Game Revisited*, 135–60. New York: Freedom House, 1987.

Assifi, A. T. "The Russian Rope: Soviet Economic Motives and the Subversion of Afghanistan." *World Affairs* 145, no. 3 (1982–83): 253–66.

Azari, E. "Afghan Refugees: A Tragedy Created by Communism." *Writers' Union of Free Afghanistan Journal* (Peshawar), March–April 1991, 62–83.

Azizi, H. "Guardianship or Looting of a City?" *Afghanistan [Journal]*, published by Afghan Information Center, Peshawar, No. I (April 1994): 66.

Baha, S. "From the Cruel Executions to the Flight from the Crucible of Communism." *Pen in the Service of Jehad Journal* (in Dari), March 1990, 3–7.

Barth, F. "Cultural Wellsprings of Resistance in Afghanistan." In R. Klass, ed., *Afghanistan: The Great Game Revisited*, 187–202. New York: Freedom House, 1987.

Bilolavo, F. "One Man's Sentence in Afghan Hell." *The Insight*, 4 July 1988, 8–16.

Bisharat, M. N. "The Stormy Developments of the Coalition of the North." *Hurriyat*, nos. 1–2 (1992): 10–17.

Canfield, R. "Ethnic, Regional, and Sectarian Alignment in Afghanistan." In B. Banuazizi and M. Weiner, eds., *The State, Religion, and Ethnic Politics: Afghanistan, Iran, and Pakistan*, 75–103. Syracuse: Syracuse University Press, 1986.

———. "Islamic Sources of Resistance." *Orbis: A Journal of World Affairs*, spring 1985, 57–71.

Deac, W. P. "Sky Train Invasion." *Afghanistan Forum*, no. 3 (1993): 22–24.

Dobbs, M. "Dramatic Politburo Meeting Led to End of War." *Washington Post*, 16 November 1992, A1, A6.

———. "Secret Memos Trace Kremlin's March to War." *Washington Post*, 15 November 1992, A1, A32.

Edwards, D. B. "The Evolution of Shi'i Political Dissent in Afghanistan." In J. R. I. Cole and N. R. Keddie, eds., *Shi'ism and Social Protest*, 201–29. New Haven: Yale University Press, 1986.

Emad, S. N. "The Impact of Jehad on the Local and National Customs of Afghanistan." In *The Future of Islamic Afghanistan* 1:31–41. Islamabad: Cultural Council of Afghanistan Resistance, 1980.

Ermacora, F. "The Situation of Human Rights in Afghanistan." *Afghanistan Forum*, January 1994.

Farr, G. "The New Afghan Middle Class." In G. Farr and G. Merriam, eds., *Afghan Resistance: The Politics of Survival*, 127–50. Lahore: Vanguard, 1988.

The Front of Afghanistan's Militant Mujahideen. *Watan* [underground periodical], 1981.

Garver, N. "What Violence Is." In R. Wasserstrom, *Today's Moral Problems*, 410–23. London: Macmillan, 1975.

Ghani, A. "Afghanistan: Islam and Counterrevolutionary Movements." In J. Esposito, ed., *Islam in Asia: Religion, Politics, and Society*, 79–95. New York: Oxford University Press, 1987.

Girard, Sylvie. "Afghanistan: The Will, but Not the Means." *Refugees*, July 1992, 13.

Hyman, A. "The Afghan Politics of Exile." *Third World Quarterly* (London), January 1987, 67–89.

Ivanov, N. "Revelations on the Soviet Invasion of Afghanistan." *Afghanistan Forum*, no. 3 (1993): 16–20.

Kakar, M. H. "Central Asia: The Opening of A Closed Region." *Writers' Union of Free Afghanistan*, special issue, April–December 1992, 159–71.

———. "Constitutional History of Afghanistan." In *Encyclopaedia Iranica*, 158–62. Costa Mesa, Calif.: Mazda Publishers, 1992.

———. "The Failed Coup of 6 March." *Afghanistan Mirror* 1, no. 4 (March–April 1990): 111–115.

———. "The Fall of the Afghan Monarchy in 1973." *International Journal of Middle East Studies* 9 (1978): 195–214.

———. "The Policy of Intrigues, Myopia, and Hatred." *Jirga* 1, no. 5 (1993): 10–19.

———. "Time for Choice." *Jirga* 1, no. 6 (October 1993): 2–9.

———. "Trends in Modern Afghan History." In L. Dupree and A. Albert, eds., *Afghanistan in the 1970s*, 13–33. New York: Praeger, 1974.

Khan, M. A. "The Emergence of Religious Parties in Afghanistan." In F. R. Marwat and S. W. A. Sh. Kakakhel, eds., *Afghanistan and the Frontier*, 1–21. Peshawar: Emjay Books International, 1993.

Kornienko, G. M. "The Afghan Endeavor: Perplexities of the Military Incursion and Withdrawal." *Journal of South Asian and Middle Eastern Studies* 17, no. 2 (1994): 2–17.

Ludin, A. "Economic Conditions and the Future of Development in Afghanistan's Economy." In Cultural Council of Afghanistan Resistance, *The Future of Islamic Afghanistan* 4:242–64. Islamabad: Cultural Council of Afghanistan Resistance, 1991.

Mackenzie, R. "Brutal Force Batters a Country." *The Insight*, 5 December 1988, 8–16.

Magnus, R. "The Constitution of 1964: A Decade of Political Experimentation." In L. Dupree and A. Linet, eds., *Afghanistan in the 1970s*, 50–76. New York: Praeger, 1974.

Majid, M. A. "The Impact of Jehad on the Local and National Customs of Afghanistan." (In Dari.) In Cultural Council of Afghanistan Resistance, *The Future of Islamic Afghanistan* 1:38–47. Islamabad: Cultural Council of Afghanistan Resistance, 1980.

Majruh, S. B. "Past and Present Education in Afghanistan." In B. Huldt, *The Tragedy of Afghanistan*, 75–92. London: Croom Helm, 1988.

Malik, I. H. "Issues in Contemporary South and Central Asian Politics: Islam, Ethnicity, and the State." *Asian Survey* 32, no. 10 (1992).

Marwat, F. R. "Waiting for the U.N." *WUFA* incidental issue 1 (July–August 1994): 43–49.

Morozov, A. "Between Amin and Karmal." *New Times*, no. 38 (1991): 36–39.

———. "A Night Visit to the *Tass* Villa." *New Times*, no. 39 (1991): 32–33.

———. "Shots Fired in the House of the Nation." *New Times*, no. 41 (1991): 32–35.

Noorzoy, M. S. "The Economic Policies of Afghanistan after World War II." (In Dari.) In Cultural Council of Afghanistan Resistance, *The Future of Islamic Afghanistan* 4:377–81. Islamabad: Cultural Council of Afghanistan Resistance, 1991.

Payand, A. "Soviet-Afghan Relations: From Cooperation to Occupation." *International Journal of Middle East Studies* 21 (1989): 107–28.

Popal, Z. "How and Why Was Ali Ahmad Khurram Killed?" *Writers' Union of Free Afghanistan Journal* (Peshawar), July–December 1989, 32–43.

Poullada, L. B. "The Road to Crisis 1919–1980: American Failures, Afghanistan Errors, and Soviet Successes." In R. Klass, ed., *Afghanistan: The Great Game Revisited,* 37–69. New York: Freedom House, 1987.

Rais, R. B. "Afghanistan and Regional Security after the Cold War." *Problems of Communism* 41 (May–June 1992): 82–94.

Rashid, A. "The Green Revolutionary." *Afghanistan Forum,* July 1993.

Roy, O. "The Origin of the Afghan Communist Party." *Central Asian Review* 7, nos. 2–3 (1988): 41–57.

Rubin, B. "Political Elites in Afghanistan: Rentier State Building, Rentier State Wrecking." *International Journal of Middle East Studies* 24 (1992): 77–99.

Shah, M. H. "The Soviet Interferences in the Education and Culture of Afghanistan." *Afghanistan Mirror,* nos. 21–29 (January 1992–March 1993).

Shahrani, N. "Response to the Saur Revolution in Badakhshan." In N. Shahrani and R. Canfield, eds., *Revolution and Rebellion in Afghanistan,* 139–69. Berkeley: Institute of International Studies, University of California, 1984.

Shepard, W. E. "Islam as a System in the Latter Writings of Sayed Qutb." *Middle Eastern Studies* 25, no. 1 (January 1989): 31–50.

Shroder, J. F., and A. T. Assifi. "Afghan Mineral Resources and Soviet Exploitation." In R. Klass, ed. *Afghanistan: The Great Game Revisited,* 97–134. New York: Freedom House, 1987.

Sliwinski, M. "Afghanistan 1978–87: War, Demography, and Society." *Central Asian Survey Incidental Papers,* no. 6 (London, 1988).

Wasserstrom, R. "The Laws of War." In Wasserstrom, ed., *Today's Moral Problems,* 482–98. London: Macmillan, 1975.

Wassil, A. "Opinion." *Afghanistan Forum* 1 (January 1993): 26–27.

Wolasmal, M. H. "Foreign Interference in the Afghan Problem." (In Pashto.) *Mojahid Wolas* (newspaper), November–December 1991, 1.

Yapp, M. E. "Contemporary Islamic Revivalism." *Asian Affairs* 11 (June 1980): 178–95.

Yusufzai, R. "Dostum." *Afghanistan Forum,* no. 5 (September 1993): 8–68.

Zurmulwal, G. M. "Know the Khalqi and Parchami Factions." (In Dari.) *Aerman-e-Shaheed* (New Delhi: Islamic Unity of Afghanistan Mujahideen), no. 69 (Aug.–Sept. 1988): 1–10.

Index

About the Author

Mohammad Hassan Kakar holds a B.A. from Kabul University and an M.Phil. and Ph.D. in history from the University of London. He has been a Visiting Research Fellow at the Middle Eastern Centers of Princeton University and Harvard University in the United States. For many years he taught history at Kabul University, where in 1981 he became a professor. He has also served as chair of the history department there. In 1982 the Kabul regime arrested him for his opposition to the Soviet invasion of Afghanistan. The London-based human rights organization Amnesty International declared Dr. Kakar a "prisoner of conscience." Along with other human rights groups, Amnesty International, the International PEN, and scholars and human rights activists in Europe and the United States (among them the late Professor Joseph Fletcher of Harvard University, Dr. Crystal A. Leslie of the Medical Center of Boston University, and, in particular, Professor Felix Ermacora, the special rapporteur of the United Nations Human Rights Commission on Afghanistan) pressured the Kabul regime by continually writing to it about him.

After his release from prison, Professor Kakar fled with his family to Peshawar in Pakistan. There, as a member of the Writers' Union of Free Afghanistan, he served as an analyst of Afghan political developments. Before immigrating to the United States in 1989, he was elected the first president of the Association of the Professors of the Universities of Afghanistan (in exile). In the United States he served first as a Fellow at the East-West Center in Hawaii and then taught at the University of California, San Diego. Meanwhile, as chair and a founding member of the Movement for a Representative Government in Afghanistan, he kept abreast of current Afghan affairs and wrote about them for Afghan journals. He adds this book, a result of his scholarship, professional knowledge, observations, and personal experience, to the many others that he has written or translated. Dr. Kakar now lives in San Diego with his wife, Maryam, their two sons Kawun and Sabawun, and their daughter Khwaga. Their two daughters Palwasha and Wagma are married and have five children between them.

PUBLICATIONS

BOOKS

Afghan, Afghanistan, and Afghans and the Organization of the State in India, Persia, and Afghanistan (Dari)
Afghanistan: A Study in Internal Political Developments, 1880–1896
The Afghan Problem (Dari)
The Afghans in the Spring of 1987 at War with the Russians (Pashto)
The Geneva Compromise on Afghanistan (Pashto)
Government and Society in Afghanistan: The Reign of Amir Abd al-Rahman Khan, 1880–1901
The Second Anglo-Afghan War (Dari)

ARTICLES

"Constitutional History of Afghanistan"
"The Fall of the Afghan Monarchy in 1973"
"Trends in Modern Afghan History"
"The Pacification of the Hazaras of Afghanistan"

TRANSLATIONS INTO PASHTO AND DARI

An Account of the Kingdom of Caubul, by M. Elphinstone (2 vols.)
The British Approach to Politics, by M. Stewart
The Contemporary World, by W. MacNeil
Letters on Literature, by M. Gorky
Medieval Europe, by S. Painter
The Real World of Democracy, by C. B. Macpherson
What Is History? by E. H. Carr

Composition: Graphic Composition, Inc.
Text: 11/13 Bembo
Display: Bembo
Printing and binding: Thomson-Shore, Inc.